ı 22 | | | rl

PRAISE FOR *ANGELA MERKEL*

'This eye-opening biography, drawing from rich behind-the-scenes knowledge, is necessary reading'   *Kirkus* (starred review)

'A well-written and informative tribute to an extraordinary political leader'   *Booklist*

'An absorbing, wide-ranging and detailed account of European power struggles over the last 50 years'   *Marxist Review*

'A sympathetic, engaging and informative political biography of one of Europe's foremost contemporary leaders. Qvortrup's highly readable prose leads one on a dramatic, whirlwind tour of a history that is still unfolding before us'

Aviel Roshwald, Professor Department
of History, Georgetown University

'Lively and engaging... a joy to read. It is an extraordinary and incisive book, which gives us a unique insight into the life and times of the woman who almost single-handedly transformed the politics of her country and of the world'

Arend Lijphart, Research Professor Emeritus of Political
Science, University of California, San Diego

'Qvortrup masterfully weaves together the key episodes of this turbulent life and most unlikely political career, and provides compelling evidence that there is no better way toward a deeper understanding of the present than revisiting the past'

Professor Ludger Helms, University of Innsbruck and author of
Presidents, Prime Ministers and Chancellors

'In a world full of disappointing national leaders, Matt Qvortrup provides us with ar ⋯⋯⋯⋯⋯⋯⋯⋯⋯⋯g of a leading woman who tons th⋯

⋯⋯⋯⋯⋯*ive Society*

© Fred Qvortrup

Matthew Qvortrup is an award-winning political analyst and Professor of Political Science at Coventry University, and a Fellow of the Royal Society of the Arts. First elected to a full Chair at the age of 36, he earned his doctorate in politics at Brasenose College, Oxford. He frequently features as the expert on Angela Merkel and world politics on radio and television, including the BBC and Al Jazeera, and has written for and been interviewed in *The Times*, *Guardian*, *New Statesman*, *Newsweek*, *Bloomberg*, Chatham House's *The World Today* and others. He lives in London.

ANGELA MERKEL

EUROPE'S MOST INFLUENTIAL LEADER

Matthew Qvortrup

DUCKWORTH

This edition published in the United Kingdom by Duckworth in 2021

Duckworth, an imprint of Duckworth Books Ltd
1 Golden Court, Richmond,
TW9 1EU, United Kingdom
www.duckworthbooks.co.uk

For bulk and special sales please contact
info@duckbooks.co.uk

A catalogue record for this book is available from the British Library

Book design and typeformatting by Bernard Schleifer

Printed and bound by Clays

9780715654378

To Anne

CONTENTS

ACKNOWLEDGEMENTS   9

PREFACE   11

1 A Childhood Under Communism   17

2 In the Shadow of the Berlin Wall   41

3 Angela in Leipzig   63

4 The Unbearable Boredom of Being: A Squatter in Berlin   89

5 Angela Becomes Merkel   111

6 Kohl's Girl   131

7 The Politics of Patricide: How Merkel Became Party Leader   151

8 Waiting Game: The Patient Party Leader   171

9 Merkel Loses and Becomes Chancellor   191

10 The Making of the Queen of Europe   209

11 Potato Soup, the Pope and Re-Election   231

12 The Euro-Crisis and Afghanistan   251

13 From the Jaws of Defeat and Beyond   271

14 Ukraine, Greece, Refugees and Brexit   293

15 The Last Liberal...   333

16 The Plague   351

EPILOGUE   371

GLOSSARY   373

NOTES   377

INDEX   393

ACKNOWLEDGEMENTS

I would like to thank friends and family members, especially my father Steffen (who always reminded me if I failed to conjugate German verbs correctly) and Nina, Sebastian and Fred, who read early drafts.

While this is not an official biography, Angela Merkel's office in the Kanzleramt has been helpful and courteous and has responded promptly to emails and clarifying phone calls. I am also grateful to my German colleagues Dr Barbara Hans (*Der Spiegel*), Dr Monika Pater (Institut für Journalistik und Kommunikationswissenschaft, Hamburg University) and Professor Dr. jur. Hellmut Wollmann (Humboldt University, Berlin) for suggestions. I would like to thank Professor Lutz Hagestedt, Universität Rostock, for providing me with evidence and facts from Merkel's Hinterland, and for encouragement.

I want to thank my editors Peter Mayer and Nikki Griffiths for stimulating and valuable conversations. I am very grateful to my agent Michael Alcock, whose patience and professionalism is legendary. Above all I am grateful to Anne, who endured the presence of another woman in the household for several years: Angela Merkel. I dedicate this book to Anne.

Preface

It might all have been very different if Angela Merkel had not arrived at exactly the same time as Chancellor Schröder on the election night of 18 September 2005. In fact, as if by fate, the two politicians turned up simultaneously for the traditional post-election debate between the party leaders at the Zollernhof television studio in Unter den Linden, a famous avenue in Berlin. An usher opened the door for Mrs Merkel, the Leader of the Opposition, with a 'Welcome, Mrs Chancellor.'

'She's not the Chancellor, I am,' erupted Gerhard Schröder, the incumbent Chancellor of Germany since 1998. Flustered and enraged, the Social Democrat politician entered the television studio in a state. 'Do you seriously believe that my party will enter into negotiations with Mrs Merkel?' thundered Schröder. He was used to testosterone-fuelled, bare-knuckle political brawls. But Angela Merkel just sat there as if to say, 'That's no way to speak to a lady.' She won the sympathy vote of the people. Schröder effectively lost the chancellorship when he lost his temper at the entrance to the Zollernhof.

Not for the first time, Merkel had used her political intuition to outsmart her opponent. The woman who had not managed to win the election outright suddenly had the upper hand in the negotiations. She had won the approval of the public. A few weeks later Angela Dorothea Merkel (née Kasner) was sworn in as the first female federal Chancellor of Germany and began her journey to become the most powerful politician in the Old World, effectively the Queen of Europe.

The first major biography written in English, this book tells the story of a professional and focused leader, sometimes referred to as 'the mathematician of power', revealing the personality, passions and past of the nondescript, meek quantum physicist who rose from political nothingness to the summit of power in only a matter of months. It traces the life and times of a woman of Polish origin who grew up in a Communist dictatorship, a one-time squatter and barmaid who became Chancellor of Germany. The story has not often been told, certainly not in English: 'People know practically nothing about 35 years of my life,' she said in an interview with *Stern* on 18 November 2004. Twelve years later this is still substantially true. Many will know that she grew up in East Germany, that she studied natural sciences and that she is Germany's first female Chancellor. But other parts of her life are less well-known. The fact that she has a wicked sense of humour and a knack for imitating voices – including the Pope's – may come as a surprise to many. It might also surprise some that she was shaped by a Christian upbringing. These facts, and others to be revealed in this book, have not previously been discussed in the shorter books about her, written or published in English.

At the end of 2015 Angela Merkel's image changed: once the tough taskmaster of austerity, she was now the only major leader in Europe to open her country's doors to large numbers of refugees. Germany took in more than a million refugees in 2015. Merkel, who had hitherto been known as a cautious leader who preferred thorough analysis to rash and impulsive action, appeared transformed. She seemed to relish her new role as the creator of a culture of welcome for these new citizens. Was this a radical break with the past? What had happened? Had she lost her touch? Many of her own turned against her. Was this yet another proof of the iron law of government that all political careers end in failure?

Only a few months before, it had seemed she could do no wrong. Praise for her was almost universal in other Western capitals. We live in the 'Age of Merkel', as British pundit Alastair Campbell noted. Mrs Merkel had shaped Europe and become a cultural icon.

We may toy with the hypothetical question: what if Merkel had not been Chancellor? We will never know, but the fact remains that she was a prominent leader at a key moment in European history. Her style of government, and the way she steered her country and the European continent through crisis after crisis was in large measure shaped by her past and her earlier experiences as an underestimated politician who was considered a lightweight by her male colleagues. She surprised them all with her tenacity and her very different style. Of course, she too made miscalculations. Her commitment to the refugees and her newfound passion for the huddled masses from the Middle East did not endear her to the political right, or indeed to many of her party colleagues. Yet at this late stage of her career she seemed prepared to follow policies she considered to be morally right notwithstanding their unpopularity.

Can she take credit for rescuing the Eurozone? Can she be blamed for the refugee crisis? Historians are divided over the role of the individual. History is not just shaped by great men and women: 'Men make their own history, but they do not make it as they please; they do not make it under self-selected circumstances.' Angela Merkel has probably read this remark by the German philosopher and Communist Karl Marx, though it is unlikely that it made much of an impression on her – she barely achieved a pass-mark in the compulsory Marxist-Leninist module as an undergraduate at Karl Marx University in Leipzig.

Merkel too was a victim of fate and fortune. But chance and luck alone do not determine our lives. Statesmen and stateswomen are individuals who seize the opportunity when given the chance. 'Destiny and character are the names of one single notion,' wrote the romantic German poet Novalis, who was fascinated by the grand sweep of history.

Merkel's deeds shaped the future, creating a new set of political circumstances in politics and economics that everybody had to accept whether they lived in Berlin, Brussels, Moscow, Athens or the refugee camps scattered across Europe and the Middle East.

This book gives an account of German history seen through the life of a demure former research scientist who, against all odds, rose to become the most powerful woman in the world. It chronicles the transformation of a woman who personified caution but who suddenly discovered her deepest convictions. It reveals how she stood up for the Christian values of her childhood home when she – to the consternation of many of her compatriots – opened the doors to refugees from the Middle East in 2015. It also perhaps explains why she spent much of her carefully accumulated political capital on a deeply unpopular policy. Why was it that a woman known for caution suddenly showed such resolve? To answer this question we need the full story of her life.

Yet, much as events earlier in her life shaped her, it was only late in Merkel's career that it all came together. It is possible to pinpoint the metamorphosis of Merkel with almost mathematical precision.

It was the end of October 2015 and the leaders of the European Union were gathered in Brussels. There was one item on the agenda: the refugee crisis. For over a month unprecedented numbers of people had been fleeing Syria and the horrors of the so-called Islamic State. Germany and Sweden were the only countries that seemed relatively open to the desperate refugees. The countries in Eastern Europe were particularly alarmed. Hungary's Prime Minister, Victor Orbán, had become an unofficial spokesperson for those opposing the intake of more refugees. He was in a confident mood, for he felt public opinion was moving in his direction. Speaking with a hint of I-told-you-so condescension the Hungarian politician said, 'It is only a matter of time before Germany will build a fence. When they have done so, then we'll have the kind of Europe I like.' There was silence in the room. Merkel looked down, paused and then spoke to her colleagues, slowly and with emphasis, 'I lived a long time behind a fence, it is not something I wish to do again.'[1]

Merkel could not be sure that she would survive politically but she was not willing to abandon her principles for the sake of political gain. While other countries devised increasingly sophisticated policies for keeping refugees out, Merkel boldly stated, 'I will not enter a competition in who can treat the refugees the worst.' She sounded defiant, but she was on the defensive. Before, the refugee crisis all seemed to be going so well, so smoothly and with such effortless ease.

ANGELA MERKEL

CHAPTER 1

A Childhood Under Communism

'I CAN TALK LIKE THAT TOO,' THE SOCIAL DEMOCRAT POLITICIAN PEER Steinbrück almost pleaded with his audience as he tried to imitate the soft conversational voice of his opponent Angela Merkel. Even the audience of party faithfuls did not like this joke. Steinbrück was hopelessly behind in the polls and everything he did seemed to fail. The year was 2013 and Merkel had been Chancellor for close to eight years. But whereas other heads of government were reeling after years of unpopular spending cuts and austerity programmes, Mrs Merkel was more popular than ever. Her nickname *Mutti* (Mummy) fairly reflected the way she conducted herself. She spoke softly, almost soothingly, to her electors. She seemed rational, calm, prudent and unflappable. No wonder Mr Steinbrück (who had served as her finance minister under the Grand Coalition from 2005 to 2009) was exasperated. He had reason to be despondent: the German economy was in rude health, and Mrs Merkel was the undisputed leader of her country and the leading politician in Europe.

The results that came in on the night of 22 September 2013 confirmed Peer Steinbrück's worst fears. Mrs Merkel's Christian Democratic Union (CDU) and its Bavarian sister-party, the Christian Social Union (CSU), won 41 per cent of the vote. Their Social Democrat (SPD) opponents won a paltry 23 per cent. A clear victory, which when translated into seats gave Merkel close to 50 per cent – only five seats away from an overall majority. This result, in a country with a largely proportional electoral system, was unprecedented.

Merkel was more popular than ever. Yet there was a small problem: the Free Democrats (FDP), the small libertarian party that had served as junior partner in Merkel's coalition from 2009, had failed to win representation to the German Parliament. Once again, Merkel had to do what she did best: find a deal. Once again, she took her time. It took over two months for her to form a government, at a time when the whole world was on the brink of several crises: the revolution in Ukraine, the unfinished business of the Arab Spring, and the never-ending saga of the Greek debt and the struggling Eurozone. But Merkel, as was her wont, remained calm. Finally, on 27 November, she presented a new government, another Grand Coalition of the CDU/CSU and the Social Democrats. Merkel remained Chancellor, Wolfgang Schäuble – also of the CDU – remained Minister of Finance, and the Social Democrat Frank-Walter Steinmeier moved into the Foreign Office, taking up the position he had held under the previous government of national unity between 2005 and 2009. It was business as usual. Continuity was the watchword. There was no place for Peer Steinbrück. Instead, the Social Democrat Chairman Sigmar Gabriel became Deputy Chancellor and Minister for Trade and Industry. He too was an old hand, having served as Minister of the Environment in Merkel's first government. Things were as she liked: businesslike, reliable and steady.

It was not to last. Two years and several crises later, Merkel was facing one of her sternest tests yet: the refugee crisis.

The August sun was shining in Heidenau, Saxony, one of the least prosperous states in the southeast of Germany, as Angela Merkel stepped out of her BMW 7 limo. It was a warm day, warmer than usual, and the local dignitaries were sweating in the afternoon sun as they greeted the Chancellor of Germany. The woman who usually wore brightly-coloured pantsuits was dressed in grey. She looked grave and concerned but also focused as she greeted Jürgen Opitz, Mayor of Heidenau, and Stanislaw Tillich, Governor of the state of Saxony. The security guards watched anxiously as the three politicians walked past the armed policemen, through the fortified gates, and into the asylum centre.

Europe's most powerful politician had been head of government for nine years and nine months. She was the undisputed leader of her country and the foremost politician in Europe. Everybody – even her opponents – agreed that she had reformed Germany from being, according to many economists, 'the sick man of Europe' into the richest and most powerful economy on the continent. Unlike her mostly male colleagues in other countries, Mrs Merkel had stratospheric approval ratings. 'Without alternative' was how her political opponent Peer Steinbrück had described her a few months earlier. And the voters mostly liked her, though recently she had come in for some criticism.

On this day, her critics were out in force. Only a hundred yards from the Chancellor a gathering of angry protesters was shouting, 'Go home!', 'Foreigners out!' 'Traitor' read a sign carried by a large woman with dyed red hair and fading tattoos.

It had been a testing summer. Earlier in the year Mrs Merkel had negotiated a peace deal of sorts with the Russian President Vladimir Putin, an agreement that temporarily halted Russian incursions into Ukraine. And during the summer months, when she would normally have been on holiday, Mrs Merkel and her European colleagues once again had to deal with Greece's troubled finances and the potential meltdown of the European Monetary Union.

Now she was facing an immigration crisis. Hundreds of thousands of refugees from Syria, Libya and elsewhere were flooding over the borders. Europe was overwhelmed. Yet Mrs Merkel remained calm. In the face of the unprecedented influx of migrants she had responded 'We'll sort it out' – a mantra she would reiterate throughout the autumn with a consistency reminiscent of the Roman Senator Cato the Elder, who finished all his speeches with the sentence 'Carthage must be destroyed'.

Germany was in ferment. The number of attacks against refugee centres stood at a disturbing 460 per month – more than the total number of attacks for the whole of the previous year. And to add to her problems, Horst Seehofer, the leader of the Christian Social Union and Governor of the southern state of Bavaria, openly defied the Chancellor, suggesting that he would introduce martial law.

To add yet another dimension to Merkel's woes, it was revealed that Volkswagen, the German carmaker, had fiddled its environmental test results, suggesting that their cars were less polluting than was actually the case. VW's deception led to the dismissal of its CEO Martin Winterkorn, an ally of Merkel's, and the company's share price nosedived. The near collapse of Germany's largest car manufacturer was a political challenge for the Chancellor. Moreover, the allegation that the federal Minister for Transport, Alexander Dobrindt, might have known about VW's practice of fabricating the CO_2 test results added yet another dimension to the tense political situation.

Still, politics is a game of blaming opponents, and Merkel was fortunate that Mr Dobrindt was a member of Horst Seehofer's CSU party. If the Bavarian Governor got too cocky, Merkel could conveniently use the VW scandal as a bargaining chip. Cynical? Perhaps, but such is politics. The fact that she had something on Dobrindt, Seehofer's protégé, gave her a bit of breathing space. It was needed. Her hitherto high poll-ratings had dropped. Her encounter with the angry mob in Saxony was not unusual at the time.

Mrs Merkel seemed unperturbed, perhaps even emboldened, in the face of the jeers. Politicians learn to live with the abuse hurled at them; it is part of the job description. And there was a certain defiance in the way Merkel reacted; a sense that she acknowledged the angry crowd and wanted to confront them, though always in her own soft-spoken style. Normally, politicians would feign deafness and pretend to ignore the angry cries. Merkel did not. Her deputy, Sigmar Gabriel, had described the protesters as 'trash'. Merkel chose a different strategy. There is no point in getting into a slinging match with the mob. Much better to set out a positive vision, especially if you are the leader. And so she did. 'Welcoming people who flee tyranny is part of what we are all about, part of our understanding of who we are,' she said to the television cameras. Then she paused, looked up, squinted as the sunlight hit her eyes, and said, 'There is no tolerance for those who question the worth of other people, no tolerance for those who are not willing to help, when helping is right and humane.'

She was not only standing for dignity, she was also upholding Germany's self-respect; she was personifying the new, open and tolerant country – one that distanced itself from its dark history of genocide, tyranny and the unspeakable horrors of the Nazi concentration camps. The demonstrators were not. Swastikas had been painted on the walls, many asylum centres were ablaze and neo-Nazis were shouting slogans not heard for decades. Mrs Merkel left the impromptu podium and posed for a photograph with a young mother carrying a small baby.

Angela Merkel too had once been carried by her mother past armed border guards in a harsh and hostile world; she too had been like the refugees who were now entering her country. Maybe it was the stories Angela Merkel had heard as a child, stories about the millions of refugees who crossed the borders of Europe after the Second World War, that spoke to her sense of humanity.

INTO THE HEART OF DARKNESS

It was in 1954 that Angela Merkel's mother, Herlind, left the city of her birth with her eight-week-old daughter to travel east. The young mother must have looked apprehensive and helpless as she and baby Angela boarded the train to Perleberg, a nondescript town in the Communist zone in the east of Germany. There was something almost biblical about the way the 26-year-old mother carried her firstborn in a basket, rather as Miriam carried Moses in the Exodus story. Herlind was entering a land of darkness, the Communist state ruled by Walter Ulbricht, the despot who had been installed by the Soviet dictator Josef Stalin. Herlind and her daughter were travelling east to meet up with Horst, the child's father and Herlind's husband, who had gone ahead to take up a calling as a pastor in the officially atheist state.

They were not coming to a happy place. Germany had been divided since the Second World War ended in 1945. The Western allies – the USA, Britain and France – controlled the west; the east of the country, by contrast, was held in an iron grip by the Soviet Union.

The East Germans were not happy. In 1953 the workers rebelled against the Soviet puppet regime. Walter Ulbricht, the son of a carpenter from the southeastern city of Leipzig, had received no formal education apart from a stint at the International Lenin School, Moscow, in the 1920s. Having worked with Josef Stalin during the Second World War, Ulbricht was uniquely suited to the task of establishing a new totalitarian state. His curriculum vitae read like a long preparation for the task. In 1936, in the first year of the Spanish Civil War, he had served as an informer for the Communist Party and had identified and helped eliminate German volunteers in the war who were not true to Stalin. He subsequently moved to Moscow, where he lived from 1937 to 1945.

After the collapse of the Nazi regime in May 1945, the Soviet Union occupied the eastern part of Germany, though the western part of the capital Berlin was controlled by the Western allies. It was Ulbricht's task to create a state. He had learned from his master and idol Josef Stalin. 'It must look democratic, but we must control everything' was Ulbricht's motto. As the leader of the Communist Party (KPD), he was aware that not everybody was committed to what Vladimir Lenin, the founder of the Soviet Union, had called 'the dictatorship of the proletariat'. Indeed, the Communists lost the election in the then still unified Berlin in 1946. Unperturbed and true to his strategy that the new Communist state should look like a constitutional democracy but would, in reality, be governed by the iron will of the Marxist-Leninist regime, Ulbricht forced the Social Democrats (SPD) to merge with the Communist Party and created the Socialist Unity Party (SED). The regime even established a political party aimed at former National Socialists (the National Democratic Party of Germany, or NDPD) in order to incorporate their former foes into the system.

In the subsequent rigged elections the smaller nationalist and nominally liberal and conservative parties such as the Christian Democratic Union (CDU) and the Liberal Democratic Party of Germany (LDPD) secured token representation. But the smaller parties always lost to the larger SED, who miraculously won over 90 per cent of the votes on a 99 per cent turnout.

The system was democratic – on paper. In practice the smaller parties – known as the *Blockparteien* or 'block-parties' – all accepted the leadership of the SED. And those, especially Social Democrats, who opposed the system were dealt with harshly, normally ending up in Hohenschönhausen, the regime's prison for political opponents. Thus the German Democratic Republic, the official name of the new state, was a bit of a misnomer. It was Russian rather than German, dictatorial rather than democratic, and was far from being a republic, if we define that type of political system as one in which supreme power resides in a body of citizens. All power was centralised. The previous federal structure consisting of several states was abolished, even though those states were supposedly protected by the East German constitution established in 1949.

However, all was not going to plan for Walter Ulbricht. There was opposition to the SED; he was concerned that the process of establishing a Communist state was going too slowly; and his targets for massive increases in production were unrealistically high. The living standard of the Germans who resided in the Western Zone was rising rapidly, not least as a result of the Marshall Plan. The European Recovery Program, to give it its official name, was an American initiative to rebuild Europe. The US government gave $13 billion (approximately $120 billion today) in economic support to help the western European countries after the war. The scheme, named after US Secretary of State George Marshall, did not benefit workers in the East, who experienced no improvement in their standard of living. They were fed up with the empty promises of the Ulbricht regime. The Communists were not willing to budge – if anything, the opposite. In early June 1953, Walter Ulbricht issued a decree that the workers, supposedly the backbone of the so-called 'State of Workers and Farmers', had to increase their production output.

This demand led to riots and uprisings. For a few days from 12 to 16 June 1953 there were running battles on the streets of Berlin and Leipzig and protests in all major cities in East Germany. On 17 June the revolt was crushed when Soviet tanks and the East German police forcefully brought the protests to an end. Bertolt Brecht, the playwright who had returned from exile in the USA and settled in East Germany after the war, summed up the situation with customary wit in his poem 'The Solution':

> After the uprising of the 17th of June
> The Secretary of the Writer's Union
> Had leaflets distributed in Stalin Street
> Stating that the people
> Had lost the confidence of the government
> And could win it back only
> By redoubled efforts. Would it not be easier
> In that case for the government
> To dissolve the people
> And elect another?

Ulbricht was no longer able to pretend that the masses were with him, though the Communist regime did its utmost to blame the disturbances on alleged infiltration by 'Western Fascists'. Whether the Communist leadership believed this propaganda is an open question. The people were in no doubt that things were taking a turn for the worse. Unable to vote in free elections, or indeed exercise any other basic democratic freedoms, they opted for the only possible solution open to them at the time: they left.

'To vote with your feet' has become a common expression, but it was originally coined by the Soviet Communist leader Vladimir Lenin to describe the desertion of soldiers from the Tsarist Army in the First World War. The saying gained currency in Germany in the 1950s when hundreds of thousands of East Germans left for the Western land of plenty.

In those days, a decade before the building of the Berlin Wall, it was relatively easy to escape. If fleeing constituted a kind of referendum on the regime, the mass emigration amounted to a vote of no confidence in Ulbricht. In 1951, 165,000 fled the regime; in 1952 the figure had increased to 182,000; and in 1953, the year of the uprising, the figure reached a zenith of 331,000. Out of an estimated population of 18 million, this mass migration was bound to have economic consequences.

As the masses were travelling west, Herlind and her daughter Angela were, as we have seen, going east. Horst, Herlind's husband, had left the northern city of Hamburg a few months earlier, and now he was to see his daughter for the first time. Hamburg, the largest city of the Hanseatic League (a commercial and defensive confederation of merchant towns in northern Germany established in the Middle Ages) was a proud place. The city had been one of the earliest seats of financial capitalism in late medieval times, when trade and industry bloomed. However, it had been almost completely destroyed in Operation Gomorrah in 1943 when British and American bombs levelled the city centre. Over 40,000 civilians had died during the attack, 214,350 out of 414,500 houses and apartments were destroyed in a single raid, and there was little left of the once prosperous city.

Pastor Horst Kasner – or Horst Kaźmierczak as he was baptised – was a theologian of Polish descent who had trained in the university town of Heidelberg on the upper Rhine plain in the southwest of Germany. Horst had passed his theological exams and married Herlind Jentzsch, an English teacher.

We know very little about Kasner's early life. He was born in 1925 and his father, Ludwig, was a senior police officer in Pankow, in the capital Berlin. The family was originally Catholic but had converted to Lutheran Protestantism and changed their name to the more German-sounding Kasner when Horst was four years old. The Kasners were religious, and their conversion was not merely opportunistic. Horst was confirmed in the Lutheran Church and decided to study theology after his military service. He won a place at Ruprecht-Karls University in Heidelberg, Germany's oldest and perhaps most prestigious university, and stayed there for four years. Soon after his graduation in 1952, Horst moved to Bielefeld, a northwestern industrial town, where he studied 'practical theology' at the Kirchliche Hochschule Bethel, a Lutheran theological seminary. The young man was subsequently offered a temporary position as deputy pastor at the Church of the Epiphany in the small suburb of Winterhude in the north of Hamburg. This was an industrial area and as such had been the target of many of the air raids during the war. There was much to do for a young pastor with a social conscience. But it was not all work. Horst met Herlind in 1952.

Herlind Jentzsch was a northern belle from a middle-class family, and she too was of Polish descent. She was born in 1927 in Danzig – present-day Gdansk – where her father, Willi Jentzsch, was a prominent politician and principal of a *Gymnasium* (an academic secondary school). Danzig, a port on the Baltic Sea, was a German city within Poland that had been allowed to remain German after the First World War.

Herlind's upbringing was reminiscent of that described in Thomas Mann's novel *Buddenbrooks*; hers was a family of comfortable businessmen and civil servants, struggling at a time when the old established order was rapidly changing. After the hyperinflation of the 1920s and the economic crisis, the family threw in the towel and moved to Hamburg.

Herlind, a petite blonde with blue eyes, must have been smitten by the exceptionally tall and rather athletic young clergyman Horst. Maybe she fell for his determination, enthusiasm and zeal. At a time when the world was heading for a confrontation between the Soviet Union and the USA, now both armed with nuclear weapons, Horst Kasner, seemingly unperturbed, wanted to preach the word of the Lord and spread the message of Jesus Christ in the atheist Communist state of East Germany.

Horst and Herlind got married in 1953 and lived in the vicarage close to the Church of the Epiphany. Life was spartan, but comparatively comfortable. The Lutheran Church had a strong network and funds to draw on. But it was a time of exceptional tensions. Josef Stalin's death in March 1953 had not fundamentally altered the political situation: if anything it had made it worse. Nobody in the West – let alone in the East – was clear what the Soviet Union would do next. The new Soviet leader, Nikita Khrushchev, was an unknown quantity. At this stage there was no indication that the Ukrainian-born Soviet dictator would change the foreign policy goals and strategies of the world's second superpower. His 'Secret Speech' to the 20th Party Conference, in which he denounced the 'Cult of Personality and its Consequences', was not to be given for another three years.

Horst Kasner was not unaware of the situation in the East. Some have even suggested that he at least sympathised with the main principles of Socialism. He was later known as 'Red Kasner', but he was not, as we shall see, a Communist. His sympathy with Socialism – which neither he nor his daughter denied – was of a humanitarian and democratic nature. His was the sort of Socialism espoused by US Senator Bernie Sanders, not the kind pursued by the East German regime or North Korea today.

The young pastor's main motivation was religious, indeed evangelical: 'I would have travelled anywhere to preach the word of our Lord, even to Africa,' he said.[1] But his calling lay closer to home. The Church wanted him to return to the East whence he came.

East Germany was predominately a Lutheran Protestant country. Martin Luther, whose revolt against the Pope had started the Reformation in the sixteenth century, was from Wittenberg in Saxony, in the southern part of what became East Germany, and his twentieth-century compatriots – insofar as they were allowed to do so – followed his teachings. But the Communist regime was not making life easy for believers. Karl Marx famously declared that religion is the opium of the people, and the regime of Walter Ulbricht was eager to make it as difficult as possible for the Lutherans to practise their religion. Several Christians – not only pastors but also other employees of the Church – were victimised. Indeed, a festival for young Christians had been banned on the grounds that the Christian association Junge Gemeinde, an organisation not unlike the YMCA, was illegal, when, in fact, no such law had been passed. The cherished ideal of the rule of law was not in vogue among the Communists, and by 1953 over 3,000 students had been expelled from their respective schools for belonging to the Christian youth organisation. At the end of the same year the harassment of Lutherans was stepped up yet further when the Communist youth organisation Freie Deutsche Jugend (FDJ) forcefully took over Schloss Mansfeld, a castle belonging to the young Lutherans.

The Evangelical Church in Germany (EKD), the organisation representing the Lutheran Church throughout Germany, sent a strongly worded letter to the East German leadership in which they begged the government to stop prosecuting Lutheran youth work and to cease to discriminate against Christian students. The regime responded by raiding the offices of Junge Gemeinde in Dresden. Not surprisingly, the number of clergymen in the Soviet-occupied zone was dwindling. It was to address this problem that the Lutheran Church sought to recruit pastors in the West who were willing to risk life and limb in the East.

Hans Otto Wölber, one of Kasner's senior colleagues in Hamburg (he later became bishop of that city's cathedral), told his young colleague that he was needed in East Germany. As Kasner was originally from the East, he was easy to persuade – though he joked that those who travelled to the East were 'normally total idiots or Communists'.[2] We do not know how Herlind reacted. She was expecting her first child and the prospect of leaving the West couldn't have been easy. The family started to make preparations. Horst went ahead but Herlind stayed behind to have her baby.

Angela Dorothea Kasner was born in the Elim-Krankenhaus, a highly regarded hospital in Hamburg-Eimsbüttel, on 17 July 1954. Being born at Elim, a state-of-the-art hospital with close ties to the Lutheran Church, was a good way to start life. Even today the hospital (renamed Diakonieklinikum Hamburg in 2011) proudly stresses its religious roots and its commitment to 'medical excellence and care combined with the Christian tradition of loving thy neighbour'. Originally built in 1927, it had been partly destroyed during the war and was still being rebuilt at the time Angela was born. Elim belonged to the Lutheran Communion in Northern Germany. Having a husband who worked for the Protestant Church had helped Herlind secure a place at the hospital: being a pastor's wife had certain benefits.

Just eight weeks after Angela's birth her mother travelled to East Germany. Little Angela was in a basket as the family could not afford a pram.

THE ABSENT FATHER

Life was tough in the Communist part of Germany, and not just economically. The newcomers were not welcomed by the Communist regime. Herlind was banned from teaching as her subjects, English and Latin, were perceived as counter-revolutionary and bourgeois. That she had gone to the East was only 'out of love for my father', her oldest daughter later said.[3] Reading between the lines, it is evident that she was anything but enthusiastic about the move. Whether she had wanted to work full-time is not known. In the 1950s only about 45 per cent of women over eighteen had joined the labour force. Herlind, therefore, was not exceptional in being a stay-at-home mother. But the fact that she had no choice in the matter and suspicion that she was being discriminated against because she was from the West made it harder for her to live under the ever-watchful eye of the Stalinist Big Brother state. She coped, however, and concentrated on raising her three children, Angela, Marcus (born 1957) and Irene (born 1964).

Herlind did her utmost to make sure that her children were not too indoctrinated by the Communist regime. She had reason to be anxious. Having grown up in Nazi Germany (she was four years old when Adolf Hitler seized power in 1933), she had first-hand experience of how that most totalitarian and repressive regime had encouraged children to spy on their parents and how its organisations infiltrated the everyday life of citizens. Every day, after school, Herlind Kasner gathered her children around her and went through all they had been told at school that day. In a way she was asking her children to give her a debriefing and giving them an opportunity to speak out. Her daily talk served to limit the deliberate brainwashing in the East German schools.

Her daughter later told a newspaper, 'Each day my mother spent two hours during which we "despoke" – as I call it. I am grateful to my parents for having given me this opportunity to talk.'[4] Despite the hardship and the discrimination, Herlind was according to most accounts 'a spontaneous, hospitable, undaunted and open woman' who, like her daughter, 'liked to tell jokes'.[5]

The young family had initially settled in Quitzow, in Perleberg, 70 miles Northwest of Berlin and only 20 miles to the east of the West German border. The parish was small, approximately 400 souls. A hard life awaited the young couple. Angela Merkel later recalled – though she cannot possibly have remembered it herself – that her father 'had to learn to milk goats and an old lady taught my mother how to make nettle-soup. The only means of transportation was a kind of moped and bicycle.'[6]

The young pastor and his wife got on with things. Alongside the local teacher, they were the only residents with further education, so in addition to their pastoral duties for the Church they helped the local population with their paperwork and generally supported them at a time when the regime was consolidating its grip on the country. The local farmers were under constant suspicion of being counter-revolutionaries, the regime forcibly expropriated four hundred hectares of land from one of the landowners, and suicides were becoming increasingly common.

The maltreatment of Christians somewhat eased off in 1955. At the same time tensions rose between the two Germanys. On 6 May 1955 West Germany joined NATO, a defence organisation established to prevent Soviet invasion. A few days later, on the 14th, the Soviet Union established the Warsaw Pact, with East Germany as a founding member. The Pact was officially established to protect Communist countries from the alleged aggression of the West. In fact it was yet another means of controlling the countries under Communist rule.

It was becoming clear that the division of the country was likely to be, if not permanent, then at least long-lasting. In the West the Christian Democrat Konrad Adenauer – the almost 80-year-old West German Chancellor who had returned from political obscurity to lead his country – had made speeches aggressively attacking the East German Communists. He and his economics minister Ludwig Erhard, an economist with free-market leanings, had issued shares to ordinary citizens (so-called 'people's shares'). Adenauer and Erhard were building a system of popular capitalism which combined the former's ideal of Catholic social ethics with the latter's model of free enterprise. This social market economy and an alliance with America became the new basis of West German politics.

Many, including Horst Kasner, had been sceptical of Adenauer and Erhard. Kasner and others like him felt that the West German Chancellor's adoption of American values was at odds with German tradition, history and culture, and that it ran counter to the ideals of social democracy that had existed prior to the Nazi takeover. Perhaps above all, many felt that the deployment of American troops on West German soil smacked of ill-disguised warmongering on Adenauer's part. This perception was particularly strong among Protestant theologians, who were inclined to be leftist liberals sceptical of the Catholic Chancellor. Adenauer's religious affiliation was another reason that he was relaxed about the division of his country. After all, without the East the Catholics would be in a permanent majority.

The Soviets, and particularly the KGB, were not blind to this dynamic. They sought to exploit the internal divisions and naïvety of some of the Protestant pastors, among them Horst Kasner. The Communists realised that it would be impossible – perhaps even counterproductive – to persecute the Christians; indeed over 70 per cent of the members of the Communist Party were themselves Christians. It made more sense to incorporate the Lutherans, or at least their leaders, into the system, for in this way the East German secret police (the infamous Stasi) would find it easier to monitor their movements.

In early 1958 the Communists organised a conference on Christianity and Peace in the Czechoslovakian capital, Prague. Horst Kasner was invited and took part in the forum. It was rich in rhetoric about the 'peace-loving Soviet Union' and the 'aggressive West'. Officially the gathering was organised by the East German theology professor Werner Schmauch, but behind the scenes the East German Communist party and the Minister for Church Affairs, Klaus Gysi, were pulling the strings. Klaus was the father of Gregor Gysi, later a member of the federal Parliament for the Left Party and the last chairman of the SED. Unlike his mild-mannered humanist son five decades later, however, Gysi Sr. was a hardline Communist. He used the gathering to identify leading Christians who could be used by the party. Unwisely Kasner allowed himself to be used. To save their churches, and naïvely believing that the Communist Party was on their side, Kasner and some of his colleagues became what Lenin reportedly called 'useful idiots'.

While the rhetoric grew increasingly harsh, the citizens of the two Germanys could still move relatively freely across the border separating East and West. Politicians still tried to find some common ground: German Chancellor Konrad Adenauer visited Moscow in 1955 and the Soviet Union recognised West Germany in the same year.

COUNTRY LIFE IN EAST GERMANY

Not all was politics. Horst and Herlind were able to go to the West and visit family, and their little daughter often stayed with her grandmother Gertrud in Hamburg. When Angela was about two years old, she came home from a visit speaking in an almost perfect Hamburg accent. While she learned to speak sooner than most, she did not learn to walk. Her parents were concerned that something was wrong and her mother would carry her downstairs. 'I was a bit of a spastic,'[7] Angela later acknowledged. Throughout her childhood climbing up stairs and even walking were a challenge for her.

The stay in Quitzow was short. Three years later the Kasners moved to Templin, a medium-sized town of 20,000 people 100 kilometres north of Berlin. Unlike their former abode, Templin was not a totally nondescript provincial backwater, but a town with a history and a place that was very much shaped by current events. In the 1930s the leading Nazi Hermann Göring lived in a purpose-built château just outside Templin. In the mid-1950s, around the time the Kasners arrived, a military airbase was established there for the 16th Air Force of the Soviet Red Army. By East German standards Templin was almost cosmopolitan, and the presence of many Russian speakers was one of the reasons Angela Merkel learned that language to perfection.

Kasner must have done a good job in his first parish in Quitzow. He was promoted, perhaps because he was well connected. Albrecht Schönherr was the general superintendent of the Lutheran Churches in East Germany. He was a clergyman who cooperated with the regime, though more out of necessity than as the result of any commitment to the Communist cause. The young pastor Kasner impressed Mr Schönherr as a man who had an intellectual interest in theology as well as being committed to preaching. Schönherr later remembered that young Kasner was

a gifted teacher. He was a natural choice for head of the newly established Templin Theological Seminary, a training establishment for theology graduates who wanted to become pastors in the Lutheran Church.

The family moved into the second floor of a complex called the
Waldhof, which also housed a school for children with special needs –
a demographic the Communist regime found difficult. Unusually for the
time, the children at the Waldhof were allowed to wander freely around
and take part in various activities in the garden and the workshops run by
the church. The centre was dilapidated and run-down when the Kasners
arrived but little by little they restored it, often with the help of those with
special needs. Angela's friends did not like to come over to 'the crazy bats'
as the locals called the residents, but being with those with special needs
had a formative effect on little Angela. She later said she learned to appreciate that 'happiness has got nothing to do with health', and that those
who are the least fortunate often have the most positive outlook on life.[8]

Pastor Kasner excelled in his new post, where his pastoral duties
were limited and the main task was to train future pastors. 'Kasner was
really something else,' an associate remembered. 'When he spoke you listened. He had authority.'[9] A relatively young man (he was only 31 when
he became head of the college), he had charisma. Had he lived in an open
society he would probably have become a professor, but the system did
not afford him the opportunity.

Although Kasner was not adverse to the ideas of Socialism, albeit
in a democratic form, the Communist regime did not welcome the pastor. The Stasi kept a detailed file on his every activity. The fact that he
was appointed by Schönherr, a well-known sympathiser with the regime,
did not seem to matter to the ever-vigilant secret agents. Kasner seems,
at this stage at least, to have been relatively naïve. In 1957, according to
the dossier on him in the Stasi archive, he warned against the militarisation of the Communist state and against being 'fascinated by uniforms,
lametta and shining military decorations'. And, in what seems a clear
reference to Ulbricht, he also cautioned against 'trusting those whose
words are not matched by their deeds'.[10] Kasner was assigned a special
agent who duly reported all this back to headquarters. He might have
been suspicious – he certainly was later – but at this stage he was igno-
rant of his surveillance by the Stasi.

In totalitarian regimes the leadership is obsessed with showing the magical unity of leader and led. Totalitarian politics is an all-encompassing activity and anyone who does not wholeheartedly commit himself or herself to the historical mission of the party is mistrusted. Kasner was in this category, at least until he learned to conform. 'He never takes part in any elections', was the indictment in another of the dossiers on him in the late 1950s.[11] Pastor Kasner was clearly in the class of individuals to be watched. He was, as another Stasi file stated, a potential threat to the regime, a 'pastor for young people who uses all available means to win over young people to the Church. His attitude towards our state is negative. He displays an extremely negative attitude towards the policies and the measures undertaken by our state.'[12]

It was because of these attitudes that Kasner was selected to go to the 1958 Peace Conference. 'Hug them close' goes the political slogan. Rather than treating the rather idealistic pastor harshly, the Stasi reckoned it could turn him into an asset. While being allowed a modicum of freedom, Kasner – without knowing it himself – could be useful to the regime.

It was sensible of the regime to allow the Theological Seminary to exist, as it was cost-efficient for the spies and special agents to have all the potential counter-revolutionaries in the same place. The Seminary soon became a pivotal institution in the Lutheran community in the region of Brandenburg, and even beyond. Most pastors in northern East Germany would stay for longer or shorter periods at the Waldhof. There they would be housed in large dormitories and could develop a kind of community spirit as they attended short courses and seminars on writing sermons, pastoral care and liturgical issues. Sometimes more political topics would be discussed. Many of the pastors who attended later became open critics of the regime, including Rainer Eppelmann, who was one of the most outspoken at the time of the fall of the Berlin Wall and became a politician after German reunification (see Chapter 3).

Whether Kasner was responsible for this critical attitude among the students and, indeed, whether he directly encouraged it is difficult to say. There has been no shortage of criticism of his conformist attitude and of the way in which he seemingly went along with the regime. Most fail to appreciate the difficulties practising Christians faced in a dictatorship of that type. To be sure there are always critics who are willing to risk life and limb, but not everyone is destined for martyrdom. Sometimes it is better to make your peace with the mighty foe lest you be crushed altogether.

Kasner's non-confrontational style and his good relations with Bishop Schönherr paid off, at least up to a point. The authorities allowed the Templin Theological Seminary to be a sort of haven in the totalitarian state. And the institution, though under constant surveillance by Stasi agent 'Zentrum', nevertheless became something of a refuge for those who were critical of the regime. The students were able to read and discuss books, even ones that were not available, and sometimes even banned, in East Germany. Former participants remember that discussions in the Waldhof were spirited. '[Kasner] was not a true critic of the regime, but he was open to discussion,' said Rudi Pahnke, a theologian who later became a vocal critic of the communist system. Kasner, Pastor Pahnke continued, 'did not mince his words when he spoke about the authorities and argued like a critical rationalist and had the appearance of a Prussian officer. [He] was a typical representative of Protestantism as a rationalist religion.'[13]

Kasner was not a happy man, and at times he seems to have regretted having returned to the East. Another one of the participants in the seminars at the Waldhof remembers how, 'after we had been drinking wine', Kasner told his colleagues 'how he had left the West out of free will and about how hard he had worked and he nevertheless was convinced that all was in vain and that the Church – even in his lifetime – would shrink and most parishes would lose their pastor.'[14]

Maybe his despair was the result of stress, anxiety and a heavy workload. Kasner worked hard, maybe too hard. He was often away and both his wife and his elder daughter – who had seen a lot of her father when the family lived in Quitzow – found it hard to cope with his absences. When he came home late in the evening, little Angela would often walk up to the gate to wait for him. In her own words: 'The worst thing was that he said he would come at this time and then he wouldn't arrive until hours later. But when we were all together and all ate supper as a family then everything was wonderful.'[15]

There was, by all accounts, a lot of unrequited love. Sigmund

Freud would have had a field day reading Angela's descriptions. 'My father always worked a lot,' Merkel later said in a frank interview:

> Work and leisure became indistinguishable and became as one. And sometimes, I think, the responsibilities were, possibly, sacrificed for the sake of his work. Dad was busy and extremely meticulous and showed attention to detail. As a child, sadly, it is not always easy when everything has to be perfect. Towards other people he was always understanding and open, but when we children screwed up [etwas verbockt hatten] he always reacted in a completely different way.[16]

Do children become like their parents? Are there other reasons why they develop habits or behaviours? Whatever the answers to these questions, it seems clear that Angela inherited her father's perfectionism and his total dedication to work when she grew up.

This dedication and eagerness was also what she displayed when she began school in 1961. Angela was exceptionally gifted and did her homework. But in a Stalinist state, school is not just about academic achievement. Children and the young are always the first targets of relentless indoctrination, which accompanies other more direct forms of repression and coercion. In a totalitarian dictatorship the educational process is used to bolster the propaganda efforts of the regime.

East Germany was no exception. When Angela began in the local primary school, the Goethe Schule, she was immediately confronted by the omnipresent Big Brother state. The pastor's daughter, who was barely six years old at the time, was urged to join the Young Pioneers. This organisation instructed young children in the virtues of Communism. Angela was not allowed to join. Horst and Herlind told their elder daughter, 'Although everyone must go to school, not everyone has to be a pioneer.'[17] The Kasners' decision on behalf of their daughter had consequences, if subtle ones. The Communist regime knew how to exert pressure without resorting to brute force, and Angela's case was a typical example. She did well at school, being quiet, diligent and of good conduct. She was the best in her class. But she did not win the prize for Pupil of the Year. Why? Elementary: she was not a Pioneer. Angela's classmate Bodo won the accolade. But as a true friend and with that inborn sense of justice and fairness that often characterises young children, the little boy asked the teacher, 'Angela gets the same grades as me, so why isn't she getting a prize?' The teacher coldly responded that Bodo, unlike Angela, was a Pioneer.[18] Even at that early stage no further explanation was necessary.

A few weeks later the class again discussed membership of the Pioneers. Angela wanted to join. Her parents, knowing full well the consequences of not falling into line – after all, both Horst and Herlind had been forced to join Hitler Jugend, the youth organisation of the Nazis – allowed their daughter to join. So Angela, a girl who, according to her father, always wanted harmony, joined the Pioneers, who prided themselves on being the 'fighting reserve of the party'.

As a Pioneer – and later as a full member of the FDJ (the young Communists' association) – Angela was allowed to shine, and eventually to collect prizes. Her classmates remember her as 'the best student by some considerable distance'. One of her teachers, who was interviewed when Merkel had become a household name, remembers her as carefree and happy and recalls that she ran around in the school hall 'wearing the blue shirt of the FDJ'.[19]

It is unlikely that this choice of attire signified a deep ideological commitment, after all she had only just started school. It seems doubtful that she succumbed to the indoctrination of the Ulbricht state. She did, of course, take part in Pioneer activities, and showed a considerable talent for organising small events. But her main focus was on schoolwork. She excelled at Russian, the language of the country known as – without any hint of Orwellian irony – 'our great Socialist brother'. Her Russian teacher recalls how the little Fräulein Kasner studied diligently and tirelessly and showed early signs of the dedicated and indefatigable adult politician, Angela Merkel. 'She was', remembers the teacher, 'exceptionally hard-working . . . She would be studying her vocabulary while waiting for the bus. She never allowed herself to make mistakes, and yet she was sometimes a bit withdrawn.'[20]

That Angela learned fluent Russian at a young age was not, one assumes, simply of her own volition. She herself seems to suggest that she learned Russian from Grade One. However, a careful reading of the school curriculum suggests that Russian was taught only from Grade Four upwards. According to a decree issued by the Ministry of Education, Russian was the only foreign language taught, and students received six hours of instruction in the subject, the same as in mathematics. Arts, drawing (a separate subject), history and sport were taught for one hour every week. The students received seven hours of instruction in German and literature.

Her parents must have encouraged her, for learning Russian was not just an opportune way of conveying that she – and by implication her family – was toeing the party line, it also allowed her the opportunity to read critical authors, such as Leo Tolstoy, later in her education. But much as Angela's parents may have thought strategically about their daughter's education, little Angela clearly enjoyed learning the language of the great Russian writers Feodor Dostoevsky, Leo Tolstoy and Alexander Pushkin. She was rather nostalgic about her Russian classes when she was asked about them later. 'Russian,' she said, 'is a beautiful language, full of emotion, a bit like music, [but also] a bit melancholy.'[21]

The other subject she excelled in from an early age was mathematics. Intellectuals in totalitarian regimes often study the hard sciences and mathematics. Just think of Andrei Sakharov in the Soviet Union, a brilliant physicist who became critical of the regime. This was, perhaps, not only because this exceptionally intelligent man had a deep desire to understand the laws of nature and abstract algebra, but also because the 'objective' natural sciences could not easily be incorporated into Marxist 'laws of motion of society'. Marxists held that Communism was a science; an infallible doctrine on how history would progress. While sociology, history and even biology could be – and were – taught in a way that conformed to the basic tenets of Marxist-Leninism, the natural sciences were out of bounds of the thought-control of the state. To study mathematics was 'safe'. Angela, like her brother Marcus, was exceptionally good at maths and numbers. Marcus later became a natural scientist and a university professor in physics in Frankfurt. Angela's, much younger sister Irene did not go to University but instead trained to become an occupational therapist. Angela's mathematics teacher was Wolf Donath. He was a card-carrying member of the SED, yet he was enthusiastic when, many years later, he was asked what he remembered of his now famous former pupil: 'She was wonderful, calm, logical, willing to put in an effort'; 'to teach her made it fun to be a teacher'.[22] Angela duly delivered and flourished. Indeed, she was a finalist in the national mathematics Olympiad a few years later. The Pastor's daughter was very much the model pupil that the East German state could parade to the wider world as proof that Socialism worked.

THE LAST HOLIDAY IN THE WEST

Meanwhile in the wider world the Cold War was warming up. In November 1958 the Soviet leader Nikita Khrushchev had demanded that the Western powers withdraw their forces from Berlin within six months. They did not. The city's Social Democrat Mayor, Willy Brandt, was defiant and won support and respect from the allies, especially the Americans. The ultimatum sparked a three-year conflict that deepened the divisions between East and West still further.

Families could still travel from West to East – and from East to West (though with some difficulty). The Kasners could still go to Hamburg to visit grandmother Gertrud. That the Ulbricht leadership would permanently close the border, let alone erect a wall, was not on the cards. Indeed, at a press conference the East German leader, speaking in his slightly eerie, shrill voice, had clearly stated: 'No one has the intention of erecting a wall.'

Whether Ulbricht was truthful when he made his comment is a matter that has divided historians. The Communist leader was certainly concerned by the exodus of well-educated East Germans from the country. But that a wall around Berlin and a heavily fortified border from Czechoslovakia in the south to the Baltic Sea in the north was the answer is disputed. There is some evidence to suggest that the Berlin Wall was built in response to a direct request from Khrushchev. According to subsequently published minutes, Ulbricht had a long telephone conversation with the Soviet leader on 1 August 1961.

Khrushchev was not in a happy mood. The most recent figures suggested that more than 200,000 East Germans had left the Stalinist state in 1960 alone. This angered the General Secretary of the Soviet Communist Party: 'Two years ago, when I spoke at your party conference, everything was under control. What has happened?'

Ulbricht, who knew the Ukrainian-born Soviet dictator from his time in Moscow, was remarkably matter-of-fact about the situation. He replied: 'The people are making demands that we simply cannot meet.' Even Communists can be realists and acknowledge that no political system, no matter how authoritarian, can survive mass dissent.

But Khrushchev had no time for this. Ulbricht's explanation did not satisfy him. Coming from a system where the will of the General Secretary is law and insubordination is punished by a long stay in Siberia or worse, he thundered back that Berlin had to be cut off from the rest of the country, and that Ulbricht should build an iron wall around Berlin forthwith.

Ulbricht, who had lived in Moscow in the years of Stalin's pogroms, obeyed the order. Construction began. This is the politics of totalitarian autocracy. In this short phone conversation, as a result of Khrushchev's losing his temper, a momentous geopolitical decision was made.

Ten days later, on Friday 11 August, the Kasners were returning from holiday in Bavaria with Herlind's mother. They had driven there in their Volkswagen Beetle. Horst noticed that there were an unusual number of soldiers about. As they crossed the border he saw large rolls of barbed wire being stored in the woods. He was uneasy; something seemed about to happen. This was the last holiday the Kasners were to have with Grandmother Gertrud. Two days later, on the morning of Sunday August 13, as the Kasners were preparing to go to church, they received the news that the Communist regime had erected what they called an 'anti-fascist protection wall'.

Angela, who had just turned seven, remembers the earth-shattering day: 'My father was preaching on that Sunday. The atmosphere was horrible in the church. I will never forget it. People cried. My mother cried too. We couldn't fathom what had happened.'[23] What had happened was almost unprecedented in human history. A whole country had been turned into a prison. In addition to fortifying the border with barbed wire and control towers, the whole of West Berlin was surrounded by a 155-kilometre-long wall four metres high. In democratic states the first duty of government is to protect its citizens, but the rulebook in East Germany was different. Many of her subjects were killed by the state when they tried to escape. Over the 28 years of the wall's existence 173 East Germans were shot dead while trying to scale it.

Willy Brandt named the Berlin Wall 'the wall of shame'. And in a brilliant move of political symbolism he put up posters showing a photo of Walter Ulbricht with his own words, 'No one has the intention of erecting a wall.' The posters were clearly visible from the East, but the West was powerless and could do nothing of substance.

The erection of the Berlin Wall was, so she later said, Angela Merkel's 'first political memory'.[24] The Cold War had entered a new phase and life would never be the same again. Not until 1989, at any rate.

CHAPTER 2

IN THE SHADOW OF THE BERLIN WALL

'IT'S PRONOUNCED ANGEELA,' THE LITTLE GIRL INSISTED, 'WITH EMPHASIS on the second vowel – Ang*ee*la.' Helga Gabriel, the music teacher, sighed and looked a bit tired. She had called the seven-year-old '*Ang*ela', with emphasis on the first vowel. But her pupil was something of a perfectionist and could sometimes be a bit of a pain; she was a girl who displayed many of the traits of Lucy from *Peanuts* or Lisa from *The Simpsons*. Music was not her best subject, though Mrs Gabriel admitted that little Miss Kasner 'didn't have a bad singing voice'.[1] She could be a bit too eager, she always wanted to be the best, and she talked a bit too much. But the teacher was not too distressed. Angela – or 'Kasi' as her friends called the pastor's daughter – was normally a good pupil. She was the sort who would continue to write when the other children became unruly and noisy; an old head on young shoulders who could seem a bit self-righteous. But all in all she was rather sweet, in her own bossy way. The teacher could put up with a bit of attitude from time to time.

Life in the Goethe School was uneventful and having a pupil who showed a bit of assertiveness and initiative was always welcome. Angela showed both. She continued to excel in mathematics and Russian and even participated in the countless competitions organised by the ever-competitive East German educational system. But sometimes she could be unrealistic. For someone who was naturally clumsy and who walked in a slightly uncoordinated way, Angela's ambition to become a figure skater was met with silent amusement.

But no one underestimated her determination or the way the seven-year-old meticulously prepared for everything. Absolutely nothing was ever left to chance. Her motto – which the other children found slightly annoying – was 'never show incompetence'.[2] Annoying or not, it was a fair description of how she approached everything. Many decades later, when Angela had become Chancellor Merkel, her attention to detail and her obsession with getting the facts right became almost legendary. And many of the character traits that were later associated with the most powerful female politician in the world were in evidence. Her behaviour as a schoolgirl, even when she was in primary school, was similar to the way she behaved and acted when she reached the pinnacle of her political career.

One example, often quoted by Angela, was the story of the diving board. In Grade Three, her PE teacher, who was under pressure to identify sporting talents for East Germany's successful Olympic team, suggested that Angela try the three-metre diving board. She knew that diving head first into the water could be painful, and the teacher probably expected her to make a jump feet first and then declare that this was not for her. That would save him time. Angela was not on his longlist of potential future Olympians, so he wasn't too fussed. But Angela always did as she was told. She climbed up the twelve steps, took a hesitant step and peered into the water. It was frightening. She turned back. But she didn't go down. She walked to and fro, analysing the situation. The other children were amused, and some of the boys started laughing. But Angela continued her analysis. Finally, just as the bell rang to signal that the class was over, she dived head first into the water. She never made it as a diver but she had summoned the courage to dive. The other pupils didn't laugh; none of them had dived in. Angela did – after she had analysed the situation.

Fast forward 44 years and German Chancellor Angela Merkel was in a difficult situation, once again analysing whether to take the plunge. This time the decision had implications for people other than herself – hundreds of millions of them, in fact. The German government had believed itself to be relatively immune to the financial crisis that engulfed the world after the collapse of the American investment bank Lehman Brothers in 2008. They were gravely mistaken. Within weeks the economy of the largest country in the Eurozone felt the aftershock of the debacle in the USA.

Merkel had little experience of dealing with economic issues. She had served as Minister for the Environment and before that as Minister of Women and Children. Her familiarity with complex economic issues was about as extensive as her experience of diving as a schoolgirl. As all those years before on the diving board, she vacillated, procrastinated and seemed to waver. And as at the school swimming pool back in Templin, some of the boys (in this case seasoned politicians from her own CDU and from the Social Democratic Party) began talking about her: she was 'scared', 'not up to the job', 'out of her depth'.

But then, just as time was about to run out, she made a surprise decision. Having considered all the possible consequences, she announced that the German government would guarantee all savings in German banks. Her announcement came with a confidence and a determination that surprised her colleagues. It created stability and earned her respect.

Later in life Merkel would recall the story of the diving board when her compatriots – and indeed the foreign media – criticised her for being indecisive. Like little Angela who did not care what her classmates said, the adult politician was unmoved by criticism. Indeed, she saw hesitancy as a virtue. Analysing every angle of the situation was a sign of strength and sure-footedness rather than the opposite, she said: 'I am quite brave when a decision has to be made. But I need a bit of a run-up and I like – if possible – to think before I jump. I always like to know what will happen to me, even if this means that I am less spontaneous.'[3] The German media continued to criticise her for her tendency to over-analyse. But she does this all her life. A political journalist from the sensationalist newspaper *Bild* described her as 'a woman who has turned procrastination into an art-form'.[4]

As a schoolgirl Angela was a bit of a character. She wasn't weird or odd, nor was she a social outcast, but she was different. There is no indication that she was bullied, though some of the boys liked to tease her. Most of the time she was in a little clique of four girls, but the other children – even the boys – seemed to like her too. A very organised girl, she was good at arranging parties. And, perhaps most importantly, she was always willing to help the students who were not quite as gifted as herself. A former classmate recalls: 'She was always helpful, and if someone had problems they could always come to her. If someone was a bit slow, Angela would explain it to them without being overbearing.' As she approached her teenage years her slightly bossy demeanour gave way to that of a girl who liked to laugh, joke and imitate voices. Not surprisingly, the photos of the prepubescent Angela are of a girl with a cheeky smile.

PASTOR KASNER'S BALANCING ACT

It wasn't always easy to be the pastor's daughter. Unlike the other children in the Goethe School, Angela wore jeans and often western trainers. This was not really a fashion statement, though undoubtedly it was perceived as such. It was a sign of necessity. Angela's mother was still not able to work – the authorities wouldn't let her – and her father received a rather modest salary of about 600 East German Marks from the Church. This was slightly below the average wage of 655 Marks in the mid to late 1960s. However, a large number of East German women started working after 1960, giving many families two incomes, and Pastor Kasner's family needed help. *Westpakete* – gifts sent from their friends and family in Hamburg – provided an important addition to his modest salary. These parcels were also a symbolic reminder of the political situation, being the only link to Grandmother Gertrud in Hamburg, whom Angela had not seen since the Berlin Wall was constructed in August 1961.

In some ways, though, Horst was better off than many of his compatriots. The family had two cars. Most East Germans had to wait for up to ten years for a Trabant, an exceptionally polluting East German car that was prone to break down. The Trabant was powered by a two-stroke engine and symbolised the difference between the primitive East German car industry and its suave West German counterpart, which provided virtually every working family with an Audi or a BMW – or even a Porsche. The Kasners had a Trabant but they had not had to wait for it for years like other families. Moreover they were allowed to have a second car, a Volkswagen, which they had bought with money sent to them by their family in the West.

There was a reason behind this favouritism towards the pastor. The Communist government was constantly short of hard currency, and one way of getting hold of it was to allow carefully selected citizens to receive money from abroad. Also, by giving the Lutheran pastor the chance to buy a second car the authorities could create resentment among his parishioners and thus drive a wedge between him and his congregation. Using the same tactics, the regime gave Pastor Kasner permission to travel to the West – to Italy, West Berlin and even to the United States. They knew he wouldn't defect. The right to travel was not extended to his wife and children. The SED and the Stasi were nothing if not cunning, and normally such tactics worked.

The Kasners were not suffering in East Germany, but they were kept on a tight leash. Life had generally improved for Christians in East Germany but, while they were no longer officially branded as 'enemies of the working-classes', they were still subject to subtle discrimination and watched as never before.

As we have seen, Horst Kasner had already tried to accommodate himself to the regime, though the Stasi files on him suggest that he had harsh words for the Communists behind closed doors. Even before the Wall was built he had attended a Peace Conference in Prague organised by the regime. In the same year, 1958, he had accepted an invitation from Pastor Schönherr, the head of the Lutheran Church in East Germany, to join the Weißenseer Arbeitskreis (WA), a formal discussion forum for divinity professors and Lutheran pastors, which, according to the ever-watchful Stasi's files, represented so-called progressive theologians – in other words, those who were willing to work with the regime.

The authorities took a keen interest in finding such potential collaborators, and Kasner was a leading light in the WA. Nothing was left to chance in East Germany, and everything had a political dimension in some way linked to the East-West conflict. Unlike most other organisations, The Lutheran Church, or EKD, had not been split up after the two Germanys had been established. It had influence over the hearts and minds of many East Germans.

The Politbüro, the highest organ of the Communist Party, was particularly concerned about the very outspoken bishop of Berlin. Bishop Otto Dibelius formally led the Church in Brandenburg (the area around Berlin) where Templin is situated. A fierce critic of the Communist regime, he had written an open letter to the East German authorities in which he bluntly declared that 'there could be no justice in a totalitarian state'. The East German authorities responded that the Bishop Dibelius was representing 'the Church of NATO'. But the Communists knew that simply branding the leader of the Lutherans a 'fascist imperialist' could be counterproductive. No dictatorship can survive if it relies on repression alone. Sometimes it is necessary to allow a small amount of dissent in order to avoid serious opposition. Repressive tolerance is often an effective weapon.

Walter Ulbricht was a master of such schemes. In a reversal of his previously harsh stance against the Christians, he told the East German Parliament that there was no conflict between Christianity and the humanitarian goals of Socialism. This was tactical rather than real, of course. In reality the clergymen were under constant surveillance and described in derogatory terms in the endless reports prepared by the Stasi. And the secret police were everywhere. Hannah Arendt, a German-American philosopher and writer who made a name for herself by analysing totalitarianism, observed in *The Origins of Totalitarianism*, that the secret police was the most deviously effective part of the otherwise dysfunctional totalitarian state: 'Above the state and behind the façade of ostensible power, in a maze of multiplied offices, underlying all shifts of authority, and in the chaos of inefficiency, lies the power nucleus of the country, the superefficient and supercompetent services of the secret police.' It was this organisation that stepped up its surveillance of Kasner and his family.

In the early 1960s, when Angela was about ten years old, a special agent assigned to her father infiltrated the Templin Theological Seminary and duly reported on the pastor's every move. Perhaps because he was slightly gullible, perhaps because he was clever, but perhaps also because he had no choice, Horst Kasner went along with Ulbricht – at least officially. At home and even in conversations with his colleagues at the Waldhof he was more critical. Officially, alongside Bishop Schönherr, Kasner began to propagate what became known as 'a church within Socialism'.

Kasner did a good job of deceiving the Stasi informant. By around 1967 the Stasi had come to see him as a nonthreatening, conformist individual. Thus when he participated in an EKD meeting with pastors and bishops from the West – many of whom were critical of East Germany – the ever-watchful Stasi informant reported that Kasner 'publicly denounced Bishop Dibelius' and was willing 'to work for our [the East German Politbüro's] policies'.[5] So great was the regime's trust in Kasner that they even assigned him a central role in one of their schemes. Not, it should be said, as a paid agent but merely as someone whom they trusted. The matter was once again the tensions between the two parts of the Lutheran Church. Bishop Dibelius was about to retire and a replacement had to be found.

One would have expected a break; that the authorities in the East would simply forbid East Germans from associating with the EKD. But such brute force was always a last resort. The SED preferred a more subtle form of control, and had a cunning plan. At a meeting of the Politbüro on 18 January 1967 it was agreed that instead of splitting, the East should put forward a candidate to become bishop of Berlin. Having an East German in that position would be a bit of a political coup.

And this is where Kasner came in. The SED used their influence – and a modicum of threats and intimidation – to get the leading lights of the Brandenburg Church to nominate Günter Jacob, a theologian and a member of the SED, for the post. Kasner was one of them. Watched by a Stasi mole, Angela's father and his colleagues travelled to West Berlin and duly – and apparently convincingly – argued the case for Bishop Jacob. According to the informant they made a good fist of it.

However, it wasn't enough. The EKD did not take the bait and chose Kurt Scharf. The new bishop proved to be a thorn in the side of East Germany. While his tone was less vociferous and perhaps more diplomatic than that of his predecessor, it was clear that he was equally unwilling to condone the deeds of the Ulbricht regime.

The failure to infiltrate the EKD forced the Politbüro to change tactics. Now they wanted to break with the 'capitalist' and 'fascist' rogues. Bishop Schönherr, who was increasingly acting as a mouthpiece of the regime, was charged with setting up a separate Lutheran Church in East Germany. Kasner played along with the idea. He did a good job convincing the Stasi that he was a genuine convert. The agent who reported on his every move now praised Kasner. The man who had once been described as 'an enemy of the Socialist State' was now praised by the Stasi as someone who 'defended the policies of our state'.[6]

Whether he had duped them or was becoming a true believer is a matter of some debate. Many denounced him for his willingness to compromise. Kasner's reportedly rather aloof and arrogant attitude did not earn him many friends and seriously annoyed many of his colleagues. His attempts to perform a delicate balancing act between being a critic of the regime and a man who was trusted by the ruling party rubbed many a clergyman up the wrong way. Pastor Rainer Eppelmann, Kasner's younger colleague, was particularly incensed by his former mentor: 'I thought to myself, "what a complete ass!".'[7]

Was this criticism fair? It is easy to be holier-than-thou, and to seek martyrdom is not always the most moral course of action. For a man who had a family to look after, willingness to compromise was not a sign of complicity with the dictatorship. Eppelmann's criticism of Kasner may have been heartfelt and understandable but even he stopped short of accusing his older colleague of being an official agent of the regime.

Kasner may have been more willing to compromise and collaborate with the regime than some others, but he was not in its pay. Richard Schröder was another critic of the regime who often came to the Waldhof. Schröder, who became a theology professor at the prestigious Humboldt University after 1989, defended Kasner against accusations of complicity, though he admitted that Angela's father had been someone who was considered 'trustworthy' by the regime. 'He [Kasner] was not conformist. The Pastoralkolleg was a window to the West [with guest] speakers and books from the West [and] the visitors were not carefully selected to ensure that they kept to the [Communist] party-line.'[8]

Perhaps just as importantly, at the time there was no indication that the Communist regime would collapse in the foreseeable future, if ever. It was understandable that Kasner wanted to secure and consolidate the shaky foothold the Lutheran Church had in the still officially atheist regime.

SOCIALISM WITH A HUMAN FACE, AND THE DEATH OF A DREAM

The later 1960s saw an easing of the relations between East and West. The imminent threat of nuclear war – which had reached its climax in 1961 when US President John F. Kennedy threatened to use nuclear weapons to stop the Soviets from stationing ballistic missiles on Cuba – had receded. There was a sense of guarded optimism; a feeling that the relations between Moscow and Washington were improving. The two superpowers agreed to treaties to limit the use of the atom bomb, high-level visits were organised, and Khrushchev donned a stetson on a visit to America in 1964. It seemed possible – if only just – that the countries in the Soviet Bloc could develop into something resembling a humanist version of Socialism.

East Germany was not a Communist state like the Soviet Union under Stalin, or like present-day North Korea. The citizens of the 'Workers and Farmers' State' were able to listen to foreign programmes and could receive Western television. As Angela recalled, 'Whenever representatives from the state, such as for example teachers, came to our house we would change television stations from Channel 7 [West German television] to Channel 5 [East German state television].'[9] So although East Germany was a dictatorship – and a cunning one at that – its citizens were not unaware of what was going on in the wider world, let alone in the Western part of the country.

The Kasners were interested in politics and followed the news from the West. By all accounts – including her own perhaps slightly rose-tinted recollections – Angela was exceptionally interested in current affairs: 'I sneaked into the girls' toilets [with a transistor radio] and listened to the debate in the Electoral College debates prior to the election of the West German President Gustav Heinemann.'[10] The fact that Angela had a small radio is indicative of the more relaxed attitude in the 1960s.

In 1963 the aging West German Chancellor Konrad Adenauer reluctantly retired at 87 and was replaced by Ludwig Erhard. In 1965 Erhard offered the Kremlin a loan of $25 billion in return for political liberties and eventual reunification. He even let it be known that he didn't expect the money to be repaid. The offer was rejected by the Soviets and generally not taken seriously by either of the sides in the conflict. Above all, the offer showed Erhard's naïvety as an international statesman. The corpulent economist was good with numbers and finances but an amateur when it came to high politics, diplomacy and international affairs. In any case, his tenure as Chancellor was short. After less than three years in office he stepped down and was replaced by Kurt Georg

Kiesinger, a conservative who was forced to join the Social Democrats in a coalition government. Willy Brandt became Deputy Chancellor and Minister of Foreign Affairs.

Kiesinger was controversial to many on the left. He had worked in the Nazi propaganda ministry and was a personal friend of the controversial philosopher and Nationalist Socialist Carl Schmitt. His deputy Willy Brandt's credentials were impeccable, unlike Kiesinger's. Not only was Brandt a man who had actively resisted the Nazis, he was also an anti-Communist who had spoken out against East Germany. He was Mayor of Berlin when the Wall was erected, and it was he who had stood by John F. Kennedy when the US President uttered the famous words, 'Ich bin ein Berliner.'

Whether all this mattered to those living in the East is debatable. German reunification was not on the cards and those living in the East were looking elsewhere for hope. Indeed, some were not even that keen on a united Germany. Kasner – though he was assuredly *not* a Communist – was lukewarm about it, and he cherished the idea of a German state based on some form of humanitarian Socialism. Kasner was ostensibly inspired by the developments in Czechoslovakia, where the reform-minded Slovak Alexander Dubček, the Communist Party leader, was building a state that was very different from the semi-Stalinist regime of Walter Ulbricht.

As a member of the Central Committee of the Czechoslovakian Communist Party (KSČ), Dubček had spearheaded a revolt against Antonín Novotný, the hardline leader of the party. The Soviets seemed to trust Dubček. His parents had been Communists and he was born in the Soviet Union. This pedigree gave him a bit of leeway. Novotný was caught unawares. As someone who had always followed the party line and never disobeyed his masters in the Kremlin, he did not fear the Russians would depose him. Assuming wrongly that Moscow would back him, he invited Leonid Brezhnev – who had replaced Khrushchev in 1964 – to Prague to quell the palace coup.

The Soviet leader, a dull technocrat with massive trademark eyebrows, was unimpressed by Novotný, and was taken aback by the opposition to him. Sensing that the personable Dubček, who spoke perfect Russian, was more capable, Brezhnev abandoned Novotný. Dubček became first secretary of the KSČ in January 1968. He immediately began reforms. It was a period of euphoria, later recounted in the Czech author Milan Kundera's novel *The Unbearable Lightness of Being*. In the spring months of 1968 Dubček and his reformist colleagues coined the phrase 'Socialism with a human face'. These events became known as the Prague Spring, named after the Czechoslovakian capital where the experiment in humane Communism unfolded.

Horst Kasner was inspired, even enthused, by these developments. So were many intellectuals in the West. Helmut Gollwitzer, a theology professor in West Berlin, wrote an influential essay with the title 'Why I am a Socialist as a Christian'. Many protestant theologians followed Gollwitzer and became critics of capitalism and defenders of Socialism, though they maintained their opposition to the Soviet Union's version of Communism.

Kasner was a vocal critic of excessive greed and the consumer society. True to his Christian Socialist beliefs, he criticised the prevailing system of capitalism: 'All that matters is money. For the producers to make profits and for the consumers to buy – and to buy more than you need. The market economy is being beaten into us and should not be questioned. Everything is being turned into a "market", even nature itself.'[11]

For someone who fundamentally believed that the capitalist system was wrong and who longed for a sort of humanitarian Socialism that combined Christian brotherly love with social justice, the Prague Spring was attractive. All Kasner's compromises, he believed, had been worth it. Finally, after initial hardships, Socialism with a human face was on the cards; his belief in some form of humane Christian Socialism seemed to have come true.

Inspired by Dubček, in July 1968 the Kasners went on holiday to the Krkonoše in north Czechoslovakia, renting a little apartment from a Czech family. Angela, now 14 years old, relished the opportunity to travel and enjoyed a bit of time with her otherwise ever-busy father, and her mother was looking forward to a bit of a rest from her domestic chores. The family from whom they rented the apartment had a son who was the same age as Angela. She was becoming increasingly extroverted and never missed an opportunity to speak to all and sundry. So naturally she talked to the son. He collected stamps and told her that he had one with Antonín Novotný's face. Angela later recalled the rest of what happened:

> I saw that the boy was tearing up the stamp and I rushed over to him and asked why he was destroying one of his stamps. And he told me that Dubček now was the great hero and that the stamps with Novotný's portrait, therefore, belonged in the rubbish bin.[12]

That the new regime was promoting Dubček as 'the great hero' and even the leaders of the Prague Spring subscribed to the cult of personality should have given Horst and Herlind cause to think. It did not. They were swept away by the tide of enthusiasm and the prospect of a new dawn of democratic Socialism. The Kasners asked the Czech family to look after the children for a couple of days while they went to Prague to experience the revolutionary air for themselves. There they experienced first-hand that indefinable spirit of liberty and hope that characterise all true revolutions. After two days in the Czechoslovakian capital the pastor and his wife returned to their three children with a proverbial spring in their step. Excited and enthused, the Kasners went back to Templin. It was not to last.

The following week Angela went down to visit her grandmother in Berlin for the weekend. Early in the morning of Wednesday 21 August she heard the news. The Prague Spring was over. Soviet tanks and cold-hearted repression shattered the dream that had seemed so real, so tantalising and so touchingly near. Television programmes from the West, which all East Germans watched, showed the familiar images of the Red Army beating up citizens who pleaded for mercy, just as Soviet troops had done in Berlin in 1953 and in Budapest in 1956.

The French philosopher Bernard-Henri Lévy dubbed Communism 'La barbarie à visage humain' ('barbarism with a human face'), cleverly paraphrasing Dubček's catchphrase 'Socialism with a human face'. Lévy's essay signalled the broken hopes of the left. But unlike Lévy, Kasner and his family could not criticise the regime.

Horst and Herlind were devastated by the Soviet invasion. This was noted by the ever-vigilant Stasi informer, who told his masters that Pastor Kasner had expressed the opinion that the invasion 'could only lead to suppression of democracy in Czechoslovakia'.[13] A statement of the obvious, but in East Germany enough to put him under renewed surveillance.

Perhaps characteristically, Angela was able to see the irony in the situation, and was amused that the boy in the household they had visited had immediately discarded the stamps bearing Novotný's portrait. On the first day of school, a couple of weeks later, the students were asked the innocent question, 'What they had done during their holiday?' Angela began to tell the story about the stamp-collecting boy in Czechoslovakia who had torn up the stamps. But the teacher fixed her with a steely gaze: 'I immediately realised that this was not to be talked about, so I quickly changed the story.'[14] Angela knew how to behave and how to avoid getting in trouble. Life went on as usual. She continued to work hard and to stay out of trouble. No one, least of all her teachers, suspected her of harbouring 'unsocialistic' sentiments.

THE RUSSIAN LANGUAGE OLYMPICS

After the Prague Spring, Pastor Kasner kept a low profile. While the family was careful not to rock the boat, they quietly stuck to their beliefs. Angela was confirmed, like other practising Christians. She reaffirmed her belief in God when she was 15 years old. She also continued to organise activities for the FDJ. Above all she excelled at her schoolwork. But she probably would not have made it if the authorities had been more suspicious of her father. Other children of Lutheran ministers and pastors were not quite so fortunate. Those who showed signs of dissent were dealt with swiftly, effectively and without mercy. Not – or not in most cases anyway – by imprisonment, torture and the like, but by effectively blocking any career prospects.

Christians – the regime's protestations notwithstanding – were still being singled out. One such victim was Ulrich Schoeneich (who became Mayor of Templin after the fall of Communism in 1989). The son of a non-conformist clergyman, Schoeneich was not a member of the FDJ. Consequently, although he got exceptionally good grades, he was deemed unsuitable to attend the EOS, the elite high school, and was effectively barred from receiving a higher education.

Angela too lived in fear; she was constantly worried that a small false step might destroy her. Every day her mother told her that she had to behave – and indeed that she had to behave better than other children – if she was going to get into university. She knew that the system discriminated against the children of clergymen. Asked what her father's profession was, Angela could hardly deny that he was a pastor. But the German word *Pfarrer* (pastor) is pronounced in almost the same way as *Fahrer* (driver). By slightly mispronouncing the former word, Angela could make it sound as if her father was working-class and not something as decidedly bourgeois and reactionary as a Christian clergyman. Whether she actually convinced anybody we cannot tell. Her father was quite a well-known figure, and it is unlikely that the teachers were unaware that Angela Kasner was the daughter of Pastor Kasner. But making the effort to play along with the regime's fetish for all things blue-collar and working-class certainly did not hurt her, and showed that she knew her place.

East Germany was a society run by a political party that spied on its citizens and was willing to kill them if they tried to escape. If a totalitarian government is one where the regime seeks to control not only people's lives but also their thoughts, then East Germany certainly was one. It was one of the most sophisticated autocratic states in human history. The fictional accounts in Florian Henckel von Donnersmarck's 2006 film *The Lives of Others* and the description in the television series *Deutschland 83* are not wide of the mark, as anyone who has visited the Stasi archives will testify. Yet even Angela Merkel has acknowledged that it was not all bad. 'I had a wonderful childhood. And that is a thing that people from the West often overlook, namely that not everything was political in East Germany,'[15] she insisted years later. It was as if she felt a strange need to defend the state that had done its utmost to control her life.

Whether or not East Germany was a totalitarian state in the sense used by historians and social scientists is ultimately a question of semantics. The regime certainly did its utmost to shape its citizens by indoctrination and intimidation. Education was an important part of the coercive machinery of repression. The schools left nothing to chance, and the school Angela attended was no exception. It has often been said that totalitarian regimes wanted to create a new type of human that fitted the image of historical materialist ideology. Angela and the other pupils were told in no uncertain terms that they were attending an educational institution 'that was a forge and that those who were not willing to be moulded would have to go'.[16]

Angela went along with the indoctrination, at least outwardly. Her diligence as a student and her quiet demeanour helped her. Another thing that didn't hurt her was her ability to speak almost flawless Russian. Every year the school would organise competitions in this language. Angela had a competitive spirit: 'whatever she does, she always wants to be the best', one of her classmates recalled. In Russian she definitely was the best, and no subject was allocated more time than the language of the Soviet Union. In 1969 Angela got a dispensation to enter the national Russian competition for Year Nine even though she was only in Grade Eight at the time. She won a bronze medal. The next year she won gold medals in the 'Russian Language Olympics' at the city, county and national level. As a reward she won a trip to Moscow in the year when the Soviet Union was celebrating the hundredth anniversary of Lenin's birth.

AT THE *GYMNASIUM*

Angela's junior school results in Russian and Mathematics ensured her a place in the highly elitist EOS High School, or *Gymnasium*. When they started there, Angela and her classmates were informed that they had to behave in a way becoming to selected pupils in a Communist elite school. Herr Gabriel, the Principal (who was married to the music teacher who had taught Angela in primary school) was a Communist to the hilt. He bragged that he returned the gifts sent by his brother in 'the non-Socialist part of the country', and he made it clear that he expected his students to do the same. This was a particular problem for Angela, who dressed in Western attire courtesy of relatives in the West because the Kasners had so little money.

To hammer home his uncompromising stance, Herr Gabriel even suspended students who turned up with shopping bags from Karstadt Warenhaus, a well-known German department store: 'What more proof do you need? Isn't a shopping bag from a capitalist Warenhaus evidence of anti-Socialist leanings?' By all accounts he took a leaf out of the Stasi book of subtle terror and intimidation. One anecdote will suffice. One of Angela's classmates, Bodo Ihrke (who after 1989 went on to be a middle-ranking local politician for the Social Democratic Party) was an entrepreneurial boy. From his family in the West he had received copies of Bravo, a harmless if slightly low-brow magazine that reported on the latest pop songs and the private lives of Western celebrities. Sensing that he could make a profit, the enterprising schoolboy sold photocopied pages of the magazine to his fellow students, who were willing to pay considerable sums for the latest updates on the likes of David Cassidy, Donny Osmond and the Bay City Rollers. Herr Gabriel caught him in the act. He was suspended and was informed that a repetition would lead to permanent expulsion. He did not re-offend.

It was a different Angela who attended the Gymnasium. No longer the goody-two-shoes she had been at the Goethe School, she now liked to party and secretly smoked cigarettes with her friends. 'We liked to go to the woods for a smoke' and Angela brought the cigarettes, a friend later remembered.[17] After the birth of her younger sister, Angela got a room of her own in a small shed-like building adjacent to the Waldhof. Her grandmother in Hamburg sent her postcards of impressionist paintings, and Angela, who particularly liked the French impressionist painter Paul Cézanne, plastered the wall with them. Like any other teenager in the sixties she was interested in pop music. Some of her friends liked the Rolling Stones, but Angela did not (it is perhaps ironic that her party, the CDU, would use the Stones' song 'Angie' as the theme tune for her election campaign four decades later). Instead, Angela liked the Beatles, particularly Paul McCartney. The first single she ever bought, on her trip to Moscow after she had placed first in the Russian Language Olympics, was the Beatles' 'Yellow Submarine'.

Her classmates and other friends from school and from the FDJ liked to come over. Bodo, who had been Angela's classmate since primary school, admitted that Pastor Kasner was a bit 'intimidating' and 'stern'.[18] But then again he was 'old', as anyone over thirty is to a teenager. However, the pastor was rarely there, and Angela's mother was 'nice' and 'friendly'. The Waldhof – and especially Angela's post-card-covered room – was a popular hangout.

Like all youngsters, Angela occasionally worried her parents. She wanted to go out with her friends in the evenings, but her mother forbade her to go riding mopeds with the other teenagers and in any case she had to be home at a certain time. Did she rebel? Not overtly. She found a compromise that didn't involve confrontation, a trait that characterises the later politician. To escape the control of her parents Angela would often go to Berlin to visit her paternal grandmother. Her grandfather Ludwig had died in 1959, but his widow Margarethe was a carefree older lady who, perhaps because she was lonely, allowed her teenage granddaughter a considerable degree of autonomy when she came to visit. The increasingly extroverted Angela was allowed to stay up until 10 pm and sometimes even later. She would visit museums, hang out in East Berlin, and eagerly talk to anyone she met. She was not much of a one for going out on the town, however. Drinking and boys were not her kind of thing.

As we know, Angela was to become the leader of a political party with the abbreviated name CDU. One of her former schoolfriends later played on this when he jokingly told a reporter: 'Angela was already a member of the CDU back at school; it's just that this one was the *Club der Ungeküssten* [club of the unkissed].'[19] Her physics teacher had the same impression, though he expressed it differently: 'Well she wasn't the kind of girl who made the boys turn their heads.'[20] Angela readily admitted that her love life was a bit unexciting in her *Gymnasium* years: 'When I was at school I fancied boys from time to time but it was all rather innocent. Back then things didn't happen quite so quickly. We did not get on with the business as readily as today. And I was not an early starter, at any rate.'[21] With certain exceptions, she fitted the expectations of a pastor's daughter. The school principal Herr Gabriel did not recall that Angela Kasner had been a troublemaker: 'She was respectful towards adults' and if she was critical it was 'in the way that all young people are critical of authority.' She was not critical of the regime, the former Communist later confided.[22] In some ways Angela seemed rather conformist, and she certainly did not show any sign of being critical of the Stalinist state when she took part in the carefully choreographed events organised by the FDJ. The woman who would later become the leader of Germany's largest conservative party was the deputy secretary of the local branch of the Communist youth organisation. 'I recall that she rather uncritically played along,' another of her teachers remembered.[23]

It is doubtful that this was a sign of devotion to the regime. In a dictatorship you have to keep up appearances, and Angela never tried to hide the fact that she played a role in the FDJ. 'Yes,' she said, 'I enjoyed being in the FDJ.' Why? 'Because of the leisure activities. In East Germany such activities were only organised by this group.'[24] In all likelihood she kept a low profile and heeded her mother's counsel not to appear suspicious lest the authorities should discriminate against her. This went well until the last week of school.

At the end of Year Twelve Angela, now 18 years old, was about to graduate with her Abitur – roughly the equivalent of a *Gymnasium* Certificate, though with an emphasis on more academic subjects. Her class, 12b, was a group of exceptionally high achievers. Angela was one of the best students, and at the end of her time at the *Gymnasium* she received the top grade in Mathematics, Physics and, needless to say, Russian. These grades ensured her a place at university. All looked settled and rosy. However, a single incident threatened to undermine all her hard work.

At the end of the year, just before graduation, the class had to carry out a joint project, a kind of theatre performance to show that they valued and understood the basic tenets of Communism. The project was called 'Kulturstunde', but it was not, as a literal translation would suggest, 'an hour of culture'; rather it was devoted to informing, or indoctrinating, the students. Passing Kulturstunde was normally a formality, but Angela and her class almost threw it all away.

The students were tired after months of exams. Tiredness sometimes leads to mischief and a failure to think things through, and Class 12b was no exception. The pupils had been asked to prepare and perform a play about a people that struggled against 'imperialists'. It was clear from the context that they were expected to prepare a play about Vietnam. The Southeast Asian country was in the middle of a war against the United States, and the Communist regime wanted to use the war between the Vietcong insurgents and American-backed South Vietnam for propaganda purposes.

The class, of course, understood what they were meant to do. But they wanted to show a bit of spirit and felt that they were relatively safe as they had all been offered university places. They decided to test the limits. Instead of organising a play about the Vietcong, they chose to put on an event dedicated to their solidarity with the Frente de Libertação de Moçambique (FRELIMO), a leftist but not unambiguously Marxist rebel organisation fighting against the Portuguese colonial power in Mozambique. On paper a sensible choice, and one that was consistent with the question.

However, some of the students got cold feet; reportedly Angela was one of them. The students may have realised that performing their play might not be a good idea. Peter Bliss, who was the chairman of the FDJ in the school and one of Angela's classmates in 12b, went to their teacher Charly Horn and told him that, alas, they had not been able to finish the play and that they couldn't perform it.

'Well, that's your problem, then,' said Herr Horn, who was less than impressed. 'You announce it yourself and you explain to the whole school why you haven't finished the play.'[25]

Shortly before two o'clock the whole class went on stage. Peter Bliss stepped forward. 'I expected that he would say why it was cancelled,' said Charly Horn.[26] But instead of announcing the cancellation of the programme Bliss announced that they were going ahead. 'We will *not only* show solidarity with the Vietnamese people, but *also* with FRELIMO, which struggles for the liberation of Mozambique,' the young man declared before the class performed the play.

As if this introduction wasn't enough, the class went further. In addition to stating their support for their struggling African comrades, they sang The Internationale (the official anthem of the international Communist movement), but they did so in English, the language of the 'imperialists' and the arch-enemy, the United States. To add another twist to their protest, one of the students recited a poem by Christian Morgenstern, an irreverent writer whose verse always seemed to have a hidden meaning. True to the spirit of the poet, the students cheekily recited his poem about pugs from the collection *Gallows Songs*: 'Human being, watch out or you will just be another pug sitting on the wall.' To mention the word 'wall' in a play devoted to Socialist solidarity, and to recite from a collection of poems that poked fun of authoritarian systems, was unwise. Class 12b was playing with fire.

The school's response says a lot about the jittery nerves of bureaucrats and officials living in a totalitarian state. Principal Gabriel – whose tolerance for dissent, as we have seen, was very low – reacted with fury. 'This will have consequences,' he screamed. His line-manager, Klaus Flemming, the local director of education, was informed. Flemming demanded that immediate action be taken again the youngsters and suggested they be denied their places at university. Dissent could not be tolerated. The risk of losing their university places was not an abstract or theoretical possibility. Denying students their hard-won places was not unusual. Indeed, as the teacher Charly Horn later recalled, 'at a nearby school in Greifswald all students at the *Gymnasium* there had lost their places after a similar incident'.[27]

Angela was shocked, her parents no less so. For years they had played along with the system, and Angela herself had joined the FDJ, excelled in Russian and been a model Socialist pupil. And now a momentary provocation threatened to undo it all. Kasner was despairing: 'I was desperate, terribly frightened. I reasoned that I had to turn to those whom I knew higher up in the system.' He contacted Bishop Schönherr and pleaded with his old friend to help.[28] The senior clergyman did what he could. After all, Angela was not – so it seemed – one of the ringleaders who had instigated the fateful play. And perhaps she had even tried to avoid the confrontation, or so the Bishop argued when he contacted the authorities.

But there was another matter that finally saved her. The students were, of course, selected for the *Gymnasium* on the basis of their grades, but they were also chosen because many of their parents belonged to the Nomenklatura, the ruling party elite. This posed a problem for Flemming, the local bureaucrat in charge of education. To deny the top party officials' children a place at university would be politically difficult. Upsetting these influential parents could have unforeseen consequences. The ambitious Flemming also feared that the implications of the episode might harm his further rise in the party. If a whole class from his elite school were suddenly denied their places at university he could – at least potentially – be blamed, especially as it had happened on his watch. If he wasn't held responsible now, this sort of dirt could be used against him later. He reversed his initial decision to deny the students their university places.

Herr Flemming and Principal Gabriel decided to let the matter rest, but there was one casualty. Something serious had happened and to do nothing at all would be a sign of weakness. Someone had to be sacrificed. A few weeks later the teacher Charly Horn was called to the Principal's office: 'They gave me a piece of paper with a confession and a statement to the effect that I would leave the school immediately. And they said, "We'll remain here until you have signed it."'[29]

Horn was demoted and moved to a junior school, but all things considered he got off lightly.

CHAPTER 3

ANGELA IN LEIPZIG

ANGELA WANTED TO STUDY MEDICINE. IT WAS A GOOD, SOLID PROFESSION. She had the grades and the determination, and had proved that she was in possession of the necessary attention to detail. Her parents were, therefore, rather surprised when she told them that she was going to Leipzig, a large city in the south, to study physics at Karl Marx University. Whether it was a free choice, we do not know. It is possible, plausible even, that an over-controlling regime such as that of East Germany 'encouraged' her to study this subject. But it is also possible that she opted for Leipzig as a welcome opportunity to leave home. The nineteen-year-old Angela was feeling stifled in the vicarage at the Waldhof and found Templin positively claustrophobic; 'I wanted to be away' and 'above all, I wanted to get out of this small town', she later said.[1]

There are many very good reasons to criticise East Germany and all other Communist states, but one has to admit that their students were given economic support that few other countries provided. There were no tuition fees and all students were given a non-repayable stipend of 190 Marks – roughly a third of the average wage for a skilled worker. Moreover the education Angela and her fellow students received was of a very high standard. Karl Marx University, which had changed its name from Leipzig University in 1953, had an enviable reputation. Its alumni surpassed those of most German – and, indeed, British and American – universities. Among its former students were the philosophers Gottfried Leibniz and Friedrich Nietzsche; the composer Richard Wagner; Johann Wolfgang von Goethe, Germany's national poet; the historian Leopold von Ranke; and in the natural sciences the Nobel Prize-winners Werner

Heisenberg and Gustav Hertz. The last – the nephew of Heinrich Hertz, the physicist who proved the existence of electromagnetic waves – had only recently retired. Angela was to attend a university with centuries of tradition for excellence and a recent reputation for world-class scholarship in the natural sciences in general and physics in particular.

Angela and her 70 fellow freshmen (63 of them were indeed men) were relatively sheltered from ideological influence on the subject they were studying. The laws of physics could not easily be incorporated into what Friedrich Engels had called 'Scientific Socialism'. As Angela later said, 'I wanted to study physics because the East German regime couldn't simply suspend the rules of elementary arithmetic and the laws of physics.'[2] In spite of, or possibly even because of this, the students at the Faculty of Physics and Earth Sciences were required to follow compulsory courses in Marxist Political Economy and Russian and engage in elementary military training on top of studying subjects such as Quantum Mechanics, Mathematics, Classical Physics and Electronics.

The university was keen to tell its students that academic prowess had to go hand in hand with an active commitment to Communism. Prospective students were told that they had to 'prove their willingness to work for a Socialist society'. Most of them were members of the FDJ and a large number were also members of the DSF, a propaganda organisation that facilitated the 'friendship' between East Germany and the USSR through scholarships for travel and studying.

Angela was not a member of the latter, but she later openly admitted that she was active in the former: 'While I was a student, I was indeed a member of the FDJ. I even served as culture secretary and I was in charge of purchasing theatre tickets,' she said when a journalist asked uncomfortable questions about the past many years later.[3] Some may have seen this answer as a tacit admission that Angela was more than just a culture secretary. However, there is good circumstantial evidence to suggest that she was not just toeing the party line, and, indeed, that she even departed from it on occasion. For example, she intermittently went to meetings in the Lutheran student society. She did this notwithstanding the university's at best ambivalent attitude towards organised religion. However, her commitment to her Christian faith did not mean that she was willing to sacrifice her career for her religious beliefs. Thus she reportedly declined an invitation to be a student representative for the Lutheran society. Whatever she may have said later, her commitment to Christianity was far from being the driving force in her life.

Angela was not overly bothered with politics. But then again, why would she be? Political engagement in East Germany was not like that in the West. Yet she remained interested in political matters and followed developments on the other side of the Iron Curtain. One politician in the West who caught everybody's attention was Willy Brandt.

WILLY BRANDT: EIN HELDENLEBEN

Ein Heldenleben – 'the life of a hero' – is the title of a tone poem by the German composer Richard Strauss. The phrase is often used in German to signify greatness, and one individual whose life has been described in this way is former German Chancellor Willy Brandt.

Politically the early 1970s were eventful years in East as well as West Germany. In the West the Grand Coalition between Conservatives and Socialists had faltered in 1969, and Willy Brandt from the Socialist SPD had formed a coalition with the FDP, a party that championed civil liberties and free markets. But more importantly – at least for those living in the East – Brandt had launched his new Ost-Politik (policy towards the East), which sought to develop a pragmatic relationship with the Ulbricht regime without in any way condoning the Communist system.

Previously the West German government had been hard-line and uncompromising towards East Germany. As Mayor of West Berlin, Willy Brandt had been at the vanguard of the opposition against Ulbricht's regime, taking part in all 'the obligatory anti-Communist rituals and the accompanying rhetoric', as a historian later put it.[4] To understand the significance of Brandt's Ost-Politik it is necessary to understand the context of his new direction.

The basic tenet of West Germany's foreign policy up to 1969 was the so-called Hallstein Doctrine, according to which West Germany would never have diplomatic relations with any country that recognised East Germany. Named after Werner Hallstein, the Deputy Foreign Secretary in the West German Foreign Office, the doctrine was inflexible in theory and followed inconsistently in practice (West Germany had diplomatic relations with Moscow notwithstanding the fact that the Soviet Union recognised East Germany, and the Grand Coalition between CDU and the Social Democrats even recognised the Communist states of Czechoslovakia, Romania and Yugoslavia).

Under the slogan 'Change through Rapprochement', Brandt sought to work with the East without formally recognising the Communist regime. In part this was an acceptance of the realities in the world; East Germany existed and reunification was unlikely in the immediate future.

A politician who shared many of John F. Kennedy's characteristics – from telegenic charisma to womanising – Brandt became an iconic figure in German politics in the 1960s and early 1970s, and arguably beyond, and a brief account of his life is useful here.

Born out of wedlock in the northern city of Lübeck in 1913, he was christened Herbert Ernst Karl Frahm. He graduated from the *Gymnasium* in 1932 but was denied a place at university for political reasons. Unable to pursue an academic career, he trained briefly as a shipping clerk, but spent most of his spare time writing articles for various newspapers.

A Social Democrat since his early youth, he fled the country after the Nazi takeover in 1933. He ended up in Norway, learned the language of his adopted country to perfection, and changed his name to Willy Brandt. As a Norwegian citizen he became a prominent critic of Nazi Germany. In several articles, written in Norwegian, he lampooned the Hitler regime and became a thorn in the side of the National Socialists. When Hitler invaded and occupied Norway in 1940, Brandt escaped to Sweden and learned to write in Swedish so that he could work as a journalist. He also worked clandestinely for Politiets Overvåkningstjeneste (the Norwegian secret service) and even went to Nazi Germany disguised as a Norwegian exchange student.

After the war, Brandt renounced his Norwegian citizenship and once again became a German citizen. His impeccable war record as someone who actively resisted the tyranny catapulted him to the forefront of German politics. Many politicians – especially in the Christian Democratic Party – had been uncomfortably close to the Nazis. Not so Brandt, who used his reputation to good effect. In 1957, aged only 42, he became

Mayor of West Berlin. As the city is a state as well as a town he was effectively its Governor and as such a member of the German Senate.

Brandt was not loved by all. He became the victim of smear campaigns conducted by his political opponents when he ran for the chancellorship in 1961. CDU Chancellor Konrad Adenauer, while recognising the younger man's talent, referred to him as a 'bastard' and as 'the so-called Willy Brandt'.[5] The latter epithet was intended to brand Brandt as a traitor who had deserted the Fatherland. The same tactic was used by Franz-Joseph Strauss – a corpulent, boisterous, up-and-coming politician from the Bavarian CSU party in the south of Germany. The Bavarian politician asked what Brandt had actually been doing during his exile, and insinuated that Brandt might not even be German.

Meanwhile Konrad Adenauer continued his assaults, alleging rather implausibly that the building of the Berlin Wall was part of an attempt by the Soviet Union to get Brandt elected as Chancellor (the Wall was built during the federal election campaign of 1961).

None of this was based on anything as inconvenient as facts. On the contrary, the top brass in the Stasi were terrified of what a Brandt chancellorship would mean for East Germany. Having a warmonger and a cold warrior like Konrad Adenauer in the Chancellor's office rather served the Communists' propaganda purposes. Brandt, on the other hand, would be a threat. The East Germans had a selfish interest in getting the conservative government re-elected. They even helped them, it was later revealed. Markus Wolf, one of the leaders of the Stasi, was personally in charge of feeding fabricated disinformation to the CDU and to the German press, material that purported to show that Brandt had been anything from an American spy to a Gestapo agent. None of this was true, but it helped Adenauer and served the interests of Ulbricht's Communist regime.

After two failed attempts to become Chancellor (he ran again in 1965), and having served as Foreign Secretary in the Grand Coalition, Brandt finally won the federal election in 1969. He immediately began a reform process intended to show that his part of Germany had better and more social policies than the allegedly 'Socialist' East, and – as importantly – that West Germany was willing to confront and apologise for the Second World War. This was long overdue.

In their influential book, *The Inability to Mourn,* the psychologist couple Alexander and Margarete Mitscherlich had argued that most Germans were in denial about the past and had gone to great lengths to establish a kind of collective amnesia about the Nazi years. They encouraged their compatriots to come to terms with the past – to begin a process of what became known as *Vergangenheitsbewältigung* ('coming to terms with the past').

The Mitscherlichs had a point. Immediately after the Second World War many of the captains of industry who had been card-carrying members of the Nazi Party continued in their roles, and did so with the blessing of the Western allies, the USA, Britain and France. To a degree this is understandable and pragmatic as it enabled Germany to get back on its economic feet, and contributed to creating a level of prosperity that prevented the radicalisation caused by austerity in the 1920s and early 1930s.

Politically, the acknowledgement that the Germans had to atone for past sins suited Brandt. His political opponent and predecessor as Chancellor, Kurt Georg Kiesinger, had worked in Josef Goebbels' propaganda department and still socialised with former prominent Nazis. The failure to come to terms with the past also characterised the policies of the East German Communist regime. Ulbricht, as we have seen, had incorporated former Nazis into the regime by establishing a political party for them, the NDPD.

The collective denial was no longer tenable, however. Even those who had been passive bystanders were guilty of having accepted the crimes of the Nazi regime. Brandt wanted his compatriots to confront their past but, being a politician, he also wanted to score political points; he wanted to show that he was moving on and facing up to Germany's guilt. His opposite number in the East, on the other hand, was not able or not willing to do so. This gave Brandt the upper hand.

Politically Brandt was under pressure to do something. Politics never takes place in a vacuum. The student revolts that hit the world in 1968 had many different causes and targets; the protesters at the American universities of Berkeley and Columbia were protesting against the Vietnam War. In Paris in 1968, the so-called *Mai français* was a protest against the increasingly autocratic tendencies of the war hero General

Charles de Gaulle's presidency. In West Germany, the '68 generation rebelled against the collective obliviousness of the older generation. Above all, the young protestors were appalled that they were being taught by professors who had once been Nazis and that they were governed by politicians who – to put it diplomatically – had gone along with the Nazi regime.

The fact that the police dealt with student protests in Berlin in a way that brought back memories of the dictatorship in the 1930s did not help. The police even shot dead a student. That the East German regime actively fanned the flames of discontent was rumoured but not proven at the time. It was later revealed that the West German police officer who killed the student Benno Ohnesorg was a secret agent of the East German Stasi and a member of the East German Communist party, the SED.

It was in part to deal with and pacify the sentiments that grew out of the protests that Brandt was elected Chancellor the following year. And it was the concerns of the student movement as well as collective German guilt that he addressed in his inauguration speech before the German Parliament, using the slogan '*Wir wollen mehr Demokratie wagen*' ('Let's dare more democracy' is the literal translation, though it doesn't really convey the poetic sense of Brandt's slogan). This commitment to democracy and his record as 'a good German' made him a credible leader – and at the same time put the regime in the East on the back foot.

Brandt was a journalist by trade. He knew the power of the media, especially television, and he used it to great effect. In 1970 he travelled to Warsaw, having just completed a peace treaty with the country, which recognised the Oder-Neiße-Line as the final German border with Poland. As was customary for a visiting head of state, he went to the memorial for the victims of the ghetto uprising in the Polish capital during the Nazi occupation. This was where the Germans had indiscriminately killed Jewish citizens – in all 13,000 were slaughtered in the ghetto during the uprising, of which 6,000 were burnt alive.

It was a grey, rather miserable rainy day and only the usual press pack of political correspondents and a handful of paparazzi had followed him. Nobody expected anything to happen. But suddenly Brandt broke with the staged protocol. He knelt on the wet pavement before the memorial and looked down as if he – the good German – was atoning for the guilt of his compatriots. The 'Warsaw genuflection', as it became known in Germany, was one of the most powerful gestures of any German leader since the war.

Of course, Brandt was a consummate politician and a man with a well-developed sense for good television. Some were cynical. Günter Grass, the Nobel Laureate for Literature and Brandt's one-time speechwriter, wrote an account of Brandt's 'genuflection' in his novel *My Century*:

> My paper would never print it. They want the goody-goody stuff: 'He took all the guilt on his shoulders . . .' or 'The Chancellor suddenly fell to his knees' or – to really lay it on thick – 'Went down on his knees for Germany!' 'Suddenly' – my eye! It couldn't have been more calculated. And you can be sure it was that shady character that put him up to it – you know his personal spy and negotiator, the one who's so good at selling the German population his distasteful renunciation of ur-German territory.[6] Now the big chief – the big drunk – is playing the Catholic. Genuflecting. What does that guy believe in? Nothing. Pure show. Though you've got to hand it to him, from a pure publicity point of view it was a stroke of genius.

The cynicism of this account undoubtedly reflects the unease with which some Germans, and not just former Nazis, viewed Brandt. A poll at the time showed that most Germans disapproved of his gesture. But he had made a point: West Germany was coming to terms with its past. East Germany – by implication – was not. The rest of the world appreciated Brandt's genuflection. Not surprisingly, he was awarded the Nobel Peace Prize in 1971 and was named Man of the Year by *Time* magazine a few weeks later.

Brandt's other feat, and the other reason he was hated in the East, was his zeal as a social reformer. West Germany's economic miracle had been a problem for the Communists. Brandt wanted to show with his social reforms that the wealth of West Germany could be spread evenly, and that the social market economy did not benefit only rich 'capitalists' (as alleged by Ulbricht). Capitalism with a human face, as practised by Brandt, also benefited the poorer members of society. Through increases in spending on education, health care and above all more money to retrain refugees from the East, Brandt put pressure on the Communists.

That these reforms were founded upon a system of free enterprise – with many people owning shares – was noted by the East German leadership and hammered home Brandt's message that West Germany was outpacing its impoverished sibling. The East German Communists were in difficulties. Somewhat like a struggling soccer team, the Politbüro sacked its manager. Walter Ulbricht made way for Erich Honecker, a bloodless, aging bureaucrat with a shrill voice who was almost pitifully lacking in charisma. Some expected the new East German leader to initiate a process of reform to match Brandt's policies. He did not do the former. He was utterly incapable of the latter.

In some ways Honecker turned East Germany into a caricature of a dictatorship; a regime in which fanciful slogans and carefully choreographed 'demonstrations' sought to paper over a disastrous lack of legitimacy.

A march on 6 October 1974 organised by the FDJ to commemorate the 25th anniversary of the establishment of East Germany was a case in point. When 200,000 youngsters marched in Berlin singing patriotic and Socialist songs, Egon Krenz, chairman of the FDJ, reported that 'the youth of East Germany [had] reaffirmed their faithfulness and expressed their willingness to work tirelessly for the state'.[7] Whether Krenz actually believed this is an open question. In any case, one of the songs they did *not* sing was the East German national anthem, *Rising from the Ruins*. Honecker had banned it from being sung, and decreed that henceforth it should only be played instrumentally. This was because it contained the line 'Germany, united fatherland', which was not consistent with Honecker's politics or with his view that the two Germanys were to be divided in perpetuity – or at least until the outbreak of the Communist World Revolution.

CHERRY COCKTAILS

Whether Angela was one of the youngsters who showed their faithfulness to the East German state in the march on 6 October is unknown, but it seems likely. She was a member of the FDJ, though this, of course, does not indicate that she participated out of free will, let alone showed any kind of enthusiasm for the regime. She later said, 'I hated the unfree system in the East.'[8] Possibly so, but she did not show this hatred publicly in any way while she was an undergraduate, or even thereafter. Angela did not rock the proverbial boat. It was not worth it, and she was not consumed by a passion for dissent. Politics was not one of her preoccupations in the early to mid-1970s. Physics is a demanding subject, and she was a hard-working student.

There were things in her life other than natural sciences. She also had a social life. In her first year at university she met Ulrich Merkel and they started dating. Ulrich was a year older than her, but they were both freshmen as he had started a year later due to compulsory military service. The son of a small businessman, he seems to have fallen head over heels in love with Angela, who was moonlighting as a barmaid. He had observed her from a distance, and he made his move while they were on an excursion to Leningrad.

Angela and Ulrich shared many extracurricular interests and Ulrich remembers the time as 'very lovely'. 'We went to the movies together, we went to the theatre and we went travelling – well, as much as you could go travelling in East Germany,' he recalled.[9] The years in Leipzig were, according to Angela and Ulrich's recollections, carefree. Angela continued to run the student society and the bar and, so she says, 'had her first experience with capitalism' when she sold whisky and cherry cocktails and made a profit.[10] Whether it was whisky (which was in short supply) or vodka (which was provided in industrial quantities by the DSF) is not important. Suffice it to say that she was having fun.

Two years later, in 1976, Angela and Ulrich moved in together. They were given a small apartment. It wasn't luxury accommodation – they had to share a toilet with two other couples – but the rent was low, 20 Marks each, or a fifth of their monthly bursary. One year later, on 3 September 1977, they got married. Angela's best friend Erika Hoentsch was the bridesmaid. Angela insisted that it be a church wedding and that it take place in her father's church, though she was not married by him. A younger colleague officiated so that the pastor could walk up the aisle with his daughter.

Angela was 23 and Ulrich 24. She wore blue for her wedding, her favourite colour but also the official colour of the Communist youth organisation, the FDJ. Was it true love? Angela was a bit guarded when she was asked this question:

> We were committed to a future together but in East Germany you married early. If you were married you were also more likely to get accommodation. So we didn't have a long time to get to know each other. I think, today, people wait a little longer before they get married.[11]

Ulrich was more direct: 'Of course we were [in love],' he responded.[12]

There was no time for a long honeymoon. They were both in their final year and they both had to pass demanding exams. In addition to the academic exams, Angela had to pass a physical fitness test. She had to run 100 metres – which she did. She didn't do well. But in the laboratory she excelled. Her thesis on aspects of nuclear physics was – quite exceptionally – published in the English peer-reviewed scientific journal *Chemical Physics*.[13]

Angela and Ulrich were not overly political, nor were they conformists who always followed the party line. In 1977 the West German magazine *Der Spiegel* published an extract from the book *The Alternative*, in which the hitherto unknown political philosopher Rudolf Bahro eloquently criticised the East German regime from a left-leaning Socialist perspective, writing 'The Communist movement began by promising that it would solve the fundamental problems of mankind, that it would answer their existential questions. The countries that confess themselves to be Socialist subscribe to this but when you look at the matter in practice the story is another one.' Harsh words, but undoubtedly true, which is why the book was so dangerous for the regime. The Stasi acted swiftly. The following day Bahro was arrested. But his book had been smuggled out and became an instant best-seller. Bahro was sentenced to 30 years in jail; his defence attorney was a young man named Gregor Gysi, the son of the East German minister for Church affairs. Young Gysi later became the leader of the Left Party (Die Linken), but as an attorney he was unable to help Bahro.

Angela took an interest in the book, although she didn't agree with all of its conclusions. She remembers that 'a group of friends and I studied *The Alternative* almost scientifically. We spent several evenings discussing each and every chapter.'[14] This implies that she was less conformist than some would later suggest. Taking part in discussions about the illegal book, and still more having a copy of it, were criminal offences. Such transgressions were dealt with harshly in East Germany.

However, for all its repression, the Honecker regime found it hard to stifle dissent. Prominent intellectuals such as the scientist and philosopher Robert Havemann were put under house arrest; Rudolf Bahro and the singer Wolf Biermann (an internationally popular folk singer in the 1970s) were thrown out of East Germany. They were *Ausgebürgert* (literally 'decitizenised'), Communist newspeak for people who were expelled by the regime. Another expelled intellectual was the Marxist philosopher Ernst Bloch, author of the book *The Principle of Hope*, who became an inspiration for left-wing student protesters in the USA, France and Germany. Simply expelling the troublemakers became the regime's favoured way of dealing with dissent. It is estimated that 665 people were expelled and lost their citizenship.

Wolf Biermann, in particular, was a problem for the regime. He was a bit of a phenomenon. His father, a Communist of Jewish descent, had been killed by the Nazis. Biermann, who was born in Hamburg, had voluntarily moved to the East as a young man because he believed in its Socialist ideals. He became bitterly disappointed. Inspired by Woody Guthrie and Bob Dylan, the former mathematics and philosophy student began to write songs in the late 1960s, gaining a large following among students. Angela and Ulrich listened to his music, as did many others.

Although he claimed he was still a Socialist – perhaps because of this – Biermann was becoming an embarrassment to the regime. After a concert tour in West Germany, the East German authorities declared he had forfeited his right to citizenship because of 'obscenity' and because he was a 'class traitor'. They had expelled people before and most of the time people were happy to be exiled, so the regime had not expected the reaction to be as strong as it was. Twelve very prominent, and hitherto party-loyal, intellectuals and authors criticised the regime. Among them was the novelist Christa Wolf. She was East Germany's only internationally acclaimed writer. As author of *The Divided Heaven,* a story about a woman who decided to return to the East a few days before the Wall was built, Wolf had been a bit of a poster-girl for the Communists.

Now she was one of the signatories to an open letter to Honecker. To ensure that the open letter was published, Wolf and her co-signatories smuggled it out of the country and got the letter published by the French Press Agency AFP, in itself a sign of insubordination and dissent. The high level of support for Biermann translated into spontaneous protests which broke out at many universities, Leipzig among them.

Interestingly, there is a fragment in the Stasi files written by the FDJ Chairman Egon Krenz, which mentions that a certain 'Physics Student', 'who had been expelled from the FDJ and the SED some time ago', apparently 'tried to gather signatures for Wolf Biermann' while attending a party in the 'Thirsty Pegasus', the student bar. 'Luckily,' the report continues, 'this provocation was stopped.'[15] It is tempting to speculate that this student could be Angela, but it almost certainly was not. She had not been expelled from the FDJ and she was never a member of the SED. Furthermore, the report mentions a male student and not a female. But the student must have been known to her as he studied physics and she was a waitress in the Thirsty Pegasus.

Angela did not get involved in student protests. She admits this herself. Asked if she was part of the opposition against the regime, she answered:

> Well that, of course, depends on what you mean by opposition. But I certainly did not belong to any of the oppositional groups and I was not a civil rights campaigner. But I developed an increasingly critical view of East Germany.[16]

MEANWHILE IN BONN

While the political regime in East Germany was becoming increasingly defensive and inept, one part of the regime continued to outperform its Western counterpart. This institution was the secret service; the Stasi was second to none as a security and spy agency.

Brandt's Ost-Politik had rattled the East German regime. He was a threat, and it had proved difficult to get rid of him. After a string of defections from the SPD and the FDP to the CDU/CSU (the Conservative Party), the Leader of the Opposition, the CDU leader Rainer Barzel, moved a motion of no confidence in Brandt in 1972. But, to the surprise of many observers, Brandt survived the vote by a 260-247 majority. He lived to fight another day. Although Brandt was resilient and again and again outwitted the East by surprising moves, his ability to catch out the Honecker regime suddenly became less sure-footed. He had seemingly lost the ability to surprise his opponents in the East. Nobody knew why.

The answer came as a shock to the world. On Friday 26 April 1974, *Bild*, Germany's biggest selling newspaper, which trades in salacious detail and sensationalism, ran the headline: 'Arrested: Brandt's Confidante is a Spy for the East'. The news came as a body blow to Brandt and the West. His close advisor and political secretary Günter Guillaume was a Stasi spy; East Germany had been able to predict Brandt's moves because they had placed a mole at the very heart of the West German government in the Chancellor's own office.

It was a success for the East. But Markus Wolf, Head of Foreign Intelligence for the Stasi at the time, was nevertheless ambivalent when asked about it. 'On the one hand, it was, of course, a triumph for us to be able to place a spy in the Chancellor's office, but on the other hand, he was found out and that meant that we lost a valuable source that gave us essential information,' he reflected.[17] The latter was a serious problem, for now the West Germans were vigilant and suspicious, and Helmut Schmidt, the new Chancellor of West Germany, was – albeit in a different way from Brandt – a formidable political opponent who was able to outsmart his Eastern counterparts.

ANGELA MOVES TO BERLIN AND AVOIDS THE STASI

Gottfried Wilhelm von Leibniz was an optimistic philosopher. He famously developed the idea that we live in 'the best of all possible worlds' and that all apparent evils are part of God's higher plan. This view of the world was historically lampooned by Voltaire, who portrayed Leibniz as the naïve philosopher Dr Pangloss in his comical novel *Candide*. This philosophical perspective – though without Leibniz's religious overtones – was rather appealing to the East Germans. The Communist regime often described its own state in terms that could easily have been uttered by Leibniz. One of Leibniz's other merits was to establish the

Brandenburg Society of Science in 1701.

It was at this prestigious institution Angela began her scientific career shortly after her graduation in 1978. Ulrich got a job there too. However, the Academy of Sciences (Akademie der Wissenschaften), as Leipniz's Brandenburg Society had been rebranded, was not her first choice. Whether it was Ulrich's we do not know.

Originally she applied for a job at the Technical University in Il-menau, a small town with 30,000 inhabitants in the middle of the country in the region of Thüringen. Angela had an impressive CV, good grades and excellent references. It is not surprising that she got an interview, but the interview itself was a surprise. She was met by two Stasi officers.

A chill must have run down the spine of the 24-year-old physics graduate. Even innocents had reason to fear the secret police. The two men did not present her with incriminating evidence, nor did they try to blackmail her. They were conducting a job interview, albeit not the kind Angela had expected. They had all the necessary information in a file in front of them and they were merely trying to establish whether the facts matched up.

'Okay, and how often do you listen to Western radio? And when did you last get a pair of denims from West Germany?' they inquired. They knew the answers beforehand. They were polite, pleasant even. They were trying to recruit Angela to work for them. She was not an enemy of the state – for such individuals, they had different methods. So, they asked, would she like to become an agent?

Angela hesitated, or so she remembered. A flat rejection of the job offer would lead to suspicion, likely ruin her career, and perhaps even bring misery to her nearest and dearest. But equally, to accept the offer would require her to spy on her friends and family, and to do so for a political system she fundamentally opposed. So she opted for a different, and rather elegant solution. She said she couldn't keep a secret. This is what her mother and father had always told her to do: 'My parents always told me to tell Stasi officers that I was a chatterbox and someone who couldn't keep my mouth shut. And I also told them that I didn't know if I could keep this secret from my husband,' she later recalled.[18]

The Stasi officers were perplexed. Clearly this woman was a naïve scientist who lived in a parallel universe of molecules, atoms and neutrinos. Such an absent-minded nerd would be of little use in the secret police. They politely thanked her. She didn't get the job.

Some have found it hard to believe that Angela never worked as a spy. Whether she was or was not in the pay of the Stasi we cannot know for certain. But even her harshest critics are yet to present any concrete evidence to this effect. The Stasi archives are open to anyone. Many of her friends were informers, as we shall see. Angela, it seems, was not.

Instead of going to Ilmenau both Angela and Ulrich got jobs at the aforementioned Academy of Sciences. Ulrich became an assistant at the Central Institute for Optics. Angela got a similar position at the Section for Physical Chemistry.

All looked quite settled. They were lucky to get a flat in Marienstraße in central Berlin, not far from the Wall. The flat was spartan, but neither of the Merkels was too concerned. True, they could constantly hear the rumbling of the underground trains from the West that passed deep beneath the eastern part of the divided city. But this constant reminder of the division seems not to have bothered Angela: 'It's not my impression that she suffered particularly from living so close to the wall,' said Ulrich, when he was asked about their life together many years later.[19]

They both worked hard. Too hard, it seems. Ulrich was often away. When they were students in Leipzig they often travelled to conferences together, and never missed an opportunity to accompany each other on trips abroad. But something must have happened when they moved to Berlin. Angela would often go on trips to other Communist countries alone. Ulrich would spend most of his time in the lab. Their colleagues noted that they were drifting apart. But, diplomatically, they kept quiet. Mentioning such things is always a delicate matter.

Angela and Ulrich did not talk much. There were no rows, no shouting, just a feeling of drifting apart and of living with a stranger. But the break-up nevertheless came as a surprise one winter morning in 1981. Ulrich remembers:

> Suddenly one day she packed her bags and left the apartment we shared. She had weighed up all the consequences and analysed the pros and cons. We split up in a friendly manner. We were both

financially independent. There weren't too many things to be divided between us. She took the washing machine and I kept the furniture – some of which I still have, by the way.[20]

Once again Angela followed her usual pattern of painstakingly analysing the situation and then making a move once she had considered all the consequences. This was how she dealt with any difficult situation. And, what is perhaps more interesting, the way she analysed her own private life was similar to the way she would analyse difficult political challenges when she became Chancellor many years later.

Fast forward 34 years and Chancellor Merkel was in difficulties. For weeks on end refugees had been flooding over the borders of the European Union. The wars in Syria and Libya had prompted an exodus of biblical proportions and most of the huddled masses were heading for Germany. The right wing part of the German press called for action, other countries closed their borders, and the television screens showed footage of police beating desperate families who tried to enter Hungary and other South European countries.

But those who reached Germany were allowed to register as refugees and most were allowed to stay. Germany is no different from other countries. Politicians and opinion-formers there too are prone to angry rhetoric and to expressing fears that Germany would become a Muslim country. Ordinary citizens, especially in the east of the country, organised protests. Even the Chancellor's political friends were asking why Mrs Merkel didn't speak up? Indeed, where was she?

She was in Berlin, but she didn't say much. She was exhausted after recent and painful negotiations with the Greek government over the third bailout. Merkel had received praise for the way she had handled the – according to German media – spendthrift southern country. But now a new problem loomed. Indeed it was already a fully blown crisis of epic proportions. And Mrs Merkel? Well, she was analysing the situation. Weighing up her options, and pondering what to do next – just as she had done many years ago in the small apartment in East Berlin. The German media and the voters were not impressed. The Chancellor's otherwise stratospheric poll-ratings were taking a hit. All political careers end in tragedy, it is often said. Was Merkel just another ordinary politician? Was her number up? Was her impressive career coming to an end after a decade in power? There were indications of her demise. Symptomatically, the German word of the year in 2015 was the verb *merkeln* ('to Merkel'). It was defined as 'the highest level of passivity', and it wasn't meant as a compliment.

But Merkel was once again unmoved. After a month, she suddenly spoke. But her message was not what most people had expected, let alone what the madding crowds were demanding. She had analysed the situation, pondered the various options, and come to the conclusion that Germany not only had a humanitarian duty to take in the refugees, it also made economic sense to allow a few hundred thousand younger people into her country. Germany was facing an acute pensions crisis. There were too few young people to pay for the pensions of the senior citizens in Germany. Immigration was a challenge but it was also a necessity. Merkel had deliberated and she had made a move nobody expected. Asked if it was possible for Germany to integrate the refugees she simply said, 'We can do it.'[21]

Angela's decision was not popular and many of her nearest and dearest criticised her decision. The parallels between the immigration decision in 2015 and her decision to get a divorce in 1981 are striking. The latter was also a decision her family found uncomfortable, but Merkel made the decision anyway.

So once again we go back in time to our main character's life in East Germany. Herlind and Horst Kasner were not best pleased with the break-up. Having a daughter who got divorced was not exactly in keeping with the strict Protestant Lutheran values of the pastor. But Angela was relaxed about it, and in any case she was not particularly close to her parents at this stage even though they lived only 60 miles away. Her relationship with her parents was 'loving, friendly but with a distance. We give each other space,' as Angela put it.[22]

The divorce might have created an even greater distance between the young scientist and her parents. The marriage, Angela felt, was a mistake: 'We got married because everyone else got married. This may seem stupid today, and I don't think we had thought seriously enough about it.'[23]

Getting divorced, even moving out of the apartment in Marienstraße, was a challenge. This account of Angela's life would be incomplete if we didn't address the mundane issues, the practical matters and the challenges she faced. By looking into the seemingly unexciting matter of finding a place to live, we also learn something rather surprising about the subject of this book; Angela became a squatter.

After she had left Ulrich she went over to her friend and colleague Hans-Jörg Osten. He remembers the evening she turned up: 'She just stood there in the door and said, "I can't take it anymore. I have already left [him]. I want a divorce. Can I stay here for a while?"'[24] She could, but sleeping on Hans-Jörg's sofa was not a long-term solution. Angela's other friends were supportive and kind too. But support was one thing, finding a permanent place to live was another. There was an acute housing crisis in East Berlin. The economic situation did not allow for massive gentrification or the building of new apartment blocks. All the houses and apartments in principle belonged to the state. But the bloated bureaucracy of the Communist state was often inefficient bordering on incompetent. They were not always aware of where there were empty flats.

On his way to work, Utz Havemann, one of Angela's older colleagues and a close friend, had noticed an empty though pretty dilapidated house in Reinhardtstraße. He looked into the matter. It seemed that the Staatliche Wohnungswirtschaft – the public rental agency – had overlooked the flat. Maybe Angela could move in?

Of course, moving into an empty flat – in effect squatting – was not strictly speaking legal. And Utz knew a thing or two about illegal actions: his stepfather, the philosopher Robert Havemann, was under house arrest for having criticised the regime.

But Utz also knew how to play the system. Angela went to see the flat, and with a couple of friends they broke the lock with a power-drill and started to redecorate the run-down apartment. DIY wasn't Angela's forte, so she looked after Utz's children while he and other friends painted the walls and installed an old stove.

Angela reported that she had moved in, and the police fell for what Utz Havemann later called a 'Felix Krull story' – a fanciful fabricated tale that no sane person could possibly believe. Angela lived in the flat for a couple of years before she moved on to a more conventional apartment in Templiner Straße in Prenzlauer Berg, then a relatively run-down area which became bohemian and hip only after the fall of the Berlin Wall.

She started her new life as a single woman, went about her business, socialised with her friends and began to study for a doctorate.

COLD WAR: 'ONE HELMUT GOES, ANOTHER ONE COMES'

Meanwhile, the Cold War had once again broken out. The years of détente – the easing of the strained relations between the East and the West in the 1960s and 1970s – were ending. But something happened before the breakdown in trust edged the world closer to nuclear war.

In 1975, when Angela was still making cherry cocktails at the Thirsty Pegasus, leaders of all the European countries plus the USA and Canada had reached an agreement at an international summit in the Finnish capital Helsinki. Under the agreement both sides recognised each other's borders and pledged that they would not interfere in 'internal matters'. The mood was friendly. The world media showed photos of Helmut Schmidt chatting away to Erich Honecker.

Initially the East had most reason to be pleased. They had achieved the recognition they craved. And they had, or so they believed, accomplished this by giving very little in return. The only concession the Communists had made was to formally recognise 'human rights and fundamental freedoms'. Henry Kissinger, the German-born US Secretary of State, was none too impressed: 'It is meaningless – it is just a grandstand play to the left,' he said to US President Gerald Ford.

But history was to prove the normally razor-sharp Dr Kissinger wrong. While not binding under international law, the Helsinki Declaration provided human rights activists in the Communist countries with a powerful tool and a document to which they could appeal when their human rights were violated, as they often were. Needless to say, the declaration did not result in a sudden adherence to the rule of law, nor did it lead to the establishment of politically independent courts in Eastern Europe. But gradually the Helsinki document became a manifesto for dissident and liberal movements in the Communist countries. As the historian John L. Gaddis noted in *The Cold War*, 'What this meant was that the people who lived under these [Communist] systems – at least the more courageous – could claim official permission to say what they thought.'

The Helsinki Declaration proved to be the last of a relatively substantial number of treaties aimed at reducing the tensions between East and West. It was a decision by the Communist countries, in short the Kremlin, which began the reversal towards a new Cold War. In 1978 the Soviet Union decided to replace its intermediate-range nuclear missiles with the newly developed SS-20 ballistic missiles. The new weapons were technically unsophisticated and it seems the Russians merely wanted to consolidate what was perceived to be their conventional military strength in Central Europe. But the NATO countries – and foremost among them West Germany – were concerned about the development. US President Jimmy Carter and German Chancellor Helmut Schmidt decided to respond in kind. At the NATO Summit in December 1979, the Western Alliance said that they would start deploying Pershing II missiles in Western Europe and new cruise missiles unless the Soviets immediately started negotiations about disarmament. This became known as NATO's Double Track Decision. It started a new process of escalating confrontations between the two superpowers and their allies. A few weeks after NATO's decision, the Soviet Union invaded Afghanistan.

Again, a bit of background is necessary. After a coup staged by the Soviet-friendly Nur Taraki in 1978, the Muslim population rebelled. Taraki initially responded by mass executions. This only made matters worse. He then asked his Soviet allies for help. Brezhnev sent troops to advise and support Taraki. However, the Soviets soon realised that their ally lacked the wherewithal to deal with the situation. The 40th Army was deployed. Brezhnev ordered the execution of his erstwhile friend and installed a puppet regime headed by Babrak Karmal on Christmas Day 1979. The speed with which Brezhnev acted sent a clear signal to the West. The Soviet Union's policy towards Afghanistan showed how unsentimental and ruthless the Kremlin's approach to foreign policy could be. But there was little the West could do. The Americans and their allies initially responded by boycotting the 1980 Moscow Olympics. A few months after this, the American voters elected as president the Republican Ronald Reagan, who made it clear that he wanted to take a tougher stance against the Soviet Union.

Reagan's rhetoric went down well with Angela, now a doctoral candidate at the Academy of Sciences. After the divorce she had become more political and many of her new friends – mostly physicists and chemists – were avidly following the developments between the East and the West. But things were not looking good for Angela and her compatriots – or for anyone living under Soviet rule.

In Poland, to the east, the independent trade union movement Solidarność (Solidarity) had grown in strength and had been able to thrive under the relatively open regime of the Communist leader Edward Gierek. But the Second Cold War (as the period after 1979 is often called), and the increasing tensions between the Soviet Union and the West, ended the brief glimmer of hope that Poland could become more free. Gierek was removed by General Wojciech Jaruzelski, a Polish nobleman who had become a Communist and received his military training in Moscow. After Solidarność's membership grew to 9 million – roughly a third of the adult population – Jaruzelski declared martial law. Gierek was jailed. Angela saw this first-hand when she visited Poland as part of a scientific delegation. She was shocked and grew even more weary of the Communist idea.

The tensions between East and West took a turn for the worse. Angela and her new friends watched this on West German TV. The authorities were aware of this. Nothing escaped their attention. The Academy of Sciences was physically right next to the headquarters of the Felix Dzerzhinsky Guards Regiment, an elite motorised rifles unit with a total of no less than 11,700 officers. Unlike in Poland, however, where the Ministry of Public Security used strong-arm tactics, the Stasi subscribed to more subtle methods.

Simply alienating the whole class of nuclear scientists – individuals who were, after all, crucial for developing new and more sophisticated weapons – would be short-sighted. Moreover, resorting to traditional means of coercion risked driving the opposition to the regime underground, where they would be less controllable and more difficult to monitor. Instead, the Communist Party organised a cultural conference in which it was pointed out that many in the West vehemently opposed the military escalation. This did not convince many. Young Christians in particular began to work against the militarisation. As always, this opposition movement used clever tactics. The Soviet artist Yevgeny Vuchetich had made a sculpture called 'Swords into Ploughshares'. It was donated to the United Nations and placed in front of the UN headquarters in New York. The phrase 'swords into ploughshares' comes from the Book of Isaiah: 'And he shall judge among the nations, and shall rebuke many people: and they shall beat their swords into ploughshares.' By referring to a well-known artist from the Soviet Union, the movement could claim that they were simply paying homage to a fellow-comrade from another Communist country. But at the same time the group signalled their Christian faith by using a phrase from the Old Testament. The latter appealed to American politicians.

The independent peace movement became a thorn in the side of the East German regime, and opposition began to grow. Back home in Templin, Angela's brother Marcus began to organise seminars with scientists and doctors who were opposed to the regime. Angela was not engaged in these activities. She was trying to finish her doctorate, and above all enjoying life.

In the West, the peace movement was equally oppositional. Helmut Schmidt, the Social Democrat Chancellor, had been the architect of NATO's Double-Track Decision. But he was increasingly being met with opposition from within his own party who wanted him to pursue a more Socialist economic policy and from his coalition partner, the Free Democrats, who demanded spending cuts and a reduction in social security. The situation became untenable. On 1 October 1982, Schmidt lost a vote of no confidence in the German Parliament, when the Free Democrats voted with the opposition CDU/CSU. The conservative Helmut Kohl replaced Schmidt.

In his resignation speech, Schmidt questioned how the un-free and disenfranchised citizens in the East would see the vote of no confidence in a government that had secured an electoral mandate for its policies. As he was about to step down from the lectern he looked at the audience and said: 'And just one last word, I know that the people in East Germany are watching this too.' He paused, as if uncharacteristically overwhelmed by emotion, then he addressed the East Germans: 'We are grateful for the trust you placed in us. We will not disappoint you. Everyone can, everyone must count on our continued solidarity.'

Schmidt was bitter and perhaps a bit melodramatic. There was no suggestion that his successor Helmut Kohl would show less solidarity towards their brethren in the East. Some observers, such as the author Ernst Jünger, were laconic in their comments. On the day of the vote in Parliament the aging writer, who had seen it all, wrote: 'Three PM; *Habemus papam* [Latin for 'we have a new pope'] – a Helmut goes another Helmut comes.'[25]

The new Chancellor was outwardly very different from his predecessor. Schmidt had been – and continues to be – an urbane, cultivated, coca-cola drinking, chain-smoking so-called *Bildungsbürger*. He personifies that most German ideal of *Bildung* (education), the ideal that public servants should be intellectuals rather than businessmen (as in America) or civil servants (as in France).

Schmidt's successor was very different. Helmut Kohl, born in 1930, was the son of a junior civil servant from Ludwigshafen am Rhein, a rather dull industrial town in the southwest of West Germany. Kohl had gone to university but did not shine as an academic. Slightly clumsy and overweight, he had something of a provincial air about him. After his studies he had worked in the VCI, the Association for the Chemical Industries.

Kohl was not an intellectual but a political operator. He learned his craft lobbying and operating behind the scenes and under the radar. Parallel to his work for the VCI, he rose through the ranks of the Christian Democratic Union. He had been one of the founding members of its youth wing and at the age of 29 he was elected to the Landtag – the state parliament – of Rhineland-Palatinate, a state on the border with Belgium and Luxembourg. Within three years Kohl had risen to the position of head of the parliamentary caucus. In 1966, not yet aged forty, he succeeded the fellow Christian Democrat Peter Altmeier and became Governor of the state.

Politically it is difficult to understand why some underestimated Helmut Kohl. His early political success – he became leader of the CDU in 1973 after his predecessor Rainer Barzel had lost the election to Willy Brandt – should have earned him respect. Kohl means cabbage and many even poked fun at his name. The cartoonist Hans Johann Georg Traxler contributed to this when he drew Kohl as a pear, on account of the CDU politician's physique. 'The Pear', as Kohl was called, was from then on considered a figure of fun.

Kohl resented this, hated the urban elite and always had a chip on his shoulder, but he was an exceptional political operator and net-worker; someone who instinctively knew the political game. In 1976, Kohl lost the election to Helmut Schmidt. He sat out the 1980 election, in which Franz-Josef Strauß, the right-wing leader of the Bavarian sis-ter-party CSU, unsuccessfully ran for the CDU/CSU (the Union). Kohl knew Schmidt was impossible to beat at that time. He reasoned that a defeat for Strauß would fatally weaken his southern rival. The Union lost four per cent; the Social Democrats made gains. Schmidt remained Chan-cellor but Kohl remained parliamentary leader of the CDU/CSU faction in the Bundestag (federal German Parliament). Strauß, who was also Governor of Bavaria, went back to his home state. He was neutralised.

Kohl's calculation – and a bit of luck – paid off. It gave him an-other opportunity, albeit without an election. Following his elevation to Chancellor in 1982 he wanted to provide the Germans with a fresh start. It was a time of change, but first he needed a mandate. Kohl called new elections.

In March 1983 the CDU/CSU made considerable gains (up four per cent on the result in 1980). The Social Democrats, under their new, rather dull, leader Hans-Jochen Vogel, lost votes. Kohl had a mandate of sorts, though he still had to govern with the Free Democrats.

In Britain and America respectively, Margaret Thatcher and Ron-ald Reagan had been elected on free-market platforms aimed at trimming down the welfare state. Helmut Kohl wanted to effect a similar change, though his commitment to free enterprise never ran very deep, and the practising Catholic Kohl was more interested in what he called 'a moral and spiritual turn' rather than an economic one. The problem for Kohl, however, was that his government was a coalition, and that the junior party in his government, the FDP, had previously served as the junior party in Helmut Schmidt's government.

Moreover, and more disturbingly for Kohl, his government ini-tially turned out to be less 'moral' than its predecessor. Preaching tradi-tional values can backfire, as British Prime Minister John Major learned to his cost when he initiated the 'back-to-basics' campaign a decade later (a campaign derailed by the extramarital affairs of highly placed Conservatives). Chancellor Kohl also stood accused of hypocrisy. In the German case it wasn't the sexual urges of politicians but greed and corruption. The liberal economics minister Otto Graf Lambsdorff – who had engineered the split between SPD and the Free Democrats – was caught in a scandal involving illegal donations from the Flick Corporation (a steel and coal conglomerate). Lambsdorff had to resign, but worse still for Helmut Kohl, reports in the press suggested that he too had received money.

Kohl survived but toned down the moralistic rhetoric in favour of the pursuit of more traditional social-liberal policies. The Social Democrat opposition was in disarray and was being threatened by the new Greens, a leftist party that championed a clean environment, opposition to nuclear weapons and the abolition of nuclear power stations. The Social Democrats were forced to the left, and this allowed Kohl to capture the centre ground.

Kohl, for all his faults and his personal awkwardness, was steadying the German economy and outpacing his Eastern neighbour by a considerable distance. But much as West Germany might have been winning the economic competition, on the spying front the East Germans were still able to get access to the highest levels. In fact it later transpired that the Stasi had played a role in getting the Flick scandal publicised. Hans-Adolf Kanter, a CDU member and a lobbyist for Flick, had sold the story to Markus Wolf, the notorious head of Stasi's foreign intelligence department. The East German spymaster merely activated his network. It wasn't the last time he was to play a leading role behind the scenes, as we shall see in the next chapter.

CHAPTER 4

THE UNBEARABLE BOREDOM OF BEING:
A SQUATTER IN BERLIN

HORST KASNER LOOKED AROUND DISAPPROVINGLY. HIS DAUGHTER WAS turning thirty and her parents had come down from Templin to visit her in her flat in Berlin. Angela seemed slightly nervous and shy, as if seeking her father's approval and knowing she wasn't going to get it. She didn't.

'You haven't made it very far, have you?' Pastor Kasner said and shook his head.[1] He did not approve. He saw her life as a scientist as being 'a continuation of her carefree life as a student'.[2]

It must have hurt. Angela had always been her father's pride and joy. She was, she said, 'perhaps her dad's favourite child'.[3] And it wasn't really fair. Angela had accomplished a lot: she had graduated from Leipzig University with a first-class degree in physics, she had published papers in English peer-reviewed journals, and she had secured a job at the premier research institution in the country. What more could he want?

Well, stability for a start. Her private life was, as far as her father was concerned, a bit of a mess, at least according to his protestant values. That Angela had got divorced was embarrassing enough. When Pastor Kasner and his wife were asked by the parishioners 'how Angela was doing', they had to respond with bland platitudes. She seemed to have time to travel around the world instead of concentrating on her doctorate. At a time when her brother was becoming an established scientist, Angela was still roaming the world and living the bachelorette life in the capital. Many of her classmates from school back home in Templin were starting families. Angela – so her parents believed – was living the bohemian life as a student – and was doing this as a squatter in an apartment she technically wasn't allowed to live in.

Immediately after her divorce from Ulrich – the final paperwork was completed in 1982 – Angela went travelling. The FDJ had a good travel agency, Jugendtourist, which organised trips to foreign countries – though, needless to say, only to other so-called 'Socialist states'. Angela and her colleagues, most of whom were card-carrying members of the FDJ, travelled to Azerbaijan and Georgia, then parts of the Soviet Union. It was as if she was belatedly enjoying life and the company of other young people, though East Germany, an Orwellian *Überwachungsstaat* ('surveillance state' is not quite strong enough to convey the meaning of this German noun), made sure that her every move was recorded by the Stasi officer known as 'Bachmann'. The undercover agent had little to report. 'She travelled by train, and then later she took the bus, before she caught a plane from Sotschi to East Germany,' he duly wrote to his masters back in Berlin. Angela was not suspicious. She knew how to behave herself. Indeed, as the report went on, 'her impression of the hospitality and the nature of the Soviet Union is very positive'.[4]

Life was not always exciting, though – far from it. Her salary was 650 Marks a month, less than the average of 1,000 Marks earned by a skilled worker. This was not a lot for someone with her level of education. Besides, working at the Academy wasn't as enthralling as she could have wished. She had been the star pupil at Leipzig, and before that at home in Templin. People expected a lot from her, and here she was, still a graduate student at the age of 30. Life could have been better. In fact her father probably had a point, and she probably knew it. That is why his comment must have been so painful.

Things could have been worse. At least she was able to have a social life and being a scientist, unlike other jobs, enabled her to travel in other Socialist countries. Shortly after her 30th birthday Angela went to Prague in what was then Czechoslovakia. Her friend Hans-Jörg Osten had helped her organise a fellowship at the J. Heyrovsky Institute of Physical Chemistry. This provided her with a welcome opportunity to get away from it all, finish her doctorate, and work with Rudolf Zahradník, an international authority on quantum chemistry.

Angela wasn't going by herself. The authorities discouraged people from travelling alone, as this could give them ideas. If scientists travelled in pairs there was always the possibility that one could report on the activities of the other. Nobody knew who was a spy and this was yet another way of creating that sense of insecurity on which the Stasi thrived. Her companion on the trip to Prague was a fellow scientist, Dr Joachim Sauer. He was a couple of years older than Angela and was at the time married with two sons.

Joachim helped Angela with her thesis. Nothing odd about that; he was already a recognised authority on the subject. But 'Bachmann' – who continued his surveillance while Angela was in Prague – noted that the pair had grown a bit too close.

Angela and her new friend also talked about politics. Joachim had strong views on the subject – and, quite remarkably, views that departed considerably from those of the regime. He liked US President Ronald Reagan. Michael Schildhelm, another of Angela's friends, remembers how Angela and her friends increasingly talked about politics and rarely discussed scientific issues: 'The chemistry between Angela and I had – so to speak – very little to do with chemistry, physics and mathematics. In fact, it had everything to do with the fact that a colleague in the office next door twice every day came in with Turkish coffee.'[5]

In these extended coffee breaks the physicists and chemists would talk not about hydrogen bonds, orbitals or elementary particles but 'about the amazing developments in *Perestroika*-country and the address President Weizsäcker gave on the 40th anniversary of the end of the Second World War'.[6] *Perestroika* refers to the political and economic restructuring that took place in the Soviet Union from the mid-1980s, and Weizsäcker was the new West German President.

Things were beginning to happen, and happen fast. To understand Angela's political awakening it is necessary to look at the unique confluence of factors that shaped history at the time.

The aristocratic Richard Karl Freiherr von Weizsäcker had been Mayor of West Berlin, elected by the CDU, and became the ceremonial head of West Germany in 1984. Some had thought that the conservative Freiherr (the second lowest rank of German nobility) would be a hardliner. He was not. Unexpectedly, he reached out to the new Soviet leader Mikhail Gorbachev, who had been installed in the spring of 1985 and was signalling a change in the relationship between East and West. As Weizsäcker said:

> It is important that both sides remember and that both sides respect each other. Mikhail Gorbachev, General Secretary of the Soviet Communist Party, declared that it was not the intention of the Soviet leaders at the 40th anniversary of the end of the war to stir up anti-German feelings. The Soviet Union, he said, was committed to friendship between nations. Particularly if we have doubts about Soviet contributions to understanding between East and West and about respect for human rights in all parts of Europe, we must not ignore this signal from Moscow. We seek friendship with the peoples of the Soviet Union.[7]

It was this part of his speech that exercised the coffee-drinking scientists. They were thrilled about *Perestroika*. What was especially enticing was that the Soviet Union, hitherto the autocratic regime that pulled the strings, now seemed to be criticising the Honecker regime – and that West Germany (at least in Weizsäcker's speech) was siding with the Kremlin against the East German Politbüro. This was a new development.

The changes in the Soviet Union had a momentous impact on the process of German reunification and indirectly catapulted a completely unknown and untested research scientist into the political limelight less than a decade later.

GORBACHEV AND GLASNOST

The weather was grey and cold in Moscow on 15 March 1985. The mournful tones of the Polish composer Frédéric Chopin's *Marche funèbre* echoed across Red Square in Central Moscow as the flag-draped coffin of the late Communist leader Konstantin Chernenko was lowered into the frozen ground in the shadow of the Kremlin wall. The Soviet leaders gathered on the top of the Lenin Mausoleum, as they had done twice before in only three years.

In 1982 Leonid Brezhnev had died and been replaced by the former KGB boss Yuri Andropov, a reformer behind the scenes who had used his power over the secret services to advance to the top of the Soviet system. Andropov had not always been a moderniser. He had a reputation as an unyielding and uncompromising Communist, and it was he who – while ambassador in Budapest in 1956 – convinced Khrushchev that it was necessary to invade Hungary. It was also Andropov who engineered the suppression of the Prague Spring in Czechoslovakia in 1968. He was a pragmatist and a realist who wanted to advance the march of Communism, but he realised that methods had to be tailored to circumstances; that it was necessary to trim the sails of autocracy to the prevailing winds of world politics.

Sometimes it takes a hardliner to initiate change, as when the anti-Communist US President Richard M. Nixon went to China. As US Senator Mike Mansfield, a Democrat from Montana, said: 'Only a Republican, perhaps only a Nixon, could have made this break and gotten away with it.'[8] The same was true of Andropov. After Brezhnev's death the Soviet economy was at best stagnating. Andropov recognised the flaws in the planned economy and began to allow public discussion about how to improve it. At the same time he dismissed incompetent leaders and ministers. On his watch seventeen ministers lost their jobs. One man, however, was given favourable treatment: Mikhail Gorbachev. The young lawyer had been elevated to the Politbüro – the highest organ and in effect the cabinet of the Soviet Union – in 1979 at the tender age of 49. Gorbachev worked closely with Andropov, and the older man expected a lot from his new political discovery.

Andropov died in February 1984, aged only 69. His successor, Konstantin Chernenko, was more of a traditionalist. Dubbed 'the man from Siberia' by the West German news magazine Der Spiegel, Chernenko was a hardliner who had little time for those who wanted changes to the Communist system. Luckily for the reformers, he was too frail to push through a counter-offensive against them, which his supporters had hoped for. Rarely seen in public, and then always propped up, the 73-year-old hard-drinking chain-smoker had barely managed to wave at the crowds at the traditional parades to commemorate the October Revolution a few months after his elevation. Western reports, always denied by the official Soviet media, suggested that he suffered from a litany of ailments. These reports were accurate, and Chernenko died in the spring of 1985 only thirteen months after taking office. An autopsy reportedly found that he suffered from chronic emphysema, congestive heart failure and liver cirrhosis. No wonder he was described as 'an enfeebled geriatric so zombie-like as to be beyond assessing intelligence reports, alarming or not' by John L. Gaddis in *The Cold War*.

The high mortality rate among Soviet leaders created a problem for the Americans and their Western allies. 'How am I supposed to get any place with the Russians if they keep dying on me?' Ronald Reagan – then aged 74 – asked jokingly. The answer to Reagan's question came in the form of Gorbachev. It was he who greeted the guests at the funeral on that cold March day in 1985. Gorbachev had been in *de facto* charge for a while and there were no serious challengers in his way. The reformers had won the power struggle in the Politbüro.

As is often the case with state funerals, this one too was used as a good opportunity to meet and greet foreign leaders who were normally out of bounds. Funerals provide an excuse to speak informally to friends and especially to enemies. Chernenko's funeral gave East Germany's Erich Honecker a chance to meet Chancellor Helmut Kohl face to face for the first time. The East German leader had wanted to visit his West German colleague on a semi-official visit in 1984, but Chernenko had forbidden it. Now there was an opportunity to meet.

As a first indication of the changes to come, Gorbachev made it clear that he encouraged contacts between the two Germanys. He already had a reputation as a moderniser. 'I like Mr Gorbachev, we can do business,' the famously anti-Communist British Prime Minister Margaret Thatcher said after she had met Gorbachev in December 1984, a few months before he took office.

'Gorby' as the Western press called the new Soviet leader, wanted Kohl and Honecker to arrange a meeting at the earliest opportunity. The two German leaders were pleased. Not that they saw eye to eye, but for pragmatic purposes a meeting would be useful to sort out some of the practical difficulties.

For Gorbachev, the East/West German problem was a bit of a distraction. He had bigger fish to fry. His problems were two-fold and yet intertwined: the economy and the perceived threat from the USA. The link was the Strategic Defense Initiative (SDI), also known as Star Wars.

Ronald Reagan wanted to develop a defence system – he called it a 'peace shield' – in which lasers would be used to intercept incoming missiles. In a way, there was nothing new about this. Systems to intercept incoming missiles had existed for years. The Soviets had the ABM-1 Galosh, which could intercept ballistic missiles. But the SDI system espoused by Reagan would also be able to take down cruise missiles – guided missiles that can fly at low altitude. In truth, few scientists – among them the highly regarded German Physics Association – believed that the SDI system could be developed within the foreseeable future. But Gorbachev could not run the risk. He had to counter Reagan's proposal. Unfortunately for him, he did not have the money, the scientific prowess, or the technological facilities to start research into a Star Wars system. He needed another strategy.

Gorbachev has been hailed as the man who dismantled the Soviet Union and the statesman who sealed the fate of Communism as a political force. But it must not be forgotten that he set out to strengthen, not weaken, the behemoth Soviet state. His tactics were political. He was aware that many young people in the European peace movement were sceptical of Ronald Reagan's foreign and defence policies. His strategy was to force a wedge between America and Europe by talking about a common European destiny and common European values from which, he suggested, America was excluded. Again and again, he referred to 'the idea of the "Common European Home". . . [which] signifies, above all, the acknowledgment of a certain integral whole'.[9]

This concept of a Common European Home was not plucked out of the air; it had a certain affinity with ideas espoused by the new French President of the European Commission, Jacques Delors. The former finance minister in François Mitterrand's government of Socialist/Communist ministers from 1981 to 1984 was a dynamic and charismatic politician who wanted to transform the sleepy and sclerotic European Economic Community (EEC) into a properly functioning economic, monetary and possibly even political union.

Parallel to Gorbachev's reforms, Jacques Delors and his colleagues worked on changes towards 'an ever closer union' (to use the words of the Treaty of Rome, which had first established the goal of a united Europe in 1957). By establishing a single market for all goods and services and the freedom of movement for workers, Delors hoped to create a sense that Europe was a single entity, rather like the USA. And by establishing a proper European Parliament, with members who could influence and even veto proposals put forward by the European Commission (in effect the cabinet of the European Union), the Frenchman hoped to create a kind of embryonic 'United States of Europe'. All these ideas were contained in an agreement called the Single European Act in 1986.

One of the most enthusiastic proponents of this project was Helmut Kohl. The main aim of the Single European Act was to deregulate the markets, break down trade barriers between the countries of Europe, create binding rules for a cleaner environment and give new powers to the European Parliament. The Treaty also established a rudimentary mechanism for agreeing to a common European foreign policy.

At the same time as Gorbachev was talking about a Common European Home, rhetoric which was well received by the West European public (and occasionally even by sceptical governments), the KGB was busy following a more sinister plan to influence the peace movements in Western Europe. It did so with more success than its American counterpart, the CIA. Subsequent historical and archival research has lent credibility to the then widely dismissed assertion that leading members of the peace movement worked closely with representatives of the KGB. Under the heading 'Active Measures' the KGB and the Stasi used all manner of influence to change the tone and tenor of the debate: disinformation, infiltration and direct bribery.

Much of this succeeded. Even Angela was convinced by the arguments put forward by Gorbachev. When Ronald Reagan turned down an offer to abolish all ballistic missiles Gorbachev gained the upper hand in the publicity and media war in Europe. Reagan appeared to be a hardliner, a war-mongerer and, in the version that was dished out to the East Germans (and even the West Germans), the guilty party. 'Angela's faith in America suffered a blow', though 'this was restored a few hours later' once she had spoken to Joachim Sauer, as one of her confidants put it.[10]

The problem for Gorbachev was that many leading politicians in Western Europe remained sceptical. The Soviets had not covered themselves in glory in the preceding 40 years and many people, like Angela's friend Joachim Sauer, were reluctant to give the Soviet leader the benefit of the doubt. Getting people to see the Soviet Union in a more positive light required action, not mere words.

The authoritarian, even totalitarian, nature of the Communist regime had to be changed without relinquishing power. In pursuit of this goal, Gorbachev introduced the concepts of *Glasnost* (literally 'publicity', but generally translated as 'openness'), *Perestroika* ('restructuring') and *Demokratizatsiya* ('democratisation'). It was all very new, very exciting and very surprising for the scientists in the ramshackle barracks in Berlin-Adlershof that housed the Academy of Sciences.

RENATE'S JOURNEY

A *roman à clef* is a novel that portrays well-known real people more or less thinly disguised as fictional. Michael Schindhelm's novel *Robert's Journey* was an example of this genre, and one of the characters in the book was based on Angela Merkel.

Schindhelm, who later became Director General of the newly founded Operatic Society of Berlin, had trained as a scientist. Like Angela he belonged to the group of intelligent people who decided to study physics as that subject was less likely to be infiltrated and polluted by pseudo-scientific Marxist theories, or so he says today. He earned a degree in quantum chemistry from Voronezh State University (an elite scientific institution in the Soviet Union), returned home to East Germany and got a job at the Academy of Sciences, where he shared an office with Angela Merkel. Years later he used these experiences as the basis for his novel.

Angela – she was called 'Renate' in *Robert's Journey* – did not play a central role in the book. Schindhelm described her as a disenchanted researcher: 'Renate, with whom I shared an office, was the archetypical disillusioned young scientist. She had been awarded a doctorate a few years before and her only passion was satisfied by lonely bike rides in the Margraviate of Brandenburg.'[11]

Life was a bit dull for Angela. She got a pay increase, albeit only a modest one. She now earned 1,020 Marks a month. This was not lavish: as she noted, 'a pair of shoes cost 320 and a winter coat 400'.[12] The work was dull and there wasn't as much freedom as had earlier been the case. Life was becoming a gloomy humdrum matter of tedious routines: 'every morning I would leave early, take the S-Bahn (the local train) from Prenzlauer Berg, and arrive at 7:15 when we began to work. It was really way too early for basic research.'[13]

Whether 'lonely bike rides' were all Angela lived for is debatable. She was in a relationship at the time and she continued her travelling. But her work certainly did not fire her up: 'the prospect of another 25 years of carrying out scientific research on a shoe-string budget [was not] enticing', she later said.[14]

She had got her doctorate, and her Head of Department Klaus Ulrich praised her work. He also offered some comments on the way she worked, words that almost seemed prophetic a few years later when she had become a politician. 'One gets the impression,' said Professor Ulrich, that 'she is on to something, she works diligently towards a goal but she is also a woman who has a mind of her own.'[15]

That Angela Merkel was someone who, in the words of her boss, 'formed her own opinions' was not entirely evident to everyone in those days, certainly not in political terms. Whereas her father had dared to become more political and increasingly took part in (and even actively organised) meetings with critical and oppositional groups, Angela was still on the sidelines. Her low profile was probably one of the reasons why, at the age of 32, she was allowed to go to her cousin's wedding in Hamburg, in what the East German regime officially called the 'Non-Socialist Economic Area'. The Stasi, it seems, did not consider her a potential defector. Nor did they have reason to. Angela did not depart from her schedule. Having spent all her adult life in Communist Eastern Europe, she was a bit apprehensive before she went:

> I didn't know if I as a woman from the East was able to stay overnight alone in a hotel. It was, when you think of it, a bit silly of me. After all, I had travelled alone to Budapest, to Moscow, to Leningrad, to Poland, I had gone hiking through the Soviet Union, but it wasn't clear to me – not back then anyway – if a woman could simply book a room in a hotel. I guess it had something to do with the crime shows I had watched on television.[16]

She duly went to the wedding and after that travelled to Bodensee, one of the most beautiful places in the south of West Germany. There she visited a colleague at the University of Konstanz and did a bit of shopping: 'Although I had very few Deutschmarks [West German currency] I was able to pick up a few bargains in the Konstanz summer sale; I got a handbag for 20 Marks, reduced from 50, and two shirts for my man.'[17] Who this man was she didn't say.

Having done her shopping, she travelled the hundred or so miles north to Karlsruhe in the middle of Germany to meet Professor Reinhard Ahlrichs, an expert on nanotechnology, then a new cutting-edge area of research in which she took a keen interest. However, it was not the research findings of the professor that impressed her, it was the public transport system. The contrast between the ramshackle East German trains and the smart, fast, streamlined West German ones astonished her: 'My first experience was the Inter-City trains of the Bundesbahn. What technological wonder! Oh me oh my, that was amazing.'[18] Observing how people behaved in the West was a bit of a culture shock for someone who was used to regimented everyday life in East Germany: 'the students [in Karlsruhe] and the other youngsters were sitting in the trains with their feet on the seats! On the seats! In these wonderful trains. I found that so outrageous.'

Back home, Angela began to read *Pravda*, the official newspaper of the Soviet Union's Communist Party. Not because she had become a stalwart Communist, but because the Gorbachev regime was rattling the Communist cage, and the East German Politbüro with it. *Pravda* was not printing critical stories, but it was no longer merely recycling unrealistic rose-tinted stories about the wonders of Communism.

THE END OF COMMUNISM

Gorbachev's new focus was met with opposition in the Communist satellite states. Turkeys don't vote for Christmas. The Honecker regime was particularly concerned. It had no inclination towards democratisation and even less interest in this new fad from the East. Gorbachev wanted to achieve the impossible; he wanted to maintain the Communist Party's grip on power while at the same time opening up the system.

In a return to politically gentler times under Khrushchev, the Soviet Union accepted dissent and even allowed other political voices to be heard. The Communist leaders in East Germany were in a bind: they disagreed with Gorbachev but they could not say so. Their statements, however, contained a clear message between the lines. Kurt Hager, the member of the Politbüro with responsibility for culture, asked rhetorically: 'When your neighbour decides to change the wallpaper in his apartment, are you then obliged to change the wallpaper in your own flat?'[19] His question was supposed to be answered with a near inaudible 'no'.

At first the East German regime had gone along with Gorbachev. Erich Honecker's long overdue visit to the Federal Republic finally took place in September 1987. Though not technically an official visit, since the two States did not recognise each other, Helmut Kohl pulled out all the stops to make his East German counterpart feel welcome; the red carpet was rolled out and the military band played the East German national anthem. And the East German leader who, as we have seen, had banned the words of his own country's national anthem because it contained lines about a united Germany, now himself expressed the view that 'there will be a day when borders do not divide us, a day when the border between East Germany and the People's Republic of Poland unites us'.[20]

Honecker seemed confident in public. Maybe he was deluded; maybe he really believed that the laws of history were destined to result in a unified Socialist Germany. If this was his belief, he was gravely mistaken. 'The standard of living in the East had not improved since the early 1970s and was considerably below that in the west,' a historian observed.[21] What Angela had witnessed on her trip a year before was accurate: West Germany was outpacing its smaller and impoverished sister in the East.

The people in the East were getting unhappier and they were demanding more. Some of them were becoming more daring. The ruling elite in East Germany was split but the hardliners still had the upper hand. Erich Honecker, his heir apparent Egon Krenz (the former FDJ General Secretary), Erich Mielke (the Politbüro member responsible for state security known as 'Mr Fear') and Prime Minister Willi Stoph were against any concessions and wanted to suppress every kind of dissent, if need be with force. After all, repression had worked in East Germany in

1953, in Hungary in 1956, in Prague in 1986 and in Poland in 1981. So why not in East Germany?

For now the hardliners had the upper hand. In November 1987 the Stasi raided the Environmental Library, a book collection established by environmentalists in the Zion Church Society, an organisation affiliated to the Lutheran Church. But even this hardline tactic was not enough. A month later the opposition turned up with banners at the official Rosa Luxemburg Demonstration. Rosa Luxemburg was the poster-girl for Communism and the closest the atheistic state came to having a female saint. A martyr for Socialism, Luxemburg had been killed by nationalist First World War veterans (ostensibly with the blessing of the Social Democrat government) in 1919. She had believed in some vague but critical version of Communism, no doubt, but the inconvenient truth was that Luxemburg was a maverick who had criticised the supposedly infallible Vladimir Lenin and the Russian Revolution. Luxemburg had even defended freedom of expression. It was a quote from Luxemburg's book with the telling title *The Russian Revolution: A Critical Assessment* that the opposition groups were brandishing on placards while they marched through Berlin: 'Freedom is always the freedom of those who think differently.'

The protesters didn't last long. The ringleaders were arrested and sent to jail, and some lost their citizenship and were sent to the West. Nothing much had changed in East Germany, and the regime was certainly not interested in debating what Luxemburg had actually written.

However, developments in the Soviet Union merely strengthened the resolve of the opposition groups. They could follow how Mikhail Gorbachev was reforming the Soviet Union. Hitherto the 'Big Brother' in the East had been a source of guidance on how to be a good Communist. Previously, reading publications like *Pravda* and *Sputnik* (a Soviet magazine translated into German) had been a sign of support for the regime. Now the opposite was true. Erich Mielke, with the blessing of Erich Honecker and his designated successor Egon Krenz, simply banned *Sputnik*. *Neues Deutschland*, the newspaper that performed the role of mouthpiece for the regime, wrote that the ban was necessary because the Soviet magazine was guilty of a 'distortion of history'.

It was clear to some of the younger and more enlightened members of the Communist elite in East Germany that this approach was not sustainable. The Soviet Union was not to be messed with. One man in particular was concerned: Markus Wolf, the Head of the Stasi's foreign espionage department.

Wolf fancied himself as a bit of a reformer in the Andropov mold. Like the late KGB boss and Soviet leader, Wolf had been a hardliner but realised that the winds of change were beginning to pick up. Wolf, whose Jewish father had escaped to the Soviet Union after Hitler's takeover, spoke perfect Russian. He relished showing off his linguistic skills in his daily contacts with Soviet colleagues. The Russians liked him too. 'Mischa', as the graduate of the Moscow Aviation Institute was called by the Russians, was well regarded in the KGB.

Another favourite of the KGB was Hans Modrow, Head of the SED in Dresden. As early as 1987 Mikhail Gorbachev had, albeit unsuccessfully, sought to engineer a palace coup which would have seen Modrow take Honecker's place. Honecker knew that Gorbachev wanted him gone. And he knew from recent history that Soviet leaders were unsentimental when it came to retiring unwanted leaders; after all the Soviets had executed Afghan leader Nur Taraki in 1979. But Honecker reckoned it would be difficult to do the same to him. It wasn't Gorbachev's style.

So what was he to do? In an ideal world Honecker would have purged Markus Wolf and Hans Modrow, but this was not possible given the circumstances; to be a client king is difficult if you disagree with your political overlord. Honecker decided to sit back and wait. Gorbachev could not last forever, or so Honecker thought. Moreover, problems notwithstanding, East Germany was economically much stronger than the Soviet Union. Reforms were not needed. He could tough it out, or so he believed. That the economic situation in East Germany was in fact disastrous and on the verge of collapse was a truth Honecker chose to overlook.

For now, in any case, Honecker was safe. The result of the aborted palace coup in 1987 was a stalemate. Honecker continued as Head of State, but his opponents remained within the SED leadership. At the same time the situation was becoming increasingly problematic for Honecker. The Stasi was not as willing to do the bidding of the SED as it had hitherto been, and certain opposition groups were allowed to organise.

In politics context is everything. What happened 7,353 kilometres east of Berlin, more precisely in Beijing, was to be of great significance. In spring 1989 student protests broke out in Tiananmen Square in the Chinese capital at exactly the same time as Mikhail Gorbachev visited the country. The Chinese strongman and leader Deng Xiaoping responded resolutely. He declared martial law on 20 May and sent in 300,000 soldiers from the People's Army to break up the protest. Over 200 people were reported dead. Egon Krenz, Honecker's heir apparent, defended the action as 'a simple act to restore order' – and even went to Beijing to deliver that message to the Chinese leaders himself. That sent a signal to Moscow, and to people in East Germany.

Many feared the SED regime would use methods similar to those used by the Chinese when they were faced with mass protests in Leipzig in the autumn of 1989. Every Monday, thousands of people gathered shouting the slogan 'We are the people', a not too subtle reference to the US Declaration of Independence's 'We the people'. The protests, known as Monday Demonstrations, spread to other cities too. (Those in Rostock, a city on the northern coast of East Germany, took place on Thursdays and were consequently known as Thursday Demonstrations. They were organised by Pastor Joachim Gauck, who later became President of Germany.)

Honecker, Krenz, Stoph and Mielke considered their options and discussed the matter with the Soviet leader, who was in Berlin as a special guest to commemorate the 40th anniversary of East Germany. Perhaps not surprisingly, they got little help. Gorbachev was blunt in his comments. The transcript of the German translation of his conversation with Honecker and his cabal contains a line that later became famous: 'Life punishes the one who comes late.'

The celebrations on 7 October 1989 were a bit of an anti-climax for Honecker. He had wanted a party to hail the achievements of East Germany, instead he watched as even the carefully choreographed parade descended into spontaneous cries of 'Gorby, Gorby, Gorby', Gorbachev's endearing nickname.

Krenz – who hitherto had been an unfaltering authoritarian and apologist for Communism of the most uncompromising kind – knew that he had to act fast lest he too was swept away by the tidal wave of political reform. Gorbachev was once again pushing for Hans Modrow to be installed as leader. Krenz was running out of time. He spoke to Günter Schabowski, another Politbüro member who had previously supported Honecker. Schabowski agreed that time was up for the old guard. On the morning of 17 October 1989 Krenz went to see Erich Honecker and told him to go. Honecker defended himself and refused to resign, but he knew that resistance was futile. The old man had to give in.

The action was timely – Krenz and Schabowski and other members of the Central Committee were due to meet that same afternoon. It was just a routine meeting. Nothing pressing was on the agenda. That changed after the brief *tête-à-tête* between Honecker and Krenz. The latter had been like a son to Honecker. Now, like Brutus, Krenz wielded the political dagger and finished the career of the man who had shepherded him to the top. The Central Committee met at 2 pm as planned. At 2.15 the meeting was over and at 2.16 the Allgemeiner Deutscher Nachrichtendienst, the official East German Press agency, issued a telegram: 'Egon Krenz has been elected as Secretary General of the Central Committee of the Communist Party of East Germany.'

Gorbachev was incensed. He had not been informed. He had wanted Modrow but he got Krenz. The 46-year-old was not a popular choice among the people either. With a permanent tan, a double-breasted suit of the type worn by used car salesmen and a smile to match, the new Communist Party boss seemed a bit of a charlatan. The protest-singer Wolf Biermann did not offer a kind appraisal of the new Secretary General, describing him as 'a laughing idiot'. Suffice to say that Biermann and other oppositional East Germans did not like Comrade Krenz.

Krenz seemed oblivious to the critique and genuinely incapable of understanding why anyone had anything against him. Like the rest of the Politbüro he had lived a life sheltered from criticism. Unperturbed, he immediately went to Moscow. When a journalist asked him what he thought of the protests against him which had broken out on the day he was elevated to Secretary General, Krenz seemed surprised: 'Protests against me? I don't think so. But what is important here is that we have a unique opportunity to build a democratic Socialism'[22] – a Socialism under which he would be unchallenged and remain leader, of course. He was living in cloud-cuckooland.

Krenz paraded himself as a reformer but it was difficult for him to be taken seriously or, indeed, to be seen as someone who wanted to break with a past that he had done so much to shape. Day by day his power-base eroded, not just because his every attempt at calming the situation was being challenged by the growing number of protests, but also because Markus Wolf and Hans Modrow actively used their positions to undermine the new leader.

Krenz was in a bind. On the one hand he had to attack the old guard and appear as a new man, but he also had to watch his rivals. He decided on a strategy of 'hug them close': give your opponents influence and make them responsible for their actions. It wasn't a bad tactic, and had been used before. Consequently, Krenz proposed on 7 November 1989 that Modrow replace Prime Minister Willi Stoph and that Erich Mielke, the feared Minister for State Security, be sacked. The post of Prime Minister was relatively meaningless. The tactic seemed prudent and well considered. But Krenz's plan was soon overtaken by events.

One of the most pressing political problems for the East German regime was the steady exodus of its citizens into Czechoslovakia and through Hungary into the West. Honecker had temporarily thwarted the relative ease with which East Germans could travel to neighbouring Communist countries. Krenz's first action had been to lift the ban on travel to Czechoslovakia. The new leader wanted to be a man of the people; he craved popularity and thought he had found a solution. He decided to open the borders to the West.

On 9 November 1989 at 6.30 pm Günter Schabowski – by now Krenz's unofficial spokesperson, gave a press conference. He reported that travel restriction to the West had been lifted. He was not specific. He merely said that henceforth 'private journeys abroad can be undertaken without proof of eligibility'.

Riccardo Ehrman, a 60-year-old correspondent for the Italian News agency Agenzia Nazionale Stampa Associata, asked a simple question:

'When will this take effect?'

The Communist bureaucrat looked perplexed, paused and said, 'As far as I know it takes effect immediately,' and then he added, 'without delay'.

The announcement came as a shock, but a welcome one for the citizens of East Germany. As one eyewitness observed:

> We couldn't believe the news we heard on the radio and [saw] on TV. We drove to the border and when we reached Schönhauser Allé we got out and followed the masses down Bornholmer Straße to the wall. When we reached it a couple of hundred people were still standing in front of the barrier and some of them were even leaning on it. They were chatting to the guards and avoided any kind of aggression. They realised that the men in uniform who for decades arrogantly had shuttled them around, no longer knew what they were supposed to do. In one single instant all the self-importance and arrogance of the uniformed guards had evaporated. Suddenly the gate opened and we all scrambled across the Bornholmer Brücke.[23]

AN EVENING IN THE SAUNA

It was a Tuesday evening, and every day of the week had a routine in Angela's life. Tuesday she went to the sauna, and then afterwards she would have one beer – not two! – with a friend. On Wednesday morning she had to be back at work at quarter past seven.

Tuesday 9 November 1989 would be no different, or so she thought. Sure, she noticed that a large number of people were walking towards Bornholmer Straße. Earlier in the evening she had watched the press conference with Schabowski on the news, but had thought nothing of it. However, she must have been aware that things were changing rapidly for she rang her mother:

> We had always said, 'when the wall falls we'll go and have dinner at the Kempinski [a luxury hotel in West Berlin]. I said to my mother, 'now it seems to have happened'. But it wasn't at all clear that it was happening immediately, so I went to the sauna with my friend as I always did at six o'clock.[24]

Angela must have got the time slightly wrong. Schabowski's press conference did not start until 6.53 pm, when Merkel would have already been sweating in the sauna. But such details are of minor importance.

When she left the tavern at 9 pm after having a beer, the streets were in frenzy. Literally thousands of people were flowing, meandering and strolling across the border over the Bösebrücke. Angela went along with them over the bridge that had hitherto been out of bounds for East Germans, crossed the border and went into West Berlin. At first she looked for a payphone. She wanted to ring her aunt in Hamburg but then realised that she didn't have any West German coins. She takes up the rest of the story:

> I met some people and somehow I ended up in a family's apartment. I was able to make a phone call from there. They wanted to go back on the Ku'damm [Kurfürstendamm, the main street in West Berlin] and celebrate. But I said that I'd rather go home. I had to get up early the next morning. So many new people and so much company was a bit too much for me at that moment. I had already got rather too carried away by my standards.[25]

Whether this is an accurate description of what she felt at the time, or a reconstruction of her thoughts many years later, we can never know. But it is interesting that even this most euphoric moment in recent European history was described in such restrained tones. Angela did not get carried away. She stuck to her routine.

On the next day she duly went to work. And after she had carried out all her duties in the lab she went across to West Berlin with her sister Irene. They didn't stay long as Angela still had work to do.

Two days after the opening of the border she went to Poland to give a talk at a seminar on quantum chemistry. She was surprised when she met her colleagues on the train: 'many were really depressed. "Now there will be no 'third way', all will go towards reunification and the East will be domesticated by the West",' one of her acquaintances said.[26]

Her Polish colleagues at the Nicolaus Copernicus University in Toruń, a town in the northern part of Poland, were surprised to see her. 'Why did you come here when there are so many exciting things happening?' she remembers one of her Polish colleagues asking. 'They went on to say that now German reunification would come very quickly, and that by their next visit to Berlin there would be one united Germany. That astonished me. But it also opened my eyes.'[27] It was as if 'those who were watching the events at a distance had a clearer view of what was going to happen'.[28]

And things were going fast. 'We are one people' the demonstrators began to sing in Leipzig on 10 November. Egon Krenz was losing power fast. As if he didn't have enough to worry about, he also received a sombre report written by Paul Gerhard Schürer, the director of the Central Planning and Economic Agency. The document painted a depressing picture of East German finances. East Germany was bankrupt and without an injection of money would default on its loans. Yet the report did not present any solutions. The proposals – such as they were – could not be described as constructive, let alone realistic. The only concrete solution proposed in the report was that East and West Berlin could jointly organise the Olympic Games in 2004.

Unless an emergency loan of 123 billion Deutschmarks could be secured, it would be curtains for the regime. Krenz, believing that the West would reward him for opening the border, dispatched Alexander Schalck-Golodkowski to the West. He was the chairman of the Department of Commercial Coordination (KoKo), the government body in charge of the import of Western goods. Schalck-Golodkowski was a powerful man and a shady character, able to supply anything at a price. He allegedly earned a bit on the side by monopolising the distribution of pornography and had allegedly provided Erich Honecker no less than 4,864 pornographic videos.

It was not the first time Schalck-Golodkowski had been dispatched to negotiate with Western politicians. He had successfully negotiated with Franz-Josef Strauß (then the finance minister of West Germany) and secured a loan in 1983, a payment that reportedly prevented his country from going bankrupt. But the situation now was different. Helmut Kohl sounded conciliatory; he would gladly give the East Germans the much needed injection of West German Deutschmarks, but the conditions he set out went far beyond what the East German Communist Party had expected and even beyond what the protesters in the streets of Leipzig had demanded.

Addressing the West German Parliament, Kohl said: 'The SED must give up its [political] monopoly and must commit to free multiparty elections. Under those conditions we would be willing to discuss economic help.' These conditions were tough. But Kohl didn't stop there. After a brief pause, he looked up and he added, in his distinct dialect, 'It is also clear that financial help is conditional upon a fundamental reform of the economic system; the abolishment of the planned economy and the development of a market economy.'

This was not received kindly by the Central Committee of the Communist Party. Krenz got the blame and had to resign, and Modrow became Prime Minister. The predictions of Angela Merkel's colleagues in Poland were about to become reality. On 28 November Helmut Kohl proposed his 'Ten Point Plan' for German reunification.

A month beforehand only 28 per cent of West Germans believed that the two Germanys would unify within the next ten years. Now the figure had risen to 48 per cent. Helmut Kohl was surfing the wave of history and had seized an opportunity that nobody had foreseen.

South of the border, in Czechoslovakia, the Communist regime of Gustáv Husák, the hardliner who had been installed in 1968 after the Soviet invasion, was forced to resign. The rule of the Communists was collapsing and within days Alexander Dubček, the hero of the Prague Spring, had returned as speaker of Parliament. Before the end of December Václav Havel, a playwright and one-time political prisoner, had become President. Gorbachev's attempt to build a Common European Home was succeeding, but not in the way he had hoped or expected.

The fall of Communism was a momentous, historical and completely unexpected event. 'In Poland it took ten years, in Hungary ten months, in East Germany ten weeks,' quipped Timothy Garton Ash. One could add, perhaps, that in Romania later in the year it took merely ten hours from the people protesting till Nicolae Ceaußescu was ousted, and a couple of days later executed. It was hard not to get carried away in those halcyon days. Lines written by the nineteenth-century historian Jacob Burckhardt, who witnessed the revolutions of 1848, seemed appropriate, perhaps even prophetic: 'History suddenly moves with breathtaking swiftness; developments that previously would have taken centuries appear like fleeting phantoms and come into being within weeks or months. A message is buzzing through the air . . . everything must change.'

A new chapter was about to be opened, and a hitherto unknown research scientist was about to enter the scene in a way that no one – least of all herself – would or could have expected.

CHAPTER 5

ANGELA BECOMES MERKEL

O NE FRIDAY, EARLY IN THE EVENING, A TRABANT 601 HUFFED AND puffed as it slowly made its way through the northeastern suburbs of East Berlin. It reached Highway A114, continued past Naturpark Barnim and onto Zehdenicker-straße, turned right on Dorfstraße and then drove the last few kilometres to the town of Templin. The driver was invited but her arrival was not expected. Angela's brother Marcus and her father Horst Kasner had often asked her to take part in the seminars they had organised for political dissidents and intellectuals. They had done so for years, but hitherto she had always had an excuse: 'she was busy', 'sorry but something came up', and so on. In other words, excuses, excuses, excuses.

But on this day, 23 September 1989, she turned up to the innocent and rather philosophical-sounding seminar 'What is a human being?' It was a thinly veiled cover for a political discussion of the situation in the country. Nobody at this stage had any inkling that the Berlin Wall could fall, and many of the participants were concerned that things – in Horst Kasner's words – 'could get out of hand'.[1] As recounted in the previous chapter, protests had broken out in several East German cities and it was as yet unclear what would happen.

Both Horst and Marcus had been involved in establishing Neues Forum (NF), an oppositional group set up by Katja Havemann (widow of the dissident Robert Havemann), whose son was a colleague of Angela's at the Academy of Sciences.

Maybe it was because of this connection that Angela began to take a more practical interest in politics. To date politics had mainly been a matter she had discussed in the (very frequent) coffee breaks in the lab. As the reform movement gained traction, Angela started to go to seminars in the Gethsemane Church in Berlin, where the participants discussed human rights issues at a rather abstract philosophical level. Angela, by her own account, was bored stiff with the rather metaphysical discussions: 'I believe politics is about results.' The idea of anarchistic grassroots democracy was not for her: 'without power there is chaos', she concluded.[2]

Perhaps it was for this reason Angela didn't say much at the seminar in Templin a few weeks later. Most of the participants were busy discussing exactly those very philosophical questions she found so tedious.

One of the other participants in Kasner's seminars, the prominent West German theologian Professor Christofer Frey, remembers a woman with 'a round and friendly face' who was quiet during the meeting.[3] Only on the Sunday 'as we were driving to church in her *Trabi*' did Angela speak, saying something to the effect that 'if East Germany were to change it would not be into something like West Germany'.[4]

Some might draw the conclusion that Angela was a bit tentative in those days. To be sure, she was starting to get engaged in the reform movement, which was brave enough in itself. However, she was not yet ready to speak out against the regime. She remembers it a bit differently herself: 'In my own mind, I had given up on Socialism. This idea that we could mix things together and create another kind of Socialism [with a human face] did not appeal to me.'[5]

In reality matters were a bit more complex than Angela would like us to remember. When the prominent writer Christa Wolf had the audacity to question whether East Germany should remain a Socialist state, Angela and Erika Hoentsch, the friend from university who had been her bridesmaid, wrote a strongly worded letter, which – apparently through the wise intervention of Horst Kasner – was never published. In the letter, Angela and Erika wrote: 'if you still believe in Socialism, then it is important to contribute to its realisation and to stop the polemics'.[6] Not exactly the words of someone who had resolved to reject Karl Marx's philosophy, let alone a response one would have expected from someone who less than a year later was elected to the German federal Parliament on a conservative ticket.

These were different times, however, and it is difficult to fault someone who had grown up in a brainwashing dictatorship. In any case, at this stage Angela could not possibly have foreseen that one day she would be a democratically elected conservative politician.

What Angela may have thought about the future of Socialism in those days remains an open question. It is probable that her renunciations were not quite as cast-iron as she would later have us believe. But it is difficult to think clearly when things happen at breakneck speed. And to suggest that she was a turncoat, as some of her critics would have us believe, is unwarranted. One thing Angela certainly knew was that politics was interesting and that she wanted to get involved in it in a practical way.

Soon after her visit to Templin, Angela went to the offices of Demokratischer Aufbruch (Democratic Awakening, often shortened to DA). This was a small group of intellectuals headed by the lawyer Wolfgang Schnur. Angela knew about the organisation from her brother and volunteered, though she wasn't particularly active. The association she joined was still balancing on the edge of illegality.

The DA was formally established in an apartment belonging to Ehrhart Neubert, a Lutheran pastor, on 1 October 1989. At this stage, about a month before the fall of the Wall, the Stasi was still keeping matters under control, or trying to. The secret police had got wind of the meeting and, true to form, blocked the entrance to the church where it was to take place. The participants had expected this and congregated in the clergyman's flat. Four weeks later the DA finally agreed on a mission statement, though this soon changed in response to the rapid political changes. It is illustrative to compare the two versions. That of 30 October 1989 stated: 'The DA's critical attitude towards actually existing Socialism does not imply that we reject the ideal of a Socialist society.' A month later, and notably *after* the fall of the Berlin Wall, the DA was singing from a different political hymn-sheet. Now all talk of Socialism had been left to one side and the party was committed to a 'social market economy with a high level of ecological consciousness'. The party was further committed to a transformation of the economy under which 'different forms of ownership will exist side by side'.

INTO POLITICS

As we saw in the previous chapter, Angela went to Poland for a conference two days after the Berlin Wall had fallen. Her conversations with her Polish colleagues made her think. Her affiliation with the DA had been non-committal and in any case it was, at this stage, more a political debating club than a real political party. If Angela were to get involved in politics proper, it had to be in one of the actual political parties. The question was which one? She first went to the Social Democrats, the newly reformed Sozialdemokratische Partei in der DDR (SPD). She did not go there alone but with her line manager and friend Klaus Ulrich. He immediately signed up, but Angela was more sceptical: 'At first everything was fine. Someone had come in from the West to organise it all. Everybody said "*Du*" [the informal "you"] to each other.' That people whom Angela had never met used the informal personal pronoun and not the more formal '*Sie*' annoyed the 35-year-old physicist. 'They started singing "Brothers, to the Sun, to Freedom",' she remembered with some disdain. This was a Russian song that became popular during the October Revolution in 1917, though it had also been sung during the Leipzig Monday demonstrations in 1989. 'That was not for me,' Angela concluded.[7]

To add to her annoyance, the Social Democrats from the West addressed each other as 'Comrade'. No wonder she was alienated. It is not entirely clear whether she considered joining any of the other relatively established political parties, such as the CDU and the Liberals (FDP). Her brother Marcus, who was committed to environmental issues, joined NF, which intended to contest the elections. Angela went along to an NF meeting, but once again she was disappointed. She had already experienced grassroots democracy in the Gethsemane Church a few months before. She was sceptical but maybe things had changed, she thought. They had not:

> I went to one of these meetings. There were all these people who shared Bahro's [the left-wing critic of the regime] ideas about Socialist society. I had absolutely nothing in common with them. I went to the meeting to show solidarity with the opposition movement in East Germany but I didn't like what I saw.[8]

Angela was perplexed. It looked back then as if the Social Democrats would be the strongest party, but she had dismissed them. What was she to do? Luckily for her, the DA decided to transform itself into a proper political party, holding a conference in Leipzig on 17 December at which the delegates decided to contest the democratic elections to the East German Parliament, which everyone believed would be held in May 1990.

Angela volunteered to work for the organisation, and although she was vastly overqualified, she was happy to do the boring jobs no one else wanted to do. She started her political career by distributing leaflets in Marienstraße in the centre of Berlin.

Less than a year later the political novice who volunteered for these tedious and uninteresting tasks was a cabinet minister, but before her career could take off a constellation of coincidences had to align and Angela had to show a new side of herself that nobody had ever seen.

HELMUT KOHL AND THE REUNIFICATION PROCESS

What happened in the political world that Angela was soon to join was characterised by a breathtaking pace rarely seen in political history. At the end of November, on the 28th, Helmut Kohl had taken everybody by surprise and proposed that Germany be unified. Without a particular timetable, Kohl presented a ten-point plan he had drawn up with the help of Dr Rupert Scholz. The latter had been a defence minister in Kohl's government but the Chancellor had sacked the bookish law professor in the spring and sent him back to his Chair of Jurisprudence at the University of Munich. The two had made up, however, after Kohl had eaten a bit of humble pie.

Kohl proposed that the two countries should gradually merge into one and that East Germany simply be incorporated into the Federal Republic, something that could be easily accommodated under Article 23 of the Basic Law, which had been established for this hitherto hypothetical eventuality. Kohl had not consulted Mikhail Gorbachev, nor his friend the French President François Mitterrand, let alone the British Prime Minister Margaret Thatcher or the American President George H.W. Bush. Sometimes politics is a game of action in which one must seize the moment.

Before the great powers had a chance to react, however, the East German regime disintegrated. On 3 December the Politbüro resigned. Those who had cowered before them a few weeks earlier now subjected their hitherto untouchable and feared Communist masters to humiliating denunciations. Under normal circumstances the members of the East German Parliament did as they were told, performing the role of a rubber stamp. But things had changed. The *Blockparteien* – the hitherto lame bourgeois parties – broke ranks with the East German Communist Party and a number of Communist deputies joined them. A barely audible Erich Mielke, the Minister for State Security, pleaded with his colleagues: 'But I love mankind, I love, I love all people,' he said. His pitiful words were drowned by scornful laughter and cries of derision.

The East German Parliament passed a resolution to the effect that the SED's monopoly of power was to be broken, and three days later, on 4 December 1989, an angry mob stormed the Stasi headquarters in Leipzig. On 7 December the political parties met for the first round-table talks and decided that free elections should be held.

When Helmut Kohl visited East Berlin on 19 December this most uncharismatic of political leaders was treated like a rock-star. His son Walter, who accompanied his father on the trip, remembers: 'What I saw was breathtaking. From our elevated position I could see far into East Berlin, and all the way down Unter den Linden there were people as far as the eye could see to witness this historic event.'[9]

Kohl acted fast. The Chancellor who had been a political liability a few months before, when the papers openly wrote about a possible 'regicide', was now in his stride. 'Because virtuosity is the excellence we ascribe to the performing arts, politics has often been defined as an art,' wrote Hannah Arendt, the German-American political philosopher, in *Between Past and Future*. In those December days of 1989 and in the early months of 1990 Helmut Kohl, so long the laughing stock of the intelligentsia, was a virtuoso in the performance art of politics. His Ten Point Plan had taken everybody – friend and foe – by surprise. The Social Democrats, with the very notable and vociferous exception of former Chancellor Willy Brandt, were sceptical of the virtues of reunification. But Kohl's policy was slowly but steadily winning support.

Kohl was not the only one who acted fast and showed political initiative. It had been loosely agreed with Hans Modrow, now the Prime Minister of East Germany, that the elections to the East German Parliament should take place in May. But after a trip to Moscow, Modrow returned with the message that the elections would take place on the earlier date of 18 March. The Communist leader knew that the SED controlled a vast network of local organisations and he was quietly confident that more people than expected would vote for the East German Communist Party.

His Western opposite number had no choice but to accept the earlier date. Kohl's greatest concern, however, was not the Communists but the resurrected Social Democrats. It was widely believed that East-SPD would do well in the elections. This could be a problem for Helmut Kohl's plans for speedy reunification. Indeed, it could even put the whole idea of reunification on the back-burner for a while.

Kohl was also aware that East-CDU was carrying heavy baggage, having been one of the *Blockparteien* that supported and collaborated with the SED during the years of dictatorship. This problem could partly be neutralised through an alliance with DA and the other right-wing party, the DSU (Deutsche Soziale Union, established in Leipzig in December 1989). On the other hand, working with East-CDU – a party that formally was a different legal entity than the CDU in the West – also had advantages. East-CDU had a vast network of members and over 5,000 locally elected politicians in municipalities all over East Germany. If these individuals could somehow be mobilised, the CDU would have a grassroots organisation that the Social Democrats did not possess. For although West-SPD poured money and expertise into the East, the Social Democrats lacked the all-important organisation of experienced local campaigners.

Kohl and his allies had an organisational advantage, but he had to be careful not to be seen as a colonial master. While he wanted to stay in control it was important that he maintain a distance and allow the East Germans to run the election themselves – at least nominally. He teamed up with Lothar de Maizière, an accomplished musician (he played viola in the Berlin Symphony Orchestra before he trained as a lawyer). The diminutive, bespectacled, bearded de Maizière had been close to the regime but had also been a leading member of the Lutheran community and even acted as an attorney for his religious brethren. This had brought him in contact with Angela Merkel's father Horst Kasner, and it also meant that he fitted into the image of the CDU Kohl wanted to portray in the East.

Kohl needed to broaden his appeal. The CDU was – at this stage at least – unlikely to win enough influence on their own; hence the alliance with the DA. By campaigning for election with recognised oppositional groups, Kohl could further neutralise the charge that the CDU was turncoats. The DA, East-CDU and DSU agreed to come together into a coalition called The Alliance for Germany. The formal meeting took place on 30 January 1990.

Kohl ran the risk that his new 'friends' in the East might develop delusions of grandeur, but he had already thought of this and had a back-up plan in the event that Lothar de Maizière, DA leader Wolfgang Schnur or DSU leader Pastor Hans-Wilhelm Ebeling should become difficult. Kohl and his advisors did their homework and carried out due diligence. As early as February he had evidence that de Maizière had worked as a Stasi agent under the alias 'Czerny'. The West German Chancellor did not have a lot of time for de Maizière, Schnur or Ebeling. In his diaries Kohl found it mildly amusing that the three political novices were fighting over the spoils even before the elections had been held. As Kohl remembers the meeting:

> After a little while a virtual fight broke out because Kirchner [of East-CDU] said that de Maizière should become Prime Minister in the event of a CDU victory, but Diestel [Ebeling's understudy] would have nothing to do with someone with 'red socks', and he even called him [de Maizière] a traitor.[10]

Kohl knew that he could neutralise each of them with a stroke of a pen, but allowed them to play around.

At this stage Angela Merkel was but a very little political fish. She had caught the political bug and was determined to take part in the new democratic experiment. She asked for – and was granted – three months' unpaid leave from her position at the Academy of Sciences. Her role was not glamorous but it was not unimportant, and for the first time in her ultra-short political career she was elected to a formal position. On 23 January 1990, the DA in Berlin held its local conference. It was agreed that they needed a spokesperson. Angela volunteered. A vote was held and she won, though no one stood against her. Compared to the elections she was to face in the future, the one in Jugendclub Gérard Philipe was a formality.

It was a subordinate role that was insignificant in the greater scheme of things, but not just a backroom position, and it soon became clear that Angela was more than capable of doing her job. Joining the DA was not at first sight a good career move, but in a roundabout way it gave Angela a chance to shine. Being part of a small party allows one to get noticed.

Wolfgang Schnur, the leader of the DA, had a rather inflated opinion of himself. His flashy ties and his hairstyle, which resembled that of a 1950s American rock 'n' roll star, probably said it all. In any case, Schnur did not hide his light under a bushel, declaring early on in the campaign that he considered himself an obvious choice for Prime Minister of East Germany. It was perhaps unsurprising that a man with such a high opinion of himself did not make time to meet the lowly party functionaries and officials whom Helmut Kohl had sent over to help DA, such as the political consultant Hans-Christian Maaß.

Schnur had shared a platform with Kohl and considered himself Kohl's equal. This, once again, provided Angela Merkel with a chance. When a delegation from Konrad Adenauer Stiftung, the CDU's official think-tank, came to see him, he told Angela to talk to them. 'But I don't have any legitimacy,' she responded. Schnur reacted promptly: 'Then I make you the spokesperson for the whole party.' As Merkel remembers, 'from then on it all went rather well'[11] – or, to be more accurate, it went rather well for her. Poor Schnur was not quite so fortunate. He was getting too big for his boots and hubris overcame him. Only four days before the election, on 12 March 1990, *Der Spiegel* published an article that provided incontrovertible evidence that Schnur had been a secret Stasi agent. His friends, especially Pastor Eppelmann, refused to believe the story. How could his friend over many years have betrayed him? Impossible. Whatever misgivings and doubts the clergyman may have had disappeared when he read the Stasi file, which *Der Spiegel* had acquired from a defected former spy. On joining the Stasi, Schnur had been ordered to 'actively influence negative and enemy forces in East Germany, and in particular Pastor Eppelmann'.[12]

The revelations resulted in hysterical scenes and chaos at Party HQ in Haus der Demokratie. Schnur himself had a nervous breakdown and was taken to the psychiatric ward of St Hedwigs Hospital. After reunification he was disbarred by the German Bar Association and later received a sentence for having broken Paragraph 241 of the Criminal Code when he gave information about his clients to the Stasi.

Eppelmann and the others were depressed, petrified and shocked. Something had to be done, and it was to everybody's surprise that Angela Merkel took action. 'I threw all Western journalists out so that we could start to think clearly,' she remembers.[13] This could be a politician's attempt to paint a positive picture of her ability to act under pressure, but, if anything, Merkel's recollection of the day is rather subdued when compared to the account of one of the journalists who witnessed her determined action. Thomas Schwarz, a radio journalist, recalled: 'It was complete bedlam in the office, everybody was down and out, and the media were baying for blood . . . But Angela Merkel was concentrated and focused, and as if it was the most natural thing in the world, all the men who held high office looked to this young woman.'[14] Her ability to clear up the mess was noted elsewhere. The revelation that Schnur had been a Stasi agent did not help the DA. The party polled just 0.92 per cent of the vote, and managed to win a handful of members in the East German Parliament only due to its alliance with CDU. It was a massive disappointment. Some optimists in the party had predicted that the DA could win upwards of 20 per cent, and even the opinion polls had the party at 10 per cent. The big surprise in the election was that de Maizière's party succeeded where his allies failed. With 40.8 per cent of the vote against the SPD's meagre 21.9 per cent, the CDU could form a majority government that was committed to speedy reunification. In the election the SED won a seemingly impressive 16.9 per cent, but it was less than a year since a beaming Egon Krenz had declared that the SED had won 99.9 per cent of the vote in the municipal elections. Everything had changed.

The result was unexpected. The SPD had been the favourites; now de Maizière had to learn to govern and take part in negotiations about reunification. It was chaotic and challenging for the small-town solicitor. Once again the unexpected was to be Angela's opportunity, but the road ahead was rocky and it was only as a result of determination, networking and sheer luck that she succeeded.

ELECTION NIGHT AND THE RISE OF ANGELA

Angela was disappointed but not surprised by the election result. It made her more determined. The DA had gathered at the restaurant Zur Mühle in Prenzlauer Berg, in the northeast of the city, but she soon left for the Palast der Republik, the seat of the East German Parliament. She knew that the DA would play only a subordinate role in the months to come, and she had set her sights on higher goals. It was essential that she met the winners. All was chaos at the Palast when she managed to get in. She witnessed Lothar de Maizière being interviewed, though she was unable to speak to the man himself. Determined not to miss out, she walked to Großgaststätte Ahornblatt, a concrete monstrosity of a Soviet-style shopping arcade and self-service restaurant on the Fischerinsel in the centre of Berlin where the CDU was celebrating its victory with a massive party. Angela tried to get in but was turned away by the bouncers as she had neither a press-card nor a ticket. Depressed, dejected and disappointed, she walked the four kilometres back to Zur Mühle. It was past midnight when she arrived.

Much to her surprise, the crestfallen DA members had a prominent guest, Lothar de Maizière. She immediately started talking to him. He wanted to show solidarity; she wanted to get close to his inner circle. He promised her that the DA would not be forgotten, then he left. Angela was in a better mood now. Once again she went back to the CDU party at the Fischerinsel and this time managed to get in. Her determination and tenacity paid off and her luck was changing. She met another de Maizière: Thomas. He was to play an important role later in her life as well as being instrumental in getting her career started. In her own words, 'I went to the CDU election party, and there I met Thomas de Maizière, Lothar de Maizière's cousin who also served as his advisor, and we spoke about the policies to be pursued and he promised me that DA would not be forgotten.'[15]

Angela was turning networking into an art form and she must have made an impression. In any case, her name came up when Thomas and Lothar de Maizière met the following day. The newly elected Prime Minister of East Germany was beginning to connect the dots. He remembered that he 'knew a rather liberal Lutheran pastor who had a daughter' who had been recommended to him, and he now realised that this daughter was none other than the enthusiastic young woman he had spoken to at the DA the night before. By coincidence – and through her persistence – it was the same woman his cousin had spoken to at the CDU party. But could she be trusted? Would she be someone who would fit the bill as de Maizière was putting his team together? He began to ask around. Hans-Christian Maaß was a political advisor to the West German Ministry of Development who had been dispatched to the East to help the embryonic political parties to establish themselves. Maaß, who was one of de Maizière's consultants, was helping the CDU politician to put a team together. He had a clear idea of whom he wanted in the Prime Minister's office. He was determined to find local talent that represented a broad spectrum of political opinion. At one of his meetings in December he remembered a woman who had all the qualities needed to stabilise the seemingly weak and inexperienced de Maizière. But who was she? The woman, Herr Maaß explained, 'was a scientist, she was disciplined, focused and was a doer. She was from the DA, so she fitted perfectly into the coalition arithmetic.'[16] It turned out that they were all talking about the same person, Dr Angela Dorothea Merkel.

Hans-Christian Maaß, a pastor's son who had escaped East Germany as a student, was a man of action. He got Angela's address in Prenzlauer Berg, drove there, and rang the doorbell. She was surprised to see him. Technically she was out of a job, and she was not enthusiastic about the prospects of going back to the Academy of Sciences and writing articles about obscure aspects of quantum molecular dynamics, vibronic couplings and the other esoteric issues that had occupied her only a few months before. She was glad but also intrigued to see Mr Maaß. 'Do you remember?' asked Maaß. She did indeed remember that they had met. As Maaß later recalled, 'Merkel had hardly finished her answer before she was in my car on the way to the East German Parliament.'[17]

Three days later Angela was offered a post as deputy spokesperson for the new East German government – in effect number two to the new director of communications, Matthias Gehler. It was a substantial promotion and it also gave her a considerable pay rise; she now earned the princely sum of 2,500 Marks per month, twice what she had been paid at the Academy. It took a couple of days to get the paperwork sorted out as the procedures for employing civil servants were not yet established. On 9 April 1990 Matthias Gehler received a letter from Italy: 'I hereby accept the offered position with thanks', it said. Angela had gone away on holiday to Italy, in itself an indication of how much things had changed. Six months before a trip to the West would have been an impossibility. 'My partner had received an invitation to go to a conference in Sardinia and I wanted to come with him. I had worked hard and I had earned a couple of days in the sun.'[18] Her work began immediately once she returned.

Her linguistic abilities meant that she was in higher demand than she had expected. There was a lot of travelling required, and the now former research chemist had not been particularly concerned about her wardrobe. This somewhat amused her colleagues and endeared her to Lothar de Maizière: 'She looked very much like a student and had all the mannerisms that went with it.' Compared to the other females in their pantsuits and stilettos, Angela's sandals and jeans did not quite fit the dress code. 'On a trip to Moscow we had to go out to get her a coat and a new pair of shoes,' de Maizière recalled.[19] Angela may not have looked the part as a professional diplomat, but no one could find flaws in her work: 'As a government spokesperson she was the best and the most helpful official source in East Berlin,' said Detlev Ahlers, chief correspondent of *Die Welt*. Angela's network and her reputation for professionalism increased by the day, but she was still a comparatively little fish.

The election gave the new government a mandate for reunification, but the great powers were not united in being happy at the prospect of a reunited Germany. Gorbachev had not given up on his idea of a Common European Home. He still envisioned the 'New Germany' – to use the Communists' expression – as a neutral country, which implied that US nuclear weapons would have to be removed. George H.W. Bush, the US President, wanted the opposite: a united Germany in NATO.

From the point of view of international law, the two superpowers were obliged to reach an agreement with France and the United Kingdom, the two other victorious powers in the Second World War. The last was not pleased. Margaret Thatcher never made any secret of her dislike for Germany, and Helmut Kohl in particular. After the East German election the British Prime Minister was unable to contain herself: 'France and Great Britain should pull together today in the face of the German threat,' she told the French ambassador to London. 'Kohl is capable of anything. He has become another man. He doesn't know himself any more. He sees himself as the master and is starting to act like it.'[20]

Things were not going Thatcher's way, however. She had underestimated the skills and determination of the man from Rheinland-Pfalz (Rhineland-Palatinate), as the Chancellor liked to call himself. That Kohl was a bit of a country boy and as such was underestimated by his cultured colleagues was to his advantage. Gorbachev described him as a 'hick from the countryside' and told Mitterrand, 'Here [in the Soviet Union] even the humblest politician in the provinces thinks six moves ahead. Not him.'[21] The Russian underestimated Kohl to his cost.

Mitterrand was more amenable in principle, though he feared the consequences of rapid reunification. In a conversation with President Bush, who had asked if Mitterrand 'as President of France' was 'for [reunification]', the Frenchman responded that he 'was not against it, given the changes in the East' and that 'if the Germans want it, we won't oppose it'.[22]

Mitterrand's greatest concern was for the future of Gorbachev. He had reason to be fearful. The Soviet leader himself had asked Mitterrand to help him avoid German reunification, and had warned him that if he did not, Gorbachev risked being replaced by a military regime. As the Frenchman grew ever more sceptical he was even able to calm the fears of Margaret Thatcher. 'Gorbachev will never accept a united Germany inside NATO and the Americans will never agree to Germany leaving the alliance, so let's not worry,' he told his British counterpart.[23] Increasingly confident that reunification would not happen, Mitterrand played the European card: that seemed safe. He proposed that if the European Union were strengthened then a united Germany would not be a problem. Hence 'all we can do is to make [the European] Community more attractive so that an eventually reunited Germany will prefer the Community [EU] to balancing between East and West'.[24]

This was the brilliant idea Kohl needed. If the EU became stronger Germany would not constitute a threat but would merely be the largest state in the 'United States of Europe'. France would share a currency with Germany and the rest of the continent and, to complete the picture, Gorbachev would get a version of the Common European Home. George Bush, who supported Kohl, was happy too. Germany would remain a member of NATO, though with certain conditions.

Everyone was happy, with the notable exception of Margaret Thatcher. The British Prime Minister had once again overestimated her strength. Her obdurate opposition to German reunification had sidelined her and the other countries were able to go ahead.

Of course, Kohl had to pay a price for the deal. But given his earlier concerns Gorbachev demanded less than Kohl had initially feared. The two Germanys agreed that no NATO troops would be stationed on former East German soil, that Germany's eastern border would not be challenged, and that Germany would pay the Soviet Union 55 billion Deutschmarks in gifts and favourable loans. This was a considerable sum – the equivalent of eight days of West German GDP – but a small price to pay in the scheme of things.

ANGELA AND THE TWO PLUS FOUR NEGOTIATIONS

Did Angela get involved in these talks? Given her lowly status as a deputy spokesperson to Lothar de Maizière, it is surprising that she got anywhere near the negotiations at all. But she did, and once again it was a combination of tireless networking and sheer good luck that helped her. Under what was known as the 'Two Plus Four' format, both Germanys had to be represented in the negotiations alongside Britain, France, the USA and the Soviet Union. While Kohl and his foreign secretary, the Liberal Hans-Dietrich Genscher, were the leading negotiators, de Maizière – who held the offices of both Prime Minister and Foreign Minister – attended the negotiations in Moscow. As he did not speak foreign languages, Angela's ability to speak both Russian and English came in handy. She was able to help her boss during the negotiations, and she was also able to present information to the press. Lothar de Maizière, who had nothing like the impressive entourage enjoyed by Kohl, increasingly relied on Angela's analytical ability:

'early on she was able to formulate answers to complicated questions', de Maizière remembers.[25] When the German negotiators wanted to gauge the attitudes of ordinary Russians Angela was sent out onto the streets to talk to all and sundry. What the ordinary Russians told her was not what her masters wanted to hear: 'Gorbachev is giving away what Stalin had won' was one comment, another was that 'Gorbachev is in the process of losing the Second World War'. Lothar de Maizière was concerned about these sentiments. Helmut Kohl decided to ignore them and press ahead. The latter's determination won out, and on 12 September the parties approved the Two Plus Four Agreement. The British had opposed the ban on NATO troops in the former East Germany up to the end, but George Bush ordered Thatcher to fall into line and she reluctantly did. Bush was facing another problem with Saddam Hussein's invasion in Kuwait and had little time for Britain's opposition to German reunification.

TWO BECOME ONE

Kohl was not the only one who was active in the reunification process. The Chancellor might have been instrumental in getting the consent of the foreign powers, but he was less engaged in domestic negotiations about a merger of the two Germanys. These were undertaken by the newly appointed Wolfgang Schäuble, long seen as Kohl's heir apparent, and the East German politician Günther Krause. The latter had been the star of the reunification process, though later he was to fall from grace, as we shall see. A civil engineer with a PhD, Krause had, rather exceptionally, been appointed to a chair of computer science when he was still in his early 30s. He had been active in the East German CDU since the mid-1970s, and combined his scientific prowess with political skills. After the election he became leader of the CDU in Mecklenburg-West Pomerania. Lothar de Maizière, who admired the younger man, made him minister without portfolio with special responsibilities for negotiating the finer points of reunification.

Dr Wolfgang Schäuble was no less impressive. The cerebral lawyer had been Kohl's minister without portfolio and was considered his problem solver. When Kohl inadvertently compared Mikhail Gorbachev to Joseph Goebbels in 1986, it was the young lawyer's job to sort out the problems, and in 1987 it was also Schäuble who had organised Erich Honecker's visit to West Germany. Now Minister of the Interior, Schäuble was a safe pair of hands.

Within a few months, Krause and Schäuble had reached agreement on a social and monetary union which meant that virtually worthless East German Marks could be exchanged for West German Deutschmarks. While monetary sovereignty was transferred to the Bundesbank in Frankfurt, the government in Bonn also began to transfer subsidies to the impoverished cities in East Germany. By early June 1990 the two Germanys were in all but name a unified state, though the formal merger was only finalised after the Treaty of Unification was agreed on 31 August 1990. It was formally approved by the East German Parliament on 20 September, with 299 votes in favour, 80 against and one abstention. The West German Parliament approved the treaty on the same day, with 442 votes in favour, 47 against and three abstentions.

The reunification was legally in accordance with provisions in the Constitution, and this proved important later when the authorities in the new Germany were able to use provisions in West German law to prosecute officials and politicians in the erstwhile GDR for crimes committed during the years of Communism.

Where was Angela Merkel in all this? Again she played a role – an important but not essential one. She was not, of course, formally part of the negotiation team, but her role as spokesperson was highly prized by Krause. Angela was there at 2.08 am when the negotiations were concluded and it was she who briefed the press on the 1,000 pages of dense legal prose that constituted the Treaty of Unification. She had done her duty but she could not go home: her talents were needed elsewhere.

PROSPECTIVE PARLIAMENTARY CANDIDATE FOR STRALSUND-RÜGEN-GRIMMEN

After the signing of the Treaty of Unification on 31 August, Angela needed to move on. She did not need to worry about unemployment. Günter Krause, who was appointed to Kohl's cabinet, secured her a job. Angela's dedication and diligence were rewarded: through Krause's intervention she was given a position as a senior communication officer in the Government Information Service (BPA) with the same rank and pay as a chief executive of a hospital or a chancellor of a public university. Krause, being a politician, did not appoint her out of the kindness of his heart. Now that he was a cabinet minister in the federal government it was understandable that he wanted – at the very least – to consolidate his position. As one of the very few '*Ossis*' (the new word for Germans from the East), he needed friends, allies and a network. Angela Merkel had many contacts and she was well liked. Having her as, in effect, a publicly paid spin-doctor would be very useful for Krause.

What Krause needed, however, was not just a press officer but also an ally in the parliamentary group once the first All-German Parliament was elected in December. He needed to find a safe electoral district from which Angela could be elected to Parliament. Krause's eyes fell upon the constituency of Stralsund-Rügen-Grimmen in Mecklenburg-West Pomerania by the Baltic Sea in the north of the former East Germany. As Chairman of the CDU in Mecklenburg-West Pomerania, Krause needed to build a local base in his own district. It was one of the CDU's strongholds and whoever won the nomination would – barring a disaster or the embarrassing revelation of a Stasi past – be certain of becoming a member of Parliament.

Two candidates had already presented themselves: Klaus Herrmann, a CDU advisor who had spent his entire career as a backroom boy in the party HQ, and Hans-Günter Zemke, director of a savings and loans bank in Bremen, in northwest Germany. The latter in particular had established himself as a strong contender, being well known for having facilitated much needed investments in the area.

A meeting had already been held on 16 September to select a candidate, but several questions about the selection of candidates were raised and there were some irregularities in the voting process. Zemke requested that the matter be investigated to determine whether the correct legal procedures had been followed, and it was decided to postpone the selection meeting until 27 September.

At this point Krause decided to pounce. He called Wolfgang Molkentin, a leading CDU member in the area, and cut straight to the chase.

'Just choose Merkel,' he said.

'Who is Merkel?' asked the bewildered local politician.

Krause went on to tell him that Merkel was the candidate favoured by the party hierarchy. He didn't stop there. No sooner had he put the phone down than he rang Friedhelm Wagner, the local party chairman on the island of Rügen. Wagner had been a staunch supporter of Zemke and was not impressed. He was not persuaded by Krause and called his preferred candidate to warn him and to reassure him. Zemke was relaxed about Krause's lobbying. 'They [the local party] did not want some Mrs Merkel they had never heard about,'[26] he said.

However, Krause was more determined than most. Next on his list was Udo Timm, a local politician who fancied himself as a candidate for high office. He was keen to get Krause's backing to run for a seat in the Landtag (state legislature). Timm had the local contacts to make a deal possible. He got in touch with Andrea Köster, a former representative of the Farmers' Party and now an influential chair of one of the local CDU party organisations. The two decided to invite Angela Merkel to a kind of job interview in Timm's house.

Only a week before the scheduled selection meeting on the 27th, Merkel went to Timm's small villa in Bergen, the picturesque capital of Germany's largest island. She was focused and determined. She knew that Krause had presented her as Helmut Kohl's favourite candidate and that this could be an advantage, but she also knew that some might consider her arrogant. She decided to play a different hand. In her usual understated attire she came across as unthreatening, and she stressed again and again that she was not a carpetbagger. Köster was impressed: 'She came from the East, just like us.'[27]

Molkentin, Timms and Köster went into action. They organised buses to the selection meeting in the Haus der Armee on the 27th. At a quarter to six Angela Merkel turned up. Wearing a plain dress, minimal make-up and with a functional 'pixie' haircut, she didn't intimidate Zemke, who met her there for the first time.

In the first round of voting Zemke won the support of 45.9 per cent. Angela Merkel polled 31.5 per cent and Herrmann secured only 21 per cent and was therefore eliminated. As Zemke had not won a majority in the first round a second round of voting was necessary, but given the financier's lead in the first round, he seemed unworried. His supporters underestimated Merkel's support. Some of the delegates left. It was already

11 pm and they had to be at work the following morning. When the votes were finally counted at ten past midnight Zemke was no longer in the lead. Having secured 309 votes in the first round, Zemke only got 274 votes. Merkel got 280 votes and was declared the winner. Less than a year after she had attended her first political meeting, and only a month after she had become a member of the CDU, she was now in pole position to become a member of the federal Parliament of a reunited Germany. Her brother Marcus, who had always been the politically active member of the family, could find only one word for his sister's rapid rise: astounding.

Those who had helped Merkel did rather well too. Andrea Köster became Mayor of Bergen, a position she holds to the present day, Timm became a candidate for the CDU and was duly elected to the Landtag in October, and when Angela Merkel became Chancellor she bestowed the *Bundesverdienstkreuz*, the highest order in the country, on Wolfgang Molkentin. Whether this was a kind of belated *quid pro quo* or merely a happy coincidence is an open question. But having friends in high places is always useful.

CHAPTER 6

KOHL'S GIRL

'SO YOU CHECKED, DID YOU? DID YOU ACTUALLY CONSULT WITH MI-CHAEL Glos and Hermann Otto Solms?' Helmut Kohl, normally an avuncular figure, looked sternly at Angela. She found it difficult to answer. She hesitated. Her other colleagues looked at her too. She felt her emotions overcome her. She was not used to getting things wrong – she normally checked everything. And now Helmut Kohl had made her look like an idiot in front of her colleagues. She felt alone, abandoned, as if they had all turned on her. She couldn't take any more: 'I felt they had played me a fool. I think a man would have shouted. But for me it was different. I couldn't hold back the tears,' she reflected.[1]

She knew that such signs of emotion could be fatal in the male-dominated environment that was Helmut Kohl's cabinet. It was now the early summer of 1995 and the ministers were discussing her proposals to put restrictions on cars to alleviate the unprecedented smog levels that plagued the country. But her cabinet colleagues Matthias Wissmann (Minister for Transport) and Günter Rexroth (Minister for Industry) were opposed to her plan. And Helmut Kohl, who normally regarded Merkel as his *protégée*, seemed to be siding with her two male colleagues. The situation was not good. Crying would be a sure sign that she had lost it, that she was a hysterical woman. She had to keep it together. She wiped the tears away and put on a brave face.

It was not the first time Angela had felt she was being picked on, and she knew that this was her weakness. On her first foreign trip – she went to Israel in the spring of 1991 – she had also cried when she had been overlooked by the ambassador who let her collague steal the limelight. The press, in this case the regional *Stuttgarter Zeitung*, almost pitied the young minister, writing on 15 April that year:

> While Heinz Riesenhuber [minister of scienific research] waxed eloquently about scientific cooperation under the watchful eye of Ambassador Otto von der Gablentz, Angela Merkel was just sitting there without uttering a word. She must – just like many other East Germans – have felt that she once again was being outshone by a pushy Westerner.

But the fact that she shed tears was not reported. Merkel's network of friends in the media did not dish out the same level of cruelty to her as they did to any other novice. But she was vulnerable and she did appreciate that she had a problem. She knew that her propensity to cry and show emotion was a disadvantage. She had even told a journalist as much in an unguarded moment: 'I have to be tougher, otherwise it won't work,' she had told the weekly magazine *Der Spiegel*.[2] But it was difficult to be tougher, no matter how much she tried.

THE YOUNGEST MINISTER IN GERMAN HISTORY

Angela Merkel had been a cabinet minister for five years and six months, but still felt as if she was a bit of an outsider. It had been a mad and unbelievable period since, aged only 35, she had become Germany's youngest-ever cabinet minister. She had joined the cabinet only a month after she had been elected as a member of parliament in 1990, and only two months after she had become a member of the CDU.

Some have spoken of Angela Merkel's meteoric rise. Whatever metaphor is appropriate, she darted skywards at a pace that had never been seen before. Angela had not rested on her laurels after she narrowly defeated Hans-Günter Zemke to become the prospective parliamentary candidate for Wahlkreis Stralsund-Rügen-Grimmen on 27 September 1990.

Less than a week later the two Germanys were to be reunified at a ceremony in Berlin. Before that, the CDU would hold a party convention in Hamburg on 1-2 October to merge East-CDU and West-CDU into one political party both formally and legally. Angela, as a prospective candidate, was invited, but she was not content with merely coming along as a delegate. She wanted to get into the inner circle and to climb the ladder to higher things. She decided to use her network to set up meetings with powerful individuals. She asked her former colleague Hans Geisler if he could help her: 'Could you get me introduced to Helmut Kohl?' is how Geisler, later Minister for Social Security in Saxony, remembers her request.[3] He was happy to oblige. Unbeknownst to Merkel, Kohl had already spotted her talent and was on the lookout for a young woman to improve the male-dominated public image of his government.

They met on 30 September in the Rathauskeller, a rather traditional restaurant to Helmut Kohl's liking. Kohl, whose imposing physique owed much to his love for traditional German food, ordered *Labskaus*, a signature casserole dish of mashed potatoes, corned beef and beetroot. It was meant to be a brief natter, but they talked for longer than planned and he invited her to Bonn. He had a plan.

'I remember that I went to Bonn and that I had to wait in Juliane Weber's office,' Merkel remembered years later.[4] Juliane Weber was the head of Helmut Kohl's private office, an immensely influential and politically astute woman who had worked as the Chancellor's right-hand woman since he was a rising star in local politics. Angela's waiting time in Frau Weber's office was part of the examination, though Angela did not know this. Any other would-be politician would have been petrified and awestruck, but Angela did not know much about Weber's power and reputation. They just made small talk.

When Angela finally met Kohl the small talk continued. As she recalls, 'We talked a bit about the election campaign and Kohl was apparently rather pleased.'[5] Her impression was right. Kohl certainly was pleased. He had already asked the security services to check if there was anything incriminating about her in the Stasi archives. There wasn't, so he could put his plan into action. However, first Angela had to get elected.

Unaware of Kohl's plans, Angela continued her election campaign. She won her constituency with an impressive 48.5 per cent of the vote. The national election was a landslide; indeed, it was reminiscent of a coronation. Helmut Kohl easily vanquished the left-leaning social democratic challenger Oscar Lafontaine. A new chapter was opening for Angela Merkel.

Coming to Bonn – a small, bustling, political town in the state of North Rhine Westphalia, in the centre of the former West Germany – was a culture shock for Angela. She tried not to be awestruck. Sitting at the same table as famous and influential politicians whom she had previously known only from mass media was still rather overwhelming. A few days after her election she found herself sitting next to Norbert Blüm, the only cabinet minister to be a member of all of Kohl's cabinets from 1982 to 1998. Blüm was one of Kohl's most influential ministers. Angela was determined not to show any signs of timidity. 'I found myself next to all these people I only knew from the television. It was intimidating, but then I thought to myself, "You know integral calculus, so talking to Norbert Blüm shouldn't be that daunting, should it?"'[6]

The rumour spread quickly that Angela Merkel was in the running for one of the positions in the cabinet. If this was the case, which position did Kohl have in mind for her? The answer was unknown. It was certain that the CDU/CSU would continue the pre-election coalition with the Free Democrats but the party leaders of the three parties were still discussing the finer points. Meanwhile Angela was talking to the few journalists she knew in the federal capital. They discussed what portfolio Kohl might give her. Merkel's friend Detlev Ahlers, a senior correspondent for *Die Zeit*, recalled that Merkel said she 'wasn't interested in family and women's issues'.[7]

A few days later, Helmut Kohl appointed her as federal Minister for Women and Young People. Angela Merkel immediately seized the opportunity and totally forgot what she had told Ahlers, though she did admit that this was an area that was new to her:

> I didn't have time to meditate over such matters [as to my lack of expertise]. What was clear to me was that there was a constellation of factors that favoured me: being a woman, being from the East and being young – none of that hurt me. The policy area itself was not one that I had spent much time thinking about – the theme women and children was not one that interested me during the period of reunification.[8]

But, she went on,

For me this challenge was a great opportunity. I could learn the game and the mechanisms of power, and I could do so without too many dangers, unlike, for example, Günter Krause in the federal Ministry for Transport, who was in a ministry with lots of money to allocate and an army of lobbyists to battle with.[9]

Hitherto, the ministry Merkel took over had been part of a larger department that incorporated health, family and women's issues. But Kohl wanted more women in his cabinet for political reasons and to counter the critics who claimed that his cabinet was dominated by old men. The former ministry was consequently divided into Health (headed by Gerda Hasselfeldt, CSU), Family and Seniors (headed by Hannelore Rönsch, CDU) and lastly Women and Young People (headed by Angela Merkel, CDU).

She was sworn in on 18 January 1991. Her first task was a reform of the abortion legislation – a testing assignment for any politician, let alone a young woman who had been in politics for less than a year.

REUNIFICATION CRISIS AND ECONOMIC DOWNTURN

It was a time of tension and upheaval elsewhere in the world. The Soviet Union was in the early stages of its disintegration, which would be completed when Gorbachev resigned at the end of 1991. Earlier that year, on 17 January 1991, a coalition of troops led by the United States had begun Operation Desert Storm to forcibly remove Iraqi occupying forces from Kuwait. For historical reasons Germany was reluctant to take part in the operation, but Helmut Kohl once again got out the chequebook to pay for part of the operation. In this way, he hoped, the US President George H.W Bush would be satisfied that Germany had done its bit to maintain and strengthen the 'New World Order'.

'It would have been much easier and indeed much cheaper for us to simply dispatch a division of paratroopers, but constitutionally we can't do this,' an apologetic Kohl told the US Secretary of State, James Baker III.[10] The American appreciated the position, but demanded that Kohl contribute financially rather more substantially than under normal circumstances. However, there was a problem for Kohl. He was running out of money. His standard response to the Soviet Union during the Two

Plus Four negotiations had been to offer money. He responded the same way with the Americans, but it was becoming increasingly clear to finance minister Theo Weigel that the incorporation of the five new federal states was much more expensive than the optimistic Kohl had told the voters during the election campaign. East Germany had been days away from bankruptcy when Egon Krenz had been forced to resign, and only the intervention of West Germany had kept the erstwhile Communist state afloat.

East German industries were far from being competitive. The products they manufactured were of poor quality and were plainly unsaleable. Helmut Kohl was aware of this and knew that many of his new colleagues from East-CDU, to say nothing of their constituents, were less than impressed by his broken promises. Kohl had been crystal-clear during the election campaign: 'Tax rises are not necessary in connection with German reunification. We don't want to raise taxes. I do not believe that we need [to increase] taxes.'[11] His campaign had promised that reunification would be cost-free and that East Germans could look forward to a standard of living that was as good as that enjoyed by citizens in the West.

These promises could never have been fulfilled, and privately Kohl was willing to admit this. At a meeting with the Conservative British Prime Minister John Major, a soft-spoken son of a circus artiste who had taken over from Kohl's nemesis Margaret Thatcher in November 1990, Kohl did not mince his words. The minutes from the meeting suggested the situation was dire – so dire that Kohl felt it necessary to share the bad news with his English colleague:

> We've had a collapse in the economy of the former East Germany, and it has been worse than expected. We had expected that the Eastern economy would have contributed thirty billion Deutschmarks in export revenues, but that figure is now converging towards zero.[12]

There was only one thing to do: raise taxes in the West to pay for the impoverished new fellow citizens in the East. But even this could not disguise dismay among the *Ossis,* who felt that Kohl had broken his promises. The unemployment rate, an unknown phenomenon in the

Socialist planned economy of the erstwhile East Germany, rose to double figures and was in the low twenties in 1991. The Treuhandanstalt – the federal agency trusted with the privatisation of some 14,000 state-owned enterprises – was facing massive opposition and its director Detlev Rohwedder was killed in late 1991 by an unknown assassin thought to be from the Marxist terror organisation the Red Army Faction.

The malaise in the German economy led to clashes between West-CDU and cabinet members from the East. Lothar de Maizière, who became Deputy Chancellor after reunification, and Günter Krause, the Minister for Transport, loudly protested against the policies and made no secret of their dislike of Kohl's programmes. And more to the point, Kohl was critical of Krause's ideas, especially regarding toll-roads and the idea that motorists would have to pay to drive on the motorways. As the infighting reached fever pitch it was suddenly revealed that de Maizière had been a Stasi agent – something the East Germans vehemently denied. Helmut Kohl had been aware of these allegations since March 1990. That the revelations came out as de Maizière was locking horns with the Chancellor seemed to be more than a coincidence.

Where was Angela in all this? She was certainly not siding with her East German colleagues. She did not criticise them; she just didn't get involved. She had work to do. The media described her as 'a grey mouse'. Others observed that she seemed un-ministerial and that she still smoked in public.

SELECTING A TEAM

Angela was aware that she owed her political career to Helmut Kohl, but she also acknowledged that she had to break free from *Der Dicke* ('Fatty'), as the corpulent Chancellor was known in government circles. 'To put it diplomatically,' she said, 'I knew that I had to fight to be seen as an individual. Not in the eyes of Helmut Kohl, but in the eyes of other people. People already had a fixed and predetermined view of who I was; a token woman on the left. All this annoyed me.'[13]

If the media had cared to look at how she ran her first department, their judgment might have been more respectful. Angela Merkel was determined to establish her authority and to make a mark. German cabinet ministers are advised by two principal advisors, a head of department (a career official who has risen through the ranks of the civil service) and a parliamentary secretary. The former is responsible for the practical, legal and non-political issues, whereas the latter is a politician tasked with political assignments, including contact with representatives in Parliament. In addition to these, a minister will have a personal secretary and advisor, a chief of staff and a press spokesperson.

Merkel replaced all the top civil servants. All her advisors were close and trusted individuals, people she had met and not individuals who were loyal to her predecessor. There was good reason for this. She was well aware that it was not easy to get to grips with running a department and she feared the arrogant bureaucrats who treated her with overbearing condescension.

Unlike in America, where bureaucrats are seen as dull pen-pushers and are even a byword for slackness and incompetence, German state employees have a prestige that goes back to Frederick the Great in the eighteenth century, who modelled his civil service on the hierarchy of his efficient armed forces. Respect for civil servants, who are well paid and have life-long careers, was further strengthened at the beginning of the twentieth century by the sociologist Max Weber, who stressed that bureaucracy was government by rational principles carried out by competent, highly educated and well-paid individuals. Consequently, civil servants in the highest echelons of federal politics were individuals with immense self-confidence who often did not think highly of elected politicians.

Merkel was certainly different from her predecessors, which rather baffled her civil servants. Unlike Rita Süssmuth, Merkel's predecessor but one, who was now the Speaker of the German Parliament, the new minister was not in the mood for small talk. She was determined, goal-oriented and – according to one of the officials – 'not the kind of person who would go for a beer after work'.[14] Rita Süssmuth, by contrast, was the life and soul of the party and would routinely invite her advisors home for dinners in her apartment.

While the media were still describing her as 'Kohl's girl', Merkel impressed even the harshest critics within the system. Some of the civil servants at the more junior levels had to admit that she was able to get things done, albeit in her own sort of way. 'Her ability to concentrate, her intelligence and her knack of understanding the essentials. This has really impressed me,' said one. She has 'developed the instinct of a "political animal" when she discusses complex issues with her staff,' said another.[15]

Angela Merkel's first year as a cabinet minister was uneventful in terms of policy. The political debate was dominated by the rising costs of reunification and the increasing tension between the CDU ministers from the East and their colleagues in the West. Lothar de Maizière's difficulties grew ever deeper. Initially Helmut Kohl tried to prevent him from resigning. He even sent his embattled deputy an open letter in which he ostensibly begged him to stay. This was all show. As pressure continued to grow de Maizière's position was becoming untenable – thanks to strategic leaks from Kohl's office, it seems. On 23 November 1991 East Germany's last and only democratically elected Prime Minister threw in the political towel and resigned his position.

He was a bitter man. He complained that Angela Merkel had failed to come to his aid in his hour of need: 'I have a feeling that Angela does not want to be associated with anyone who has ever helped her in the past.'[16] Whether this embittered lamentation was fair is a moot point. Angela showed some empathy. She even pointed out that de Maizière had been treated worse than other politicians, but she maintained that her former benefactor and boss 'had been registered as an undercover employee for the Stasi'. However, she went on, 'whereas Stolpe [another politician with a past] was allowed to stay de Maizière was found guilty before he was able to defend himself'.[17] Rather kind words, but words that were only uttered a couple of months after her former boss had left the fray.

Angela's failure to speak up for de Maizière was politically understandable though not particularly endearing. She immediately realised that his fall opened the door for her own career prospects. She had impressed Volker Rühe, the CDU's General Secretary, by her no-nonsense approach. Rühe suggested to Helmut Kohl that she become Party Chairman in Brandenburg – in other words that she take over de Maizière's last remaining post. Rühe told *Frankfurter Rundschau*, 'It is important for the internal development of our party that de Maizière's successor [as the next party chairman for Brandenburg] comes from one of the new states.'[18] And Angela Merkel, of course, was from the East.

In reality there was another agenda. Such is politics. Sinister and ulterior motives get dressed up in principled arguments and are wrapped in idealistic words. Helmut Kohl and Volker Rühe were keen to reduce the influence of the former CDU general secretary Georg 'Heiner' Geißler, whose right-wing views often had clashed with Kohl's consensus policies. Geißler became a prominent spokesperson for anti-globalisation after he retired, but in the 1980s he was considered to be a hardliner on the right.

Ulf Fink, a known supporter of Geißler, had declared that he would stand for the vacancy. Although Fink had served as a Senator (a member of the City Legislature in Berlin), he was born in Freiburg in the south of Germany. Formally, therefore, he was not a local boy. Merkel, by contrast, was an *Ossi*. However, her campaign started too late. In retrospect, Rühe did not act quickly enough. He did not have time to prepare the ground or knock heads together. The local party was not keen on someone who was described as 'the favourite of Adenauer House' (the CDU HQ).[19] A candidate who had the backing of the increasingly unpopular Helmut Kohl did not go down well in Brandenburg, where ordinary citizens were experiencing a worsening of their standard of living and were now poorer than they had been under Communism. The result was not a surprise. Merkel lost the vote by 67 votes to Fink's 121. She was defeated, but learned a lesson.

The defeat was not fatal. Standing against Fink had earned her brownie points in the leadership. As a consolation prize, Rühe and Kohl suggested that she be made Deputy Chairman of the Party. This was within their gift. The position was not one that gave her power and responsibility, but it sent a clear signal to others that she had the goodwill and the support of Helmut Kohl and that he had rewarded her loyalty. In December 1991, 621 of the 719 delegates at the CDU Annual Conference in Dresden voted for her.

Merkel's problem was that, notwithstanding her steady rise in the party hierarchy, she still had to prove herself as a politician and as someone who could solve problems and get results. Her first challenge was Paragraph 218 of the Criminal Code, the section that dealt with abortion.

PARAGRAPH 218

Abortion was a tricky issue for the Christian Democratic minister. A protestant from the East, and a liberal one at that, Angela Merkel was bound to meet opposition in a party founded and in large measure supported by conservative Catholics. In East Germany the abortion laws had been relatively liberal. Following a vote in the East German Parliament in 1972, abortions could be performed up to the twelfth week of pregnancy. A similar law was introduced and passed by the West German Parliament in 1974. But unlike in America, where the Supreme Court ruled that abortion was consistent with the Constitution, the German Constitutional Court ruled in 1992 that abortion 'violates the right to life of the life developing in the mother's womb'. West Germany was not 'pro choice' and the issue remained controversial, with many on the left pressing for more liberal legislation and even a constitutional amendment. As part of the Treaty of Unification it was agreed that the whole issue should be debated in the first German Parliament after reunification. It fell to Angela Merkel to square the complex political circle.

Privately, Merkel was in favour of considerable relaxation of the rules. The positions, however, were polarised. On the right – especially in the Bavarian CSU and on the right of the CDU – many deputies wanted what was known as the 'Polish solution', a complete ban on all forms of abortion. On the other side, the Social Democrats, Free Democrats and representatives of *Bündnis90/Die Grünen* (an alliance between the Greens in the West and the Civil Rights movement in the East) wanted complete liberalisation. Philosophically Angela Merkel sided with the latter, but she was aware that this could have political consequences for her future career, and that it would be difficult to win majority support for a more liberal law. On the other hand she acknowledged that polls showed 78 per cent of East German women and 56 per cent of their West German sisters in favour of complete liberalisation along the lines that existed in East Germany before reunification. She was aware that it was necessary to make concessions: 'I belong to those who would rather develop some sort of compromise instead of presenting a position in public as it is more practical and politically more likely to be implemented,'[20] she said at the time.

In the parliamentary debate she sounded a conciliatory note, arguing that the aim was to find a way to help mothers get through pregnancy
without having to resort to an abortion, 'hence it was inappropriate to
use the Criminal Code'. The new law was intended to 'work with mothers and not against them'. As a compromise she proposed that women
who wanted an abortion would first have to receive counselling from a
doctor. By offering this concession she hoped the more conciliatory of
the members of her own party would be able to support the Bill, though
in reality the new law liberalised abortion. The stratagem succeeded.
Merkel and the liberal wing of the CDU voted for the Bill, which also
received slightly grudging support from the SPD and the FDP.

Helmut Kohl, perhaps surprisingly for a practising Catholic, was
not particularly concerned about the Bill. He personally believed that
abortion was a private matter, not an issue that belonged in the political
sphere. But he too had to appease his supporters, so – as the politically
cunning individual he was – he proposed that the enacted law be challenged in the courts. He used legal procedure to get out of a tricky political situation. If the members of the German Parliament have any doubts
as to the constitutionality of a law they can send it to the Constitutional
Court before it takes effect. Schäuble suggested to Angela Merkel that it
might be politically opportune for her to sign an appeal to the Constitutional Court. She did as she was told.

Not all in the media were impressed. 'There is no end to the hypocrisy', opined *Die Zeit* on 3 July 1992, accusing Merkel of following
a wavering course. Politically, however, the passage of the law was seen
as a triumph for the young minister. She had proved that she was able
to get a controversial law enacted, which, moreover, was popular with
the public and even supported by 67 per cent of CDU/CSU voters. At
the same time she was able to appease her colleagues in the CDU/CSU.
Everybody knew that the Constitutional Court in Karlsruhe was unlikely
to strike down the new law (it was declared compatible with the Basic
Law a year later). Once again she was duly rewarded for her loyalty and
hard work, and in this case the support came from an unexpected quarter: the Lutheran-Protestant caucus in the CDU Parliamentary Party. In
September 1992, Merkel was elected as chairwoman of the Evangelical
Working Group (EAK), not a powerful position to be sure, but once

again one that had previously been used as a springboard for prominent politicians like Gerhard Schröder, CDU Foreign Minister in the 1960s (not to be confused with the later Social Democrat Chancellor) and the later federal President Roman Herzog.

Merkel immediately focused on 'Christian values' and pledged to put the 'C' back into the Christian Democratic Party. Coming only a few months after she had been the architect of one of the most liberal abortion laws in Europe, some of her fellow brethren could be justified in concluding that there was no end to the hypocrisy. But such is politics.

Merkel was re-elected as Deputy Party Chairman at the Annual CDU Conference in Düsseldorf. She was slowly but steadily edging up the steep slope towards the higher echelons of federal politics.

KRAUSE'S FALL

'No one has risen so high and fallen so deep,' concluded the newspaper *Frankfurter Allgemeine Sonntagszeitung*. The person in question, Günter Krause, could do nothing but watch and resign, though he did his utmost to survive. Two years earlier he had been the architect of the Treaty of Unification. He was considered the most shining and talented of the new politicians from the East. And now, without prior warning, he was found to have broken elementary rules. As is often the case it was a trivial matter that ended his career. Evidence had come to light that Dr Krause had used public funds to move his family. Not, it would seem, a capital offence, but after Krause had fallen out with Helmut Kohl over his controversial policy to introduce tolls on motorways he was fair game. The German interstate highways are considered sacrosanct by the car-loving Germans, and Krause's career had hit the rocks. Kohl was waiting for an excuse to sack him, and he found it in a bill from the removal firm, or so it is alleged. That the media also found evidence that Krause had used state funds to employ a cleaner made it impossible for him to stay in his post.

Angela Merkel, who owed her seat in Parliament and much else besides (including her job in the civil service) to the intervention of Günter Krause, was supportive at first. In September 1991 she told the regional paper *Ostsee-Zeitung* how she valued his work and supported him. Soon afterwards, however, she became more careful and responded to questions about her erstwhile supporter by resorting to politician-speak, such as 'I value the work *done* by Krause' (note the past tense).[21] As Krause's position within the cabinet became more precarious she denounced him as 'unpredictable', in other words a loose cannon and a liability to the party. Krause was disappointed and angry, but could do nothing but decry Merkel's unprincipled opportunism in embittered terms, describing her as career-obsessed.

There was a reason for Merkel's lack of empathy and support, even if it may appear cynical and heartless. She knew that Helmut Kohl and Volker Rühe had a plan to make her party chairman in her home state. The party hierarchy ensured that no serious politicians challenged her. Governor Bernd Seite was not in a position to make objections. In June 1993 she added yet another title to her business card when 135 of the 159 delegates voted for her at a special conference in Schwerin, capital of Mecklenburg-West Pomerania.

To concentrate on her more powerful position, she resigned from the position as chairman of the EAK and stopped talking about her desire to put the 'C' back into the CDU. She was learning the craft of being a politician. It seems that the description of her as the 'dutiful pastor's daughter' who acted 'without any unpleasant ulterior motives' was in need of revision almost two decades before he put pen to paper.[22]

ELECTION 1994

'It is not only those from the West who can be selected for the National team,' said Angela Merkel. But her tone was not as confident as it could have been. It was not clear what she meant. She was wavering.

The issue was the selection of a candidate for the post of President of Germany. Helmut Kohl, 'who tried to appease discontent in the new states through symbolic politics',[23] had suggested that Steffen Heitmann, a staunchly conservative minister of justice in the new federal state of Saxony, should be the next German President. Heitmann was a controversial figure. In an interview with the left-leaning *Süddeutsche Zeitung* in September 1993, he had expressed the view that 'the Germans would not be expected to atone for the holocaust in all eternity'. This view was shared by many, but the way Heitmann had phrased it had upset even more people. Rita Süssmuth, tentatively supported by Merkel, had opposed the appointment.

Heitmann had withdrawn his candidacy and Angela was now, as Chairwoman of Mecklenburg-West Pomerania, trying to step out of Kohl's shadow by arguing that although Heitmann was the wrong man for the job, it was wrong that the post should automatically go to a Westerner. After a bit of rambling, clearly intended to please everyone, she concluded that people in the East were 'happy that the highest office should go to a Westerner for now'.

Merkel was not a natural speaker. Her interventions seemed stiff and calculated not to upset the leaders of the party. The party chose Roman Herzog, a judge at the constitutional court and unusual in being a protestant from Bavaria. Herzog's election to office, or Merkel's involvement in it, was not the main issue of the day. Not that Herzog's election by the Electoral College was a shoo-in. It was not. The FDP supported the Social Democrat Johannes Rau, and Herzog was only elected after the third round of voting. All eyes were on the election to the German Parliament in 1994.

Under normal circumstances Kohl would have lost. The economy had not recovered, he had broken scores of promises, and he had lost several ministers due to scandals and abuse of power in the period since the reunification. But once again luck was with the 'eternal Chancellor', as he was becoming known.

The Social Democrat candidate, Björn Engholm, a photogenic Governor of Schleswig-Holstein, a state bordering Denmark in the north of Germany, was popular, moderate and oozed confidence by appearing as a laid-back pipe-smoker. Engholm had succeeded the disgraced CDU Governor Uwe Barschel, who had committed suicide after it was revealed that he had orchestrated a defamation campaign against Engholm. However, sadly for Herr Engholm, two years later it was revealed that he too had used dirty tricks. During the hearings concerning his disgraced predecessor's conduct, Engholm had lied. He was forced to resign. The Social Democrats, who thought they had finally found a winner, were back to square one.

In the internal party elections Rudolf Scharping, Governor of Helmut Kohl's native state of Rhineland-Palatinate, was chosen as contender for the office of Chancellor. But the former army officer and avid cyclist (he later became chairman of the German Cyclists Association) found it hard to run an effective campaign. His two colleagues, the leftist Oskar Lafontaine (who had lost the 1990 election) and Gerhard Schröder, a more business-friendly Governor from Lower Saxony in the north, made it impossible for him to follow a clear course. The Social Democrats presented their candidate as part of a troika, but it was unclear who would do what after the election. The overall impression was that the somewhat demure Scharping was not strong enough to subdue either of the two factions in the SPD.

The Social Democrats and their allies, the Greens, won 288 out of the 672 seats in the German Parliament. Kohl had a majority of 10 seats. Not a solid majority, but enough. Kohl could continue for another term. 'He admitted that 'yes, it would be difficult, but so is life'.[24] Angela was re-elected; she won 0.1 per cent more than the 48.5 she had won in 1990. But compared to the national result (the CDU secured only 41 per cent of the vote) hers was a minor triumph. Things got better still when she returned to Bonn. Helmut Kohl had a surprise for her – a new job.

Before the election she had feared that her ministry would be disbanded. In fact she was succeeded by fellow East German Claudia Nolte. Angela's new job was a promotion: she was offered the post of Minister of the Environment. This was in every sense a senior position. The environment was – and is – one of the most important policy issues in German politics. Kohl was rewarding her loyalty. But the Chancellor always had several motives. In this case his main aim was to remove the hyperactive and extremely competent Klaus Töpfer, who had held the post of federal Minister of the Environment, Nature Conservation and Nuclear Safety since 1987, only one year after the ministry was first established. Alongside his head of department, Clemens Stroetmann, Töpfer had established a very effective ministry for the environment. The two had successfully introduced regulations that limited pollution from several German industries. And this was the problem. Many of the captains of industry felt that Töpfer was a bit *too* efficient. They wanted someone less bent on environmental protection. Kohl, who was aware of the importance of 'green' issues among voters across the spectrum, wanted someone with expertise but also someone who was politically pragmatic. As a scientist and as a loyal follower, Angela Merkel was ideal for the post.

She began her career in the ministry as she had begun her tenure in her previous post. She was even more aware that it was necessary to make a break with the past. She knew that Clemens Stroetmann – the strong head of department – had effectively created the ministry and that he was the most competent and knowledgeable civil servant in Bonn. It was for this reason he had to go. Merkel did not want an expert in environmental affairs. She wanted an administrator. Stroetmann was given a golden handshake and replaced by Erhard Jauck, an expert in public administration. That Merkel very publicly decided effectively to fire the heavyweight Stroetmann received considerable coverage in the media and was a surprising move from a woman who was considered to be timid and keen to avoid battles.

What was not noted was that Angela Merkel had appointed a new chief of staff. Her name was Beate Baumann and she would go on to become Merkel's most trusted advisor for the rest of her political career. The 31-year-old linguist had been a card-carrying member of the CDU since her teens. She was fired up by the anti-nuclear demonstrations (she denounced the idealist peaceniks) and was a conservative with a high opinion of the USA and the Anglophone world. She briefly studied in Cambridge and had intended to become a *Gymnasium* teacher. However, after a brief internship working for Christian Wulff (then a junior politician in Lower Saxony), she was recommended to Angela Merkel. The two got on well and shared the same philosophical outlook. Merkel hired her, and thus began a historic partnership.

THE CLIMATE CHANGE CONFERENCE, APRIL 1995

In the spring of 1995 Germany was the host of the first of the United Nations Climate Change Conferences. Klaus Töpfer had looked forward to welcoming colleagues from all over the world. Instead he was now serving in a more junior post as federal Minister for Regional Planning. The host was Angela Merkel. Her difficult task was to reach a deal on legally binding obligations for developed countries to reduce their greenhouse gas emissions. The Kyoto Treaty, agreed a year before in Japan, had laid out the framework. Now it had to be put into practice. It was a tall order for a politician who had little international experience. As in the negotiations over Paragraph 218, Merkel opted for a conciliatory strategy, and as in other policy areas she sought the advice of more experienced politicians. In the first days of the conference she developed a close professional relationship with India's Kamal Nath, who had headed his country's Ministry of Environment, Forests and Climate Change since 1991. The soft-spoken Indian politician gave his new German colleague a piece of advice, which she would use on many later occasions: 'divide the delegates into groups; one for developing countries and one for industrial countries'.[25] She did as Nath suggested. Once the delegations were in their respective rooms she personally shuttled between them, comparing notes and trying to iron out differences. At six o'clock in the morning of 7 April 1995, she emerged with a result. The delegations had agreed that the industrial nations must sign on to a binding timetable for reducing carbon emissions by 1997. This was not impressive in itself, but it paved the way for better deals later on. As such, it was hailed as a small triumph for the new minister for the environment.

Her civil servants, who were upset and sceptical after she had fired Stroetmann, had to admit that she had achieved more than they had expected, and perhaps even more than Töpfer would have achieved. Once again pragmatism won out over dogged determination and inflexibility. While she was criticised for the modest result – especially by the opposition Social Democrats – Merkel made a virtue of her pragmatic approach:

> Of course one can go insisting on optimal results for several years and be determined not to compromise. I like to take things forward one step at a time even if I don't get unanimous applause for it. Perhaps a compromise is only a good one if everybody is a bit disappointed at the end.[26]

BLOOD, SMOG AND TEARS . . .

Notwithstanding her relative success at the climate negotiations in April 1995 – or perhaps because of it – Merkel was still viewed with suspicion.

As recounted at the beginning of this chapter, she shed tears over her colleagues' opposition to imposing a driving ban on certain cars and she was scolded by Helmut Kohl for not consulting with ministers. Two days after the cabinet meeting Rexroth and Wissman agreed to a compromise: there would be a ban on cars without catalytic converters if the ozone or smog levels reached a pre-set maximum. Tears or not, Angela got her way once again.

Not everybody was impressed by Merkel's style. Gerhard Schröder was one of her harshest critics. The Governor from Lower Saxony considered her the weakest link among Helmut Kohl's ministers and rarely missed an opportunity to criticise her for alleged incompetence. Shortly before the German Parliamentary elections in 1998, Schröder (now the Social Democrat candidate for the chancellorship) found yet another reason to criticise the minister for the environment when new data emerged about problems with the transportation of nuclear waste.

In May 1998, only four months before the federal elections, it emerged that the radiation from the transported material exceeded the legal limits. As Minister for the Environment Merkel was ultimately responsible. It was clear that the government – and in this case her ministry – should have known about this earlier. The opposition called for her resignation. Merkel was furious: 'I felt I was treated like a fool'.[27] Gerhard Schröder, sensing the vulnerability of his younger colleague, changed tack. Instead of attacking her alleged incompetence, he now described her as 'Not commanding, just pitiful.'[28]

The debacle could have cost Merkel her job and with that her career. But Kohl was determined not to lose a prominent minister only a few months before the election. She survived, and she vowed that Schröder would pay for his condescension and his arrogance.

The woman who cried at a cabinet meeting and who had confided to a journalist that she 'had to be tougher' was making strides towards her goal. While her party was facing near certain defeat in the upcoming elections, Merkel had been transformed; she was now the woman who had stopped crying.

CHAPTER 7

THE POLITICS OF PATRICIDE:
HOW MERKEL BECAME PARTY LEADER

HELMUT KOHL TOWERED OVER 'JOSCHKA' FISCHER. THE FORMER AN-ARCHIST and *Gymnasium* dropout looked anxious for a moment when the Chancellor approached him in the television studio. Kohl's physical size (6ft 5in tall, and weighing in at an estimated 266 pounds) seemed to overwhelm the younger man, but there was more to it than mere physical presence.

Kohl spoke in a low voice that accentuated his humble southern roots, in the dialect for which he had so often been mocked by political opponents. But this evening Kohl seemingly did not care.

'Herr Fischer,' said the Chancellor.

'Yes,' said the Green Party leader with a hint of trepidation mixed with a trace of surprise.

Kohl smiled in a grandfather-like fashion. 'Well, congratulations, Herr Fischer!'

'Thank you, Chancellor,' said Fischer. He looked rather like an embarrassed schoolboy in the principal's office. The often foul-mouthed Fischer, who held the dubious distinction of having been the first politician to address the speaker of the German Parliament as 'asshole', was unchar-acteristically quiet in the presence of the Chancellor. The two shook hands and Kohl strolled away, nodding, smiling and chatting to all and sundry. The Green politician was left standing in the middle of the busy television studio before being ushered off to celebrate with his party comrades.

'Joschka' (full name Joseph Martin Fischer), born in 1948, stood for everything Kohl loathed. An irreverent and often bad-mannered representative of the '68 generation, Fischer had been a member of the Proletarian Union for Terror and Destruction, and in 1973 had attacked and beaten a police officer, though he later apologised to the man in question. Although he now pranced around in a three-piece grey designer suit and claimed that the Bible was his favourite book, it was difficult for the likes of Kohl to see him as a serious democratic politician.

It was this individual whom Kohl had just respectfully congratulated. Kohl might have been ambivalent towards Fischer's policies, but behind the scenes he was 'impressed by Fischer, especially because the Green politician was so cheeky'.[1] Fischer was a bad boy with attitude, but also someone who could get things done. He had been Minister of the Environment in Hesse, one of the largest states in Germany, in the 1980s and latterly had served as Deputy Governor there. Much as Kohl disliked Fischer's policies, he also admired him.

The unwritten rules of the political game dictated that Kohl should be magnanimous in defeat. The result of the election was clear. The Social Democrats had won 40.9 per cent of the vote, five per cent more than Helmut Kohl's Christian Democratic Union (CDU) and its Bavarian sister-party the Christian Social Union (CSU). Joschka Fischer's Green Party, though it had won only 6.7 per cent of the vote, was to join the Social Democrats in a Red-Green coalition government.

It was the worst result for the CDU since 1949. The election was historic, being the first national German election since the introduction of universal suffrage in which the parties of the Left gained an absolute majority. Kohl had campaigned on an uninspiring theme of 'German world class'. But there was precious little world class about the way he was running his government. The cost of unification had been higher than estimated and considerably more costly than Kohl had promised in the 1994 election. Voters in the East were disappointed that their standard of living remained so low almost a decade after East Germany was amalgamated into West Germany. Voters in the West were disgruntled that they had to pay more via taxation to their impoverished new compatriots than the CDU had promised in both 1990 and 1994.

Kohl, however, seemed relatively relaxed, even relieved. As the longest serving Chancellor since Otto von Bismarck, he had won a place in history. It was true that CDU/CSU had lost, but the defeat had not been catastrophic. His party had not been trounced as the Conservatives in the UK had been the year before, when Prime Minister John Major's Tories had been all but annihilated by Labour under Tony Blair. Kohl would, or so he thought at the time, go down in history as a great statesman on a par with Nelson Mandela or Mahatma Gandhi. And, indeed, for a period after the election it seemed that he was right.

The 'Chancellor of the Unification', as he was often described, was made an honorary citizen of Europe a few months after the electoral defeat, a distinction that has only been bestowed on one other person, Jean Monnet, the founder of the European Union. Even his successor Gerhard Schröder was present when all Europe's prime ministers and heads of state awarded him the accolade.

Less than two years later, Kohl was not even invited to the festivities organised to celebrate the ten-year anniversary of the unification. His wife Hannelore had committed suicide and Kohl was vilified by the party he had served for over 40 years. What happened in the two years after the defeat was of momentous importance for Kohl, for Germany, and for Angela Merkel.

CHANGING OF THE GUARD

Wolfgang Schäuble, Kohl's heir apparent, moved quickly to consolidate his position. Seen as a 'Prince Charles figure', he had been lobbying hard to become leader of the party, and Chancellor Kohl had – albeit reluctantly – given the wheelchair-bound parliamentary leader his blessing. On election night, 27 September 1998, Schäuble – apparently uninvited – turned up with defence secretary Volker Rühe at Kohl's private bungalow on 139 Adenauer Allé in Bonn. The mood was subdued and sombre but not depressed. Angela Merkel was there too.

It is a truism that acts of friendship and kindness in politics are at best skin-deep. Although Schäuble and Rühe had arrived together, the former feared that the latter, a former school-teacher from Hamburg with a conceited demeanour, was his main political rival for the top job. With hindsight Rühe was probably not interested in becoming leader, but Schäuble did not know this. He was keen to neutralise his presumed opponent, and suggested that Rühe become Secretary General. Rühe, who had already served in this post before, declined the offer. Schäuble was relieved. With Rühe out of the way, he could choose Angela Merkel, whom he regarded as a gifted moderniser but not a potentially threatening rival.

The Secretary General's role is to coordinate and consult with local party organisations, which provide delegates to party conferences and choose the party leader. In his later years Kohl had neglected the grassroots, and Schäuble needed someone who could reconnect the parties in the federal states with the leadership in Berlin. Schäuble had been impressed by the pragmatism and work ethic of the 44-year-old Secretary of State for the Environment. As someone from the East, and as a woman, Merkel would help to appeal to parts of the electorate who had deserted the CDU. Further, as someone with a green agenda she presented a new and modernised face of the party. Above all, she was not a threat. She did not seem to harbour personal ambitions that could threaten Schäuble's dream of becoming Chancellor. She was, in other words, an almost perfect Secretary General.

At the Party Congress in Bonn on 7 November 1998, a tearful Helmut Kohl handed over the party leadership to Wolfgang Schäuble. On the same day, Angela Merkel was endorsed by 874 of the delegates for the post of Secretary General. Only 68 voted against her. Schäuble had achieved his ambition of becoming party leader and felt that he had a united party behind him. A year later things began to take an unexpected turn.

THE RED-GREEN GOVERNMENT: WAR AND PEACE

Burgfriedenspolitik literally translates as 'castle peace politics', but it is more adequately described as a truce. It was the term used when different factions of the Social Democratic Party disagreed over German involvement in the First World War but agreed to disagree for the greater good. Back in 1915 the main characters in the drama were the likes of Karl Liebknecht (the leader of the Marxist wing of the Socialist party) and Friedrich Ebert (the leader of the reformist faction of the same party). The main characters 83 years later were Gerhard Schröder (on the right) and his finance minister Oscar Lafontaine (a left-wing firebrand). The latter had long wanted to have another go at beating Helmut Kohl, to whom he had lost in 1990. But 'Red Oscar' was aware that he did not have the support of the country at large. Until a few months before the election the prospect of yet another power struggle loomed. It was still unclear who would be the leader of the SPD in the election. When Schröder was re-elected as Governor of Lower Saxony on the first of March 1998, Lafontaine reached for the telephone and personally called his rival, greeting him with 'Hello, Candidate.' In return for his support, Schröder promised Lafontaine that he would be Finance Minister. This was *Burgfriedenspolitik* in practice.

Once the Social Democrats were in office things began to take a different turn. Lafontaine had evidently hoped that he would be able to change things from the inside, but he was disappointed. To be sure, Schröder stressed that social issues were important and made unemployment the centrepiece of his administration, saying in his inaugural address, 'If we cannot accomplish the feat of reducing the unemployment rate significantly then we will not deserve to get re-elected.' But the new Chancellor's means of reducing unemployment was more neo-liberal economic policies. Willy Brandt had talked about '*Mehr Demokratie wagen*' – 'daring more democracy'. Schröder, who had nothing but contempt for such idealistic niceties, privately suggested that '*Mehr Volkswagen*' would be more appropriate[2] – in other words it would be better to be inspired by the business model of the successful car company than to get hung up on democratic dreams. Only five months after the Red-Green government had taken office it became too much for Oscar Lafontaine. 'Most esteemed federal Chancellor,' he wrote on 11 March 1999, 'I hereby resign as federal minister of finance.' *Burgfriedenspolitik* was well and truly over and Lafontaine could now criticise the Chancellor from the backbenches on the left. The opinion polls immediately nose-dived for the largest governing party. For Schröder, however, the departure of Lafontaine was not the disaster the latter had hoped. It enabled the new Chancellor to appoint Hans Eichel, a more centrist politician who was as enthusiastic about market-based reforms as his boss.

The other issue facing Schröder was the international situation. After the end of the Cold War ethnic conflict had broken out in several of the former Communist countries. In 1998 Kosovo, formally part of Serbia-Montenegro, had declared independence. The separatist aspirations of the majority of the people in Kosovo were met with brute force by the Serbian nationalist leader Slobodan Milošević. The Western powers, especially the British, suggested that military action was the only possible solution.

Under normal circumstances Germany would not have supported such a course of action. As we have seen, Helmut Kohl, though sympathetic towards the war to throw Saddam Hussein out of Kuwait, offered money but no troops. And this was the case even though the United Nations Security Council sanctioned the War against Iraq in 1990. The bombing of Belgrade – proposed above all by British Prime Minister Tony Blair – was not sanctioned by the UN; indeed two permanent members of the Security Council, namely Russia and China, were against the intervention. The bombing would be in clear violation of UN Charter 2(4), which clearly states that all force 'against the territorial integrity or political independence of any state is inconsistent with the purposes of the United Nations'. Germany had always – and for obvious historical reasons – maintained that the UN was to play a crucial role in international affairs. That this was to change under the new Red-Green government seemed improbable. Joschka Fischer and the Green Party had become a political force as a pacifist party and had always opposed war and the use of force. Faced with another genocide in the Former Yugoslavia, however, Joschka Fischer told his party of former peaceniks and environmental activists that their party and its coalition partner could send German soldiers into battle to keep the peace and protect the civil population in Kosovo, and that they would do so by sending German Tornados on bombing raids over Belgrade even if this was not sanctioned by the UN. On 25 March 1999, German fighter planes carried out the first attacks since 1945. In June Milošević admitted defeat and accepted a peace plan proposed by the Finnish President, Martti Ahtisaari.

THE CANADIAN ARMS-DEALER

It was almost Christmas and most of the newspapers were preparing for the inevitable slowdown that characterises the festive season. 1999 had been an eventful year. The federal government had moved from Bonn to Berlin, the new Red-Green Coalition had struggled to find its political feet, and the former Chancellor, Helmut Kohl, had become embroiled in a scandal concerning apparently illegal party donations of up to one million Deutschmarks from a Canadian arms-dealer and lobbyist, Karlheinz Schreiber, who reportedly had handed over these illicit funds in a parking lot in Bodensee in the south, near the Austrian border.

On 5 November, a lower court in Augsburg, a small city in the southwest of Bavaria, issued a warrant for the arrest of Walter Liesler Kiep, who had been treasurer of the CDU from 1972 to 1992. It was suspected that the CDU bureaucrat had failed to declare donations from the lobbyist Schreiber to the Federal Election Commission. Schreiber was extradited from Canada in 2009 and sentenced to over six years in jail. Kiep was found not guilty. Other party workers, including the son of former CSU leader and Bavarian Governor Franz-Josef Strauss, were found guilty. Shortly after Kiep had surrendered to the authorities and been released on bail, Schreiber alleged that the money was a bribe intended to persuade the government to rubber-stamp a sale of German tanks and airbus planes to Saudi Arabia, and that he had merely been a go-between between the Arabs and the CDU. The story was reminiscent of the Flick Scandal in the early 1980s, when the industrialist Friedrich Karl Flick contributed money to 'cultivate the political landscape'.[3]

It was further reported that the CDU had not paid taxes or reported the donation to the tax-authorities. In short, during the years when Helmut Kohl was in charge the CDU had violated election laws and the tax-code, and – so it seemed – accepted a bribe. Then events started to unfold quickly. For understandable political reasons (the coalition government was not popular and found governing difficult) the leader of the SPD caucus, Peter Struck, acted quickly, calling for the establishment of an investigative parliamentary committee.

The committee summoned Helmut Kohl and the party's former Secretary General, Heiner Geißler, to appear before the representatives. The hearings revealed that the money had not been registered in accordance with the strict rules of party donations. On 26 November Geißler testified that 'the party [CDU] had accounts at the federal headquarters, but also accounts in addition to these'. 'The individuals who were responsible for these accounts,' he continued, 'were the federal party leader and the party's bursar.'[4] More damaging still, Kohl's less than convincing explanation seemed to confirm that the hitherto unknown secret parallel set of accounts in the CDU headquarters was at best unethical and politically damaging and at worst against the law.

The Social Democrats, who had struggled in the polls, now had strong evidence if not outright proof that Helmut Kohl had been aware of criminal breaches of the law. The new situation was already translating into miserable poll ratings for the CDU. The party had dropped 15 percentage points in two months and the Social Democrats were getting stronger at their expense.

Shortly before the Christmas break Kohl gave an interview to the television station ZDF in which he had refused to answer certain questions, saying that he had given the arms-dealer his 'word of honour'. The matter would slowly be forgotten, thought Kohl's advisors. After all, the former Chancellor had not personally made any money from the deal. Matters regarding party finance do not exercise voters as much as political insiders, and with at least three years before the next federal election it was unlikely it would have electoral implications.

This was also what Karl Feldmeyer, the chief parliamentary correspondent for the conservative *Frankfurter Allgemeine Zeitung* – or *FAZ* as it is commonly called – believed when he received a phone call from Angela Merkel. The two had known each other since she was a deputy spokesperson for DA in the months after the fall of the Berlin Wall when he was a junior correspondent covering the breakdown of the East German Communist state.

Merkel is known for cultivating her contacts in the media. The phone call did not surprise Feldmeyer. It was expected and indeed legitimate that Merkel, as General Secretary of the CDU, would use her contacts to spin a story to become less embarrassing for her party and her old colleague Helmut Kohl. But the story she was about to offer was a different one. She cut straight to the chase, asking her old friend if he was interested in an interview about the illegal party donations. Feldmeyer was slightly surprised. The paper didn't normally carry long interviews with leading politicians, and Merkel surely knew this. But he would, he told her, be happy to publish an opinion piece, or op-ed, about the story when or if she wrote one. The article arrived by fax five minutes later.

Feldmeyer had not expected anything before Christmas, and he certainly did not expect an explosive article that would reverberate for months. As Secretary General, it was Merkel's job to defend the party line and write op-eds to that effect. Such an article would rarely be newsworthy in itself, but something the paper was duty-bound to publish in the interests of fairness.

Nobody was prepared for what happened next. Few articles by a politician have caused a greater stir in the history of the Federal Republic than Merkel's 1,017 words of carefully crafted political malice. The article was a surgical denunciation of Helmut Kohl and indirectly of his successor Wolfgang Schäuble. With one clinical stroke, Merkel undermined the former Chancellor and made life impossible for his successor as party leader. The woman who had been called 'Helmut Kohl's girl'[5] and even his 'political stepdaughter',[6] had morphed into a Machiavelli.

Politicians normally deploy oblique language coached in diplomatic code. Merkel departed from protocol and told it straight. The headline, 'Kohl has caused damage to the Party', showed no signs of reverence, loyalty or solidarity with her mentor. 'The party,' she wrote, 'must learn to stand on its own feet, it must have the confidence to face the future without Kohl.'[7] After he had admitted the party had received funds 'totalling more than a million Deutschmarks', it was 'necessary' to make a break with the former leader. For, as she concluded, 'the Party must, like someone in puberty, learn to break free and leave home'.

The article was a stroke of political brilliance, though also one of cynicism and perhaps disloyalty. But such is politics. As Merkel said on an earlier occasion 'only he who wins does not follow the rules of the game'.[8] By breaking the rules, by doing something totally unexpected, 'the game' itself had changed.

Schäuble was dumbfounded when he read the article the following day. 'I immediately rang Mrs Merkel and expressed my surprise . . . that she had published this article without informing me.'[9] He had selected Merkel as Secretary General precisely because he did *not* expect her to be disloyal and because she was no threat to his leadership. This belief was shattered in the morning of 22 December 1999. Had Schäuble been a resolute leader he could, of course, have sacked his Secretary General for insubordination, though such an action would smack of panic. And, perhaps more importantly, Schäuble feared that Merkel was aware of *his* knowledge of the illicit party donations. Only three weeks before Schäuble had told the German Parliament that he knew nothing of the illegal money transfers. He admitted that he had met the arms-dealer Karlheinz Schreiber, but strenuously denied that he had received money from the Canadian. But he had been somewhat economical with the truth and Merkel knew this, or so Schäuble believed. Firing the Secretary General – one of the party's few trusted and popular politicians; some-one who had no involvement in the case – would free Merkel to tell the press what she knew. Schäuble was in a bind. He could do nothing other than say that he knew nothing about the article before he read it.

Schäuble was not the only one to be surprised. Helmut Kohl too was astounded. But the former Chancellor refused to even contemplate that the woman he had called '*mein Mädchen*' ('my girl'), the young politician whom he had plucked from total obscurity and thrust into the limelight of German politics only days after she was first elected to the German Parliament, could have acted alone. As the former Chancellor wrote in his diary, it was 'unthinkable that Schäuble had not known about this action'.[10] Moreover, Kohl was less than impressed by Merkel and did not think highly of her political abilities. She had, as far as he was concerned, been the token women and token East German in his cabinet. In an unguarded remark that he did not intend to be published, the former Chancellor described Merkel and Friedrich Merz (the latter was the leader of the CDU Caucus in the German Parliament) as 'people who are incapable of doing anything'. Indeed, he went on, 'Merkel is clueless and Merz is a political baby'. That Merkel further was 'someone who never quite learned to eat with a knife and fork'[11] was a clear indi-cation of Kohl's ill-disguised disdain for her. What exactly he meant by the reference to Merkel's apparently limited ability to use cutlery is not entirely clear. But he was clear that it was not a compliment: 'this woman is not burdened by a strong character', he said.[12] One often runs the risk of reading too much into off-the-cuff remarks: there is always the risk of over-interpretation and one must always be open to the possibility that Kohl did not choose his words carefully. Still, it is worth pointing to the subtleties of his remarks and the fact that in them he used the mildly condescending title '*Dame*' rather than the more respectful '*Frau*' when referring to Merkel. His opinion of her was patronising. This woman could not possibly have come up with such a daring plan.

Like a boxer who struggles to stand after an unexpected blow, Kohl was befuddled and perplexed by the situation. Hurt, shocked and anxious that his 'little mistake', as he called it, should not undermine his historical legacy as the statesman who unified Germany, he began a personal vendetta against Schäuble. Countless leaks to the press, orchestrated by the former Chancellor himself (so the ghost-writer of his biography later revealed[13]), undermined Schäuble's professed innocence day by day and blow by blow.

In response, an increasingly desperate Schäuble expressed his bitterness and denounced his former boss as someone who had been engaged in an 'intrigue with criminal elements', in which 'new lies and fabrications are constantly being taken out of the handbook of conspiratorial disinformation'.[14] But Schäuble's position was undermined by the fact that he – though not deeply implicated in the scandal – had been privy to more information than he had admitted to the parliamentarians in December. He knew that he was living on borrowed time. On 10 January 2000, in an interview with the television network *ARD*, Schäuble admitted that he had indeed known more than he had said earlier, and that he had in fact himself received money from Schreiber.

Did Merkel know that the article would have this effect? Was the *Frankfurter Allgemeine* article intended as a *Putsch* – a coup? Merkel had certainly prepared well. In her brief period as Secretary General she had consolidated her power-base. The Secretary General's post is an organisational one. Unlike the party-leader, the Secretary General is constantly in touch with regional and state-party organisations, and Merkel had established a network of sympathisers among the rank and file members who choose the party leader. While Schäuble, who never had a regional network in the first place, was focused on consolidating his position in Berlin, Merkel toured the country and was involved in successful regional elections (the CDU won an absolute majority in the state parliament election in Hesse in the west and repeated the feat in Saxony-Anhalt and Thuringia in the east before the scandal broke out). She also built up a small inner circle of advisors headed by Beate Baumann, who would later become her chief-of-staff. But building a strong power-base and support was not enough. Politicians – especially female ones – need to cultivate their images and shield themselves from attacks on their private lives. Merkel knew this all too well.

MERKEL'S UNFINISHED BUSINESS: JOACHIM SAUER

One of the things that we should never forget is that Merkel is the leader of a political party that is socially conservative. This was a cause for concern for the 45-year-old divorcee. As early as 1993, Cardinal Joachim Meisner, the Catholic Archbishop of Cologne (and someone close to the social conservatives in the Christian Democratic Party), had told the tabloid newspaper *Bild* that 'apparently there is a female minister of the Christian faith who lives in sin'[15]. There was nothing 'apparent' about it, and there was no doubt who the 'female minister' in question was. Merkel immediately responded to the Cardinal that she 'found it prudent to be cautious' when she already had been married once.[16] Although not a Catholic herself, Merkel was aware that her private life was a matter that could harm her, especially vis-à-vis rivals from the Christian-Conservative heartland in the south of Germany. More than any other politician, Merkel had to constantly fend off questions about her private life; questions that would, in all likelihood, not have been asked if she had been a man. 'No, I had not concluded that I did not want to have children,' she said exasperatedly to a journalist who asked her the question for the umpteenth time. 'But when I went into politics I was 35, and now it is out of the question.'[17] Whether that explanation satisfied her foes within the party is doubtful. As a leading figure in a party that appealed to the conservative values of *Kinder, Kuche, Kirche* (children, kitchen and the church), Merkel, a career woman who had grown up with a more enlightened view of the role of women, found it hard to be continually bombarded with questions about her family and private life, especially as she felt them to be irrelevant. But like the questions she had faced about her image, she knew that she needed to neutralise those about her marital status if she were to have any chance of playing a truly leading role as a federal German politician. So what did she do? She got married.

On 2 January 1999 a small notice in the announcement pages of the *Frankfurter Allgemeine Zeitung* read: 'We have married. Angela Merkel and Joachim Sauer.' The event was almost peculiarly low-key. *Bild* informed its millions of readers that nobody, not even the couple's parents or siblings, were informed of the nuptials, let alone invited to the wedding.

The private lives of political figures are often the source of endless fascination. Whether this is warranted is an open question in the case of Merkel's husband Joachim Sauer. At the risk of oversimplifying, partners of powerful figures often either play the role of adoring wife (like Nancy Reagan, Lady Bird Johnson – and, indeed Helmut Kohl's late wife Hannelore) or are pushy figures that harbour ambitions on behalf of their spouses akin to those of Lady Macbeth – though rarely with the murderous determination of Shakespeare's villain. It is difficult to place Professor Sauer in this scheme. Merkel's partner is her equal and an impressive individual in his own right. It says something about Merkel's self-confidence that she was attracted to a man who was her intellectual equal, but there are drawbacks too, especially for Sauer. The holder of the Chair in Inorganic Chemistry at Humboldt University and winner of the prestigious Friedrich Wöhner Prize, Sauer is a renowned chemist. He has been described as 'one of the top 30 theoretical chemists worldwide but just below the rank of those who tend to win Nobel Prizes'.[18] Perhaps not surprisingly, a man of this stature was often annoyed by all the focus and attention afforded to his wife. German professors are important figures who are accustomed to being shown a level of respect and reverence that would be almost surreal to their American colleagues. To be a professor in Germany is an esteemed and prestigious position that is held in the highest social regard. A professor has the same social status in Germany as CEO of a blue chip company in the United States, and Sauer is no exception.

His name, literally translated, means 'sour'. Perhaps an odd name, especially as his father was a patisserie chef who specialised in sweet cakes and biscuits in the southern part of East Germany. But the name is less inappropriate if we are to trust the following anecdote reported by *Bunte*. According to the women's magazine, Merkel had invited the liberal party leader Guido Westerwelle to the couple's apartment in Berlin. 'Mr Merkel, I presume,' said the liberal politician to Merkel's husband. The latter, according to the magazine, 'responded in a way that was consistent with his surname – sour'.[19]

Merkel had met Joachim Sauer, who was five years older than her, at the Academy of Sciences in Berlin. At that time, in the early 1980s, he was married to a university lecturer and the couple had two sons. There has been endless speculation as to whether meeting Merkel led to the breakdown of Sauer's first marriage. There is some evidence to suggest this. As Sauer's divorce was finalised in 1985, their cohabitation began two years before his first marriage officially ended. Sauer had proofread Merkel's doctoral thesis in 1986, in which she thanked him for 'critical scrutiny of the manuscript'.[20] Whether this is an indication of an intimate relationship cannot be determined with any certainty, though the popular press reported that the couple had known each other for 17 years when they tied the marital knot at registry office Staatsamt-Berlin-Mitte on 30 December 1998.

Perhaps more than his future wife, Joachim Sauer had been remarkably open about his opposition to the Communist state and his high regard for America (he went to the USA to teach in San Diego as soon as the Berlin Wall fell). The scientist had even told friends and colleagues that Ronald Reagan's decision to station cruise missiles in West Germany was justified. Thus Merkel did not just marry a remarkably successful scientist, her new husband was also a politically engaged individual with strong opinions and the courage of his convictions.

Did Angela Merkel get married just to make sure that nobody could attack her for not being true to the party's values? Political observers are often guilty of reading a political message into seemingly trivial and unrelated events. Merkel and Sauer might just have wished to formally seal their relationship. Even politicians and theoretical chemists can be romantic souls; there is nothing to suggest that Merkel and Sauer are not – the patisserie chef's son apparently bakes tarts for his wife when they stay in their summer residence. On the other hand, politicians – especially those in Merkel's league – never stop thinking about politics. 'Merkel is a politicoholic – 7 days a week, 24 hours politics', one observer concluded.[21] It is almost certain that the future Chancellor and her spouse discussed the political implications of the nuptials. Merkel – though she is an extremely private person who rarely talks about her private life – has been surprisingly candid about the role played by her husband in her life as a politician. 'It is often said that my husband does not play any political role. This perception is in no way a reflection of the reality.'[22] That Merkel got married may not have been a result of political calculation alone, but it is extremely unlikely that strategic considerations were absent from her and her husband's minds. When she made her move almost a year later, she was in a stronger position now that she was a married woman.

SCHÄUBLE'S FALL

Did she act alone when she decided to send her op-ed to the Frankfurt newspaper? It is unlikely. Merkel has refused to talk about the genesis of the article, but it is evident that she discussed it with her inner circle, above all with Beate Baumann, and, of course, before that with Joachim Sauer. But there is no evidence of a long-planned takeover. Indeed, it was not clear that Schäuble's position was shaky before his testimony on 2 December. After his elaborate and unconvincing performance before the parliamentary investigative committee, however, Merkel knew that an opportunity had come her way. She had come a long way since she was the young Minister for Women and Children who was prone to cry in public when she felt snubbed or was stressed by the hurly-burly of high-octane power politics. The woman who watched the two senior politicians tear each other to shreds in the first weeks of the year 2000 was 'harder' than they could have imagined, and she acted with steely resolve.

On 18 January, in the midst of the battle royal between Kohl and Schäuble, Merkel told the press that she had reviewed the party's accounts for the years 1991 to 1992 and had found donations of over two million Deutschmarks from unknown sources. This was another deadly and calculated body blow. What had at first seemed a matter of a couple of hundred thousand Deutschmarks was now a scandal involving literally millions, complete with secret Swiss bank accounts, money in brown envelopes and clandestine meetings in car parks. On the same day as she presented these new revelations Merkel demanded – with the support of the board of the federal party – that Helmut Kohl resign from his position as honorary party chairman. His place in history was tarnished, and Schäuble was further undermined.

Were these acts of disloyalty? Kohl and Schäuble believed so. But, as Merkel was careful to point out at every opportunity, she was merely acting in the interest of the party; acting in the interest of something that was greater than herself. She was doing her job, she said. Kohl and Schäuble, by contrast, were apportioning blame to save their respective political skins. Whether this is entirely accurate is a moot point. As someone who had cultivated her contacts in the media, Merkel was better at selling and spinning her version of the story to the press than were her reserved, often arrogant and frequently condescending older colleagues. Merkel must have known that when the story broke she would have to distance herself from Schäuble or fall with him. Her act of disloyalty was also an act of self-preservation, and, of course, a way of winning power.

Schäuble was suffering. In what must have been a coordinated attempt by Kohl and Schreiber to involve the party leader in the scandal, the Canadian issued statements which mysteriously seemed to implicate Schäuble. These continued smears fatally undermined his position. Mocked by the Chancellor Gerhard Schröder, deserted by the tabloids – especially the influential *Bild* – and with no support from his deputy let alone other members of the CDU, Schäuble resigned on 16 February 2000 with the parting remark that 'the CDU is in its worst crisis in its history'.[24] Cometh the hour, cometh the woman. Merkel had outmanoeuvred the 'old men'. 'Kohl's little girl' had, to quote a headline in the magazine *Focus*, become the 'refined queen of power'.[24] The 'underestimated woman', as a regional paper called her,[25] the junior politician who had been treated with condescension, was suddenly one of the most powerful politicians in the party and the country. The CDU was in the doldrums. 'Mrs General, could you please take over?' was the headline in the magazine *Stern*. An editorial inside the magazine opined that the 'woman who was once known as a docile woman who laughed like a little girl . . . was the CDU's only saviour'.[26]

It was dawning on Merkel's opponents that this story was the result of intensive lobbying by the aspiring party leader. They were not prepared for it. On 27 February Volker Rühe, Friedrich Merz and CSU leader Edmund Stoiber met at the Ratskeller, a well-known traditional German restaurant in the northern city of Lübeck. There was one item on the agenda: Merkel and how to stop her. Stoiber was keen to be nominated as the Union's candidate for the federal elections in 2005, and feared that Merkel might prove an obstacle. Rühe's motives are unclear, but he seemed keen to support Friedrich Merz and was never a great fan of Merkel's in the first place. Merz wanted to succeed Schäuble, but he knew that he had started his campaign too late and that he was in a weak position. Stoiber, though he reigned supreme in Bavaria, did not have a strong network in northern Germany, let alone in the East. Rühe did have the contacts, but was not in a strong position as he had just failed to become Governor in Schleswig-Holstein in the north of Germany.

They were too late. Merkel had planned a series of regional conferences in February. This does not seem coincidental. The conferences were intended to inform local party branches of developments at the centre. They cannot make binding decisions, but those attending the conferences were to a large extent the same as the delegates to the federal party conferences who would elect the party leader. As Secretary General, Merkel had become the centre of gravity of a party in flux. None of the politicians who harboured ambitions of succeeding Schäuble had anything like the exposure, let alone the network Merkel had built in the preceding year. The regional conferences cemented her grip on the party organisation. Moreover, other potential challengers, such as Roland Koch, the populist and upwardly mobile Governor of Hesse, and Volker Rühe, who served in a largely ceremonial post as Schäuble's deputy, were implicated in the scandal. This, admittedly, was not public knowledge at the time, but with her access to the party accounts none of the potential challengers dared to stand lest Merkel should use the information against them. This fear among her rivals, alongside her uncompromising championing of the interests of the party, made it almost inevitable that she would become the first woman to lead a political party in Germany. On 10 April 2000 she was elected as party leader with the backing of 95 per cent of the 935 delegates at the special party conference in Essen, a large city in the West of Germany.

If there is anything that characterises the public's perception of politicians it is their disingenuousness, their ability not to give a straight answer, their assurances that even their worst enemies are really their trusted friends. As a part of a kind of established ritual journalists persistently ask questions to which they know they will never – or rarely – get a straight answer. Shortly after she became party leader Angela Merkel agreed to be interviewed by *Der Spiegel*. The interviewers Tina

Hildebrandt and Hajo Schumacher, both seasoned professionals, asked the usual questions. However, they did not get the usual answers.

'So, Mrs Merkel,' asked *Der Spiegel*'s journalists, 'How are you personally getting on with Helmut Kohl? What is your relationship?'

'Tense,' she answered.

A 'normal' politician, one trained through years of apprenticeships in local party organisations and the youth organisation, would have answered like a politician, expressed their closeness, their undying friendship. Merkel did not.

'Are you in touch?' The journalists continued their probing.

'What do you mean, in touch?' Merkel asked back.

'Well, do you talk to each other?' they tried. Once again, Merkel gave them a straight answer.

'No we don't talk. I have not spoken to him since I was elected party leader, nor have I approached him personally.'[27]

It is hard to read between the lines in a printed interview. The awkward silences, the body language and the intonation are lost on paper. We do not know the tone of the questions, but it is clear that Merkel did not provide the standard run-of-the-mill answers. This apparent honesty, the very human acknowledgement that the relationship with Kohl was 'tense' could be seen as inexperienced, even naïve. Politicians are supposed to stick to the unwritten script, and Merkel did not. Yet years later this propensity to give straight answers became one of the reasons for her popularity, a strength rather than a weakness.

Merkel was not a 'normal' politician, and it is an open question whether she ever became one. But one thing had changed in the months from late December 1999 to early April 2000. She had shown herself to be a ruthless Machiavellian politician and not at all a meek follower.

Her male colleagues had not been fully aware of the metamorphosis she had undergone in the years since she first went into politics; it was as if they did not appreciate that sometimes the apprentice can become the master. They had misjudged her at their peril.

Michael Schindhelm, Merkel's former colleague at the Academy of Sciences, once commented of his former colleague, 'She is the half-sister of Parsifal.'[28] Like the eponymous hero in Richard Wagner's opera, Merkel was an underestimated newcomer who suddenly seized the chance to grasp the Holy Grail. Perhaps, as Schindhelm suggested, she was successful because she was a novice who was not frightened by 'the dangers that lie in wait in the dark undergrowth of the forest of German politics'. But unlike Parsifal, Merkel was yet to be crowned. And unlike the Arthurian knight in Wagner's opera, Merkel still had some way to go. Being leader of the party was one thing, becoming the political leader, let alone becoming Chancellor, was quite another. Her rivals were queuing up, and her start was not an easy one. Not for the first time, a politician learned that it is more difficult to govern than it is to be elected.

CHAPTER 8

WAITING GAME: THE PATIENT PARTY LEADER

JOHANN WOLFGANG VON GOETHE, THE GERMAN NATIONAL POET WHOM Germans hold in the same regard as Shakespeare is held in the English-speaking world, must have been spinning in his grave. 'Only he deserves freedom who has to conquer it anew every day,' the great man wrote in his tragic play *Faust*. His compatriots had conquered their freedom, rebuilt their country after total destruction in the Second World War, and thrown off the shackles of state Socialism. But now, a decade later, dignity had all but disappeared. The Romans were nourished on a diet of bread and circus; the Germans were content with discourses about hairspray and highlights. As always, *Bild* was leading the charge and the politicians were playing along. 'Yes, I do dye my hair,' Angela Merkel admitted to the sensationalist newspaper in May 2002.

So the secret was out. The woman who was famous for not wearing make-up or bothering with other distractions had gone to a stylist. Hold the front page! The Leader of the Opposition's hairstyle was deemed an important issue during the silly season in 2002. The debate continued unabated for years and even evolved into a full-blown spat between stylists and hairdressers anxious to claim credit for Angela Merkel's transformation from a frumpy *Frau* to something approaching a style icon. Martina Acht, one of the world's leading hairstylists (according to her own website she won the world championship aged 29), was the first to enter the fray and claim credit for Ms. Merkel's hairdo.

Just before George Bush visited Germany in February, Mrs Merkel came to me for advice. I wanted her to look her best for 'Georgie

Boy', so I did her hair, and gave her a bit of encouragement in the looks department. I wanted her to look a bit younger, a bit saucier, but not too girlie, so that people would still take her seriously.[1]

Martina Acht admitted that Mrs Merkel was sceptical at first, saying '"I've never looked like this before", but she seemed to like it. She returned in June.' This statement was greeted with barely controllable rage and incredulity by Acht's rival Udo Walz, the star of Berlin hairdressing who had styled Marlene Dietrich, Maria Callas, Twiggy, Claudia Schiffer, Heidi Klum, Julia Roberts, Naomi Campbell and, somewhat bizarrely, the terrorist Ulrike Meinhof. He, so Walz claimed, had cut the CDU leader's hair. The stylist told the press that Martina Acht was trying to 'jump on the bandwagon' and that 'about a year ago, with her agreement, I started slowly changing [Mrs Merkel's] style'. Acht was clearly lying, for Mrs Merkel 'comes to me every four weeks for a cut and colour', said the Berlin star-stylist.[2]

It was at this stage that Lee Stafford felt called upon to join in. The English hair maestro, based in the central German city of Cologne, did not claim credit for Merkel's hairdo. Far from it: he didn't like her style at all. 'This short bob makes Frau Merkel look too serious; too aggressive', sighed the stylist. And 'the hair colour! Dear God, not sexy at all. I would categorically recommend blond highlights finished off with a spray wax'.

Now some might think that this issue would not have exercised the minds of the Germans if the Leader of the Opposition had been a man; that the whole thing was yet another proof, if such were needed, that politics is a sexist game. But another possible explanation is that the Germans were just obsessed with hair. Chancellor Gerhard Schröder was so concerned about his hair colour that he got his lawyers involved. When the news agency Deutsche Depeschendienst (DDP) suggested that the Chancellor dyed his remarkably full head of auburn locks to maintain his youthful looks, he sued for defamation and won.

No amount of wax spray could alter the fact that Germany was going nowhere fast, however. In March 2005 *Die Welt am Sonntag* reported: '5.2 million unemployed, the recovery is further delayed, the Germans are getting poorer according to UNICEF and the children are getting dumber according to PISA [the OECD's league table of educational performance in developed countries].'[3] The *Economist* dubbed Germany 'the sick man of the euro'. The once rich country was still struggling with the unusual economic problems created by reunification. Helmut Kohl's 'blossoming landscapes', as a historian observed, had 'failed to bloom (or even bud)'.[4]

Maybe it was this sorry state of affairs that prompted Germans to talk about bobbed hair, highlights and hairspray. None of the political parties seemed to have a solution to the crisis, and both Schröder and Merkel were probably rather pleased that the voters were distracted.

WORLD POLITICS VS. PAROCHIALISM

In the wider world matters were happening at breakneck speed. Many in the Green Party were still finding it difficult to come to terms with the surprising fact that they were members of a government that had sent German soldiers into battle. And many of them were finding it equally difficult to stomach Gerhard Schröder's unequivocal support for George W. Bush in the wake of the 9/11 terror attack on the World Trade Center in 2001. In November of that year, Schröder, who sensed that the issue was becoming politically dangerous, challenged the German Parliament with a vote of confidence. His 'back me or sack me' tactic worked and he won the vote, though with a rather thin majority of only 336 out of 662. Like Brandt in the early 1970s, Schröder had proved to his compatriots that he was in control and, by implication, that the Opposition had no alternative strategy.

Angela Merkel did not find it easy to go from the backroom to the front office. Once elected to the leadership she had to appoint her team, and the first thing she needed was a good, efficient and above all loyal Secretary General. She thought she'd found him in Ruprecht Polenz. The 54-year-old father of four was a soft-spoken lawyer. He was not regarded as threatening and he came from North Rhine Westphalia. Merkel was aware that the mathematics of politics was important, and to have a representative from the most populous state in the Western part of the now reunified country could, so to speak, balance the ticket in the same way as a US presidential candidate needs a running mate from another part of the country. The problem was that the somewhat self-effacing Polenz was a bit too timid. In fact he never really wanted the job: 'I couldn't really say no out of convenience,' he said, and mentioned his loyalty to the party.[5] Any sense of burning passion was absent, but he was popular among the press and well liked. 'Polenz is thoughtful. He is a very competent Secretary General but he is not someone who can go on talk shows,' was the verdict of *Süddeutsche Zeitung*.[6]

The problem was that Merkel needed a tough guy. She was not the most combative politician herself, and her attempts to sound tough and oppositional did not come across as genuine. She needed a loyal lieutenant, to be sure, but also someone with a bit of a profile who could perform well in television studios and fulfil the role of a political Rottweiler. Polenz was not performing as expected. On 20 November 2000, Merkel summoned him to her office and told him without further ado that she wanted a different Secretary General. Conscious that she didn't need more enemies on the backbenches, she had lined up a lucrative position for him on the board of the national television broadcaster ZDF. In this way he could be silenced and could save a bit of face. Polenz accepted with good grace. Later in his political career, Merkel rewarded his loyalty by making him chairman of the Foreign Policy Committee in the German Parliament. Polenz remained loyal.

His replacement, Laurenz Meyer, could not have been more different, though like his predecessor he too was from North Rhine Westphalia. Meyer and Polenz knew each other from their time as students at the University of Münster. But that is where the similarities ended. Meyer, an economist who had served as leader of the CDU faction in the local legislature in the state capital of Düsseldorf before he was elevated to his new post, was prone to speak his mind and got off to a rather shaky start by saying that Merkel could not 'afford to make a second mistake'.[7] The party leader was embarrassed, but she pretended to ignore the ill-judged comment and let Meyer loose. This proved both entertaining and efficient. Meyer, it would later turn out, was a bit too inclined to cut corners and often a bit too creative, but this was in the future. What mattered at the moment was that he had the common touch. 'We must end the torture of the [German] people,' he shouted when he was elected.[8] An exaggeration, of course: Chancellor Schröder was hardly a crackpot dictator. Yet the comment was indicative of Meyer's no-nonsense combative style and his philosophy of 'attack, no matter how'. Merkel had found her Rottweiler.

Every blue-collar German worth his salt has a *Stammtisch* (a regulars' table) at his local pub or tavern. Here he can discuss the world over an Altbier, a Weizenbier, or whichever regional brew is appropriate. To engage in *Stammtisch* politics and even more so, to stoop down to *Stammtisch* level, has become a cliché for engaging in populism. Meyer, playing on the associations, made clear that 'We [the CDU] will not blindly repeat what has been said at the *Stammtisch*, but we must be understood at the *Stammtisch*.'[9]

That Merkel needed someone who could address even the darker parts of the CDU's electoral heartland had much to do with the debate about preserving German culture in a multicultural society. It also had a lot to do with the main political proponent of this concept, Friedrich Merz.

MULTICULTURALISM

Upon coming to power the Schröder government wanted to change Germany's notorious citizenship laws, which bluntly stated that German citizenship referred to a 'community of descent, with little regard for birthplace and residence'; in other words it was confined to those of German blood. This definition, enshrined in law in 1913, was rather similar to a Nazi law of 1935 which stated that 'Only *Volk*-comrades can be citizens. And only persons of German blood, irrespective of confession, can be Volk-comrades.'[10] Schröder's progressive government regarded this as unacceptable. The coalition wanted to make it possible for those of non-German blood who were born in Germany to become citizens. This was not popular among politicians on the right.

Roland Koch had won the state election in Hesse in 1999 on the back of a campaign against the proposed Dual Citizenship Law, but the most surprising turn was the attitude of the educated elite. After several decades during which intellectuals in Germany were almost automatically proponents of liberal and leftist causes – just think of the leftist or even Marxist writers, the philosopher Theodor W. Adorno, the Nobel Prize winning author Heinrich Böll and the social philosopher Jürgen Habermas – thinkers and writers had begun to take positions in support of traditional values and to cherish classical German culture. Now intellectuals on the political right began to toy with ideas about the nation and once again voiced opinions that at the very least came close to sympathising with illiberal and nationalist virtues. The term *Neue Rechte* was coined. Rather paradoxically, this New Right based their strategies on those of the Italian Marxist leader Antonio Gramsci, who had stressed that it is necessary to break with the ruling-class ideological 'hegemony'.

The New Right wanted to fundamentally challenge the liberal consensus. In 1993 the playwright Botho Strauß had published an oddly entitled essay in *Der Spiegel*. In typical German intellectual fashion, the essay's title alluded to classical Greek culture. In a rather pompous allusion, rather typical of German intellectuals past and present, the title of the essay was inspired by the etymological root of the Greek word for tragedy (*tragos*) which means 'goat'. In 'Swelling Billy-goat Song' Strauß made this politically incorrect statement:

> The fact that a people is ready to claim superiority of their own culture and is willing to shed blood for this, is something we no longer understand; it is something that we, in our liberal-libertarian self-centredness, regard as reprehensible and wrong.[11]

Rather predictably, perhaps, the stalwarts of the left were shocked and appalled. The social philosopher Jürgen Habermas even wrote an entire book about it.[12] Yet in the decade that followed more and more writers on the political right joined in to express sympathy with Strauß's view. In an anthology entitled *The Self-Confident Nation*, authors and philosophers of a right-wing and nationalistic persuasion expressed sympathy for the view that German culture was under threat from massive immigration. Politicians being what they are, namely creatures who want to win elections, it was not surprising that this theme began to feature strongly in the political rhetoric. It was to come up again in 2015.

No one was more articulate than Friedrich Merz, who emerged as Angela Merkel's main rival within the CDU. The razor-sharp politician had sensed that playing the nation-card could be a vote winner. In full pursuit of his strategy he stated that 'foreigners have to accept our

Angela Merkel was a model student and her best subjects were Russian and mathematics. Here she is (circled) as a participant in the East German mathematics Olympiad. She didn't win on this occasion but went on to win the prize for best Russian student in 1970 and was awarded a trip to Moscow.

The German-speaking former KGB man and Russian-speaking chancellor never liked each other. Putin knew Merkel was scared of dogs after she had been bitten in 1995. The Russian leader delighted in letting his dog into his office on Merkel's first visit in 2006. Later Merkel got her revenge and outsmarted Putin when the EU imposed sanctions on the Kremlin strongman.

She was Wolfgang Schäuble's deputy, orchestrated his fall as party chairman, and then made him finance minister. Merkel and Schäuble showed mutual respect but never affection. They tried to establish a better relationship by going to the cinema to watch the movie *The Untouchables*—the German title of the movie is *Ziemlich beste Freunde* ('Apparently Best Friends').

Italian Prime Minister Silvio Berlusconi uttered unflattering remarks about the German chancellor. Two weeks later the Italian tycoon and politician resigned as prime minister.

Pastor Horst Kasner (1926-2011) and wife Herlind—both of Polish descent—moved from West Germany to Communist East Germany to preach the Gospel in the atheist state. It was no easy task and they had to make compromises. Here they are in the gallery when their oldest daughter, Angela, was inaugurated as the first female chancellor of Germany.

Merkel was the eighth Chancellor of the Federal Republic of Germany. The photo from top left to right shows Konrad Adenauer, Ludwig Erhardt (formally independent supported by CDU/FDP), Kurt Georg Kiesinger (CDU), Willy Brandt (SPD). Second row (left to right): Helmut Schmidt (SPD), Helmut Kohl (CDU), Gerhard Schröder (SPD), and Angela Merkel (CDU).

Guido Westerwelle (1961-2016) was the openly gay leader of the liberal FDP party and was often bulldozed and undercut by Angela Merkel. Here they are at a cabinet meeting during the years of the CDU/CSU-FDP coalition 2009-2013. Bottom left is Ursula von der Leyen, who for a long time was tipped to be Merkel's successor.

In 2015 Merkel opened the borders to refugees from Syria and Libya. Her popularity dropped from 70 per cent to below 50 per cent in a matter of months. The poster reads: "When is an individual brain-dead? Yes to help, no to immigration chaos". With 90 per cent in favour of helping those in need but over 50 per cent against mass immigration, the caption on the poster summed up the mood in Germany at the beginning of 2016.

Angela Merkel broke with protocol and supported French President Nicolas Sarkozy's unsuccessful bid for re-election. The two developed a close partnership during the Euro crisis. Afterwards Merkel found it difficult to develop a close relationship with Sarkozy's successor François Hollande.

Barack Obama and Angela Merkel were not always close but her initial skepticism towards the American president gradually evolved into a pragmatic and warm relationship. Under Merkel, Germany solidified its position as America's most important ally in Europe. 'You're on the right side of history on this', Obama told Merkel when they met in Hannover at the international trade fair in April 2016, praising her decision to open Germany's borders to over a million refugees.

Even before she became chancellor, Angela Merkel supported President George W. Bush. While the German government opposed the war in Iraq in 2003, she supported it. While they disagreed on the economic crisis, Merkel was personally close to 'Dubya'.

During the early weeks of the refugee crisis of 2015, Merkel opened her country's door to over a million refugees. This made her a hero among those fleeing the war in Syria. This photo sums up the hope many refugees placed in her. After the protests at home in the spring of 2016, Merkel tightened her immigration policy somewhat at the insistence of the sister party CSU, but Merkel stood firm that those seeking refuge from persecution could seek asylum.

In the 2013 election, Merkel was at the height of her popularity. The way she held her hands in a diamond shape signified stability and calm competence to such a degree that her CDU party simply used an image of her hands in Merkel's successful bid for re-election.

In 2011 and in 2015 angry Greek voters turned their anger towards Germany and not at their own government. The leftist SYRIZA party claimed the Germans still owed them war reparations from the Second World War and implied that Merkel and Germany had the same ambitions as the Third Reich.

norms, customs, habits'.[13] Although Merkel won the leadership election easily, her position within the parliamentary group was far from secure. She was not the only politician to have risen through the ranks almost by stealth. Merz, a youthful lawyer from Rüthen in North Rhine Westphalia who had become a judge at the tender age of 30, had also manoeuvred his way to the top of the party without attracting too much attention.

After Kohl's retirement, Merz had become Wolfgang Schäuble's deputy in Parliament. A relatively meaningless post in terms of work-load, but a prominent one all the same. Unlike other members of the CDU, Merz – like Merkel – was untainted by the scandal. He kept a low profile during the battle between Kohl and Schäuble, and only made his move after Merkel had declared that she would stand for the leadership. Merz, then aged 44, was in no rush. Like Merkel, he too needed to build a power-base. When Merkel became party leader, Merz took over Schäuble's other post as parliamentary leader.

While Merkel was leader of the Party and ruled over the rank and file, Merz was the *de facto* Leader of the Opposition. It was he who was tasked with exchanging verbal blows with Chancellor Schröder, and it was he who, in the eyes of the public, was the challenger, the contender. In any parliamentary system the legislature is the main arena for political battles. This is particularly the case in Germany, where the federal Parliament has been described as 'the most powerful legislature on the continent'.[14]

Building up a power-base among members of parliament is nec-essary in order to establish the credibility that, among other things, can take you all the way to the Chancellery. Merz had several advantages. In a conservative party strongly dominated by Social Catholics, the former leading member of the German Catholic Student Organisation appealed to many of the core voters. Another advantage was that he was a man. Further, while Angela Merkel had been careful not to make comments about Germany's growing Muslim minority, Merz had no qualms about expressing opinions that at best raised questions about multiculturalism, and at worst deliberately targeted a vulnerable minority. Shortly after he had become parliamentary leader Merz made it clear that Muslims 'have to adopt our values, our character and our way of life'. He criticised Muslim teachers who wore the headscarf.[15] Previously something of a bookish character, he came out – perhaps a bit opportunistically – as a supporter of the soccer team Borussia Dortmund. He also established himself as a proponent of neo-liberal policies, particularly privatisation, deregulation and less generous welfare payments.

There can be no doubt that Merkel considered Merz a threat to her ambitions, but unlike her rival, she was less clear about her position. Moreover, while she had previously been a somewhat anonymous character, she was now firmly in the public spotlight. Whereas Merz played to the gallery by flagging up his past in the Catholic Student Organisation, Merkel rarely spoke about her past and her upbringing in the East. She was aware that she could be interpreted negatively. Her background was one thing; the more important question was what she stood for. Some suggested that she was 'Maggie Thatcher from Uckermark'[16] but to most she was a mystery, a 'lady with a mask' behind which nobody had been able to see.[17]

THE K-QUESTION

Die K-Frage (the K-question, short for the Chancellor-question) – began to hot up. Who would challenge the incumbent Social Democrat Chancellor? Not unexpectedly Friedrich Merz was the first to come out of the starting blocks. A headline appeared in *Der Spiegel* on 1 February 2001: 'Merz wants to become Chancellor'. In fairness, Merz did not express himself this categorically. All he actually said was that 'it is in the nature of things that the leader [in Parliament] is a contender'. But the message was clear. He would run.

In fact it was not 'in the nature of things'. In the post-war era, the most successful Chancellors had come from positions as Governors in one of the states: Schröder had been Governor in North Rhine Westphalia, Kohl held the same office in Rhineland-Palatinate, Kurt Georg Kiesinger had been Governor in Baden-Württemberg, Willy Brandt had served as leader in West Berlin, and Helmut Schmidt, though he had not been the leader of his state, had been an influential minister of the interior in the city state of Hamburg. A track record of dealing with real practical issues at the state level was considered an apprenticeship for would-be Chancellors. By contrast, Ludwig Erhard, who had no experience of regional government, had failed to make an impact and was regarded as weak.

History does not repeat itself, and political leaders are not critical historians, but the past is an important ally for those who know how to use historical facts to get their way in politics. The fact that Merz had no experience of running a public bureaucracy did not rule him out *per se*, but it was a hindrance for reasons other than merely historical. As in America, experience of running a state, and familiarity with the art of governing, is regarded as essential and something very different from the business of debating in Parliament. Merz's problem was that he had little experience of public administration. Without this he was untested, just like Angela Merkel.

Edmund Stoiber, the leader of the CSU (the CDU's sister party in Bavaria), had plenty of experience. A federal minister of the interior from 1988 to 1993, he had been Governor of Bavaria since 1993. Being a member of the CSU he had not been implicated in the party finance scandal, and as the Governor of Bavaria he had the administrative experience Merkel and Merz lacked.

For the first time since Franz Josef Strauß had unsuccessfully challenged Helmut Schmitt in 1980, the prospect of a challenger from the CSU was being increasingly talked about. The problem for the Bavarian politician was that he repeatedly had ruled himself out. As late as December 2000, only a month before Merz indicated that he would run, Stoiber had made what he called 'the definitive' decision not to be a contender. He spelled out his decision in a radio interview, and did so in rather impatient terms: 'You know very well that I am not available for that position because I am the Governor of Bavaria and I would like to remain in this position for a little while when I am re-elected in 2003.'[18] It was difficult to retreat from that categorical position. Although going back on such statements is quite common in politics, Stoiber's had been more than definitive than most. This left the field open for Merz and Merkel, though the former was regarded as too right-wing, too nationalistic and too polarising for the centrist voters.

Where was Angela Merkel in all this? Nowhere, it seemed. She had not said directly that she would run. She had merely noted that she hypothetically had 'a clear idea of how [she] as Chancellor – alongside others – would make this country a better place'.[19] It was becoming clear that she was failing in her attempt to build momentum for her candidacy.

'Who are still behind Angela Merkel?' *Die Welt* asked rhetorically on 28 August 2001. The answer was implied: nobody important.

The impression that the party leader was not suited to challenge Schröder was reinforced by prominent politicians, notably those who did not rely on the support of Merkel for their positions. Thomas Goppel, the general secretary of the CSU, was quick to denounce Merkel in a rather cavalier fashion when he told a newspaper: 'Merkel does not have a profile, and nobody is rallying behind her.'[20] It was pretty obvious that this action was coordinated with Stoiber, but the Bavarian Governor was still reluctant to break his earlier promise and avoided the K-question.

Gerhard Schröder was not getting any more popular, and it was beginning to be a problem for CDU/CSU that they had not agreed on a candidate to take on the Chancellor. But what were they to do? Could Stoiber be made to stand? What could convince him? Or were there other candidates?

There was one: Wolfgang Schäuble. The wheelchair-bound former party leader had been left for politically dead after he resigned from his position in the wake of the party finance scandal. But now – seemingly defying the laws of political gravity – some of his parliamentary colleagues began to toy with the idea that the former party leader could challenge Gerhard Schröder. At first it was only a rumour, but in November 2001 the leader of the CSU faction in Parliament, Michael Glos, stated: 'For me Schäuble is a possible candidate but I am not sure whether he is willing to apply.' Glos's speculation was quickly denounced, though not in categorical terms. Thomas Goppel made a routine statement pointing out that 'Glos does not speak for the party at the state level'.[21] This was a statement of fact, but not one that closed the debate.

The possibility that Schäuble could make an improbable comeback was not good news for Merkel, but it was even more concerning for the conservative Governors Roland Koch (Hesse), Edwin Teufel (Baden-Württemberg) and Peter Müller (Saarland). These influential politicians feared with some justification that Schäuble's involvement in the illicit party donations scandal, and the fact that he lied to Parliament about his knowledge, would be fatal for the party's chances.

The situation was becoming surreal. When the CDU met for their annual conference in Dresden in the beginning of December nobody mentioned the K-question. The newspapers tried to read the runes and found clues by looking at the delegates' reactions to the speeches by the various contenders. The left-leaning *Süddeutsche Zeitung* noted that the delegates spontaneously stood up to cheer Mrs Merkel, and concluded that, after all, 'she can do it'.

Whether this was a sober assessment or merely wishful thinking is an open question. And in any case, she was not the only contender, let alone the only one to be greeted with massive applause. The following day *Die Welt,* a more conservative paper, noted there was 'no end to standing ovations' during the speech delivered by Edmund Stoiber, 'Can 2000 hands lie?' But the Bavarian Governor still did not declare that he would run. This was understandable, at least from a personal perspective. In 1980 the young Edmund Stoiber, as Secretary General of the CSU, had been a chief advisor to Franz Josef Strauß. He had seen how his mentor had lost the election to his polished, eloquent, posh-sounding northern opponent Helmut Schmidt.

Stoiber did not wish to repeat history by losing to the similarly slick northerner Gerhard Schröder. Yet, at the same time, Stoiber knew that he was in with a chance; Schröder was unpopular, and on paper Stoiber's chances were better than they had been for Strauß in 1980. The possibility that he *might* beat the Social Democrat in the 2002 election could be a way of redeeming the late Franz Josef Strauß. Stoiber was tempted and was beginning to lean towards running.

Shortly after the conference, and only a week before the Christmas break, a group of Governors began to conspire. They belonged to the right of the CDU and they wanted to clear the way for Merz. Peter Müller, the Saarland Governor, was indiscreet and revealed that they would seek to prevent Merkel from running. She acted quickly; she could sense that her authority was waning and that she had to regain respect. She told the press that she had rung Müller and given him a scolding. This stopped the momentum behind Merz for the time being, but it did not help Merkel win the candidacy. The following day, 10 December, Wolfgang Bosbach (Merz's deputy in Parliament), spoke out in favour of Stoiber but denied rumours of a conspiracy against Merkel: 'No, we cannot say that anyone is plotting a coup,' he told *Die Tageszeitung*, without sounding genuine, 'the Union is blessed to have two good candidates' – though pointedly he did not reveal their identity. It was clear that he was not thinking of Merkel and that he preferred Stoiber if he could not have Merz. 'There is no denying,' Bosbach said, 'that Peter Müller and others regard Edmund Stoiber as an exceptional candidate for the federal elections, and someone who could successfully fight this. But no, there is no *Putsch* against Merkel.'

It was evident, Herr Bosbach's protestations notwithstanding, that there *was* a conspiracy against Merkel, and although he publicly supported Stoiber, it was also clear that Merz was still in contention.

Crunch time was set for 11 January. On that date the CDU Executive Board was scheduled to meet in Herrenkrug Parkhotel in Magdeburg, a retreat where Germans normally go to relax and get a break. Merkel was not in a relaxed mood. She knew she would be presented with a *fait accompli* and that the Governors would nominate Edmund Stoiber. This would all but end her chances of ever becoming a contender for the top job. A public vote for Stoiber would make her look like a loser. She had to follow Helmut Kohl's example from 1980: gracefully allow her Bavarian colleague to run, and then hope for the best. But she had to make it look as if she was in control, as if she was calling the shots.

She rang Stoiber on 9 January and asked if she could stop by for breakfast before the meeting. Stoiber was somewhat annoyed about this sudden forced invitation, but he and his wife couldn't really say no. Angela turned up at their house, Wolfrathausen. Merkel had a clear proposition for her colleague. She would support his candidacy publicly and back him during the campaign subject to one minor condition, which was unlikely to be relevant in the scheme of things. Stoiber was surprised and delighted. He had feared a showdown and was still suspicious of Merz. Now he was being handed the candidacy on a plate. He accepted.

What he also accepted, though this was only revealed later, was that Merkel, in the unlikely event of a defeat for the Union, would take over from Friedrich Merz as parliamentary leader. Merkel was upbeat when she spoke to the media after the breakfast: 'I have always said that the candidate for the Union should be the one who has the greatest chance of winning. And I believe that person is Edmund Stoiber.'

Roland Koch, Peter Müller, Friedrich Merz and the other conspirators on the right were perplexed. Merkel had acted more quickly than they had expected; she had regained the initiative at a time when they thought she was on her way out. Their tactic of humiliating the party leader – and through this removing her – had failed.

THE WAR AND THE DELUGE

The campaign was unusual. Normally the FDP would more or less blindly fall behind the candidate proposed by CDU/CSU. But the little libertarian party was concerned about Edmund Stoiber. The Catholic conservative views of many in the CSU alienated the civil rights campaigners in the FDP. Instead Guido Westerwelle (who had become chairman and leader of the party in 2001) proposed to stand for the chancellorship. He knew full well that he was not going to win a majority on his own but then nor were any of the other parties. So why not? His answer was 'equidistance' – to keep both of the largest groups at arm's length and negotiate the best result. No law said that the Chancellor necessarily had to come from the largest party. In addition, by adopting this strategy he could distance himself from both sides, and then, in the aftermath of the election, negotiate a better deal for his party.

Edmund Stoiber was not a natural. In Bavaria, where the CSU is all but guaranteed a majority in the state elections, he was able to play it safe and appear statesmanlike and dignified. Against Gerhard Schröder it was a different story. Unlike the Chancellor, he was not used to politics as a combat sport. That said, objectively speaking things looked good for Stoiber. He had a good story to tell and had been dealt a good hand. The economy was once again slipping into recession and the polling evidence suggested that Stoiber and his team were ahead on the themes that mattered most at the start of the campaign. Schröder had said that his government should be judged on its ability to reduce the level of unemployment and 85 per cent of the voters agreed that joblessness among the Germans was the main issue in the campaign. In addition, 50 per cent believed that CDU/CSU was the most trustworthy coalition on the economy against only 30 per cent for SPD/Green.

At the personal level, however, Schröder was miles ahead. Asked whom they regarded as a 'winner', 63 per cent of the voters opted for Schröder against a paltry 13 per cent for Stoiber. And when asked whom they regarded as more 'sympathetic' the figures were almost equally impressively in Schröder's favour: 61 per cent to 17 per cent. It was undoubtedly this, along with Schröder's knack for seizing any opportunities that presented themselves, which enabled the incumbent to turn a potentially catastrophic defeat into a close race.

In the wider world, US President George W. Bush had begun a diplomatic effort to win support for a war against Iraq. Although the SDP/Green government had sent German soldiers into battle in Kosovo, Schröder sensed the mood correctly. Many Germans were sceptical of Bush's motives and over 80 per cent of the voters were against involvement in a possible war, especially if this was fought without a mandate from the UN Security Council.

Schröder's main stroke of good luck, however, came with the floods in the northwestern state of Lower Saxony in the middle of August 2002. The water in the Elbe rose to over nine metres (30.8 feet) above normal and more than 300,000 citizens had to be evacuated. Always a man of action, Schröder donned a pair of wellington boots and took charge. Travelling to the area, speaking to the affected people and making sure that immediate demands for shelter and provisions were met, his hands-on approach was in marked contrast to the somewhat reserved, silver-haired Stoiber in his trademark grey three-piece suit who stayed in official residence at 1 Franz-Josef-Strauß-Ring in Munich. Even this natural disaster did not give the governing coalition a lead in the polls, however, though it reversed Stoiber's earlier lead. While Schröder had almost caught up with his opponents, he was still behind. Stoiber was confident of winning; perhaps too confident.

On election night the first exit polls suggested Stoiber had reason to be optimistic. At 6.47 pm, three-quarters of an hour after the polling stations had closed, a beaming Stoiber went on TV and said, 'We have won the election.' He spoke too soon. Very soon afterwards it became clear that the exit polls were wrong and that the governing coalition had beaten CDU/CSU with a total of 577,000 votes. Stoiber had lost, just as his mentor had done in 1980. Schröder could go on.

MERKEL POUNCES – AGAIN

Angela Merkel had – outwardly at least – been the personification of loyalty during the election campaign. She had noted that the opinion polls suggested that more women than men had voted for the SPD and that the support for the CDU/CSU had plummeted in East Germany. This gave her a potential extra card, but she did not need to play it just yet. Now was the time to call in old favours and to keep Stoiber to the promise he had made at that breakfast in January.

Merkel had given Stoiber a free run provided that he would let her become leader of the parliamentary party after the election. Friedrich Merz knew nothing about this deal and was sure his position was safe. The majority of members of parliament were conservatives like him and there was no reason to suspect that they would force him to resign. In the morning after the defeat Merkel, Stoiber and Merz met in Konrad Adenauer Haus. Merkel told the astonished parliamentary leader she was taking over from him. Stoiber said nothing. It would all be formally declared at the meeting of the CDU Party Executive Board the following day.

Merz was appalled and incensed. He called Roland Koch. The Governor of the State of Hesse in the southern part of the country was not prepared to rubber-stamp a decision to demote his ally, but he knew he didn't have much of a choice. It was dawning on Koch that Merkel had planned this long before and that he and his colleagues had again been caught unawares. Anxious to secure a position for Merz, Koch suggested that Merkel and Merz could form a double act. Whether the experienced politician believed in this strategy or whether he proposed it out of loyalty to his friend is anyone's guess. But Merkel was in no mood to make compromises. You don't make concessions when you are in a position of strength. She was dubbed 'Mistress Merciless' by the media, who were surprised to see the hitherto meek and restrained Merkel do away with a political rival with a steely determination and resolve that nobody had expected.

Merkel wanted to combine the positions of leader of the party and spokesperson in Parliament, but not everybody was happy. Her position as leader was affirmed in a party conference exactly seven weeks after the election. But, as one commentator noted, the support for her was not warm-hearted, there was no euphoria among the rank and file, and her speech was 'strangely uninspired'.[22] Merkel was supported by 93.7 per cent, but a similar percentage voted to give Merz a seat on the party's Executive Board. Merkel had completed a stage of the race to the top, but she was still not secure in her own party.

LEADER IN PARLIAMENT AND
MERKEL'S MASTERSTROKE

It was a different, more confident, Angela Merkel who turned up in Parliament after the 2002 elections. Schröder was his confident self and had given an upbeat – though perhaps rather too rose-tinted – assessment of the country's economic prospects. Merz, a skilled debater, had previously given Schröder a run for his money and had been a combative opponent in the debating chamber.

Merkel had not previously been considered a strong challenger. She was not a debater, a bit shy, not confident. The Chancellor did not expect her to be his greatest problem. Her response to his inaugural address was a surprise to him.

'Mr Chancellor,' began the pastor's daughter, 'your speech reminds me of the Gospel according to St John, "My kingdom is not of this world."' The punch-line was delivered with confidence and a hint of wit that the public had not heard from her before. The verdict among experts was that Merkel's speech – to their surprise – was masterful: 'Spirited and rhetorically beautiful', according to Thilo von Trotha, the President of the Association of German Speechwriters.

As Leader of the Opposition Merkel did not have many opportunities to prove her worth. One exception was the election to the presidency. It is a widespread view among many observers that the election of Horst Köhler to this largely ceremonial post was 'Merkel's masterstroke'. It was undoubtedly a feat to prevent the Social Democrats and their allies from choosing one of their own to succeed the Social Democrat President Johannes Rau when he was due to step down in 2004. But it is not entirely clear why this was so remarkable unless one goes behind the headlines. Merkel's achievement was that she was able to play off one faction against another and secure a majority for her favoured candidate.

In the autumn of 2003, Wolfgang Schäuble – at this stage an increasingly bitter figure – declared that he was interested in the post, and for a while he was considered the front-runner among the CDU/CSU candidates. Merkel was not interested in having Schäuble occupy the highest post in the Republic. There was still bad blood between them and Merkel's predecessor had not forgiven her for what he regarded as her betrayal during the illicit party funds scandal. Ideally she wanted a technocrat, a neutral figure who could stand above parties. Horst Köhler, the recently retired President of the International Monetary Fund and a former junior finance minister under Kohl, would be ideal. But she kept this to herself at the time.

In early December Merkel met with Guido Westerwelle and suggested that Schäuble could be the joint candidate for both the FDP and the CDU/CSU. The liberal leader flatly rejected this: Schäuble was not presidential, Westerwelle said, and reminded Merkel that her predecessor was still formally under investigation for his involvement in the scandal concerning illegal party donations. This effectively killed off Schäuble's chances, though Merkel did not tell him so, nor did she tell anyone else. The reason for her reticence was understandable. Edmund Stoiber, still a powerful figure in the CDU/CSU, had expressed strong support for his fellow southerner: 'I value his intellectual capacity. He has the courage to show the way for our country at a time when we are facing difficult changes,' the Bavarian told *Der Spiegel* in September 2003.

Merkel, much to Schäuble's annoyance, did not discuss what was becoming known as the *P-Frage*: 'the Presidential question'. She left it to the last minute as, indeed, she often did with important decisions. At a meeting with Stoiber on 3 March 2004 – just one day before the CDU executive was to make a decision as to its candidate – she acted as if she supported Schäuble for the post even although she knew that Westerwelle would never accept him.

Merkel and Stoiber's apparent agreement to propose Schäuble evidently annoyed Roland Koch. The self-confident Governor of Hesse – who had his sights on higher things – expressed frustration and ill-contained anger. He went before the cameras and stated 'I am very unhappy. This is completely chaotic.' He had walked directly into Merkel's trap. She could now tell Stoiber that, alas, Koch wasn't happy and, by the way, nor was Westerwelle. So they had to look at the alternatives. She had in fact already drawn up a list of three candidates: Annette Schavan (the culture minister of Baden-Württemberg and a Catholic theologian), Klaus Töpfer (the left-leaning former environmental minister) and, almost as an afterthought, Horst Köhler (the candidate she had preferred from the start). She knew that Töpfer was toxic to conservatives like

Roland Koch and Friedrich Merz, but she also knew that the Bavarians and Stoiber's cabal of conservative Catholics would not countenance a woman as President – not even if she was a Catholic. Thus there was only one option left: Horst Köhler.

The FDP were surprised, but Westerwelle was happy to support the economically liberal former banker. Thus Merkel – using a bit of cunning – had coaxed and cajoled her colleagues into supporting a candidate no one had even considered to be a contender. Köhler defeated the Social Democrat candidate Gesine Schwan on the first ballot in the Electoral College by 604 votes to 580 and moved into the presidential mansion, Schloß Bellevue.

Merkel had outsmarted her rivals again, and she had achieved the rare feat of securing the election of a Christian Democrat candidate at a time when the Chancellor was a Social Democrat. This had not been done before. Schäuble, not surprisingly, was angry and aghast. On 5 March 2004 a critical piece entitled 'Angela Machiavelli' by his friend Heribald Prantl appeared in *Süddeutsche Zeitung*, in which he ostensibly acted as Schäuble's mouthpiece. Merkel, wrote Prantl, was guilty of 'falsehood, deceit and fraud'; the events surrounding the presidential election were part 'of Merkel's overall plot, the CDU leader's diabolically brilliant plan, to eliminate her intellectually superior rivals'. This gained her respect, *Die Welt* concluding on 25 May that 'the transfer of power from the Helmut Kohl era is complete. Nobody in the Union can surpass her.'

MEYER AND MERZ

Not everything went to plan. Laurenz Meyer, Merkel's belligerent General Secretary, continued to attack Schröder's government. This was not a problem, as his aggressive style meant that Merkel could play the role of calm and collected stateswoman while Meyer did the dirty work. Previously, of course, this role had been performed by Merz. But he was – or rather had been – a rival and someone whom she didn't trust. Meyer, by contrast, was her personal Rottweiler, someone who could be trusted to launch attacks on Schröder on an almost daily basis. However, Meyer also had a rather unfortunate habit of not telling Merkel everything. He sometimes followed a course that bordered on the unethical and often strayed beyond it. One of the things he had *not* told his boss was that he, as a former employee of the energy company Rheinisch-Westfälisches Elektrizitätswerk AG, had been paying a lower price for electricity. This was a legitimate perk when he had worked for the company, but he had not done so for half a decade; the other problem was that he had received energy to a value of €81,800 (roughly US$ 100,000). Once again, Merkel acted quickly. Meyer was immediately sacked and in his place she appointed Volker Kauder, who tellingly originated from the town of Rottweil in Baden-Württemberg – the place where the breed of attack dog originated.

Meyer was not the only one to leave, but unlike Meyer, Freidrich Merz's departure was not linked with any scandal, political or otherwise. Merz knew that his time was up when Merkel demoted him. He had continued to play a role in Parliament as spokesperson for taxation, but his proposals for a reform of the tax code were repeatedly rejected.

In October 2004 Merz wrote a letter to Merkel using a surprisingly personal tone mixed with the formalities that go with such letters: 'Most esteemed Mrs Chairwoman – Dearest Angela,' he began, 'as I told you earlier today when we spoke, I have decided not to stand for re-election to the Party Executive and I will also retire from my current positions in Parliament.'

Another rival had fallen by the wayside; now for the greater prize, the chancellorship. Merz left politics and made a fortune. But he returned many years later, in 2019, when he once again became a thorn in Merkel's side.

CHAPTER 9

MERKEL LOSES AND BECOMES CHANCELLOR

GERHARD SCHRÖDER'S RE-ELECTION IN 2002 HAD NOT SOLVED GERmany's fundamental economic problems, above all its aging population. Schröder had never been particularly constrained by ideological baggage. His political philosophy, insofar as he had one, was close to that of the British Prime Minister, Tony Blair. Like his UK counterpart, Schröder believed that market forces should play a greater role and that social policies needed to be reformed away from a pure entitlement system. Before they had fallen out over the war in Iraq in 2003, Blair and Schröder had even written a joint manifesto in the form of a pamphlet entitled 'The New Middle', in which they attempted to translate the concept of Blair's so-called 'Third Way' into something resembling an ideological programme. These lofty justifications for reforming parts of the welfare state had little practical importance in the late 1990s when they were first introduced, but many of them resurfaced in the negotiations over the so-called Hartz IV reforms. The reforms were named after Peter Hartz, then personnel director of Volkswagen, who was put in charge of a commission tasked with proposing reforms of the labour market. The Commission came up with several ideas, among them increasing the retirement age to 67 and reducing benefits for job-seekers by paying them the same as those on welfare. It was argued that these reforms were necessary on economic grounds. Without them, Schröder alleged, the whole welfare state would eventually collapse. Schröder's philosophy was in many ways like that of Don Fabrizio Corbera, the main character in Lampedusa's classic novel, *The Leopard*: 'If you want things to stay as they are, things will have to change.'

However, just as in the case of the fictional nineteenth-century Sicilian nobleman, not all Schröder's contemporaries agreed. Schröder's first finance minister, Oscar Lafontaine, led the charge against his former comrade from within the SPD. Lafontaine had written a book, *The Heart Beats on the Left*, and had generally become the spokesperson for a perhaps rather romanticised view of the traditional West German welfare state.

The attacks from within the party made Schröder's position precarious. The SPD was losing state elections and as a result the Red-Green government was facing an increasingly hostile majority of the centre-right parties in the Senate, which is composed of representatives of the federal states. In an attempt to limit the pressure on the government, Schröder decided to resign his chairmanship of the SPD to Franz Müntefering, the chairman of the parliamentary party and, so Schröder believed at the time, a true and loyal comrade.

The aim was for Schröder to concentrate on governing the country and not be distracted by internal party bickering. In reality, of course, Schröder had a more sinister motive. He wanted to share out blame for the unpopular programmes lest he should be challenged. He avoided the latter, but he could not avoid defeats in the state elections. On 22 May 2005 he threw in the towel. The SPD had lost the election in North Rhine Westphalia, where the CDU's Jürgen Rüttgers, an arch-conservative, easily beat the Social Democrat incumbent Peer Steinbrück. The Social Democrats had ruled the state since the CDU politician Franz Meyers had lost to Heinz Kühn in 1966, and losing the majority was symbolically and politically disastrous for Schröder. Governing would be more difficult. Merkel could effectively hold the government to ransom by vetoing legislation in the upper house.

Schröder wanted new elections to Parliament. But dissolving the federal legislature's lower house is not within the gift of the Chancellor. Elections are called only every four years or when the Chancellor loses a vote of confidence. Schröder's subterfuge was to have his own party and the Greens vote against him for tactical reasons and hence force President Köhler to call new elections. The first part of the plan went ahead without problems. On 1 July 2005, in a 296-151 vote with 148 abstentions, Parliament issued a vote of no confidence. This was a highly unusual procedure and possibly unconstitutional. The Green member Werner Schulz, describing the motion as illegal, immediately challenged it in the courts: 'If the president dissolves Parliament,' he said, 'I will file suit at the Federal Constitutional Court.' Legally speaking, it looked as if he had a point. The German Basic Law, Article 67.1.1, states:

> The German Parliament may express its lack of confidence in the Federal Chancellor only by electing a successor by the vote of a majority of its Members and requesting the Federal President to dismiss the Federal Chancellor. The Federal President must comply with the request and appoint the person elected.

Nobody had expressed confidence in anyone, nor had Parliament 'elected a successor'. So was the move unconstitutional? The Constitutional Court did not find a problem with the procedure and declared that the method was acceptable. Schröder could proceed.

But why call elections? If the opinion polls were to be trusted, everything suggested that Schröder would lose to Merkel. Was the move rational? There were several reasons for Schröder's gamble. At one level he trusted his legendary abilities as an election campaigner and knew – correctly, it turned out – that his skills at electioneering were second to none, and certainly much better than Mrs Merkel's. Perhaps the other reason was that Schröder wanted to retire from politics to pursue his interests as a businessman, and to devote himself to his fourth wife and their two adopted children.

Schröder was thus in two minds. On the one hand he was looking forward to a new, more lucrative career which he could combine with more relaxation with his family. On the other hand he was a consummate politician and a skilled campaigner, and as such he relished a fight. Having secured the passage of the Hartz IV reforms and with little prospect of winning another general election, Schröder could enjoy the campaign in a comparatively leisurely fashion. To be sure, the Social Democrats could lose – in fact, he was certain they would – but he and only he would be able to minimise the damage. The CDU would win but Merkel would find it difficult to form a stable government, and the SPD would regroup and re-establish itself after a short period in opposition.

Four months later, when the first election results ticked in, it looked as if Schröder's gamble had paid off. Thanks in no small measure to his campaigning genius, the SPD had almost overcome a 20 per cent gap in the polls. The outcome was a virtual dead heat between the SPD and CDU/CSU, with the former winning 34.1 per cent against the latter's 35.2. The result was a disaster and an embarrassment for Merkel, and threatened to end her political career. Four years earlier Edmund Stoiber had polled a respectable 38 per cent. Merkel had not even matched the Bavarian's result. The outcome of the 2005 election was the worst the CDU had suffered since 1949, when the party was not properly established. Why had it gone so wrong?

THE STORY OF JUDGE KIRCHHOF:
HOW IT (ALMOST) ALL WENT WRONG

Merkel had started in an almost unbeatable position. At the beginning of the election campaign the CDU/CSU were polling 48 per cent. SPD was languishing at a pitiful 28 per cent. So strong had Merkel and the CDU/CSU's position been that some believed – or feared – that she would be able to govern alone, a feat no one had accomplished since Adenauer's victory in 1957, when CDU/CSU gained more than 50 per cent of the vote. On 16 September 2005 *Das Handelsblatt*, a newspaper that can be compared to the *Wall Street Journal*, though it is less overtly political, warned that Merkel needed the FDP to put a 'brake on her own party and to balance the egotistical tendencies of the state governors'.

Merkel's problems at the beginning of the campaign were minimal. Her greatest concern was what to do about Edmund Stoiber, who she feared could become a threat to the internal stability of the coalition. Simply handing him the keys to the finance ministry – a position the CSU had held under Kohl – risked giving him too much power over the most important policy area. Her other problem was that some considered her a political lightweight. She tried to solve both by naming the relatively nondescript academic and former judge Paul Kirchhof as finance minister designate. This gave her control over Stoiber, who was to become a kind of superminister for business, economics and technology – a post that looked good on paper but was unlikely to carry much weight in reality. She also thought that she had found in Kirchhof a credible philosophical heavyweight.

Helmut Kohl, it should be said, did had not have a particular knack for discovering intellectuals. Indeed, it was often noted that he seemed to antagonise the intelligentsia. But perhaps Merkel wanted to stand out. Margaret Thatcher, though no role model for Merkel, had succeeded in wooing intellectuals such as the Austrian-born economist Friedrich von Hayek. Closer to home, Willy Brandt had surrounded himself with intellectuals such as the novelist Günter Grass in the 1969 election campaign.

Merkel felt she needed a genuine intellectual: an academic thinker of repute, or a philosopher; someone who could add depth to her campaign. In short, someone who could put to rest the assertion that Merkel was a political dilettante. She found what she wanted in Paul Kirchhof, who after a distinguished career on the bench had become professor of jurisprudence at Heidelberg University. In addition to his glowing CV, Kirchhof had exerted considerable influence on centre-right circles with his book *The Gentle Loss of Freedom for a New Tax-Code: Clear, Understandable and Fair*.

Kirchhof's theory was deceptively simple: everybody should pay the same level of income tax and the various deductions should be abolished. This tax system, so Kirchhof argued, would result in lower levels of fraud and tax evasion as the legal opportunities for tax avoidance would be reduced. It was this man whom Merkel designated as her future finance minister; in doing so she sidelined Edmund Stoiber, who would have to accept the lesser role of 'superminister' for economics, business and technology.

At first Kirchhof's appointment was met with approval and even respect. *Süddeutsche Zeitung*, not normally a paper that cheers for CDU/CSU, found it inspiring that Merkel had 'drawn this man out of the dusty world of learning and legal reasoning'. Kirchhof was, so the paper opined, 'of a totally different calibre than the dilettante Jost Stollmann', whom Gerhard Schröder had dragged out in 1998.[1] Unlike the said Jost Stollmann, a millionaire businessman and former member of the CDU whom Gerhard Schröder had appointed to his shadow-team in 1998, but who later became an embarrassment when he expressed opinions that seemingly contradicted the SPD, Kirchhof was a much more serious and inspired choice, a man who was presented as 'a *deus ex machina* in the realm of financial policies'.[2] 'Never before has Hans Eichel [the SPD finance minister] clung more desperately to his office than in the first days of the political career of Paul Kirchhof', declared *Das Handelsblatt*.[3]

There was a certain element of hubris in Merkel's team, however, a feeling that the result of the election was in the bag. This arrogance led to near fatal mistakes, which seemed almost unfathomable. No one in Merkel's team had ensured that the Professor Kirchhof was 'on-message' or that his utterances were cleared and coordinated with campaign HQ. Merkel had not integrated Kirchhof into her team, indeed they had met only once – on the day Merkel appointed him. Early in July Merkel had rung the professor and asked him to join her team. The two had never met before, and it was unclear who had recommended him. But the professor was happy to be on board and agreed. Equally problematically, Merkel had apparently discussed the appointment only with Stoiber.[4]

Merkel must have been aware that the neo-liberal ideas and views espoused by Kirchhof were not to everyone's liking. It is an often overlooked fact that the conservatives in the CDU – and especially in the CSU – are not free-market apostles but rather sceptical of free enterprise in its unfettered forms. Capitalism is not a cardinal virtue in a party which historically and ideologically grew out of Pope Leo XIII's 1891 encyclical letter *Rerum Novarum*, in which the pontiff had attacked rampant capitalism as well as godless Communism.

Merkel, having grown up in a Protestant household – and as someone who idolised Ronald Reagan – was on the right of many in the CDU/CSU, though she was more liberal in matters such as gay marriage, stem-cell research and education. Her background and socialisation meant that she was not completely attuned to the heartbeat of the party to which she belonged. She had gone out of her way to champion a neo-liberal ideology and had even criticised the Federal Republic for being too Socialist: 'You have no idea how Socialist you actually are,' she told the newspaper *Frankfurter Allgemeine Zeitung* in the early stages of the election campaign.[5] It was as if she deliberately wanted to provoke her compatriots; as if she wanted to dare them to elect a conservative who believed in the free market and distrusted the state.

Only a year before the election, the socially Catholic newspaper *Tagespost* had warned that 'neo-liberal concepts do not win elections', and the paper had even complained that under Merkel 'the Christian social ethos in the Union has been pensioned off'.[6]

Merkel should have been more careful, and she soon learned this to her cost. After Kirchhof had made a few unscripted remarks, the press-pack smelled blood. Asked about his big idea, the flat-tax, Kirchhof maintained that everyone henceforth would pay only 25 per cent of their income, regardless of how much they earned. This was unwelcome news for Merkel. Tax policies were already a touchy subject, one that had indirectly led to the resignation of Friedrich Merz, as we have seen, and one that split the Union.

Seemingly caught unaware by Kirchhof's remarks, Merkel immediately contradicted the professor in an interview with the television network ZDF in which she maintained that the party (she didn't specify whether she meant just the CDU or both sister parties) wanted a graduated tax with different brackets ranging from 12 to 39 per cent. She also stated that 'Kirchhof's proposals would never be implemented in the next Parliament'. Edmund Stoiber, who bore some of the responsibility for Kirchhof's appointment, was equally embarrassed, stressing that 'the professor's statements were part of a mere academic debate'.[7]

At this stage Gerhard Schröder pounced. As a seasoned political pugilist he instinctively sensed his opponent's weakness. 'An academic debate' was not part of a serious programme for a would-be party of government, Schröder told his compatriots. Warming to his theme, the Chancellor spoke patronisingly about 'the professor from Heidelberg' whom he not only portrayed as an otherworldly armchair theorist but also as a mad scientist who cared more for his own theories than for the plight of ordinary folk. 'The views expressed [by Kirchhof] represent a view of human beings which we [the Germans] cannot tolerate.'[8] 'Human beings are not things, and should not be treated as such,' Schröder continued, while softly alluding to the philosopher Immanuel Kant's dictum that 'nobody should be treated as a mere means to an end'. To accomplish the feat of denouncing the professor and at the same time alluding to Germany's greatest philosopher was a measure of Schröder's skill as a campaigner: he was able to appeal both to the ordinary folk who considered Kirchhof an academic egghead and at the same time to intellectuals who, from the reference to Kant, appreciated that the Chancellor was himself a man of learning and erudition. To be able to combine a folksy touch with an appeal to the educated middle class was no mean feat. The intervention was followed up by posters with the simple message 'Merkel/Kirchhof: radically anti-social.' On 31 August at a party rally, Schröder described the professor as one who 'will use the Germans as guinea pigs for his reforms'.

Whether Schröder was in a position to preach, especially given that he himself had embraced neo-liberalism – is a moot point. The damage was being done on a daily basis. And worst of all, from Merkel's perspective, interventions from her own side threatened to undermine the support and status she had meticulously built up since 2002. Sensing Merkel's weakness, a slightly sanctimonious Christian Wulff, the Catholic Governor of Lower Saxony, felt called upon to declare that Kirchhof's economic model was 'contrary to all Germans' sense of [social] justice'.[9]

That Wulff intervened was indicative of Merkel's predicament. There was a sense that she was in the process of snatching defeat from the jaws of victory; and perhaps even a growing probability that the next Chancellor would have to be found outside the current Parliament – in short, that one of the Governors would have to step up to the plate. History was not on Merkel's side. The pattern of recent decades had been that the Chancellor had come from state politics. Four of the last five Chancellors, as we have seen, had been leaders at the state level before reaching that office. That the next one might be one of the Governors seemed a realistic prospect. The likes of Wulff felt they had to position themselves in case Merkel faltered.

Thus Wulff merely did as might have been expected. That he was able to do so by attacking the much maligned neo-liberal doctrine that Kirchhof – and by implication Merkel – espoused was just an added bonus.

Meanwhile Judge Kirchhof was not making life easier for himself, let alone for his boss. Seemingly oblivious to the subtle rules of political appropriateness, the academic continued to issue a steady stream of increasingly unrealistic policy proposals. These proposals may have been intellectually coherent, but intellectual coherence is not the be-all and end-all in politics. Public policy is not and never has been characterised by 'communicative action' or the ideal of an open discussion without prejudice as espoused by public intellectuals such as Jürgen Habermas. In politics arguments are tools of power and must fit into what is considered opportune and appropriate at any given time. Kirchhof did not appreciate this and continued to champion his ideas. Only two weeks before the election, he was at it again. Although he had been denounced by Merkel, he confidently stated that 'all the 418 legal tax-breaks and loopholes would be closed by the first of January 2007'.[10]

Kirchhof's public policy seminar, conducted complete with social science and legal jargon, was turning CDU/CSU's election campaign into a shambles. No wonder Merkel declared 'I am a rather emotional type' in one of the countless damage limitations she had to engage in.[11] A natural thing would have been to have sacked Kirchhof, but this would have smacked of panic. Another possibility was a quiet talk with the professor. But the latter, which indeed was tried, did not have much effect on Kirchhof. Some in the party – ostensibly Merkel herself – sought to convince Friedrich Metz to make a comeback, to return to the fold and be reinstated as a kind of prodigal son. Metz, after all, was still running for election. But these efforts did not bear fruit. Metz remained in semi-retirement.

In the media and in public the CDU's designated finance minister was effectively being portrayed as a cynic who cared little about individuals. This was, of course, a caricature, and a somewhat unjust one at that. Kirchhof had in fact expressed views that showed a considerable concern for social justice. But the problem with these statements was they were directed not at the SPD but at existing CDU policy. For example, Kirchhof criticised the CDU's proposal for higher General Sales Tax (GST) as this would negatively affect 'the least well-off', especially 'those who have to bring up children'.[12]

In politics, and especially in election campaigns, the nuances get lost. To make matters worse Kirchhof, who was not even a member of the CDU, showed little loyalty to the party that had appointed him as finance minister designate. As an academic he was labouring under the misapprehension that politics belongs to the sphere of calm and rational argument. This fallacy cost the CDU dearly.

At a time when election campaigns are becoming more and more professionalised, in the era of the 'war-room', focus groups and political marketing, it is almost incomprehensible that Merkel and her party could run a campaign that was as incompetent, amateurish and down-right shoddy as that of 2005. The appointment of Kirchhof had not only weakened Merkel within the party, it had also led to a drop in support among working-class voters. Blue-collar workers are a necessary constituency for the CDU, but this part of the electorate feared the consequences of the professor's tax reforms. In addition to this, the abolition of loopholes in the tax code and the phasing out of tax-breaks – as suggested by Kirchhof – raised serious concerns among small-business owners and shopkeepers, the two groups that constitute the core of CDU voters.

In the light of the Kirchhof debacle the close result was not surprising at all.

SCHRÖDER THROWS IT ALL AWAY

Schröder, who had been declared politically dead a few months before, who had been treated as yesterday's man and even as a figure of mild ridicule, had risen from the grave. But he was not destined to remain long in the land of the living.

The next scene of the drama is familiar, being the well-known story, related in the Introduction, of how Schröder bulldozed Merkel during the debate between the party leaders after the election, and how his condescending, arrogant, rude and possibly misogynist attitude towards his CDU opponent undid all his campaigning.

Whether Merkel was genuinely meek, shocked or actually felt bullied, or whether she was just tired after months of too little sleep and too much worry, is impossible to say. It doesn't really matter. What matters was that the press performed a *volte face* and abandoned Schröder after having given him positive treatment during the election campaign. While on the campaign trail Schröder, though the incumbent, was the challenger. He was campaigning in the style of Harry S. Truman in his 'Give 'em Hell, Harry' campaign in 1948, in which the Democrat President won over the people and even the press by being the underdog.

Schröder had been the underdog. He had been far behind in the polls, and he had recovered, but that is where the analogy with Truman ends. Whereas the Missouri-born American President came across as a polite and humble gentleman, Schröder did the very opposite. The press punished him and immediately turned against him. 'Even SPD women and the remaining gentlemen within that party must be appalled by his behaviour' read the verdict in *Die Tageszeitung*. The same paper summed up the general consensus that the Chancellor had acted as an 'arrogant, know-it-all, macho' man whose attitude was unbecoming and downright rude,[13] and all this because of a rant on the night after the election. His outburst saved Angela Merkel's political career.

On election night it had become evident that the Free Democrats were not willing to enter into a coalition with the Social Democrats and the Greens (a so-called 'traffic-light coalition' of red (SDP), yellow (FDP) and the Greens). However, Westerwelle was open to the possibility of a 'Jamaica coalition', so-called from the colours of the Jamaican flag, black (CDU), yellow (FDP) and the Greens. At this stage some in the SPD, though not Schröder, were willing to contemplate a Grand Coalition.

Everything was up in the air. Merkel needed to act quickly, and she did. The first task was to consolidate her position as candidate for the post of Chancellor lest one of the state Governors should seize the initiative. The likes of Roland Koch, Christian Wulff, Jürgen Rüttgers and, at a stretch, even Günther Oettinger (the new Governor of the southwestern state of Baden-Württemberg) had the potential to challenge her.

Only one day after the catastrophic result of the general election, Merkel was transformed. Gone was the timid politician who was out of her depth on the campaign trail. What emerged was the familiar Angela Merkel, the one that only insiders knew: the fixer, the politician who excelled at deals behind closed doors.

It was Tuesday morning, two days before the autumn equinox. According to ancient astrology, this is a tipping-point between something old and something new, but it is almost certain that Merkel was not thinking about such matters when she invited the 226 newly elected members of the CDU/CSU parliamentary group to elect a leader and a spokesperson. This was a risky move. Submitting herself to what was a de facto vote of confidence could easily have backfired. Indeed anything other than a victory by acclamation would have fatally wounded her and left the field open for one of the state Governors, or possibly for a come-back by Friedrich Merz. However, it was a calculated risk. Not all the cards were stacked against her. The surprise move gave her an edge and at the same time wrong-footed her opponents in the state capitals. And perhaps most important, Schröder's attacks on her had bred a kind of siege mentality and accompanying solidarity with Merkel within the CDU/CSU parliamentary group.

It would be trite to liken Merkel's political resurrection to a phoenix rising from the ashes, though in this case the cliché has a whiff of truth. Less than 48 hours after the catastrophic end to the election, Merkel was back in pole position in the race to become Chancellor; she won 98.6 per cent of the vote in the leadership election. The result was the best ever for a leader of the CDU/CSU in Parliament. The result, announced by the leader of the CSU caucus, Michael Glos, was met with a standing ovation – some reportedly standing on their chairs – and Merkel was quick to seize the result as a vindication of her right to negotiate: 'This result shows emphatically that *we* – as the strongest party in Parliament, have a claim to lead the negotiations. This will be a difficult task for us. But it is a task that can be solved.'[14] It is noteworthy that Merkel used the collective pronoun 'we'. The task was hers, but it would not have been possible without the trust and support of her parliamentary colleagues. Little things matter in politics.

The situation among the Social Democrats was different. Schröder had major problems. Having handed over the chairmanship of the party to Franz Müntefering, he was no longer in charge of negotiations with other parties. Protocol dictates that the negotiations are led by the party leader, so Schröder was no longer master of his own fate. His other problem was that the FDP, as we have seen, had rejected any talk of a traffic-light coalition. The day after the election, Westerwelle reiterated his position that he 'would not negotiate with the SPD'. Lastly, Schröder was suffering from lack of trust. Only 16 per cent thought that he would be able to solve future problems. Merkel, by contrast, was considered 'credible' by 43 per cent of voters.

Mathematically the situation seemed relatively positive for Schröder. But coalition politics – political scientists' insistence notwithstanding – is not mathematics. Numerically Schröder had a majority with the Greens and former Communists, but he was not willing to countenance a coalition with Oscar Lafontaine who, in the early stages of the election campaign, had left the SPD and entered a loose association with the successors to the East German Communist party. Political parties are relevant only if they have either coalition-potential or blackmail-potential, a shrewd observer once remarked.[15] Schröder was determined not to accord the former Communists either. He considered them a nonentity, ignored their very existence and was not even willing to acknowledge the theoretical possibility of coalition. That the PDS (the former Communists) and the SPD had been willing to share power in Mecklenburg-West Pomerania, where Harald Ringstorff had led a 'Red-Red Coalition' of Social Democrats and ex-Communists since Schröder himself came to power, and that Reinhard Höppner in Saxony-Anhalt had governed with the support of the PDS from 1994 to 1998 – all this was seemingly irrelevant for Schröder.

The Chancellor's rejection of any form of cooperation with PDS could have left the way open for a Jamaica coalition, but this possibility was almost immediately rejected by Joschka Fischer. His Green Party had come a long way from its roots in the '68 generation of aging hippies who propagated an alternative society, but joining forces with the CDU, the establishment party *par excellence*, would be a step too far for many, and not least for the party's leader. The acting foreign minister killed off all speculation concerning a black-green-yellow coalition: 'I am a dyed in the wool red-green. It is all. I have never known anything else.'[16]

The negotiations were stuck. The only option was a Grand Coalition, but Schröder had described the possibility that the SPD could enter into a coalition headed by Merkel as out of the question and had rejected it with fury. Was it the final and non-negotiable red-line for Schröder? The answer is probably affirmative. However, and this is the crucial part, what Schröder thought was no longer of paramount importance. Müntefering now spoke on behalf of SPD; Schröder didn't.

The Chancellor had expected that the new party leader would play a subdued and subordinate role, but the outwardly meek Roman Catholic Rhinelander was not the loyal foot-soldier his boss had expected him to be. Müntefering, a former industrial management assistant who had worked in industry and as a trade union official but never attended university, was a traditional Social Democrat, but he did not lack ambition. He was personally interested in a deal, although on the day after the election he too was quoted as saying that the SPD 'would never accept Merkel as Chancellor'.[17] In fact he would be happy to serve as deputy to Merkel: being Deputy Chancellor would be a considerable promotion for a politician whose highest office thus far had been that of Secretary of State for Transport.

The problem for Schröder was that several other members of his party were ready to serve under Merkel as long as they were promoted or stayed in their ministerial posts. Party loyalty and loyalty to the Chancellor were in short supply among the Social Democrats in the autumn of 2005.

Müntefering communicated this to Merkel. At first he suggested what was known as the 'Israel solution' – a power-sharing arrangement under which the two party leaders would take turns as Chancellor. This model was based on the deal agreed between Israeli politicians Shimon Perez and Yitzhak Shamir after the Knesset elections in 1984 under which they each served two years. However, neither Müntefering himself nor Merkel were particularly interested in this option; it was clearly a bargaining chip to get negotiations underway. What Müntefering wanted was to secure a prominent position for himself, and to ensure that the SPD got the heaviest portfolios other than the chancellorship.

While Merkel and Müntefering were negotiating, the incumbent was watching helplessly from the sidelines. He knew that the game was up; there was no need to prolong the pain. On 3 October, a fortnight after the election, Schröder bowed out. He issued a short statement which concluded with the statement that he 'would not stand in the way of a process towards implementing the reforms initiated by me', nor would he 'stand in the way of establishing a stable government'. In some ways it was a rather sad end to an impressive career. The right-wing British politician Enoch Powell once observed that 'all political lives, unless they are cut off in midstream at a happy juncture, end in failure, because that is the nature of politics and of human affairs'. This may seem appropriate for Schröder, but it also seems unfair. Schröder, for all his machismo and bravura – and there was much of that – had achieved much, shown bravery and forced through reforms that were later hailed as the reason for Germany's economic success and resilience during the global financial crisis. Schröder prepared the way for his successor, and for the country's future prosperity.

However at this stage, in the second week of October a month after the election, this successor had not yet been found. The process of negotiation had been slightly delayed due to a by-election. One of the candidates in Precinct 160 in Dresden had died and a new election had to be held in the area. The CDU unsurprisingly captured the seat. This did not change the overall distribution of seats, but it added to Merkel's momentum. After a meeting with both Müntefering and Schröder it was in principle agreed that Merkel would become the new Chancellor, that Müntefering would become her deputy, and that the SPD would get six of the eleven cabinet posts.

'How do you do, Madam. Are you happy now?' the Irish journalist Judy Dempsey wanted to know at a press briefing about the agreement the two parties had reached during three weeks of extensive negotiations. Merkel made no reply. Maybe she was keen not to jinx her chances, or maybe she felt it inappropriate to engage in such emotional babble. In truth, she was not yet 'happy', if, indeed, this word was appropriate. Entering into a deal with the Social Democrats was one thing, securing the backing of her own party comrades and fellow conservatives was quite another task. Having engineered a deal with the Social Democrats, she still had to divide the portfolios within her own camp, to square up to the Governors, who would want to get influence in the form of representation at the federal level.

One thing that did not concern her was the fate of Paul Kirchhof. He met Merkel and the rest of the erstwhile campaign team on the day after the election, and that was the end of the relationship. Kirchhof was not to be part of the equation. The professor, who had been such a central – and maligned – part of the campaign, was bitter. His wife had suffered health problems as a result of harassment by the press and he had been bruised by the whole experience. This was of little concern to the CDU leadership, and Merkel dropped him without a word. There was no discussion of why her finance minister designate was no longer part of the line-up, no press release. Kirchhof was informed by CDU HQ that he was no longer needed.

Merkel's immediate problem was not a disgruntled professor from Heidelberg, but Edmund Stoiber, Governor of Bavaria. Stoiber had wanted to play a role in the new government. He had even attended some of the negotiation meetings with the Social Democrats. He wanted a big post, but he was aware that the chances of becoming finance minister were limited and that the idea of a super-minister was unlikely to become a reality. In short, there was not much in it for him, or for the CSU. In theory, the CSU could – as a formally independent party – leave the negotiations and stand outside the government, but this would not bring the government down. Black-Red would still have a majority without the CSU. Moreover, if Stoiber were to withdraw from the negotiations his party would be, like the PDS, a mere obstructionist force. Worse still, leaving the negotiations would probably mean that Stoiber's party would never again be taken seriously. Lastly, and this was becoming increasingly important, Stoiber was not in control of his political troops in the way that Merkel was in control of the parliamentary party. Many CSU members in the joint CDU/CSU parliamentary faction supported Merkel, and nearly all of them had supported her for the leadership on 20 September (we do not know who supported Merkel in the vote as the ballot was secret, but the overwhelming support of the parliamentarians speaks for itself). Lastly, and more troubling for Stoiber, some of the other prominent members of the CSU leadership – the likes of Günter Beckstein and Horst Seehofer – were waiting to take over and were, albeit discreetly, making it known that Stoiber had neglected his home-turf in pursuit of his ambitions in Berlin. With little prospect of becoming a leading politician in Berlin, the disgruntled Stoiber bowed out of the negotiations and declared that he would not be a member of the new government. Like Schröder, another big beast had left the national scene.

'IT'S A LONG, LONG WHILE FROM MAY TO DECEMBER'

These words from *September Song*, the popular American tune written by German émigré Kurt Weill, seemed to fit the situation. It was almost December before Angela Merkel finally formed a government. The last stage of the negotiations had been made easier by the resignation of Stoiber. But the SPD were keen not to be sold a deal too cheaply.

Müntefering had secured the foreign affairs and finance portfolios, which created some problems for Merkel. Peer Steinbrück, the former Governor of North Rhine Westphalia, whose defeat by Jürgen Rüttger in the state election had prompted the national election – became finance minister (although he was not a member of parliament) and Gerhard Schröder's former right-hand man, Frank-Walter Steinmeier, became Foreign Secretary. Müntefering became Deputy Chancellor and Minister for Employment. But Merkel could not be unhappy. The division of posts within the Cabinet was skewed towards Merkel's more socially liberal part of the Union. Her trusted allies all became ministers: Thomas de Maizière became Minister of the Chancellor's Office; Anette Schavan, a Catholic theologian and Merkel ally, became Minister for Education; and the new rising star, Dr Ursula von der Leyen, became Minister for Family, Pensioners, Women and Youth. The last was a new discovery of Merkel's, a medical doctor and mother of seven, and her appointment was a small coup. Christian Wulff, the otherwise traditionalist conservative Governor of Lower Saxony, was keen to ensure that his state was represented in the cabinet. Von der Leyen fitted the bill. Her father Ernst Albrecht had served as Governor of Lower Saxony from 1976 to 1990 and had tried, albeit unsuccessfully, to be nominated as the Union's candidate for Chancellor in 1980. Dr von der Leyen was herself a minister of social affairs in her home state. Wulff was pleased that his minister was among the chosen ones, and Merkel was pleased to have discovered another progressive young Lutheran woman.

Other critically important Governors were pleased too. Roland Koch was happy that his friend the arch-conservative Franz Josef Jung became Minister of Defence, a position in which – so it was thought at the time – he could do little damage. And Edmund Stoiber was pleased that Merkel appointed Horst Seehofer, one of Stoiber's rivals back home in Bavaria, to the relatively toothless post of Minister for Agriculture. Seehofer was to become Merkel's nemesis ten years later, but no one could have foreseen that in 2005.

The only one who was not happy was Jürgen Rüttgers. The Governor of North Rhine Westphalia was angry that no politician from his state, the largest in Germany, was represented in the cabinet, but Merkel could afford to ignore the Governor of the industrial state in the west of the country. 'Divide and rule' has been a maxim of politics from Julius Caesar to Machiavelli; it was also applied by Merkel. Her challengers among the Governors were split; some were happy, others less so.

To complete the picture, even Wolfgang Schäuble was happy. He was allocated the important and not unchallenging post of Minister of the Interior. At a time when international terrorism was on the agenda, and with the prospect of new legislation that would limit civil liberties, Schäuble had a tough task ahead, but he accepted the position with joy. Indeed, it seemed that his appointment to the cabinet led to a rapprochement and a reconciliation of sorts between Merkel and her predecessor as CDU leader. The two could even be described as political friends, though perhaps only in the sense of friendship defined by the playwright Bertolt Brecht: 'We are friends because I don't trust him.'

At precisely 11.52 am on 22 November 2005, at the relatively tender age of 51, Angela Dorothea Merkel became Chancellor of Germany. She was the youngest ever to serve in the post: Helmut Kohl (1982) was 52, Gerhard Schröder (1998) was 54, Willy Brandt (1969) and Helmut Schmidt (1974) were both 55, Kurt Georg Kiessinger (1966) was 60, Ludwig Erhard (1963) was 62 and Konrad Adenauer (1949) was 73. But unlike them Merkel was the first woman ever to lead Germany. She was soon to prove that her gender was no hindrance to governing.

CHAPTER 10

THE MAKING OF THE QUEEN OF EUROPE

F ACING A DISCIPLINARY DISCUSSION IS NEVER PLEASANT. JÜRGEN HAD always been a good and conscientious employee. He was generally well liked, although some had mocked him for his strong regional accent. He had been with the same business in one capacity or other for close to 20 years and had never been called in to see the boss of what in effect was the holding company.

He was wearing a dark suit and had slightly loosened his matching tie. One might have assumed that he was going to a funeral. He pursed his lips and looked down as he nervously brushed his thinning blond hair forward as if to hide the balding patch. As manager he was, of course, responsible, but he looked baffled. To be called to a meeting at the head office in Willy-Brandt-Straße 1 was not a good sign, especially not when the meeting was on the 7th floor. Two hours later, Jürgen emerged from the meeting. He had been given a warning. Jürgen Klinsmann was not any ordinary middle-manager, though that is how he was treated. He was the head coach of the national football (soccer) team and had been summoned to a meeting with the Chancellor after the German team had lost a training match to Italy by four goals to one. Soccer fans – including readers of the tabloid *Bild* – will tell you that Germany often loses to Italy (indeed, three months later they would again be defeated by their southern neighbours). Such details might have been known to the Chancellor, who often claimed to be a bit of a football connoisseur, and football was part of her game plan for her second year in power.

The defeat by Italy was not part of this plan, hence the somewhat unusual disciplinary action. In 2006, for the first time since 1974, the

FIFA World Cup was to be held in Germany. The summer was intended to be a celebration, a reason to be proud to be German. Sixty years of atonement and apology for past sins could now be transformed into something approaching normality. That was the plan: Germany was to become an ordinary country again; flying the flag to celebrate the achievements of her national heroes on the football pitch was to be the new norm, just as in other countries. Merkel had reason to be optimistic. For the first time since 1990, when West Germany had won the trophy a few months before reunification, there was a real prospect of the unified Germany becoming world champions, something most German fans considered close to a birthright and a natural state of affairs. Michael Ballack – the German captain and star player – had been born Görlitz in East Germany, and in many ways he and his teammates represented the new Germany. Some (like the other star player, Miroslav Klose) had even been born outside Germany, in his case in Poland. The team personified the new integrated and multicultural Germany.

The defeat by Italy was a shock to the ruling classes and their plans. Whereas the football fans and the pundits were magnanimous in defeat, the politicians were not. Norbert Barthle, a CDU member of parliament, demanded an inquiry. The former physical education teacher and President of the German Skiing Association was appalled. He demanded action. Frau Merkel summoned Klinsmann, Franz Beckenbauer (the former national coach and the organiser of the tournament), and Theo Zwanziger, the head of the German Football Association, to the Chancellor's Office. Here they were called upon to explain themselves. Why, the Chancellor inquired, did Klinsmann change from the traditional 3-5-2 system to the 4-4-2 system, which had proved so disastrous against the Italians? In most other countries sport is sport and it would be rather unusual for the head of government to get involved in something as seemingly mundane as this. For Merkel the prospect of a fiasco at the World Cup was a project management issue – something that needed to be sorted out through rational debate and planning. Armed with statistics, graphs and comparisons with other countries' preparations, the Chancellor discussed the issue and came up with a plan. (Later in the year Germany finished third, and the once hapless Klinsmann went on to coach the American national soccer team.)

Football was a side-show, however. Other issues were on the agenda: challenges her predecessors Kohl and Schröder had left unresolved or actively ignored. In March 2006 when the meeting with Klinsmann took place, Merkel's way of solving problems had already become well established. Her careful approach to policy issues, addressing them as if they were civil engineering projects, was not limited to her dealings with Klinsmann and his colleagues. She had used exactly the same approach when she had coaxed her European colleagues into agreeing on a new budget for the European Union. This was, as usual, difficult.

MERKEL'S FIRST EUROPEAN SUMMIT

It is a common misperception, especially in Britain, that the Germans are in favour of the EU. This is not unequivocally the case. At the time when Merkel came to power 46 per cent of Germans were of the opinion that Germany had not benefited from membership. One of the reasons for this was that many – with justification – felt that Germany was subsidising the other countries in the EU. During the long reign of Helmut Kohl other countries' unease about Germany's increasingly strong role in Europe was dealt with by opening the German chequebook. Under Gerhard Schröder some efforts were made to limit Germany's contributions to Brussels' seemingly bottomless coffers. Speaking to Parliament shortly after his election in 1998 Schröder made it clear that:

> We cannot and will not solve the problems of Europe with the German chequebook. Without more fairness in our contributions the people of our country will distance themselves from Europe rather than being won over by the prospect of more integration.[1]

Schröder's problem had been that since the early 1980s the United Kingdom had paid a smaller than proportionate contribution, a so-called 'rebate'. Back then most of the common budget was allocated to subsidies for farmers. This so-called Common Agricultural Policy (CAP) disproportionally benefited countries with relatively large agricultural sectors. Because Britain had a relatively small number of farmers, Margaret Thatcher had secured a deal that ensured smaller net contributions from Britain, though the British were still net contributors to the European Community.

Though vehemently resisted by France, the proportion of the budget allocated to farmers was set to be reduced, and with this reduction the justification for the British rebate would no longer apply. But Schröder did not achieve his overall aim at the summit in 1999. Tony Blair, the British Prime Minister, was at the high point of his career and was able to block any attempts to make his country pay more. True, Schröder was able to claim some credit for having reduced Germany's overall contribution. Five years earlier Helmut Kohl had accepted that it was necessary to reach 'into a deep [German] pocket to finance a sharp rise in spending';[2] Schröder reversed this trend. But he did little else. In many ways Schröder – the bruiser who liked to play hardball-politics at home – cut a rather pitiful figure at the European summits. His command of English was poor, and for someone who acted on impulse and was used to cutting deals in the corridors of power, dealing with politicians from different countries in a foreign language was a difficult challenge.

When Merkel took over in October 2005 the budget negotiations were already in full swing. The German Ministry of Finance was fighting tooth and nail to ensure that the largest economy in Europe did not have to pay a disproportional share of the budget. The reason for the Germans' unwillingness to pay was not merely political but also financial. Having been the richest country in Europe measured by average national income in 1980, Germany had dropped to eleventh place. The cost of reunification – effectively the incorporation of a third-world country – had taken its toll. Further, the accession of several East and Central European countries to the EU had created new demands as these countries, reasonably enough, expected to get the same benefits as other newcomers, such as Greece, Spain and Portugal, had received two decades before in the 1980s.

The European Commission, in an attempt to reach a compromise, had suggested that each country should pay 1.24 per cent of its GDP into the common coffers. This was blankly refused by Germany. Merkel not only wanted to pay less, she also wanted to address the more general problems such as Britain's rebate and the bloated budget for the moribund agricultural sector which – in Germany's view – was little more than a large and unprofitable job-creation project. Expectations of what Merkel would be able to achieve were low – lower than they should have been. As we have seen, Merkel already had considerable experience of multilateral negotiations from her time as Minister for the Environment. However few seemed to be aware of this.

The negotiations did not take place in a vacuum. Another issue that complicated the debate was the fate of the European Constitution. For several years delegates from the different EU countries had worked on a document inspired by the US Constitution, which was intended to put the EU on a more formal constitutional footing. Valéry Giscard d'Estaing, the former French President who had chaired the negotiations, had not been able to come up with an elegant document. The resulting 'Constitution' was in many ways a step away from the ideal – or the nightmare – of a 'United States of Europe'. Under the new document the role of national parliaments was recognised. The much maligned phrase 'an ever closer union among the peoples of Europe', which had justified continued transfers of powers to the EU, had been amended with the caveat that all decisions should be 'taken as closely as possible to the citizen'. But this move away from centralism was poorly explained. The people of Europe still largely believed that the Constitution was yet another example of the seemingly inexorable concentration of power in Brussels. This was fatal. The problem for the drafters – and for the governments of Europe – was that many Europeans were less than enthusiastic about the document.

While a referendum in Spain in the spring of 2005 resulted in a 'yes' for the Constitution, similar plebiscites held in France and in the Netherlands in June of the same year led to clear rejections. That two of the six founder nations of the European Community (the others being Belgium, Luxembourg, Italy and Germany) vetoed the document meant that it was legally void. This was an embarrassment for the political class in Europe. Although a referendum in Luxembourg in the autumn of 2005 returned a 'yes' vote, the document was legally dead and politically on life support.

It was in the shadow of this public vote of no confidence and without a budget deal that the leaders gathered at the Justus Lipsius Building in the centre of Brussels on 19 December 2006. Only a month before, Merkel had been sworn in as the eighth Chancellor of the Federal Republic of Germany. Now, she was facing the big boys, Jacques Chirac and Tony Blair, and a cast of other seasoned politicians with years of experience negotiating at the European level.

The relationship with France was, as always, central. While nominally a conservative, French President Jacques Chirac had had a good rapport with Merkel's predecessor, Gerhard Schröder. Both men were more or less ill-disguised critics of President George W. Bush, and it would probably be possible to accuse both of a certain element of anti-Americanism. Merkel acknowledged the importance of the Franco-German relationship – as, indeed, all German Chancellors since Konrad Adenauer had done. On her second day in office, on 23 October 2005, she flew to Paris to meet Monsieur Chirac, who provided her the full treatment, complete with marching bands and national anthems.

Chirac put on a good show, but he had seen better days. The defeat in the referendum a few months before was a significant set-back, and there was something almost pitiful about the man who greeted Merkel at the Elysée Palace; something akin to an aging playboy trying to hide the fact that his charm and good looks belong to yesteryear.

Merkel was polite, playing along with Chirac's delusions of Gallic *grandeur*, and in public she kept quiet apart from reciting the obligatory platitudes of peace, cooperation and the unbroken bonds between the two former enemies. At their one-hour meeting, Merkel had elegantly avoided the thorny issue of the European Constitution, but she gave the Frenchman the support he needed and craved. The failed referendum was Chirac's greatest headache, and his mind was not focused on the EU budget. Merkel, on the other hand, was less concerned about the failed constitution since the existing Maastricht Treaty (which had been put in place in 1993) worked tolerably well. All her attention was on the EU finances. Although the meeting was short, the new Chancellor managed to nudge the French President towards a budget, though few – including Chirac – were aware of this at the time. Merkel's use of what the French call *la force tranquille* (quiet force) paid off a month later.

Tony Blair was politically a different kettle of fish. The former barrister had been a political superstar when he replaced the Conservative Prime Minister John Major in 1997. Blair had implemented a number of reforms in his home country, including a peace treaty in Northern Ireland, and had introduced a minimum wage. But many of his supporters had been left disappointed by his lack of resolve and his unwillingness to risk unpopularity on domestic issues. Elected as a liberal, his agenda had been conservative: privatisations, foreign policy adventures and the use of market forces in healthcare and education. After 2003, and his decision to join George W. Bush and the 'coalition of the willing' in the war against Iraq, many of his erstwhile voters had turned against him with a ferocity that bordered on hatred. Notwithstanding this he had managed – though with great difficulty – to win a third term as Prime Minister in May 2005.

Blair no longer had the boyish charm and charisma of his earliest years in power, but he was still a towering political figure. Merkel, though a very different politician, was sympathetic towards her British colleague. The two had met a year before the 2005 election in Germany. Blair was in Berlin on official business and a meeting was organised between him and the leader of the opposition in Parliament. Blair's chief of staff, Jonathan Powell, later remembered how Merkel made an impression on the British politician. Unlike the cigar-smoking, macho Gerhard Schröder, Merkel seemed strangely honest, meek, and yet businesslike. Without being starstruck, 'the soon-to-be chancellor plonked herself down in front of him [Blair] and said disarmingly, "I have ten problems" – and then began to list them, starting with a lack of charisma'. This, at any rate, was how Powell remembered her first encounter with her British colleague.[3] Blair was impressed. Indeed, so close were relations that Blair accepted a request that Thomas de Maizière (Merkel's chief of staff) be allowed to shadow his opposite number in London. 'For two weeks [de Maizière] accompanied Blair's chief of staff in the Cabinet Office in Downing Street, learning about the legislative process, the passing of laws, how to manage the secret service and [other] procedural rules.'[4]

Blair may have had reason to believe that he and Merkel were on friendly terms when they met again in Brussels, but in politics personal friendships are at best skin-deep. As in war and professional sport, politicians of the highest calibre double-cross and abandon their personal friends when this is required to reach their goals. That is the nature of international relations, and to do otherwise is a sign of weakness. To take advantage of a situation – even using dirty tricks – earns politicians respect.

Blair was nominally the president of the summit in Brussels. Britain had held the rotating presidency of the European Union in the last six months of 2005, but the UK government had not accomplished much. After negotiations in the evening of 16 December, Blair had withdrawn to the spacious presidential suite on the fifth floor of the building. Meanwhile Merkel was busy at work. Unlike her predecessor, Merkel was able to converse with all the other leaders in English. She spoke to almost everyone individually, including the French President who – unusually for a Frenchman of his generation (he was born in 1932) – had learned English when he was an exchange student at Harvard in the 1950s. Building on the favourable impression Merkel had made on Chirac at their first meeting, she found him receptive towards her proposals and – without saying so in public – impressed by Merkel's command of detail and professionalism.

Her tenacity paid off. At three o'clock in the morning, Chirac and Merkel reached an agreement. The money for the Common Agricultural Policy should be reduced, Britain had to give up some of the rebate, and the countries' individual contributions should be limited to 1.04 per cent, significantly lower than proposed by the European Commission.

Blair was surprised to see his German colleague in the morning. While the two were talking, Jacques Chirac was presenting the deal as 'a Franco-German agreement'. In reality he had given way on the agricultural subsidies, but he was keen to sell the deal as a success for France and as a much-needed sign that he was still a player on the European stage despite the outcome of the referendums earlier in the year. Chirac's public statement left Blair in an awkward position. As chairman he needed a deal. Without a deal he would be seen as an ineffective leader. But Blair also knew that any concessions on the rebate negotiated by Margaret Thatcher would be seized upon by the Conservative opposition back in London.

Merkel was keen not to humiliate Blair. She stated that the deal was close to Britain's 'red lines'. Before the summit, Blair had proposed an annual contribution equalling 1.03 of GDP. He had also said that Britain would only give up its rebate if the contributions to the agricultural sector were agreed. In fact, the Chancellor told her surprised British colleague, Britain had actually achieved what Blair had set out to accomplish. Basically, she had been negotiating on the British Prime Minister's behalf. He could now take the credit for it, subject to agreement by Luxembourg and Austria. Blair was persuaded by Merkel and after meeting her briefly spoke to Chirac. The two men disliked each other, and the enmity had deepened in recent months. Paris had been considered the favourite to host the 2012 Olympic Games, but shrewd tactics and behind-the-scenes diplomacy by Blair had secured the games for London. The meeting was short, polite and businesslike, as one would expect from an encounter between men with large egos who dislike each other.

The two men were assured that Merkel had negotiated a deal they had both sought. They took the lift up to the 7th floor where they were met by Merkel. She had been busy shuffling the chairs around so as to make the atmosphere more conducive to an agreement. The leaders of the big countries were joined by Jean-Claude Juncker, the Prime Minister of Luxembourg, who failed to get a deal at the previous summit, and by the Austrian Chancellor Wolfgang Schüssel, who would take over the rotating presidency after Britain. Merkel small-talked with the Austrian and the Luxembourger – they all speak German as their mother tongue. She stressed that it was important that this was a deal agreed by the whole continent, and then she presented her plan in a calm fashion and 'walled in her opponents with facts'.[5] By midday she had secured a deal.

The diplomats were impressed, probably because they had expected very little. The result of the summit was a change in dynamic, as an EU diplomat said to the *Guardian* newspaper: 'Angela Merkel has done two things at the summit: she has been constructive, and she is not Gerhard Schröder. Schröder, acting as Chirac's mini-me, used to stitch up a deal before European summits. This has not happened this time and her constructive behaviour has made everyone more constructive too.'[6] It was that afternoon, barely a month after Merkel had become Chancellor, that the world entered the 'Age of Merkel', a period dominated by a politician who was 'capable of ruthless political management of public finances and strategy but was also there at the World Cup'.[7]

After the New Year the World Cup was Merkel's next challenge. She dealt with this in the same way as she had dealt with the European budget. Internationally she was well regarded, though part of this was also to do with the novelty factor and with the tiredness – and occasionally contempt – in which the old guard, Chirac, Bush and Blair, were held. Merkel, being a woman and a plain speaker, was different, and this translated into positive poll ratings at home and respect abroad.

FEDERAL REFORM

Before welcoming the world to the World Cup, Merkel presented her legislative programme in March. What she proposed was an ambitious plan for a constitutional reform of Germany's federal system. Federalism reform was intended to redress the imbalances that had been created after the reunification of Germany, and the plan comprised a wholesale reform of the division of labour between the individual states and the federal government in Berlin.

To understand the significance of the reform it is necessary to outline the history and background of the debate about German federalism. Federalism is a system with which Americans are familiar. The basic tenet of the system is that certain policies are decided at state level whereas others are the preserve of the federal government. The system was – at least in practice – the brainchild of the American founding fathers who wrote the US Constitution, though the original inventor of federalism was the Dutch political theorist Johannes Althusius who championed the idea in the seventeenth century. But the federalism adopted by West Germany after World War II was not merely a foreign implant imposed upon Germany by the victors. Germany had always been a diverse nation, or rather a loose confederation of small kingdoms sharing a similar culture and the same language. Germany in anything like its present form had existed only since 1870, when the Prussian Chancellor Otto von Bismarck established the German Empire, a federal-like structure comprising 27 regional entities. The Weimar Republic had similar federal characteristics, but these were destroyed by Hitler, who imposed an unbending system of centralisation known as *Gleichschaltung* (making equal or similar). When East Germany was established it too adopted a centralised system based on Lenin's Soviet model of 'Democratic Centralism', a system in which the vanguard of the Communist party made all the important decisions with scant regard for local and regional differences.

The 1949 Basic Law was explicitly aimed at re-establishing the federal structures. The fact that these were diametrically different from those that had existed under Hitler's regime, and to the structures that continued to exist in East Germany, showed that West Germany was radically different from its National Socialist predecessor and its Communist neighbour. The agreement in 1949 was roughly that the central government controlled foreign affairs, immigration and defence and collected taxes, whereas the states were in charge of education, police and cultural affairs. In addition the Basic Law enumerated a number of areas in which the federal government and the states were to share powers, above all nature conservation and health.[8] While the federal system and the principle of democracy could never be changed, only a two-thirds majority was required to change all other parts of Basic Law. Now Merkel wanted to reform the Basic Law.

The American lawyer Bruce Ackerman famously observed that changes in the fundamental political and legal framework of a state take place in the 'constitutional moments', 'during rare periods of heightened political consciousness', when political parties put aside the activities of 'normal politics' and leave behind the pursuit of 'their own narrow interests'.[9] Legal scholars and philosophers will, no doubt, question whether the period 2005 to 2009 was indeed such a 'constitutional moment' in Germany. Merkel is unlikely to have given the matter much theoretical thought; that was not her style nor her inclination. But in practice her thinking ran parallel to Ackerman's. 'Only a Grand Coalition,' said Merkel at a press conference in the end of March, 'would have been able to enact such a reform.'[10] With the formation of the Grand Coalition the two largest political parties in Germany were able to put aside their narrow interests and enact the necessary reforms, and 2005 could be a 'constitutional moment' in Germany.

There was reason to be optimistic. Previous reforms had ended in failure, or at most in compromise solutions that did not address the fundamental problems. In the early 1990s, shortly after reunification, Helmut Kohl had set up the so-called Independent Federal Commission. The independence of the commission was questionable. Headed by a CDU politician, Dr Bernhard Vogel (the former Governor of Kohl's home state, Rhineland-Palatinate), its impartiality was questionable, and in any case the commission was only able to recommend small changes, such as the relocation of certain state institutions to the newly established federal states in the East and a few changes necessitated by the establishment of the European Union by the Maastricht Treaty in 1991.

During the late 1990s and early 2000s it had become clear that the existing constitutional framework was not fit for purpose, and that the Vogel Commission's proposals were woefully inadequate. The Basic Law was never intended to become a permanent feature. It had been drafted with the intention of being a stop-gap, a provisional charter that was to be revised once the two Germanys had been unified. Indeed, it was called the Basic Law rather than the Constitution to stress that it was but a temporary solution.

In October 2003, while Gerhard Schröder was still Chancellor, another attempt was made to change the constitution. Schröder appointed Edmund Stoiber as chairman of the Constitutional Convention. This was to signal that constitutional reform was a matter that cut across party lines. But the work of the Constitutional Convention came to naught. With growing disagreement between the two blocks the negotiations broke down in December 2004 when the states refused to accept that responsibility for education policy be transferred from them to the centre. The stalemate was less a result of actual disagreements than a reflection of the party political battle at the time. Neither the SPD nor the Union were opposed to reform.

Thus, during the coalition negotiations, both the SPD and the CDU/CSU stressed the need to revisit the constitutional issue. Merkel, sensing that there was common ground, seized the opportunity and was able to win a commitment to rewrite the Basic Law. However, in a move characteristic of her leadership style, she presented the new constitution as a pragmatic issue and not one of high jurisprudential theory or lofty philosophical principle. After months of deliberations within the Grand Coalition, when Merkel finally presented her plan to Parliament in March she spoke about consumer protection and the need to cut red tape, not about rights, justice or legal philosophy.

But this pragmatism and focus on 'bread-and-butter issues' was not reflected in the outcome a few weeks later. When Merkel presented the agreement, negotiated by CDU's Günther Oettinger and SPD's Peter Struck, the result was more procedural and contained few issues that interested ordinary voters. Oettinger and Struck came from polar opposite sides of politics and their careers could not have been more different. Whereas Struck had been a chief whip and in charge of party discipline in the SPD faction in the late 1990s, Oettinger had a basis in state politics as a Governor in Baden-Württemberg. Both men were partisan politicians, but they were also both protestants and neither of them represented Bavaria. By appointing Oettinger, Merkel was able to keep the three vice-chairmen of the CDU, the Governors Roland Koch (Hesse), Christian Wulff (Lower Saxony) and Jürgen Rüttgers (North Rhine Westphalia), away from the decision-making. The three state Governors could have made life difficult for the coalition and for the passage of federal reform if they had been in key negotiating positions, but they were not politically able to block a reform negotiated by Oettinger. It was 'divide and rule' once again.

The stumbling block was the German Senate, the Upper House of the German federal Parliament. Previously this chamber, composed of representatives from the state governments, had been able to veto substantial parts of the legislation passed by the Lower House. This had led to gridlock, especially in 1997 when the then Leader of the Opposition, Gerhard Schröder, as Governor of Lower Saxony and as President of the German Senate, had vetoed Helmut Kohl's tax reform. The Social Democrats too had experienced the problems posed by a recalcitrant upper house; indeed, the reason Schröder felt forced to call new elections in 2005 was in response to CDU/CSU obstruction of his policies in the Senate.

Merkel and her Social Democrat deputy Franz Müntefering were determined that something similar could not happen again, but they were equally aware that a reduction in the states' ability to block legislation came with a price-tag. Merkel proposed through Oettinger and Struck that the states be given more power over education – something that was especially popular in the south – but that the Senate in return should be limited in its ability to block legislation. The result was that the Senate would in practice be unable to block legislation dealing with economic policy. After reform the Senate would be able to block roughly only half the laws they had been able to block before.

The media hailed the result of the negotiations as something of a coup for Angela Merkel. This might seem a bit of an exaggeration as she was not, unlike in the case of the EU budget, personally involved in the negotiations. But to say that Merkel was merely a bystander, someone who was fortunate that the reform was agreed under her watch, would be equally fallacious. Leadership is not always about micromanagement and putting in all-nighters. Leaders are also measured by their ability to delegate. 'Leadership,' as US President Dwight D. Eisenhower reportedly said, 'is the art of getting someone else to do something you want done.' Merkel had succeeded in this endeavour.

THE FALL OF THE CROWN PRINCES

In December 2006, 80 per cent of her compatriots felt that Merkel was doing a good job. The reasons for this support were manifold. Gerhard Schröder had not covered himself in glory and the enactment of the controversial, but probably necessary, Hartz IV reforms meant that he was disliked even by stalwart supporters of the SPD. But the overall reason for Merkel's popularity was, so the opinion polls suggested, also related to the manner in which she carried out her newly acquired duties. Schröder's image – his uncanny likeness to a used-car salesman – did not inspire a lot of trust. Merkel had a more than 17 per cent lead over her predecessor on the crucial issue of 'solving future problems'.

Whereas Schröder had appealed to male voters and to those who liked raw, robust and traditional politics, complete with a certain misogynist attitude, Merkel had followed a pragmatic, quiet, but equally determined approach. Schröder and many of Merkel's rivals within the Union revelled in political wrestling matches. Merkel, by contrast, did not.

At the beginning of the year her rivals – the likes of Koch, Wulff and Rüttgers – in various ways fancied their chances of succeeding Merkel. The Grand Coalition was a temporary measure, a bit like the previous experiment in 1966-68. Back then Kurt Georg Kiesinger had merely prolonged the inevitable transfer of power from one block to another. Merkel, or so her rivals liked to think, was merely running a caretaker administration. After a year in power it was obvious that they too had underestimated her.

Her style of politics – meticulous preparation, a willingness to compromise and an improbably flirtatious charm – had disarmed many of her opponents, most notably her colleagues in the European Union. Her rivals in the Union were trained in the bare-knuckle school of politics: for them the essence of politics was power, intimidation and bravado. She hated all this: 'I find the tendency that certain male politicians have constantly to assert themselves unpleasant. Many people puff themselves up and try to drown out each other's voices in order to impose themselves. When that happens I feel almost physically oppressed and would prefer not to be there,' she said.[11]

That Merkel felt this way was not a surprise to her rivals. Indeed, it was merely confirmation of her perceived weakness and her inability to cope with the rough-and-tumble of politics. For these men politics *was* street-fighting. Merkel did not accept this, so she would falter, her opponents thought. Merkel was aware that they were a threat. She was also aware that she was engaged in a series of battles on several fronts: in the European Council of Ministers, in the coalition, and within her own party. The last was in many respects the most difficult one.

People join a political party because they have strong opinions. They canvas for a politician because he or she takes a strong stand on an issue. Members of political parties are therefore typically more extreme or radical than the average person. Notwithstanding her surprisingly good results throughout 2006, Merkel had reason to be apprehensive when the CDU met for their annual conference in the southeastern city of Dresden in November.

Tactically, Merkel had done a great deal to neutralise her rivals. 'Hug them close' is a standard political maxim. To prevent Roland Koch, Christian Wulff and Jürgen Rüttgers from scheming, the three had been given the relatively meaningless title of deputy party leader. Formally these deputies (there were five of them altogether) were members of the Bundesvorstand, in practice the party's executive board. This board – which also included members of parliament and representatives of other groups such as the chairman of the protestant caucus, the Speaker of Parliament and a few other dignitaries – was little more than a talking shop. But formally speaking, the Bundesvorstand decided, top-down, the priorities for the party and could even dictate how individual members of parliament should vote. Such power, even if it is rarely exercised, comes at a price. Every year the delegated representatives of the party's local chapters elect the party leader as well as the deputy party leaders. 2006 was no different.

It was on 27 November 2006 that it dawned upon Merkel's rivals that they had miscalculated her power and the support she held within the party. 'The feathers of the crown-princes were ruffled' was the conclusion of the German Press Agency. Merkel had gone to great length to cultivate the rank and file. After the policy achievements in the first half of the year the period from August to November had been relatively quiet. This paid off at the party conference where 93 per cent of the party delegates endorsed Angela Merkel and re-elected her as chairman of the party. The deputy leaders, Koch, Rüttgers and Wulff, also faced the verdict of the party members. Normally such votes are a *fait accompli,* a time to show unity and to prove to the outside world that there are no disagreements within the party. Not this time; none of Merkel's three conservative rivals received the endorsement of the conference; Rüttgers merely managed to scrape over 50 per cent and both Koch and Wulff languished in the mid-60s. By contrast, Annette Schavan – the federal education minister, who was one year younger than Merkel – was endorsed by 85 per cent of the delegates. What precise role Merkel and her cabal played in this has been debated, but few questioned her involvement. 'If this was planned, then it was a tactical stroke of genius,' was the admiring, if anonymous, comment of one of her opponents.[12] That Koch and his group were weakened and that they had underestimated the mood in the party was beyond dispute. Conservative forces within the party, groups that resisted challenges to established German culture and the conservative values that went with it, had lost. Moreover, they had lost to a woman – Dr Schavan – who was well-known for her positive attitude towards multiculturalism. Indeed, the following year the federal education minister actively encouraged immigration – again to the annoyance of both her conservative and her Socialist colleagues. And Merkel, who had urged the party to modernise, embrace globalisation and become the party of 'the workers as well as that of the millionaires' got a six-minute standing ovation for her speech. She even got endorsement for a proposal to increase employee representation on company boards. It was not conservative policy, not what her opponents on the right espoused, but a signal that the CDU was becoming the party of the centre, rather like the Zentrumspartei to which the founder of the CDU, Konrad Adenauer, belonged between the two World Wars.

PERSON OF THE YEAR

At the end of 2006, *Time* magazine named Angela Merkel a 'Person Who Mattered'. A little over a year before, the 51-year-old politician had become the first female Chancellor of Germany, which in itself was a historic achievement. But that this alone should merit the prestigious accolade seemed, perhaps, slightly disproportionate. Other countries had female presidents or prime ministers. Ellen Johnson-Sirleaf became President of Liberia, Michelle Bachelet took office as President of Chile and Han Myung-sook became South Korea's first female Prime Minister in 2006. Yet these women, impressive though they were, did not match Merkel. Being leader of one of the world's largest economies gives status. Few would have disagreed that Merkel – in *Time*'s words – was 'the most powerful woman politician in the world'.

Merely holding a position is not a source of greatness, however: politics is action, an ability to get things done, a knack for getting individuals to compromise, give way and make agreements – these are the hallmarks of statecraft. To be a stateswoman you must be able to implement the decisions and, as importantly, communicate these achievements. Did Merkel do this in the first full year of her reign?

Time clearly believed so, noting that 'Merkel mended fences with Washington' and that she 'had proved a tough and effective problem solver'. Though which problems exactly she had solved was not specified, and, to be fair, mending the fences seemed less of an achievement given that it was her predecessor Gerhard Schröder who had fallen out with George W. Bush. *Time* also pointed out that unemployment had fallen to single-digit figures, but even her cheerleaders in New York acknowledged that Merkel had benefited from some economic reforms introduced by her predecessor. Merkel became a political superstar in 2006. Not to be outdone, *Forbes* magazine placed Merkel at the top of their list. Merkel beat Condoleezza Rice, the US Secretary of State, who placed second. The business magazine enthusiastically wrote that Merkel had been 'dazzling world leaders, including Tony Blair and George W. Bush'. The voters were not quite as impressed as the foreign media. Her popularity fell to 55 per cent in the middle of 2006, following an increase in General Sales Tax from 16 to 19 per cent. In fact, she was more unpopular in the middle of 2006 than she was in January 2015 after the massive influx of refugees. But few questioned her ability to survive. To govern you have to do unpopular things – and do them early. There was no sense of crisis, let alone calls for her to resign.

But all this was politics, and most people do not think about politics all the time, at least not during normal political times. For most of Merkel's compatriots 2006 was remembered for the football World Cup which took place in Germany – and for a strange disciplinary hearing involving a highly paid middle manager who later redeemed himself (Germany finished third in the tournament and Klinsmann was awarded the *Bundesverdienstkreuz*, the highest civil honour for a German). There was a growing confidence in Germany. Unemployment fell, and citizens were taking pride in being German. Some were disturbed by this. The Centre for Football and Conflict at the Institute for Interdisciplinary Research on Conflict and Violence found that German fans grew more nationalistic during the 2006 World Cup than during past championships. And a peer-reviewed scientific study found similarities between the 1936 Olympics organised by Hitler and the more recent World Cup.[13]

Merkel's honeymoon was not to last.

THE BANKING CRISIS

The helicopter landed at the Chancellery at 2.58 pm.

'Mrs Chancellor,' said her bodyguard, 'We are back.'

'I'm sorry,' said Mrs Merkel, looking slightly startled as if she had been asleep for a few seconds.[14] She gathered her papers, greeted the crew of the blue Eurocopter Super Puma and stepped out into the sunshine. She always greeted the staff. Maybe it was her own insecurity as an *Ossi* from East Germany that made her acknowledge the myriad of ushers, drivers, security staff and secretaries that surrounded her, or maybe it was just the good manners that had been instilled into her as a pastor's daughter in Templin. Whatever the reason, it is unlikely that she gave it much thought as she walked to the office on 10 October 2008. If she had listened carefully she would have heard the gentle buzz of Berliners enjoying a blue-sky day in the Tiergarten, the large public park next to the heliport.

But the Chancellor had little time to enjoy the weather or, indeed, ponder her manners. While her compatriots were preparing for a carefree weekend, seemingly oblivious to the gathering storm on the financial markets, Frau Merkel was facing the greatest crisis of her three-year reign as head of the Grand Coalition. Barely a year before she too had been largely unaware of the finer points of international finance. Indeed, her relatively limited knowledge of economics had previously been her Achilles heel. In the televised debate before the 2005 election, Merkel had confused the basic economic concepts of net and gross national income.

But now she had no choice but to become an expert. While she was walking towards her new office building on Willy-Brandt-Straße 1, the Dow Jones Index in New York was shedding 20 per cent of its value, and earlier in the week the leading shares on the Nikkei Index in Tokyo had lost a quarter of their worth. After the collapse of the American Lehman Brothers Bank the deluge had hit Germany. The financial crisis had become international and threatened to destroy western capitalism. Some warned that the crisis could be deeper than in the 1930s. This needed to be avoided at all costs. Merkel wanted to stop the rot; hence her determination. She had already been in power for three years, but it was only now that she was really being tested. Over the following days she established the reputation that enabled her to be referred to as the most powerful woman in the world, and the second most powerful person after Barack Obama. 'This was, so to speak, my introduction to a completely new preoccupation,' she would recall years later.[15]

There was a resolve in her voice as she sat down in her office on the sixth floor and looked at the plan.

'Frau Baumann, could you please . . .' said the Chancellor to her chief of staff without finishing her sentence. Although Beate Baumann had been Merkel's chief of staff since 1995, the Chancellor still insisted on the formal tone and always addressed her trusted advisor by her surname and the formal '*Sie*'.

'Yes, Chancellor,' said Mrs Baumann.

'Get me Herr Steinbrück on the line, would you please?' said
Merkel as she flicked through a pile of papers. It was necessary that Peer
Steinbrück, who was at a meeting of G7 finance ministers in Washington, should be on board before she went ahead with the plan. Leaving
the finance minister out of the loop would not be prudent. For while the
relationship between Merkel's CDU/CSU and its junior coalition partner, the Social Democrats, was never easy, marriages of convenience are
difficult and there is always the suspicion that the other party is thinking
strategically.

Party political strategy always plays a subconscious role for politicians, but on this day there was a sense that other things were more
important. This was reflected in the conversation between Merkel and
Steinbrück. We do not know what the Chancellor said to her Social
Democratic colleague, but we know that he gave her the green light to
go ahead with the operation.

Normally, the tone in the office was jolly and cheerful. Merkel
would tell jokes and imitate voices (she has, perhaps surprisingly, a gift
for impersonating her colleagues), but not this evening. She had work to
do and it would be a long night.

This, the most difficult of crises, had started a few months before.
But Merkel, to the annoyance of her colleagues, had done nothing – or
nothing drastic anyway. This was to change now, and the cause was the
collapse of the German mortgage lender Hypo Real Estate Holding
AG, then Germany's second-largest property lender. Only a year before
Merkel had rejected the use of public money and had unequivocally
stated the neo-liberal gospel that 'embarking on an expansionary fiscal policy could prove an unnecessary and costly venture'.[16] Now she
changed her mind.

Merkel had been elected as a conservative, as someone who supported free enterprise. Now she seemed to change her spots and directly
attacked countries that had allowed the markets and the bankers a free
reign. 'Sadly, backed by the governments in Great Britain and the US,
they have resisted voluntary regulation. I strongly advocate that we use
the latest crisis to draw the necessary conclusions.'[17]

It was this package she started implementing that evening. With
one stroke Hypo Real Estate was bailed out and the government took

over large stakes in all the leading banks. Not all the financial institutions were pleased to see their assets being nationalised, and Merkel's next moves – a ban on bonuses for banks in receipt of aid and a further cap on executive pay set at €500,000 – suggested that Mrs Merkel had been more radical than any previous Chancellor. To add to this, two weeks later the government won backing for a financial stimulus package to the tune of €50 billion. As she admitted in an interview with *Bild* on 11 March 2009, the banking crisis forced her to 'overstep boundaries and do things she would otherwise not have done'. Pragmatism, not political philosophy, was the watchword.

Her moves were popular with the voters. Her party's poll rating had fallen below that of the Social Democrats, but on 7 November, three weeks after Parliament had passed the emergency package and two days after the stimulus package, the CDU was five per cent ahead of its rival and coalition partner. More importantly, the action sent a signal to the markets that the German government was ready to take extreme measures. The drop in share prices and the economic malaise was halted. The first step was taken towards recovery. And leaders around the world saw that Merkel was willing to lead the way – even when this upset business leaders who normally supported the CDU. When this author met her in Brussels a few weeks later and asked her if it wasn't odd for a conservative government to pursue a policy of state intervention, she merely responded, 'Well, I would like as much free enterprise as possible, but we should also balance this with as much state intervention as necessary.'[18] This sounded very much like the classic doctrine of the German economist, Walter Eucken:

> If there should be more or less state intervention is the wrong question. It is a qualitative not a quantitative question. The state should neither steer the economic process nor should it run the businesses themselves. The public sector make plans for the framework of the economy, but it should not plan the economy itself.[19]

Asked if this was her inspiration, Merkel looked at me with her blue eyes and smiled overbearingly but patiently, 'Perhaps.' What political or economic doctrine she was following was, so it seemed, of secondary importance. The aim was to solve a problem, not to delve into the finer points of economic theory. And rightly so.

It somehow became Merkel's fate to react to crises rather than to implement preconceived manifesto commitments or party platforms. But perhaps that suited her; perhaps her place in history was secured precisely because she had the fortune to gain power exactly as the world economy was hit by a perfect storm. 'She has no goal. No ideology,' lamented the philosopher Jürgen Habermas over breakfast in Princeton in the spring of 2013. But after a reflective pause the icon of the liberal left added, 'She is very bright. You should never underestimate her.'

CHAPTER 11

POTATO SOUP, THE POPE AND RE-ELECTION

'OH, YES, I AM A VERY GOOD COOK. POTATO SOUP AND BEEF OLIVE,' giggled Angela Merkel. It seemed a bit odd, but elections are often like this. And here she was on 16 May 2009 answering questions from listeners who had tuned in on RTL's *Bürgersprechrunde*, a programme that seemed to cater to the more senior among the voters.

Merkel was careful to sound polite and genuinely interested. She was keen to come across as knowledgeable about all manner of issues. Not that the format tested the limits of her political knowledge, let alone gave rise to many revelations. The questions were, to put it diplomatically, rather tame. This was hardly Merkel's fault. The questions had been selected by the presenters, RTL's editor Peter Kloeppel and his colleague Maria Gresz from Spiegel TV. The moderators had carefully screened the questions so as to avoid embarrassment. There was little sense that the programme served the purpose of grilling Mrs Merkel about the details of her economic programme ahead of the European elections a few weeks hence, and more importantly the federal elections, which were due in September of the same year.

Only a few weeks before Mrs Merkel had offered to step in and effectively rescue Opel – the carmaker owned by General Motors. 'I am assuring you of that explicitly, not only for the state governments, but also for the federal government. We have the tools for that,' she said, thereby giving the venerated old company a new lease of life after President Obama had declined to give financial assistance to its parent company. Public finances and economic performance in general was a tricky issue. Germany had experienced its worst economic downturn since the early 1970s. The recession was biting; the economy contracted by 3.6 per cent in the first two quarters of 2009. The only positive sign from Merkel's perspective was that she was leading her opponent, foreign minister Frank-Walter Steinmeier, by 36 per cent in personal popularity polls.

Even if the voters had grown tired of the endless debates about bankers' bonuses, financial rescue packages and negative growth rates, it would have been understandable if those who phoned in had asked the Chancellor about other issues. Above all, it would have been natural if the Winnenden School shooting; a killing spree carried out by the 17-year-old Tim Kretschmer a few weeks before, had been raised. The matter was current and took up a fair number of column inches in both the serious papers and the more colourful *Bild*. The gunman, who blamed his school for not getting the grades required to start an apprenticeship, had turned the sleepy small town in Baden-Württemberg, 20 kilometres from Stuttgart in the southwest of the country, into a nightmare. The village had been unknown to most Germans until the young man had gone on the rampage and killed 15 students and teachers before committing suicide. Most of the dead were women.

In most democratic countries such an event would have prompted an immediate statement by the President or the Prime Minister – just think of President Obama's speech after the Sandy Hook Elementary School shooting in Newtown, Connecticut in 2012, or Bill Clinton's heartfelt 'Help Us Heal' speech shortly after the Columbine High School massacre in the third year of his presidency. But Merkel had given no such speech. She had merely – through a spokesperson – issued a statement that she was 'deeply shaken and appalled'. Instead of speaking to the nation, the Chancellor left it to Ursula von der Leyen – the Minister for Women, a paediatrician and mother of seven – to speak of how the 'killing had left her speechless'.[1]

However, the Winnenden School shooting, grave and gruesome though it was, did not feature in the phone-in. Merkel did not talk about killings, nor did she touch upon the credit crunch or the car manufacturing industry. No. She talked about cooking, and a little about the good Lord above. Once again the second and third parts of the CDU trinity of *Kinder, Kuche, Kirche* (children, kitchen and the church) was taking precedence over weightier matters of politics. Now it is, of course, possible that the listeners had in fact asked more searching questions but that these had been blocked by the hosts, who showed an unusual degree of reverence for the Chancellor and few traces of critical journalistic virtues. Merkel for her part was respectful and sounded every bit the pastor's daughter – and a pious one at that. *Kirche* was given its due. In among the culinary small-talk – 'yes, my beetroot salad has been praised by guests and I hope it isn't faint praise' – Merkel spoke about God. Lowering her voice half an octave, and with an almost intimate whisper, she told one of the questioners who phoned in that 'God protects us, and that gives me strength.'

After a bruising spring with more bad financial news and the worst mass-shooting in German history, Merkel needed to reconnect with her own voters, a group of people she had somewhat overlooked in the months of crisis management that had just passed. She had been severely criticised by CSU leader Horst Seehofer for having forgotten the core voters of the CDU/CSU. 'Mrs. Merkel,' he said, 'should concentrate on her loyal customers' and 'forget about the Nirvana [of appealing to] the floating voters'.[2]

Appearing on this programme was intended to do exactly that: to appeal to – to charm – voters over the age of 50. This demographic had reason to be sceptical. True, Merkel had saved the savings and loans banks, a popular issue among the 'small c' conservatives, but she had also made gaffes that she could ill afford in an election year. Her cardinal sin? She had upset the Pope. Or that, in any case, was the way it was being portrayed by her critics within her party and by several Catholics.

Pope Benedict XVI was not only the head of the Catholic Church. He was also a German, and moreover a Bavarian from the CSU heartland. The former Joseph Aloisius Ratzinger was revered and respected and a source of pride for many lay Catholics in the south and west of the country. Many of them had never really trusted Angela Merkel. 'She is fundamentally a Prussian protestant' was one description of her in a southern newspaper.[3] For a party that had traditionally been headed by a practising Catholic, this was a problem. All but one of the previous CDU Chancellors, Konrad Adenauer (1949-1963), Kurt Georg Kiesinger (1966-1969) and Helmut Kohl (1982-1998) had been Roman Catholics. By contrast, every one of the SPD's Chancellors, Willy Brandt (1969-

1974), Helmut Schmidt (1974-1982) and Gerhard Schröder (1998-2005) belonged to the Protestant Lutheran Church insofar as they were religious at all. The only exception among Chancellors was the protestant Ludwig Erhard, who was head of a conservative government from 1963 to 1966. But, as everybody with the merest modicum of knowledge about German political history knew, the father of the 'economic miracle' after the Second World War had never been a member of the CDU.

So Merkel was the odd one out, and for this reason not entirely trustworthy. She had already had her clashes with the Catholic hierarchy – we saw in Chapter 7 how her marital status had been criticised by the Archbishop of Cologne. And now this woman – this 'Prussian protestant' – had upset the spiritual leader of the more than 26 million Roman Catholics in Germany. The issue was complicated, as is often the case, and reveals once again how Merkel had to walk a tight-rope to maintain the carefully built alliances both outside and within Germany.

The Pope was not blameless in what threatened to overshadow the run-up to the European elections. What Merkel had done was merely to ask for clarification in a matter that had been less than deftly handled by the 82-year-old pontiff.

Benedict XVI, a former professor of divinity, a genuine intellectual who habitually quoted philosophers such as Plato, Kant and Hegel and had published a book with the philosopher Jürgen Habermas, had found it hard to make the transition to the top job after he succeeded Pope John Paul II in 2006. He was a master at quoting scholastic philosophers but was not the type of person who was comfortable with spreadsheets, project management and public relations.

In his previous role as Prefect for the Sacred Congregation of Faith (the successor to the Inquisition) Josef Ratzinger had earned the nickname 'God's Rottweiler' and 'Panzerkardinal' for the overzealous way in which he had silenced critics such as the liberal theologian Hans Kung (a prominent Catholic theologian with dissenting views). But despite his harsh and often uncompromising treatment of dissenters of a theologically liberal persuasion, the pontiff was surprisingly lenient and even tolerant towards individuals who held strongly conservative and even – so it turned out – anti-Semitic views. Bishop Richard Williamson was a case in point. The English cleric had been excommunicated alongside four other members of the traditionalist Society of Pius X in the 1980s, but Pope Benedict now readmitted them to the Church. This would not have been newsworthy outside the narrow confines of the most committed readers of the *Catholic Herald* had it not been for the statement that Williamson, apparently unbeknownst to Benedict, had recorded a few days earlier. In an interview with a Swedish television station, the conservative Bishop bluntly stated his scepticism regarding the holocaust: 'the historical evidence is strongly against, is hugely against 6 million Jews having been deliberately gassed in gas chambers as a deliberate policy by Adolf Hitler'.[4]

Exactly why anyone who is not a card-carrying member of the National Socialist Party would want to make these remarks remains unclear. But the fact that the Pope did not have the sense to reverse the readmission – or rather that his advisors did not hear alarm-bells go off all over the Holy See – probably says more about Benedict and his advisors' political naïvety than about any sympathy the pontiff might have had with Williamson.

The Roman Catholic Church had suffered some rather bad press that at the very least gave reasons to be suspicious. Fairly or not, the Church had had an ambivalent and in some cases friendly relationship with both Hitler and Mussolini. At Benedict's request, Pius XII, the Pope during the Second World War, had recently been fast-tracked to sainthood. It had angered many in the Jewish community that the person who had failed to criticise the Holocaust had been beatified on Yom Kippur, the holiest day in the Jewish calendar. Add to this the rather inconvenient fact that the Pope himself had been enrolled in the Hitler Youth in 1941, and the Church had a pretty bad case. Of course, Ratzinger could with some justification claim that he had had no choice, that the so-called Hitler Jugend Act of 1936 made membership compulsory for all boys over the age of fourteen. He could also have pointed out – though he didn't – that the men who wanted to assassinate Hitler had been Catholics who acted out of religious duty. But the Pope was strangely silent about this. One question kept coming up: if the pontiff was so innocent why then did he readmit Bishop Williamson? The latter's views were far from unknown; a bit of due diligence, even a quick search of the internet, would have revealed that Williamson and his cabal held unpalatable views.

For Merkel the statement came as an unwelcome bolt from the blue. Nothing was less welcome than a reminder of Germany's dark past, and an issue that could cause infighting in the Union was equally undesirable. For a politician who had made support for the state of Israel a part of Germany's national interest[5] and had ceaselessly argued that 'Germany and Israel are and remain linked through the memory of the *Shoah*',[6] the Vatican's actions required a response lest the German government too be accused of tacit agreement. Further, in Germany denying the murder 'of the victims of the national Socialists' – whether Jews, homosexuals or political opponents – was a criminal offence that carried a prison sentence of up to five years and nothing less than a fine. (Williamson was later convicted for having violated the law.)

It was in the light of this 'internal church matter' as Merkel called it, that she answered an ostensibly planted question during an otherwise routine press conference with the President of Kazakhstan. The readmission of Williamson, Merkel said, 'must be so unambiguously clarified by the Pope and the Vatican that there can be no denial of what happened [during the Nazi period]'. And, she went on, so as to make the issue clear once and for all, 'when a decision made by the Vatican can give the impression that they could doubt the Holocaust then it is a constitutional issue'.

Legally speaking, according to the letter of the law, the government had to act. But the action did not need to be taken by the head of the government. In fact, it was wholly unusual for the Chancellor herself to get involved in what was, after all, an operational matter. The correct, or at least the normal procedural way, would have been for Monika Harms, the Attorney General, to deal with the issue. Merkel decided to raise it herself; whether this was prudent is debatable.

The few sentences uttered in Astana, the capital of the central Asian republic of Kazakhstan, caused trouble in Merkel's party and among those who normally voted for her. They even led to a rebuke from the Pope's older brother Georg Ratzinger, also a Catholic cleric and a former musical director at St Peter's Cathedral in the southern city of Regensburg. The pontiff's brother criticised Mrs Merkel in condescending terms: 'I have always thought that she was a rational person, but maybe she was under pressure and then she might have said things that she would not have said had she thought rationally about them.'[7] Even Reinhard Marx, the otherwise progressive Bishop of Cologne and author of a book about his more famous namesake Karl, felt called upon to intervene, describing it as 'outrageous to insinuate that the Pope holds these views'.[8]

That such feelings were aroused caused Merkel considerable concern, not just because of the damage it caused to Germany's reputation but also because it showed that her own party harboured members who held views that were disturbingly close to the darkest memories of the country's history.

The relationship with the Vatican was soon resolved. The Pope issued the requested 'clarification', made it clear that the Catholic Church 'in no way' questioned the holocaust, and said that he personally abhorred it. However, the Pope did not revoke the readmission of Williamson and his religious brethren. Some felt that Rome had failed to act in accordance with their professed views, although the Church made clear that Williamson would not be allowed to hold episcopal office until he had retracted his statement and apologised. He still has not.

However, the issue soon took on a life of its own. Other religious leaders entered the debate. In most cases their comments were ill-advised and rather hasty responses to phone calls from journalists. Asked by *Die Zeit* what he thought of the matter, Bishop Wolfgang Huber, the head of the Lutheran Church in Germany, initially said that it was 'an internal matter' for the Catholic Church. But then he imprudently added, 'We as Germans have joint liability with regard to the consequences of the Holocaust.' What had been a small remark – and probably a necessary one – had re-exposed long-forgotten fault-lines in the CDU. Never mind that Merkel and Benedict XVI had an apparently cordial phone conversation the day after the Chancellor's press conference. The Williamson story had become a serious threat to the Chancellor and was a reminder that some people in the CDU heartland were less than enthusiastic about her leadership.

Like Gerhard Schröder in 2005, who had won an election only to be ditched in the coalition negotiations, Merkel had reason to fear that she might suffer a similar fate if the Union failed to win a sufficiently large majority at the federal elections. Only a month earlier Roland Koch, the CDU party leader in Hesse, won the state elections in the small western state, and Merkel had reason to fear that some in the party might use the debacle over Bishop Williamson to find a more suitable candidate with proper Catholic and genuinely conservative instincts. Koch, so it could be argued, might be a better bet as Chancellor should the CDU and the FDP fail to win a majority in the federal elections.

Merkel had to put the matter to rest. To neutralise the issue she dispatched Annette Schavan, a staunch Catholic theologian who served as federal Education Minister, to defend the Chancellor's handling of the matter. Ms Schavan, who later became Germany's ambassador to the Holy See, called Merkel a 'blessing' and said that she had been 'a stroke of luck for Germany'. Ms Schavan seems to have been less than enthusiastic about entering the debate. Her article in the *Hamburger Abendblatt* showed all the hallmarks of being a response to an edict from the Chancellor.[9] Such is politics. However, it is one thing to coerce a minister to make statements that she would not otherwise have made; silencing the critics in the party by making peace with the likes of RTL's *Bürgersprechrunde* audience is another matter altogether.

It was for this reason Merkel spent an afternoon answering questions about faith and food. It is questionable whether it worked. Merkel may have sounded genuine and her profession of faith mixed with cooking tips was certainly not met with hostility. Merkel had a lot on her plate. A week after the phone-in her party faced a possible defeat in the Federal Assembly, the appointed body tasked with electing Germany's largely ceremonial President. And twenty days later she and the Union would face the voters in the elections to the European Parliament, now widely seen as a kind of dress-rehearsal for the federal elections. Neither of the two gave Merkel ringing endorsements, but it could have been worse.

KÖHLER'S RE-ELECTION AND THE EUROPEAN ELECTIONS

The presidential election was the first test facing Merkel. She had struck a deal with the FDP and had re-nominated the incumbent Horst Köhler who – as we shall see in the next chapter – was a less than inspired choice. The former head of the International Monetary Fund was also a practising Lutheran, but this was not mentioned in the debate – though the SPD had cheekily fielded Gesine Schwan, the Catholic academic whom Köhler had defeated by a narrow majority in 2004. But Merkel was determined to secure the position for one of her own. She succeeded, though only just: Köhler won 50.08 per cent of the votes in the first round. A year later she might have wished she had appointed another candidate. But for now she had won a minor, if symbolic, victory.

The more important test was the European elections. Germany is a country on a constant electoral footing. State elections flow in a steady stream all year round. Politicians are constantly being reminded about their popularity or lack thereof. The year 2009 was especially crowded and was dubbed a 'super-election year', in which no less than seven of the sixteen states held elections. But the European elections – or more formally the elections to the European Parliament – were different from the state elections. The latter are often dominated by local issues and the presence of a popular regional figure can often buck the trend.

The SPD decided to run a negative campaign directed at their main rivals. Posters with the slogan 'Those in favour of salary-cuts would vote for the CDU' were plastered up all over the country even though the European Parliament has no say in employment matters. Keen to capitalise on the perceived anger with high-paid executives, the SPD went further and declared in another poster-campaign that 'Sharks would vote for the Free Democrats'. Meanwhile the CDU played it safe with a poster featuring Merkel and the simple slogan 'Together – Successful in Europe'. The campaign did not set the pulses racing. Election observers noted that the Pirate Party (a political grouping advocating the legalisation of illegal downloading) won its first member of the European Parliament and that the anti-EU party, Alternative für Deutschland, won representation. But the overall result of the election suggested that Merkel and her favoured coalition partner FDP were on course for victory at the federal elections in September. The scaremongering and populist campaign by the Social Democrats failed to convince voters. The Union won 35.4 per cent of the vote. The SPD trailed on a mere 27 per cent of the vote. The only cause for concern was the poor result for the CSU in Bavaria. Having spent most of the spring criticising the Chancellor over her remarks about the Pope, Horst Seehofer's party lost three of their eight seats. The decision to attack Merkel over her remarks about the Pope had not benefited the

CSU. It seemed that Merkel had after all succeeded in appeasing her hinterland, exactly as she intended when she went on *Bürgersprechrunde*. Her cooking tips and her profession of faith had done her no harm, but a far greater test lay ahead.

THE FEDERAL ELECTIONS

Vera Lengsfeld had an impressive story to tell. So good, in fact, that a Hollywood producer later bought the rights to her life story. No less an actress than the multiple Acadamy Award-winning Meryl Streep was to play the role of Lengsfeld in a biopic about the latter's life in East Germany. But for now she was just a candidate for Parliament, and in a bit of hot water. 'I'm sure Ms Merkel is smiling about it. She's got a sense of humour, after all,' said the former East German civil rights activist and now candidate for the CDU. She was unapologetic. And why shouldn't she be? The former political prisoner was making light of an election poster which showed herself and the Chancellor wearing low cut-blouses that exposed their ample bosoms. Who says the Germans lack a sense of humour? Merkel herself did not comment, nor was she asked to, but a bit of comic relief was welcome after the first term. In many other ways the 2009 election was an anti-climax.

That an election campaign is best remembered for the exposed cleavages of two women in their fifties is telling, but understandable. Both the SPD and the CDU/CSU were bruised by the Grand Coalition. Governing is never easy and always costly. The caption on the aforementioned poster, 'We have more to offer', was acknowledged by the voters as a bit of harmless fun, though it did raise eyebrows in the conservative Christian heartland of the CDU.

The voters were unenthused by what the Chancellor and her colleagues had to offer. Vera Lengsfeld finished a distant fourth in her Berlin constituency, and the CDU suffered one of its worst elections ever. This was hardly surprising. 'To govern is to antagonise', as the political scientist V.O. Key observed.[10] All governments break promises, fail to deliver and enact unpopular laws. This was true too for the Grand Coalition. The CDU and CSU were suffering in the polls and losing votes to the rejuvenated FDP, which had made the most of its first period in opposition since 1968. Opposition to the war in Afghanistan, a commitment to more liberal social values and less censorship, and a pledge to lower taxes won the FDP votes from individuals who had previously not been inclined to vote for them, in particular young people, workers and people living in rented accommodation.

Losing votes is never comfortable. But Merkel's problems were minuscule compared to those of her foreign minister – and now rival for the chancellorship – Frank-Walter Steinmeier. The man who was once jokingly called 'the Grey Efficiency' was less efficient as a candidate for the chancellorship than he had been as a Minister of Foreign Affairs. Having left the economic issues to Finance Minister Peer Steinbrück, Steinmeier had been somewhat sheltered from the debacle, and had seen little direct political combat while he was travelling the world. His polite and refined demeanour was ill-suited to the campaign. Moreover, and more troubling for Steinmeier, the Social Democrats' poll-ratings were in free-fall as support was haemorrhaging to Die Linke, the far-left populist party founded by the former SPD leader and finance minister Oscar Lafontaine and the East German attorney Gregor Gysi (who had become leader of the Communist Party of the GDR after Egon Krenz had resigned in December 1989).

The reason for the Social Democrats' troubles was easy to understand. Under Schröder's firm leadership, the SPD had been turned into what the commentators called a *Kanzlerwahlverein*, an organisation devoted to winning re-election for the Chancellor. There was some truth in this. Schröder was a charismatic politician and a gifted campaigner with a folksy touch. Building the party around him had made electoral and tactical sense. Indeed, although he failed to get re-elected in 2005, he had used his rhetorical gifts and his skills as a campaigner to advocate and implement the Hartz IV laws and the accompanying increase in the retirement age. But none of Schröder's successors had anything like his charisma, let alone his ruthlessness. They were not able to come up with convincing arguments that satisfied the lowest paid, nor were they able to explain why the party of the employees had to shoulder the burden for what was perceived to be the lavish life-style of those working in the finance sector. The fact that they had propped up Merkel, who was after all a conservative, provided the SPD with few excuses. No, they were losing support, and losing it fast.

Falling below 25 per cent in the polls only a month before the election, Steinmeier's only chance was a traffic-light coalition between the Social Democrats (red), the Free Liberals (yellow) and the Greens; a coalition involving the Left Party and the SPD was out of the question even if the two parties were to win a majority. However, Guido Westerwelle, the FDP leader, ruled this out in unequivocal terms: 'I consider a coalition of the FDP, the SPD and the Greens out of the question. The policies of the SPD and the Greens are aimed at putting ever greater burdens on citizens. We won't have any part in that.'

No wonder the voters switched off before the electoral battle had commenced. There was only one possible outcome once the Social Democrats and the Union had made it clear that only a hung Parliament would result in a continuation of the Union/SPD coalition.

2009 had been an eventful year, which so far had included the worst mass-shooting in German history, a financial rescue package of hitherto unprecedented dimensions, the near collapse of the carmaker Opel and, of course, the Chancellor's clash with the Pope. Now the elections were to take centre-stage. In the middle of the dullest campaign in living memory something unexpected happened in a faraway land.

THE KUNDUZ BOMBING

The sun was shining and it was a warm day. The Khanabad River in northern Afghanistan meandered across the fertile plain as it had done for hundreds of years when first Buddhist monks in the third century and later Persian Muslims in the twelfth century had settled there. Now the capital of the Afghan province of Kunduz, the city of the same name was a haven of tranquillity, a lush area where prosperous peasants grew cotton against a backdrop of gently sloping yellow mountains. The German soldiers who had been sent there as a contribution to the war against terror were not overworked. Some were sunbathing; others were reading. Being a soldier in a faraway land is uneventful. And it was perhaps this boredom that prompted Colonel Georg Klein into action. While all was calm in the camp, there had been an alarming development the night before.

The Germans – wrongly it turned out – believed that the Taliban had been eliminated from the area. What happened next showed exactly how wrong they had been. Early in the evening on Thursday 3 September 2009 two tanker drivers had been approached by a group of Chechen volunteers and a handful of Taliban insurgents. The truck drivers did not stand a chance. They were dragged out of their vehicles, denounced as traitors and beheaded before the Taliban and their Chechen comrades drove off with the tankers. Two hours later, at 9.01 pm, Colonel Klein received the first phone call, ostensibly from an American intelligence officer, informing him of the disturbing events. Roughly sixteen hours later, at 1.02 pm, the colonel received another phone call. The tankers, the American voice at the other end of the line told him, had been located. One of them was stuck in the mud at a river crossing. Klein immediately took action. He contacted his American allies, who, without questioning the evidence – it came, after all, from a US intelligence officer – swung into action. The Americans deployed two F-15E fighters. They flew over the mountains, reached their target at 2.30 pm and deployed their weapons. The tankers exploded; and the insurgents died. More worryingly, so too did over a hundred civilians, some reports claiming many more. At the same time as the German soldiers were playing backgammon and sunbathing in their heavily fortified camp, hundreds of Afghan civilians were burning to death near the hamlet of Omar Kheil.

The news quickly reached Berlin. Defence Secretary Franz Josef Jung was sanguine about the events. Such is war. As the Prussian military theoretician Carl von Clausewitz wrote in *On War*, 'Kind-hearted people might think that there is some ingenious way to disarm or defeat the enemy without too much bloodshed . . . pleasant though it sounds, it is a fallacy.' Jung was no softie. The CDU politician was a former student at the Academy of Junior Officers (USH) and a devotee of the Prussian master, whom he often quoted. And Jung had never been squeamish about applying force or taking a tough stance. In 2007 he even proposed that hijacked planes should be shot down as a matter of policy, a suggestion that led to calls for his resignation. The Social Democrats in particular were not fond of the CDU politician, and many felt that his elevation to the cabinet in the Grand Coalition was a mistake, especially as evidence suggested that he had been involved in the illegal party funding scandal that led to Helmut Kohl's downfall.[12]

Jung's own view was probably that the resolute action by Colonel Klein was proportionate and efficient, and that collateral damage was part of the game. But others, most notably Germany's allies and European partners, were appalled. At a meeting of EU foreign ministers the following day representatives of other governments – notably those of Sweden and France, who also had troops in the area – expressed their deepest regrets. 'The West should work with the Afghan people, not bomb them,' said Bernard Kouchner, French Foreign Minister and co-founder of the medical charity Médecins Sans Frontières. The German Deputy Foreign Minister, the SPD politician Günter Gloser, said nothing. He was not amused, nor was his party, let alone the Chancellor. But Jung defended the action, 'when just six kilometres away from us, the Taliban take two fuel tankers that represent a serious danger for us,' he said on the Friday after the attack. Two days later, on Sunday, he was even more unwavering in his support for the action, telling Germany's best-selling tabloid, *Bild*, that the dead were 'Taliban terrorists'. At this stage the Ministry of Defence in Berlin already knew there were civilian casualties, though this information was not passed on to NATO, which was conducting a routine evaluation of the bombing.

Dr Jung, who holds a PhD in jurisprudence, must have known that he was on shaky legal ground. Collateral damage (as the killing of innocent civilians is called in military parlance) is strictly prohibited under international law. And the fact that the truck was stuck in the mud clearly indicated that it was not an immediate threat to the German camp. That such things happen was an example of the consequences of what Clausewitz referred to as the fog of war: the uncertainty that soldiers experience when they lose orientation in a theatre of battle. But that is not the way Jung's colleagues, among them Chancellor Merkel, saw it.

On the Monday, taking a day off from her heavy campaign schedule, Merkel expressed regret that civilians had been killed. She admitted that there were civilian casualties at the same time as the official line from Jung's department was that only terrorists had been killed. The discrepancies between Merkel's account and that of the Defence Secretary might be costly, and Merkel was aware of this. She also knew that the Social Democrats could potentially use the information to damage the CDU and the prospect of a Union/FDP coalition. Frank-Walter Steinmeier had a good alibi. The SPD politician had not been briefed – though he should have been – and learned about the bombing only when he heard it on the news. Merkel, however, was informed about the incident only a few hours later.

The Kunduz bombing was a potential liability. Of course, Merkel could, with some justification, claim that she had left matters of foreign policy to Frank-Walter Steinmeier. This was true, for she had been pre-occupied with the financial crisis and had largely left Afghanistan to the Foreign Office. But to admit that she was busy doing other things would undermine her greatest asset, the perception of her as a hands-on politician who simultaneously controlled various different agendas.

Immediate action was necessary, and she delivered it in the form of a speech to Parliament. Rather than getting involved in the detail and the shortcomings in communication that had become apparent, Merkel decided to tackle the issue head-on and defend Germany's involvement in Afghanistan. One of the main problems, especially among those voters who emphasised Germany's continued commitment to peace, was that the bombing risked raising the spectre of a remilitarised Germany. The criticism of the bombing at the aforementioned meeting of EU foreign ministers was telling. Reading between the lines, other countries had more than suggested that the Germans were warmongers who were re-gaining their confidence as military players in international affairs. This was problematic in itself, but Merkel's problem was an electoral one as well. She needed voters to defect from the SPD to the FDP and the CDU, but these voters could not be lured to vote for the bourgeois parties if there was even a whiff of a suggestion that a new Union/FDP coalition would change Germany's commitment to peace and internationalism. The speech was vintage Merkel: factual, measured – and slightly dull. 'Germany,' she said, 'is pledged to the service of world peace; it says so in the preamble of our Constitution.' And, she went on, 'the presence of the German armed forces in Afghanistan, together with that of our partners in NATO, is necessary. It contributes to international peace.' For good measure she added: 'it appears that civilian lives have been lost', though 'it is as yet uncertain'.

The speech achieved several things, though they may not have been noted by the listeners, or even by the pundits. By linking Germany to the cause of 'world peace' she was speaking the language of the SPD and the Greens. And by stressing that lives 'appeared' to have been lost she was very publicly distancing herself from Dr Jung who, she implied, had misled the public and was responsible for what had happened. The speech achieved its dual aim. The peaceniks among the SPD and Green voters could find no evidence of Merkel siding with the warmongers; as a consequence voting for Merkel was not against Germany's post-World War II commitment to peace. As importantly, by implicitly denouncing the Defence Secretary, she sealed his fate. Dr Jung had to resign shortly after the election when *Bild*, not normally a beacon of investigative journalism, suddenly discovered evidence that he had known about the civilian casualties. The Kunduz bombing, a potential electoral disaster, had provided Merkel with a welcome opportunity to show that she was as committed to peace as Frank-Walter Steinmeier – and it also provided her with an opportunity to get rid of a conservative politician from the Catholic wing of the party. Campaigning resumed and all was set for a return of a coalition between the FDP and the CDU/CSU.

The FDP were in a favourable and historically unique position. With exceptional poll-ratings and with support for their gospel of lower taxes and civil liberties (Mr Westerwelle was the first openly gay German party leader), the FDP scored their best result ever: 14.5 per cent of the votes cast. CDU/CSU won 33.8 per cent; the Social Democrats managed only a dismal 23 per cent, their worst result ever, thanks mainly to the increased vote for the Left Party, who captured 11.9 per cent. The net result was a majority of 42 members for the CDU/CSU/ FDP coalition.

There were celebrations in Konrad Adenauer Haus, the CDU party headquarters. To the sound of the Rolling Stones' 'Angie', Merkel – a woman who claimed 'never to have liked pop music' – basked in the applause of the party faithful. Her former rival, Roland Koch, was fielded to talk to the international press. Never a natural charmer at the best of times, the bespectacled Catholic politician did his best to smile but his eyes remained emotionless as he spoke to the journalists. Angela Merkel, intoned the Governor of Hesse in his usual monotonous tones, had 'achieved her goal to form the government she wants'. The outcome was 'a clear vote of confidence for the policies for which she stands'.

What exactly these policies were was unclear. Koch himself made no secret of his ideological commitment: 'You cannot create a state without values and principles' was one of his dictums and the title of a book he had published. But Merkel seemed less sure. Both the Union and the FDP had called for tax reforms, though Merkel had been circumspect and showed no sign of resurrecting the proposal for a flat-tax that had almost finished her career in 2005. The only point of convergence between the soon-to-be coalition partners was an agreement to halt a plan to shut down Germany's seventeen nuclear power plants by 2021 and extend the lives of some until more renewable energy was available. Not even this commitment, as we shall see, was kept.

Forming the government with the FDP was not expected to be taxing. In the United Kingdom, where coalitions are rare, forming a government after the 2010 election took five days and many people were impatient at the wait. In Germany, forming a government in 2009 took almost five weeks and no one was surprised. In Britain the smaller coalition party, the Liberal Democrats (which won 23 per cent of the vote), was given none of the heavy portfolios, such as foreign affairs, finance, the interior. In Germany the Free Democrats, winning roughly 10 per cent less, secured the vice-chancellorship, the foreign office, justice, economics and health.

That Westerwelle, FDP leader since 2001, was able to get top positions for his party was not just a reflection of his greater skills as a negotiator. In fact, much was due to norms. It is almost a convention of the German constitution that the smaller coalition party gets the foreign office, while the largest gets the chancellorship. Willy Brandt had served as foreign minister when the SPD was the junior partner in the Grand Coalition led by Kurt Georg Kiesinger (1966-1969), the FDP politician Walter Scheel served as foreign minister under Willy Brandt (1969-1974) and as junior partner in, respectively, the Schmidt government (1974-1982) and the Kohl cabinets (1982-1998). The FDP's Hans-Dietrich Genscher served in this role until he was succeeded by Klaus Kinkel, also FDP, in 1992. The pattern was repeated when Joschka Fischer served under Gerhard

Schröder (1998-2005) and when Frank-Walter Steinmeier served under Merkel (2005-2009).

It was therefore expected that Westerwelle would move into the Foreign Ministry. The problem, as the negotiations and his first period in office showed, was that the former contestant on the German version of the popular television show *Big Brother* and avowed proponent of what he called 'the politics of fun' had not done his homework properly.

Even before the election results were in Westerwelle used his pivotal position to great effect. He made it clear that he 'would not enter into government at any cost' and that his participation came with a price-tag. Relishing his strong negotiating position, he made it clear that he would:

> Not sign any coalition agreement that doesn't include a new and fair system of taxation. In terms of financing, among other things, we've proposed roughly 400 spending cuts in the budget – although these calculations, of course, don't include all the nonsense with the cash-for-clunkers programme or the billions in tax money wasted on the crazy health care fund. If we succeed in getting a fair system of taxation, we could bring 10-20 per cent of unreported labour back into the legal economy and, in doing so, make our national finances healthy again.[13]

But his demands in foreign and defence policy were the most troublesome for his new partner. During the negotiations he demanded that the remaining American nuclear weapons should be removed from Germany. This policy might have been popular but it involved international agreements and long-established partnerships with the USA which could not – as Westerwelle should have known – be ditched merely as part of a coalition agreement.

Merkel may have had a premonition that there was trouble ahead. The Chancellor, a devotee of the arch-German Richard Wagner, has always said that she was so fascinated by the composer's greatest work, *Der Ring des Niebelungen*, because 'if things go wrong at the start they can develop in a number of different ways, but they can never turn out well', as she summed up the opera.[14] Her hunch was correct: things did not go well. Only a few weeks after the government had been sworn in, the unfinished business of the Kunduz bombing reared its head. Franz Josef Jung, who had become minister for employment, was forced to resign.

Further trouble was to come, both within the coalition and in Europe.

CHAPTER 12

THE EURO-CRISIS AND AFGHANISTAN

WOMEN, SO PSYCHOLOGICAL RESEARCH TELLS US, ARE BETTER AT MULTI-tasking. Whatever one thinks of such research, Merkel, as we shall see, needed to display all her aptitude in this area in her second term in office. Trouble at home in the coalition with the sometimes unruly FDP, resignations *en masse*, and not least the Eurozone crisis, made the first year of the coalition more difficult and testing than anyone, including the Chancellor herself, had expected.

It began calmly. At 10.58 am on 28 October 2009 Merkel received a text message on her battered Nokia mobile: '323 members of the Parliament have voted yes [to the coalition]' it read. She smiled. The text was not unexpected. She was relaxed and for the first time was wearing the *Bundesverdienstkreuz* (federal order of merit) which she had received the year before.

If she had read the text message closely she would have learned that nine members of her own coalition had voted against her. And if she had been concerned she too would have joined in the discussions about the identity of the deserters. But she did not seem to be overly troubled. And, in any case, Thomas de Maizière (now federal Minister for the Interior) had been dispatched to spin the story. 'Well, that happens. We are a large group and not everyone thinks things through,' said the former chief of staff of the Chancellery.[1] Merkel herself did not talk to the press. Having been presented with a customary bouquet of flowers, she looked up at her parents in the gallery. Horst Kasner and his wife Herlinde were sitting next to Michael Mronz, Westerwelle's civil partner. The Kasners did not – so it seems – speak to Mzronz. But this might have been due to shyness as much as to any prejudices they might have had. The Kasners seemed reserved and were not displaying any sense of pride, but then again ostentatious displays of emotion were not their style, nor something that characterised their daughter.

Down below Merkel was chatting away to Westerwelle. The Chancellor and her new foreign minister were outwardly on good terms. Much has been made of the fact that they were on first-name terms and that they used the informal word '*Du*' rather than the more formal '*Sie*'. But using *du* is not necessarily a sign of close friendship. In recent years it has become more common for the younger generation, especially the socially liberal, to use informal greetings. Helmut Kohl, who belonged to an older and more formal generation, was appalled when a journalist failed to address him in formal terms. 'I do not want any intimacy with you,' the old Chancellor had sneered, insisting on being addressed as Herr Doktor Helmut Kohl. Merkel and Westerwelle, both urban liberals, were more relaxed about such things. Whatever their personal relations, the most important matter was the bond between the two parties. The Union and FDP were both *bürgerliche Parteien* – 'bourgeois' or centre-right parties with a commitment to free enterprise and the Atlantic alliance.

The period 2005-2009 was an anomaly, rather like the interregnum of 1966-1969 when the conservative Kurt Georg Kiesinger had governed with the Socialist Willy Brandt. In the minds of the rank-and-file members (as well as in the minds of the respective leaders) the two parties – assuming that we can view the CSU and CDU as a unit – were destined to govern together.

28 October was a day of celebration, but then the political newlyweds had no foreboding of things to come. President Horst Köhler, who was soon to play a central role, was the only one to dampen the positive mood. 'We should beware of too unrealistic growth figures,' said the former deputy finance minister and IMF chief to the Chancellor when they met up for a small ceremony at the presidential residence in the recently refurbished Schloss Bellevue. The palace had been built in 1786 as a residence for Prince August Ferdinand von Preußen, Frederick the Great's younger brother. King Frederick was a strong ruler who re-established Germany as one of the most powerful countries in Europe in the years before the French Revolution. Köhler was someone in a subordinate

role; rather like the prince, whose advice to his older brother was rarely heeded, he was a man whom Merkel could ignore.

Merkel, as a latter-day Frederick the Great, listened politely and nodded, but did not seem too concerned. Köhler was not very specific in his warning, and maybe it was just his innate sense of impending doom that prompted him to issue it on a day that was otherwise devoted to optimism and ceremony. Or perhaps the President had been following the international news while Merkel and Westerwelle had been busy negotiating the finer points of the coalition agreement.

Just ten days before, the newly elected Greek Prime Minister George Papandreou had revealed that the finances of his country were in a considerably worse state than had been expected. Greece – soon to be the *bête noire* of German domestic politics – had not featured at all in the election campaign; nor indeed had any of the other fifteen members of the Eurozone. The economic situation in Greece had gone relatively unnoticed. With an annual deficit of nearly 13 per cent of GDP, or four times more than the allowed limit under Eurozone rules, the country's debt was larger than its annual income. As a result of what he described as the 'unexpected' bad news, Papandreou announced new austerity measures. For an economist like Köhler the substance of the matter was that the Greek government had lost its credibility on the financial markets and that the implications of the situation could have repercussions in Berlin. For Merkel, now a seasoned political animal, there was nothing alarming in the statement from a political point of view. Indeed, Papandreou had merely followed rule number one of power politics as espoused by the Italian renaissance political theorist Niccolò Machiavelli: 'It should be noted that when he seizes a state the new ruler must determine all the injuries that he will need to inflict [and] he must inflict them once for all.' As a member of a political dynasty (both Papandreou's father and grandfather had served as prime ministers) the new Greek head of government was just following the rule-book. However, the situation was worse than his political colleagues in Berlin – and other European capitals – knew.

That Merkel did not seem too alarmed by Köhler's warning or by Papandreou's Jeremiads was perhaps due to the fact that she too was using the language of a latter-day Jeremiah as a justification for drastic measures. Striking a pessimistic note, Merkel's investiture speech on

10 November sounded like a prophecy of her people's imminent destruction. Dressed in black, and with a gloomy message to suit, she warned that 'the full force of the financial crisis will only hit us in the next years'.

There were, as we have seen, other things on the agenda; other matters preoccupying the political debate. Over and above all, the Kunduz bombing continued to reveal catastrophic errors of judgment; mistakes that were politically embarrassing for the new government and required the undivided attention of both the Chancellor and her new defence minister, Karl-Theodor zu Guttenberg.

Within a month of coming to power, the former Defence Minister Franz Josef Jung – who had been demoted to Employment Minister – had to resign his new post. So too did Wolfgang Schneiderhan, the army Chief of Staff. More damaging still for the German military, it was revealed that German special forces from the elite Kommando Spezialkräfte unit had been involved in the attack. Even a whiff of German involvement in military matters that involved indiscriminate killings of civilians was unwelcome for Merkel, her government and Germany's standing in the world.

Merkel survived the debacle over Kunduz in a tactically shrewd way. She went to America. Having given Dr Jung enough rope to hang himself, she flew to Washington to address both Houses of Congress. The trip served a dual purpose. With Westerwelle in the Foreign Ministry and her former Defence Minister in the dock of the court of public opinion over a foreign policy matter, she needed to reassert herself; she had to show who was in charge and make sure that her internationalist, enlightened and peaceful policies prevailed. There was no better place to demonstrate this than on Capitol Hill, just as Konrad Adenauer had done 52 years earlier.

From an American point of view Merkel was almost an ideal example of what the head of government of an allied country should be. All too often European politicians, from Charles de Gaulle in the 1960s to Gerhard Schröder and Jacques Chirac in the early 2000s, had been rather ambivalent towards their larger military ally. While officially committed to freedom, free enterprise and a military alliance, the self-same politicians had scarcely ever missed an opportunity to use the anti-American 'Yankee go home' sentiments prevalent in some countries to political effect. Merkel never succumbed to this. Perhaps largely due to her upbringing in a Communist dictatorship, she never missed an opportunity to praise America. The daughter of an English teacher who was not allowed to teach the language of Walt Whitman and Abraham Lincoln pressed all the right buttons when she called America 'a haven of freedom'. And to be absolutely sure the message was received, she declared that 'we Germans know how much we owe to you, our American friends, and we shall never – I, personally – shall never, ever forget this'.[2] The use of the personal pronoun was hardly accidental.

To a degree the US congressmen, congresswomen and senators were being used, though they would probably have forgiven her. Her story as told to the joint session of Congress was inspirational, almost a German version of the American dream: 'I lived in Brandenburg together with my parents, a region that at the time belonged to East Germany, the part of Germany that was not free. My father worked as a Protestant pastor. My mother, who had studied English and Latin to become a teacher, was not allowed to work in her chosen profession.'

One aim of the speech was, of course, to cement the ties between America and Germany, but that was not its only purpose. The real target audience was in Germany. Merkel did not sign any new political deals or trade agreements during her stay, no new joint policies were launched and no major German companies won lucrative contracts – or none were reported. So why address Congress? Because it showed she was in charge; because the address displayed the contrast between the trigger-happy conservative Franz Josef Jung and the hapless Guido Westerwelle who, as was becoming clear, did not have the experience, the gravitas or the knowledge of his predecessor, Frank-Walter Steinmeier.

2009 ended in a lull, and 2010 began with a similar sense that no major developments were occurring. While the government in Athens faced massive street protests, the German newspapers seemed more interested in Merkel's personal CV than in the calamitous situation in Greece.

Merkel, like the British Prime Minister Margaret Thatcher, was trained as a scientist. But unlike Thatcher, Merkel had practised her craft and, as we saw in Chapter Five, she practised it well. Those who follow these things – and they are surprisingly many – will tell you that Dr Merkel was a well-published, research active, quantum chemist who was awarded the German equivalent of a PhD at the Academy of Sciences on a learned dissertation entitled 'An Investigation into Radioactive Decay Reactions with Simple Bond Rupture and Calculation of their Rate Constants on the Basis of Quantum Chemical and Statistical Methods'. Her work, as befits a serious scientist, was published in peer-reviewed journals. She co-wrote a paper with her partner Joachim Sauer and two other colleagues with the tongue-twisting title 'Vibrational Properties of Surface Hydroxyls: Non-empirical Model Calculations including Anharmonicities' and a study in the journal *Chemical Physics* with some of her colleagues at the Academy of Sciences.[3] In the country of Albert Einstein, Max Planck and Werner Heisenberg, the prestige of being an academic scientist is immense. Equally, such a background could be a cause of envy and suspicion. Merkel had never been conspicuous or especially talkative about her academic achievements. Maybe she considered that she had moved on, that quantum chemistry belonged to her past and was devoid of any political importance. But this too seemed odd: politicians are thought of as vainglorious individuals who never tire of talking about themselves and their achievements. Yet Merkel, who had attended one of the best universities in Germany, was silent about her academic achievements. Could it be, some began to wonder, that she was silent about this for a reason. Indeed, could it be that she might have embellished her CV? And, if not, why was it exactly that she had refused to give the media access to her university grades and the examiners' report on her doctorate?

Like so many other sensationalist stories about Merkel, this one too turned out to be excessively banal when *Der Spiegel* – a liberal-leaning weekly with good ties to the Chancellor – finally (after persistent freedom of information requests) got access to her grades. 'Exceptional in physics – mediocre in Marxism-Leninism' read the transcript from the files. As importantly for Merkel's image – and as a rebuke to those who said that she was an opportunist turncoat who had excelled in the Communist state – the report-card revealed that she had achieved 'a bare pass' in the subject of Marxism-Leninism (a compulsory subject in Communist East Germany). Once again the conspiracy theorists had been put to shame. That the scientific achievements of a national politician could preoccupy the country in this way was an indication that most of Merkel's compatriots were relaxed and comfortable.

A GREEK TRAGEDY: ACT I

Maybe Merkel too was excessively relaxed. Some, especially her critics in the SPD (now the official opposition in Parliament), subsequently criticised her for being asleep at the wheel at the time. 'From February to May this year you had no idea of where you were going. You failed to act,' was the indictment of the SPD's economic spokesman, Joachim Poss, in the autumn.

The charge that Merkel was behind the curve, that she 'spent most of the time arguing with her colleagues and the FDP', to employ another quote from Poss's address to Parliament, was not uncommon. To be reactive, dictated to by events and not by one's own actions is a serious criticism of any politician. The good leader is resolute, proactive and anticipates the dangers before they materialise. Merkel had not displayed these qualities, or so many felt.

Some of this criticism was superficially correct. Merkel did not talk much publicly about Greece in the last months of 2009 or in January 2010, but this does not mean that she was oblivious to the situation. A case can be made for the view that Merkel and Schäuble (who had taken over from the SPD's Peer Steinbrück as federal Minister of Finance) were deliberately and studiously avoiding any mention of Greece lest the markets should take fright. Merkel rarely disguised her dislike for the investment bankers whose jittery nerves and quest for profits had in her view caused the collapse of Lehman Brothers in America and Hypo Real Estate in Germany.

Merkel and Schäuble were keen not to give the markets cause to react. There is ample evidence that Merkel, though she did not talk about Greece in public, was preoccupied with the potential dangers of Greek bankruptcy. At a private briefing organised by the newspaper *Die Welt* in January 2010, Merkel warned that Greek bankruptcy could 'put us under great, great pressures' and that the result could be that the euro would be in 'a very difficult phase over the coming years'.[4] Although these comments were published by Bloomberg – who broke with protocol by reporting from a closed event – Merkel's warning was not front-page news. If anyone is to blame for the lack of reporting about Greece it is the media, for Greece was already clearly facing massive problems.

Running battles between the police and protestors in Athens had turned the birthplace of democracy into a war zone.

Insofar as Merkel said anything about the situation, it was to try to calm it down. In early spring 2010 she said that 'Greece does not want our money'. And the woman who later became a staunch critic of Prime Minister Papandreou even said that he had 'grabbed the bull by the horns'.[5] Whether this too was spin and yet another strategy to contain the contagion is an open question. In either case, it was not enough and in March 2010 serious doubts were raised over Greece's ability to repay its loans.

If Merkel has a reputation for being ruthless, tough and someone who does not blink first, she earned it in the spring of 2010. Addressing Parliament on 17 March – two weeks after the crisis erupted – she bluntly told her fellow legislators that it was possible 'for a country to be excluded from the Eurozone if it continually fails to meet the conditions for membership'.[6] Otherwise friendly countries and colleagues were shocked. 'Merkel's lack of solidarity with Greece is shocking,' noted Belgium's centre-right Prime Minister, Guy Verhofstadt.[7] Merkel's broadsides against Greece, spiced up with denunciations of 'perfidious investors' and proclamations that 'speculators are our opponents'[8] suggested that Verhofstadt had a point when he called Merkel a populist.

Something had to be done. Behind the scenes Nicolas Sarkozy, the French President, urged his German colleague to contribute to a bailout. Wolfgang Schäuble was positive. His boss, Angela Merkel, was not. Schäuble still had an uneasy relationship with Merkel, and she cannot have been oblivious to his feelings of betrayal. But the two were professionals and Merkel had at least acknowledged the former tax-lawyer's technical expertise and immense political experience when she had promoted him to finance minister.

There were several reasons for Schäuble's support for the French plan. The Finance Minister had earned his first political stripes in the 1980s, at a time when European cooperation was in vogue. For Schäuble any political solution that was based on Franco-German cooperation was by definition a positive thing. Moreover, as someone born in Freiburg im Breisgau in Baden-Württemberg, just a few kilometres from the French-German border, Schäuble personally favoured cooperation between the two largest countries in the Eurozone. Merkel had experienced a different political socialisation. She was sceptical towards the French. Her earliest political experience after the fall of the Berlin Wall was of Paris (and London) trying to block German reunification, and of America forcing the two European countries to accept a united Germany.

While Merkel accepted and to a degree sympathised with the necessity of coordinating policies within the EU, she never fully understood the lofty ideals of European integration that characterised Helmut Kohl, Wolfgang Schäuble and other German politicians of the 1980s and 1990s. Further, for someone who saw transatlantic cooperation as an article of faith and was keen that America should maintain a role in Europe, a 'European' solution that involved only the EU countries would send a wrong political signal, and in all likelihood the 'French solution' would not calm the markets.

Merkel instead proposed a different solution, or rather her economic advisor Jens Weidmann came up with one. Weidmann, a former economist at the International Monetary Fund, suggested that his former employer contribute to the bailout. Merkel liked the idea. By involving the IMF, the plan would be more financially credible and it would, furthermore, send the signal that Greece's debt problem was an international matter and something that concerned an institution whose headquarters is in Washington and not in Brussels. The suggestion was not met with enthusiasm in Paris, let alone in Detlev-Rohwedder-Haus, the massive building on the corner of Wilhelmstraße in Berlin that houses the Ministry of Finance.

Schäuble found the proposal unusual. As a lawyer, he was concerned that a solution involving the IMF was without precedent and would therefore be legally problematic. It is debatable whether this was his true reason. As is often the case in politics, legal arguments are used to defend existing positions rather being employed as the result of an idealistic commitment to the letter or the spirit of the law. However, by framing the argument in legal terms, Schäuble felt he had the upper hand against Merkel and Weidmann, neither of whom are legally trained. The Chancellor responded that a similar solution had been tried before when Latvia, not a member of the Eurozone but a member of the European Union, had faced solvency problems in 2008; then the small Baltic country had received money from both the IMF and the European Union. The involvement of the IMF was not only politically and financially optimal, it was also legally acceptable. Merkel – who often referred to her East European roots – wanted to stress that Latvia, a much poorer country than Greece, had shown willingness to solve her own problems after she had received help from the EU and IMF. By invoking the Latvian example she hoped to send a signal to Athens.

Schäuble admitted defeat. Not that he agreed with Merkel, but the situation was getting out of hand and something, indeed, anything, had to be done. On 7 May 2010, the German Parliament's lower house and the Senate voted for a bailout according to which the Greeks would receive a €110 billion bailout, of which Germany (as the strongest economy in Europe) would provide a whopping €22 billion. The Social Democrats abstained from the vote.

The phrase 'too little – too late' gets bandied around a lot, but in this case it was true. Even before the vote in Parliament the politicians' efforts to contain the contagion received the collective thumbs-down. On Monday 3 May, four days before the vote in Parliament, the 'speculators' showed that they had no faith in the rescue plan that had been agreed. Another – more credible – plan was needed. Whose fault was it? Was Merkel to blame for the debacle? Was it her procrastination that had caused the markets to tumble?

Her hesitancy certainly had not helped, but the main cause of the sudden panic was not inaction by the Chancellor but the comments made by the EU Commissioner Dr Olli Rehn after a video-conference call on Sunday 2 May. The Oxford-educated Finnish politician had recently taken up the post as European Commissioner for Economic and Monetary Affairs. The affable Finn had played football at the elite level in his home country, written a doctoral thesis about the competitiveness of small European states, and seemed – in theory – well suited for his post. But he had always been a backroom boy and had little experience of dealing with the press. Asked why the heads of government had organised a conference call the day before, he lost his nerve and spectacularly failed to reassure the markets. His silence was interpreted as a sign; he had no answers.

Merkel was not impressed, nor were her colleagues, but she reserved her ire for the investment bankers, declaring that the world was witnessing 'a battle of politics against markets' which she was 'determined to win'.[9] 'Is commerce in the future to govern the state, or the state to govern commerce?' asked the philosopher Oswald Spengler in his book *Prussianism and Socialism* at the end of World War I. Ninety years later a conservative politician sided with the latter alternative.

For a conservative politician to declare war on the practitioners of financial capitalism may seem odd. There are two reasons why it was not out of character for Angela Merkel to go on the rampage. At the more abstract historical level, Merkel's tirade was against the real-world Gordon Gekkos – Gekko being the ruthless trader played by Michael Douglas in Oliver Stone's movie *Wall Street* in 1987. Her outburst was not an indictment against free enterprise and the market economy *per se*, but against its degeneration. Hers was an attempt to save capitalism from itself.

Her calls for more regulation were reminiscent of the Republican Teddy Roosevelt's similar concerns and policies in the late 1890s, the tail end of the Gilded Age, when he introduced regulation and anti-trust legislation to make the markets function more optimally. Her other rationale was pure pragmatic party politics. Merkel knew that giving the Greeks more money would not go down well with the voters. And although she had recently been re-elected as federal Chancellor she faced a state election in North Rhine Westphalia, the most populous state in Germany.

To American readers this concern about a state election may seem strange and illogical. In the USA state elections are a local matter. Of course, losing a state election may be embarrassing for an incumbent president of the same political party, but no more than that. In Germany it is different. In Germany the Bundesrat or Senate, the second chamber of the German federal Parliament, is composed not by directly elected senators as in the USA or Australia but by representatives of the state governments. And unlike in America, where all states send two senators to Washington, the larger German states have more votes in the Senate. This posed a problem for Merkel. If the state Governor Jürgen Rüttgers of the CDU lost the election – which was only a week away – the Social Democrats and the Greens would be able to block the government's legislation. Merkel could – at least in theory – face legislative gridlock.

Merkel was no friend of the incumbent Governor. Jürgen Rüttgers had often been a thorn in her side. His comments on citizens of a different ethnic heritage were embarrassing – he had infamously said 'Children not Indians' and confirmed that he meant it.[10] At a personal and even at a political level Merkel was closer to the SPD challenger Hannelore Kraft. But personal sympathies are of little importance in the tactical game between the blocks in the Senate. Whatever Merkel's personal views, losing North Rhine Westphalia to the opposition would make life difficult for her government. So Merkel's tough talking was above all aimed at the 15 million voters in the state. Her interventions were intended to be a reminder that the CDU was more than a conservative party wedded to neo-liberalism.

Merkel had little time to campaign. She was adamant that a new deal, in addition to the one already in the pipeline, would once and for all stop the rot. The European Commission, through the hapless Dr Rehn, had proposed a bailout of €60 billion. Merkel reportedly described this as '*lächerlich*', a slightly stronger word than 'ludicrous' or 'laughable'. She communicated back to Brussels that Germany was prepared to provide additional funds.

The public declaration that a massive sum was forthcoming calmed the markets. The approval of the first bailout on Friday 7 May somewhat reassured the markets. Merkel had bought herself a little time on behalf of the embattled continent. But the situation was tense: in Greece protests erupted and three people were killed when the demonstrations turned violent. The financial crisis was ripping Athens to pieces.

Having secured the passage of the first bailout but still in the process of negotiating a second, Merkel flew to Moscow on 8 May. Her trip had nothing to do with the euro-crisis: she had been invited to the 65th commemoration of the Red Army's victory over Nazi Germany in 1945. She could have done without the distraction. Nicolas Sarkozy had sent his apologies. He was able to do so, but Merkel was not. Failure to attend the parade would have caused considerable diplomatic fallout, something she could ill afford at a time when the economic architecture of Europe was in danger of meltdown. Her mind was elsewhere when she took her seat on the balcony in Red Square in front of the Kremlin. She excused herself several times to make phone calls to her colleagues back in Brussels who were negotiating the terms of the bailout – and to her chief of staff who was keeping an eye on the state election in

North Rhine Westphalia. The election had turned into a cliff-hanger. The CDU had been behind in the polls but seemed to be catching up. A last-minute effort by Rüttgers, and apparent satisfaction with the federal government's resolute crisis-management, suggested that the incumbent coalition was in with a chance.

While speaking on her encrypted mobile phone she missed the spectacle of endless columns of marching soldiers, nuclear missiles and tanks that trundled over the cobbled plaza in what seemed like a flash-back to a bygone age, when politics and economics were anchored in cast-iron certainties and clear-cut ideologies. Now, on this crisp spring day, the leader of a unified capitalist Germany stood shoulder to shoul-der with China's Communist leader Hu Jintao and the Russian Prime Minister, the former KGB colonel Vladimir Putin. They were all – albeit in different ways – feeling the consequences of the Greek crisis.

Merkel did not stay a moment longer than required. Her hosts understood, for they too were concerned about the situation. Merkel was committed to her plan and felt that other countries were ready to accept the solution she had proposed. Opposition to the plan was waning.

Sunday 9 May did not go to plan, however. Having returned to Berlin, Merkel issued instructions to Schäuble, who was positive about the outcome. But then something happened that nobody had foreseen. The problem was not of a technical nature, nor was it due to any unfore-seen political development. The problem was medical – or pharmaceutical to be exact. The Finance Minister, who had been on heavy painkillers since he survived an assassination attempt in 1990, suffered an allergic reaction to a new medicine he had been prescribed and was rushed to hos-pital in the Belgian capital. To make matters worse, Merkel received news from Düsseldorf that Hannelore Kraft's coalition of the SPD and Greens had beaten Rüttgers' coalition of the CDU and FDP. The opposition now controlled the Senate and could hold the government to ransom.

The situation seemed hopeless. Her negotiator was literally on life-support in a Brussels hospital and even if she were to secure a deal with her European partners, she now faced a hostile majority in the upper house of the German Parliament. Merkel had to act quickly and, unusually, she did. Her move suggested that she was capable of a large measure of political virtuosity. She dispatched Jörg Asmussen, a Social

Democrat who had served as Deputy Finance Minister to Peer Steinbrück during the Grand Coalition. Asmussen had, rather exceptionally, been kept on by Schäuble, who made the bespectacled northerner his Deputy Minister when he took over as Minister of Finance in October 2009.

Dispatching Asmussen was in many ways an inspired, indeed brilliant choice. Merkel could have sent Jens Weidmann, who had technical expertise that few could match, but Weidman did not have the necessary political clout to cut a deal. She could also have dispatched one of the FDP ministers. Rainer Brüderle, the federal economics minister, would have been a logical choice. He wasn't even considered. Asmussen had all that was needed: he knew the state of the negotiations and, having worked for Schäuble's team, he provided continuity. He was a highly regarded economist who had specialised in monetary matters, and above all – and this was the genius of the decision – he was a member of the SPD. By getting a Social Democrat to steer the deal through the European Council, Merkel's new opponents in the Senate would find it difficult to block a deal when it came to a vote in the Senate. Asmussen got a deal. The other European countries accepted the German terms, and a second bailout was agreed on 11 May 2010. Greece accepted the conditions and agreed to make the cuts required by the German government in return for the money.

And, as predicted, on 21 May the German Parliament approved the second rescue plan. Merkel had to suffer insults from the opposition: 'You have no strategy, no goal,' said the Social Democrat leader Sigmar Gabriel. But the deal was agreed in both chambers. Disaster had been averted, but the issue did not go away.

Under ideal circumstances, Merkel would have been able to rest for a few days after this, but she wasn't afforded the luxury. The next bolt from the blue was completely unexpected, and it came from the presidential palace. As we saw in the previous chapter, Horst Köhler, an unusually active President of the republic, had been re-elected in May 2009. The former head of the International Monetary Fund had considerable political experience, though not in foreign affairs and defence, and there lay his problem.

On 30 May, shortly before two o'clock in the afternoon, the President called a press conference in the Langhans-Saal, a grandiose hall on the first floor of Schloss Bellevue. Nobody knew why. 'He will probably clarify what he said on the way back from Afghanistan,' speculated some seasoned Köhler-watchers.[11] The President had been in a bit of hot water recently, so it was to be expected. But nobody knew why he had brought his wife with him. Angela Merkel had been informed of his intentions only two hours before.

'I would like to say something on the subject of the German army and Afghanistan,' began the President in a sombre tone and with his wife Eva Luise standing behind him in the choreographed stand-by-your-man-pose that indicated that this was more than a lecture about German troops on foreign soil. Köhler paused as if to summon up courage before he continued: 'My comments about foreign missions by German armed forces on May 22 this year met with heavy criticism. I regret that my comments led to misunderstandings in a question so important and difficult for our nation. But the criticism has gone as far as to accuse me of supporting armed forces missions that are not covered by the Basic Law. This criticism is without any justification whatsoever. It lacks the necessary respect for my office.' Looking up, as if to make sure that everybody was listening, he once again lowered his voice. He paused slightly, swallowed and seemed to be fighting to hold back the tears. Then he continued, 'I hereby resign the office of the presidency with immediate effect.' There was a stunned silence.

Once he had been known as 'Super Horst' – a popular President who could walk on water. But he was also a thin-skinned and occasionally vain politician who was unusually sensitive to criticism. Several of his key aides had resigned after rows with the reportedly ill-tempered head of state. Such antics are never helpful for a President. Predecessors like the aristocratic and conservative Richard von Weizsäcker (1984-1994), his successor the Christian Democrat Roman Herzog (1994-2000) and even Köhler's immediate predecessor the Social Democrat Johannes Rau (2000-2005) had displayed that stoic calm which, combined with a quantum of aloofness, constitutes the essence of being 'presidential'. Köhler, by contrast – or so his former staff had suggested – was prone to temper tantrums especially if the press criticised him. Being slated by the media is part and parcel of the game, even for a ceremonial head of state. Köhler, more than anybody, should have known this. He was not a political novice and as someone who was prone to meddling in everyday policy-making he should have been aware that decisions have consequences. That goes with living in a democracy with a free press.

Controversially, Köhler had used his insight into economic matters to challenge the government and he had done so even when this was seemingly at odds with his stated belief in the free market and a smaller role for the state. When Merkel's coalition wanted to privatise German air-traffic control in 2006, he had intervened and refused to sign the law as he considered it to be unconstitutional. This was unusual, not only because Köhler was not a lawyer, but more so because the Constitutional Court is normally considered the appropriate institution for determining the constitutionality or otherwise of laws passed by Parliament. Back then, the decision had been well received in the press and by the public. But controversial decisions cut both ways, and Köhler was, to put it diplomatically, much less happy with criticism.

On his way home from an official visit in China he had stopped in Afghanistan to talk to the German troops there. This was a sensible decision, for the soldiers had received a fair bit of bad press since the Kunduz bombing: they could do with a boost in morale and the recognition of their work that a presidential visit signified. Köhler delivered a speech that ticked all the boxes. The President was fired up as he boarded the plane. The visit had been a success. Now he could take the plaudits for a job well done and enjoy the adulation of the selected journalists who travelled with him. He should have been more careful. He should have been more subdued. He was not. Speaking in glowing and impassioned tones he laid out his thinking on foreign affairs. The man who had famously described himself as a patriot went on to praise German troops – and to say why it was necessary that they served abroad:

> We – including [German] society as a whole – are coming to the general understanding that, given this [strong] focus and corresponding dependency on exports, a country of our size needs to be aware that where called for or in an emergency, military deployment, too, is necessary if we are to protect our interests such as ensuring free trade routes or preventing regional instabilities

> which are also certain to negatively impact our ability to safeguard trade, jobs and income. All of this should be discussed and I think the path we are on is not so bad.[12]

The words had not been carefully weighed and to a degree they were taken out of context. Military involvement is a touchy subject for Germans and this came only a few months after the Kunduz bombing. Köhler seemed to be suggesting that a country of Germany's size had a right to use military force in pursuit of its economic interests. Such a suggestion all the media – whether electronic or print, conservative or Socialist – agreed was unacceptable. Köhler was severely criticised. The Social Democrats urged him to retract the comments, the Left Party likened his comments to gunboat diplomacy, and Merkel did not come to his aid. In fact, the *Frankfurter Allgemeine Zeitung*, a newspaper Merkel had previously used to communicate her true feelings, reported that the Chancellor had 'a difficult relationship' with the President.[13]

This slating by politicians and the media enraged Köhler. Rather than issuing a statement that he was sorry and then waiting for the matter to blow over, he threw his toys out of the presidential pram and resigned.

Merkel was not amused. A keen football fan, she had looked forward to visiting the German football team in their training camp ahead of the FIFA World Cup in South Africa. Her plans were interrupted by the President and she had to cancel her visit, and with it valuable photo-opportunities. Still worse, having just secured a modicum of economic stability and in the process used up a considerable amount of goodwill and political capital, she now had to find a successor for Köhler. This was not an easy task, but she had to make the most of it. What was needed was a steady operator, someone with practical political experience and someone who was unlikely to make gaffes.

Christian Wulff, Governor of Lower Saxony, seemed to fit the bill. There was, needless to say, a fair bit of politics involved in the decision. Merkel's hinterland in the Catholic part of Germany was not entirely happy with her recent dispositions. The Greek bailout had not gone down well, and some were still smarting over the way Franz Josef Jung had been blamed over the Kunduz tragedy. Merkel needed to give the conservatives a concession, but what? The presidency was a possible option.

Wulff belonged to a group of younger conservative Catholics within the CDU, also including Roland Koch and Jürgen Rüttgers, known colloquially as 'the Altar Boy Generation'. They were steeped in the established tradition of conservative Catholicism and traditional values and belonged to the old-boy network. Koch and Rüttgers had, as we have seen, conspired to bar Merkel from taking over the leadership of the CDU all the way back in the spring of 2000. For these politicians 'Merkel was someone who never really belonged'.[14]

To admit one of these 'enemies within' to the circles of power was not ideal, but giving concessions to the conservative wing of the party might buy her some internal goodwill. Moreover, the manner of Köhler's departure meant that his successor would have limited room for manoeuvre; the new President would not be able to assert himself. Wulff, after all, might not be too bad for Merkel. On the evening of 3 June – only three days after Köhler's resignation – Merkel, Westerwelle and Horst Seehofer (now the leader of the Bavarian CSU) nominated Wulff as the government's candidate for the highest office.

For many in the CDU, Wulff was an ideal candidate. Not only did he have a solid track-record as a reforming local politician who had increased the number of police officers – always a popular policy with voters – he had also balanced the bloated budget of the northeastern state. Wulff had grown up with a single mother and had cared for his younger sister when his mother had developed multiple sclerosis – at least that was what he told *Bild*.[15] In spite of this, the young Wulff still managed to serve as President of the Schülerunion (CDU's student union), had been a prominent Catholic and had later gone to law school at the University of Osnabrück. All this would indicate that he was a rather traditional conservative politician wedded to the ideal of family values. But Wulff, so it was alleged, was a bit of a playboy. On an official trip he had met Bettina Körner, a tall leggy blonde, 'who sported a tattoo – yes perhaps even two'.[16] Smitten by her and suffering from a bit of a midlife crisis, Wulff had divorced his wife of eighteen years and married the much younger woman.

Such salacious detail may seem frivolous to those interested in high politics, but such matters are important in politics. Having selected a conservative politician who was *not* whiter than white, Merkel and her circle were able to control Wulff and make sure that he would not be a threat. A gentle hint concerning the new President's 'wandering eye' and his less than squeaky-clean private life would ensure that he stayed within the boundaries of his purely ceremonial role. All in all, it was understandable that Merkel did not choose labour minister Ursula von der Leyen, who was rumoured to be a contender. Merkel could ill afford to lose an ally within the cabinet, especially a progressive woman cast in her own mould. So Wulff was almost perfect for her.

Winning the ballot in the electoral college that chooses the President was not a foregone conclusion, however. The Social Democrats – perhaps recalling the damage Merkel had done to them when she had secured victory for Köhler in 2004 – had proposed the independent East German theologian Joachim Gauck, who had been a prominent human rights activist in the Communist state. Gauck's father had survived imprisonment in Stalin's infamous Gulag prison camps, and after the fall of the Berlin Wall, Pastor Gauck had served as federal Commissioner for the Stasi Records (the body charged with the task of recording the crimes committed by the Communists during the years of the East German dictatorship). To nominate Gauck was a brilliant idea conceived by the SPD leader Sigmar Gabriel. Gauck was attractive to conservatives on account of his uncompromising anti-Communist stance and background, and he was revered by civil liberals within both the Green Party and the governing FDP. Within days, prominent politicians – including Jörg Schönbohm, the CDU chairman in Brandenburg, and the FDP politician Oliver Möllenstädt – expressed their support for the human-rights activist.

Good chess players, however, think more than one move ahead. Gabriel might have scored a few points by getting prominent members of the government to switch sides, but he had forgotten about the Left Party. Seemingly, Gabriel had assumed that the members of that party would support the candidate proposed by the SPD and the Greens. He forgot that Gauck was anathema to members of the Left Party, who largely represent the former Communist Party members in the East. While Gabriel managed to secure defections from the conservative and liberal camps, he faced opposition from the left. Instead of supporting Gauck, Gregor Gysi (the chairman of the Left

Party's parliamentary group) proposed Luc Jochimsen, a broadcaster and member of the Parliament for the Left. This killed off any chance of an upset in the presidential election, although the vote was close: Wulff won only after three ballots, and the debate was heated. Wulff then took up his post with immediate effect.

CHAPTER 13

FROM THE JAWS OF DEFEAT AND BEYOND

'I CAN'T LISTEN TO THIS SHIT ANYMORE.' ROLAND POFALLA ROLLED HIS EYES in disbelief. The debate was very heated indeed. Not all the members of parliament were convinced that the European Financial Stability Facility (EFSF) was the answer to the seemingly perennial problems that were facing the southern European countries. And they were intent upon making that point to the Chancellor. But, rather cleverly, Mrs Merkel had left it to Roland Pofalla, Minister for the Chancellery (Head of the Chancellor's Department), to face the music. He did with gusto, though often with impatience and ill-disguised annoyance.

The CDU's Wolfgang Bosbach, Chairman of the Domestic Affairs Committee, was a thorn in Merkel's side. Not that the former trial lawyer was a threat in the same way as the likes of Roland Koch or Jürgen Rüttgers, but he was capable of stirring and creating discontent within the ranks. That Bosbach criticised Merkel was to be expected. He had been one of the few members of the CDU's parliamentary group who admitted that he was a member of the Berlin Circle, a loose parliamentary group of Merkel critics. Opposed to immigration, fearful of the effects of more Muslims in Germany, these self-proclaimed defenders of small business had a sceptical attitude towards the European Union. Bosbach and his roughly 50 colleagues wanted 'a different CDU', though they claimed that they did not 'want to take shots at the Chancellor'.[1] The CDU was not just an electoral machine for the Chancellor's re-election, however. Moreover, the EFSF was a constitutional issue.

Merkel seemed relaxed about these men, treating them as she did all opponents, with a mixture of mumsiness and studious seriousness.

Most of the Berlin Circle were men (only five out of fifty were women). And the leadership, if so it could be called, consisted of the usual suspects: middle-aged men in grey suits wearing colourful ties and the obligatory signet ring on the little finger.

Pofalla was fair game; it was his job to be the lightning rod for dissent and he played along. Several times during and after the debate he uttered the s-word, apparently to the delight of Bosbach, who gleefully teased Merkel's right-hand man, telling him that 'Shit makes everybody go crazy.'[2]

All in all, the previous year had not been a good one for Merkel. Her steady, solid and competent steering of Germany through stormy waters was no longer in evidence. Many of her colleagues in the party, both in Parliament and in the states, felt that Merkel needed to be put in her place. Most of the time it was up to Pofalla to take the verbal flak.

After the eventful months in 2010, the issues seemed to continue to pile up. Germany had taken over one of the rotating seats in the UN Security Council and Merkel and Foreign Minister Guido Westerwelle knew that they would be playing a stronger and more visible role in international affairs in the near future. This was a challenge with the situation heating up in the Middle East, where the Arab Spring was in full swing. And then there was the Eurozone crisis, which refused to go away.

All was not bad, though. In some ways Merkel was strengthened internally. Her allies within the Cabinet were growing in number: Defence Minister Theodor zur Guttenberg, Education Minister Anette Schavan, Minister of Labour and Social Affairs Ursula von der Leyen, Interior Minister Thomas de Maizière and the young Environment Minister Norbert Röttgen were all her political friends. And even finance minister Wolfgang Schäuble had buried the hatchet and was content with, even relishing, his role as finance minister. Of course, there were the FDP ministers, but they were not a threat to her.

There were few problems domestically. Peter Müller, the CDU Saarland Governor who had been an earlier critic of Merkel, resigned to become a judge at the Constitutional Court in Karlsruhe, but this had no practical political impact. At most it was a positive sign that a potential rival was gone, though Müller (who was the first CDU Governor to enter into a Jamaica coalition with the FDP and the Greens, had become much less outspoken).

Then all hell broke loose in February 2011. The main character in the drama was the hitherto safe pair of hands Defence Minister Karl-Theodor zu Guttenberg. To give him his full and rather impressive name, Karl-Theodor Maria Nikolaus Johann Jacob Philipp Franz Joseph Sylvester Freiherr von und zu Guttenberg – married to a great-grand-daughter of Otto von Bismarck, and descendent of King Leopold II – had become the most popular politician in Germany. He was routinely mentioned as a possible successor to Merkel, who in turn valued him. What unfolded in the next couple of weeks seemed almost like a caricature of Murphy's Law: 'All that can go wrong will go wrong.'

In early February Professor Andreas Fischer-Lescano, an otherwise unknown though academically capable law professor at the University of Bremen, wrote a review of zu Guttenberg's doctoral dissertation, 'Constitution and Constitutional Treaties – Constitutional Steps of Development in the USA and the EU', for which zu Guttenberg had received a *summa cum laude* (an intermediary honour roughly equivalent to a B+) at the University of Bayreuth, a relatively new public university in Bavaria.

Fischer-Lescano was not a fan of the CDU. He had written a critical article about the Kunduz bombing, but he was not prepared for what happened next. As an academic he was interested in Guttenberg's doctoral thesis and agreed to write a scholarly review for the legal journal *Krisische Justiz*. He couldn't believe what he discovered:

> During the winter term in 2010 I gave a seminar on constitutional law at the University of Bremen. And naturally, I read all the literature on the topic I could get my hands on. It came to my attention that Guttenberg had earned a doctorate on a thesis in my field, and that, of course, made me interested. I wanted to take a conservative position and then develop my response in juxtaposition to his. But, when I read the passage about the lack of references to God in the European Constitution, I thought it was a bit odd and I googled it, and I found that Guttenberg had used a passage from an article [in the Swiss newspaper *Neue Zürcher Zeitung*] and when I googled more references I found more [plagiarised passages].[3]

Fischer-Lescano rang the newspaper *Süddeutsche Zeitung*. The left-leaning paper was immediately interested. As a paper representing liberal causes, anything that could embarrass the aristocratic Defence Minister was – if nothing else – a good story. Guttenberg did not take it lying down. He denied the accusations in strong and very uncompromising terms. He declared that the allegations were 'fanciful'. At the same time Professor Fischer-Lescano began to receive threats and was denounced as a Communist (in fact he had previously been a member of the SPD but had resigned in 1992).

More and more revelations began to come out. Initially Merkel defended Guttenberg: 'I have appointed him as Minister of Defence not for an academic post,' she told the press,[4] but that didn't silence the embattled minister's critics. Other parliamentary colleagues and possible rivals in a future leadership election in the CDU denounced him. Education minister Annette Schavan told the media 'stealing is not something you can be cavalier about'.[5] That this was a bit rich was only revealed two years later in February 2013 when Ms Schavan herself was found guilty of the same misdemeanour, stripped of her doctorate in theology by the University of Düsseldorf, and resigned from her post as Education Minister. But back to Guttenberg.

The young Defence Minister's position was becoming untenable. On 1 March 2011 the crestfallen Guttenberg met the press. 'This is the most difficult day of my life,' he began. 'I have just spoken to Chancellor Merkel and have announced that I will resign from all my public offices.'[6] The matter had got out of hand, and Guttenberg was a liability for the government. The word of that year was 'to guttenberg' – a new verb meaning to cheat or to act dishonestly. That the Defence Minister had copied long passages from others' work was not only embarrassing and dishonest, it was also potentially a criminal matter. The resignation left Merkel vulnerable at a time when she could ill afford it, for important events were taking place overseas.

NUCLEAR POWER

On 11 March 2011 the Fukushima Nuclear Power plant in Japan was hit by a tsunami caused by the unusually strong Tōhoku earthquake. Water flooded the plant, something that had been regarded as a near impossibility, and three of the power station's six reactors began to melt down.[7] This disaster created a huge problem for Angela Merkel's government.

Nuclear power, and the dangers associated with it, constituted a totemic issue for many Germans, especially those on the left. The Green Party had been established as a result of protests against nuclear power in the 1970s. In late 1990, the Greens made participation in the government conditional upon Chancellor Schröder's commitment to shut down the nuclear industry. Two plants had already been shut down in 2003, but the Red-Green coalition's decision to phase out the nuclear power plants met with opposition from the CDU. With some justification, the Christian Democrats pointed to Germany's reliance on energy from abroad, and Angela Merkel was also acutely aware of what political scientist Tilman Mayer called 'the negative correlation between popularity and the energy prices'. Higher energy prices equalled lower support for the CDU.

While the CDU was unable to reverse the policy when they were in coalition with the SPD in 2005-2009, they were now free to do so. In September 2010, only six months before the Fukushima catastrophe, the German government had published a rather long-winded paper which stated that nuclear power would be an essential part of German energy supply, though Merkel had stressed that nuclear energy was to be a bridging technology, to be used while renewable forms of technology were further developed.

Not all in the CDU were convinced that nuclear power was the answer. Indeed, the federal Minister for the Environment, Norbert Röttgen, had expressed reservations about the policy and was described as someone who wanted to phase out nuclear power. This dissent did not suit Merkel. She, and the leadership of the party, wanted to rely on nuclear power at least for the time being. It was not a coincidence, therefore, that Röttgen was not even present at the cabinet meeting when the decision to continue nuclear power was taken.

But there was nevertheless something a bit odd about the way Merkel defended the decision to reverse the previous government's policy. It is true that the CDU had prepared a paper on the issue before the election. This 'Thesis paper on Environmental Policy' had suggested that nuclear power was a means to meet CO_2 reduction targets, and Roland Pofalla (then CDU secretary-general) had even stated that 'For the CDU nuclear power is an environmentally friendly source of power.'[8] However, the new coalition was not terribly quick to implement the plans after the election in 2009.

Merkel had been her usual consensual self until the autumn of 2010. Now all of a sudden she was spoiling for a fight, and the issue of nuclear power was her battering ram.

The paradoxical fact was that many in Germany – perhaps even a majority – were opposed to nuclear power. But not all politics is about national majorities and debates. Politics is local, and nowhere more so than in the decentralised Federal Republic of Germany. Once again, it was a state election that concerned Merkel. The new Governor of Baden-Württemberg, Stefan Mappus, was fighting for his political life against the Green politician Winfried Kretschmann, who – according to the polls – was likely to become the first Green Governor of a German state.

Normal political logic would have dictated that Merkel's party, under these circumstances, should appeal to the average voter and try to be more green than the Greens. This tactic, after all, had worked in Hamburg, Lower Saxony and North Rhine Westphalia, where Ole von Beust, Christian Wulff and Jürgen Rüttgers respectively owed their positions to their ability to appeal to centrist voters. But in Baden-Württemberg it was different. Merkel's pollsters and political consultants advised her that it was necessary to 'solidify the base' as jargon has it. Many stalwarts, volunteers and CDU sympathisers were put off by the appeal to the centre ground and were likely to abstain. However, so Merkel was told, they could be won back with a strong message that appealed to the core voters, and nothing was more potent than a bit of Green Party bashing. Instead of appealing to the would-be Green voters Merkel targeted disaffected conservatives. This explained her tactics.

When Merkel addressed Parliament in the annual debate about the budget shortly after the decision *not* to phase out nuclear power, she went uncompromisingly for the Greens. 'The Green Party always want more railways. But when it comes to a new central train station in Stuttgart [the capital of Baden-Württemberg] then they are, of course, against it. It is this kind of hypocrisy, based on ideology, that we really don't need in Germany,' said Merkel before turning to nuclear power. '[We are] doing the people a disservice when we want to abolish nuclear power for ideological reasons.'[9] Merkel wanted to make a political splash, to draw attention to her uncompromising policy in a state where many voters were allergic to the hippy-green policies of environmental sustainability and other things which they rightly or wrongly considered to be a return to a kind of 1970s retro politics.

The state elections in Baden-Württemberg were held on the very same day as the earthquake in Japan, but before the catastrophic news hit the headlines. The CDU lost. Merkel's tactic failed. True, the Christian Democrats remained the largest party, but they failed to win an overall majority. After 38 years of interrupted rule, the CDU was forced to go into opposition and Winfried Kretschmann became Governor. Angela Merkel was less popular than ever. A year earlier 76 per cent of the voters approved of her. Now only 52 per cent believed she should play a central role in politics. Her poll rating was lower in 2011 than it would be for several years and even lower than it would be in December 2015 after the influx of a million refugees. But Merkel was less principled in 2011. She was willing to change her mind. The nuclear issue was not close to her heart.

'That was it,' Merkel is quoted as saying on the day when the news of the Fukushima disaster broke.[10] The nuclear meltdown in Japan changed everything. Massive protest marches were organised, rivalling the legendary demonstrations of the 1970s. There were calls for the reinstatement of the Red-Green policy of phasing out nuclear energy. Industry was against any decision to this effect. 'How,' asked Peter Keitel, President of the Federation of German Industry, 'will the international competitiveness of German industry be guaranteed?' He pointed out that in 2010 the nuclear plants 'accounted for two-thirds of Germany's economic upswing'.[11]

But Merkel, who was facing problems in foreign policy too, as we shall see, was evidently more concerned with electoral short-term gain than long-term energy-security pain. She decided to reverse her policy and revert back to the Red-Green promise to phase out nuclear power. Why? The imminent state election in Rhineland-Palatinate in May (yet another election) was turning out to be a political cliff-hanger. Having just lost Baden-Württemberg, the CDU could ill afford to lose the state to the Social Democrats.

Merkel announced that there would be a moratorium to ensure that all Germany's nuclear power stations were safe. She appointed Klaus Töpfer, a well-known sceptic, to head a commission. Was Merkel genuinely concerned about the dangers posed by nuclear power? Or was she playing politics with the matter?

In June, *after* the CDU had lost the Rhineland-Palatinate state elections to the SPD's Kurt Beck, Merkel told the federal Parliament that she had changed her mind and that atomic energy was no longer government policy. 'I have been personally affected by the developments in Japan,' said the former research physicist. 'Before Fukushima I believed that the risk [of a meltdown] was minuscule,' she admitted. Now she was no longer prepared to take the risk and she decided to – as she put it – come clean and admit her mistake. 'We have to admit that this disaster was possible and that it couldn't even be prevented in a technologically advanced society like Japan.' 'The use of nuclear power can only be acceptable if we are convinced that [something like this] will not happen.'[12]

Some of her critics, both within her own party and in the opposition, accused her of 'false pathos'. But the public seemed to side with her and evidently accepted her statement as genuine. No one could fairly accuse Merkel of lacking detailed knowledge of the subject. After all, she wrote her doctorate on radiation. It is possible to denounce her as a turncoat and a renegade, but we should never fail to accept that even politicians may have good reasons to change their minds. As Cicero, the Roman politician and philosopher, wrote in a letter to a friend:

> Unchanging consistency of standpoint has never been considered a virtue in great statesmen. At sea it is good sailing to run before the gale, even if the ship cannot make harbour; but if she can make harbor by changing tack, only a fool would risk shipwreck by holding to the original course rather than change and still reach his destination.[13]

The nuclear question was not the only thing concerning Merkel at the time, however. Another important concern was her relationship with the CDU's junior coalition partner, the FDP, and in particular with its leader Guido Westerwelle.

WESTERWELLE

In late November, Wiki-leaked diplomatic cables suggested that the new German Foreign Minister was considered a lightweight and an amateur in the art of foreign policy. Westerwelle was described as having an 'exuberant personality' which sometimes resulted in conflicts with Merkel, and as having 'but little foreign policy experience and an ambivalent view toward the US'.[14]

Before the election Merkel and Westerwelle were friends, inasmuch as that word has any meaning in the world of politics. After the election Westerwelle experienced Merkel as someone who would use every opportunity to score points and gain a competitive advantage over other politicians, even friends. An early example of this was the vote on whether Germany should get one of the rotating seats in the UN Security Council. Westerwelle wanted Germany to get a seat at the table. Merkel was more sceptical. Other candidate countries were Canada and Portugal, states with which the Chancellor wanted to maintain friendly, even cordial relations. Westerwelle insisted, however, and so it was that Germany's diplomats started lobbying the members of the UN General Assembly for votes in September. At the end of the month, the news came in that Germany had won a seat in the Security Council. Merkel was on a plane on her way back from America and was about to land as she received the news. She immediately asked her staff to organise a press conference in the airport as soon as she landed. Westerwelle, who had also received the news, did not know anything about the Chancellor's press conference and was in the process of organising his own. Gaining a seat on the Security Council was a personal triumph for the foreign minister and a rather rare opportunity for Westerwelle to show that he was not as incompetent or inexperienced as some in the media liked to say. It was therefore with consternation that he realised that Merkel's press conference was taking place before his and that all the media would give her the credit for his work. Westerwelle was disappointed. 'She takes all the good stuff, and she leaves the bad stuff to me,' he was reported as saying.[15]

It was to get worse for the seemingly hapless liberal politician. The situation in Libya was the issue that most vividly exposed the problem at the heart of German foreign policy in the period 2009-2013.

When Muammar Gaddafi ordered the arrest of the lawyer and human-rights activist Fethi Tarbel on 15 February 2011 the whole country erupted in riots, protests, and soon afterwards civil war. The tyrant responded in the only way he knew, with indiscriminate violence. On 26 February the UN Security Council, of which Germany had become a rotating member on 1 January, passed Resolution 1970 (2011), which condemned 'the gross and systematic violation of human rights, including the repression of peaceful demonstrators, expressing deep concern at the deaths of civilians, and rejecting unequivocally the incitement to hostility and violence against the civilian population made from the highest level of the Libyan government'.

Gaddafi took hardly any notice of this, and the human rights violations continued apace. The Security Council started to draw up yet another resolution, but its members were in disagreement as to what steps to take. The United Kingdom and France advocated military action (formally a no-fly zone over Libya), the USA was inclined to support them, and Russia and China would not vote for the use of force. Germany sided with Moscow and Beijing.

Guido Westerwelle had spoken at length with Merkel about the proposed Security Council Resolution 1973. They were in agreement that Germany should oppose military intervention. Neither the Germans, the Chinese or the Russians wanted to vote against military action; they abstained. But the symbolism of Germany's siding with those two countries looked odd.

Interestingly, Merkel did not justify the decision to abstain to the press. She left the talking to her Foreign Minister. Formally, of course, this was in line with protocol and it could even be argued that she was showing due respect to her colleague. Westerwelle was Deputy Chancellor and Foreign Secretary and this was part of his area of responsibility. On the other hand Merkel often got involved in foreign policy matters. There was in fact another reason. The German government's failure to vote for Resolution 1973 was criticised by most of the opposition in Parliament and public opinion was resolutely behind military action.

It was shortly before the state elections in Rhineland-Palatinate, and the government was looking weak. Merkel was silent for a reason: electoral politics.

When the issue of Resolution 1973 first came up, Merkel was in complete agreement with her Foreign Minister and she had not wavered when a civil servant had asked her to reconsider the consequences. Now she wanted to distance herself from the decision and her spin-doctors spread the story that Merkel had saved Germany from the embarrassment of voting against the resolution, which – thus the spin – Westerwelle had advocated. This was not true. The decision had been reached by consensus and Merkel had not given in.

Westerwelle was angry, but also surprised and disappointed. Merkel had been someone he trusted. And now she had undercut him, gone behind his back and undermined his credibility. In hindsight, the position defended by Westerwelle, that military intervention was likely to create unforeseen problems, was arguably vindicated by events after the death of Gaddafi.

At the time, however, and arguably as a result of the Chancellor's spin-doctors, the FDP leader got the blame for a foreign policy decision that both he and Merkel had made. As Ludger Helms, political scientist, observed, 'Westerwelle was soon identified by many as perhaps the Federal Republic's weakest holder of that office [Foreign Secretary]'.[16]

Westerwelle was certainly not a man without qualities, but his position was fast becoming untenable. On 3 April he handed over the reins of the party leadership to Dr Philip Rösler.

Rösler, a former army doctor, was tougher than many had expected. Born in Vietnam and adopted by a Catholic German family at infancy, Rösler was the first German Cabinet Minister of Asian background. Perhaps predictably, he was subjected to thinly veiled racism from the tabloid press, which questioned if it was possible to be 'German' with a Vietnamese background. Some of the papers thought not, and commented 'Once Asian – always Asian.'[17] Rösler, who hitherto had been Federal Minister of Health, was also elevated to the more prestigious post of Economics Minister and Deputy Chancellor on 13 May.

Westerwelle kept his position and his office on Werderscher Markt 1, the official address of the Foreign Office, for the remainder of the parliamentary term. Rainer Brüderle, who had been Economics Minister, became leader of the parliamentary FDP caucus and Rösler's former position as Minister of Health was taken over by Daniel Bahr.

Angela Merkel was increasingly making all the major decisions herself and representing Germany on the world stage. The way she sidelined and outmanoeuvred Westerwelle was a classic piece of neo-Machiavellian power politics. 'She is neither "Kohl's little girl", nor is she the Machiavella of Uckermark,' said Westerwelle before the 2009 election. A few years later he was unlikely to have been of the same opinion.

CIAO SILVIO

The debacle over Libya, the reversal of the position on nuclear power, Guttenberg's resignation and defeats in state elections: 2011 had not been a good year for Angela Merkel and her party. Things were not getting any easier in the main problem area, the Eurozone, where a second act of the Greek tragedy was looming.

Not everything went against Merkel in 2011, though. One development she particularly relished was the resignation of the Italian Prime Minister, Silvio Berlusconi. In the late summer of 2011, the Milanese politician was under increasing pressure to do something about his country's deteriorating economy lest it should end up as an oversized version of Greece.

Berlusconi had spent his years in office passing legislation to protect his media and business interests. He had done little to reform the downwardly spiralling Italian economy. Silvio was not best pleased with the pressure exerted by Angela Merkel and her European sidekick, the French President Nicolas Sarkozy. In a private telephone conversation in the late summer of 2011 he spoke his mind, referring to his German opposite number in most unflattering terms: 'Angela Merkel is an unfuckable ass.' This was not the kind of thing that the fiercely nationalistic *Bild* liked to hear about Germany's Chancellor. On 11 September the tabloid reported the story with consternation and ill-disguised rage.

What Merkel herself thought about the insult is not known. But it is remarkable how quickly the self-styled 'Il Cavaliere' Berlusconi fell from grace when the story was out, and how quickly everybody turned on the infamous Bunga-Bunga party host. A few days later, Jean-Claude Trichet (then the President of the European Central Bank) and the President of the Italian Central Bank, Mario Draghi (soon to be Trichet's successor), sent a jointly signed letter to Berlusconi in which they demanded that the Italian government implement reform of its financial and industrial policies. In the letter, which was later leaked and published in the Italian newspaper *Corriere della Sera*, Berlusconi was effectively told that he had been weighed and found wanting; he had to go, or he would be forced out. The letter was backed up by action: in the days after it was sent the European Central Bank began to buy Italian bonds, which convinced the markets that the Bank had lost trust in the Italian Prime Minster.

Berlusconi had long been seen as a joke and as an incompetent fool. 'Why does he talk so loudly?' a clearly annoyed Queen Elizabeth had asked when the G20 leaders had a group photo taken in April 2009. On that occasion the Italian Prime Minister was showing what she regarded as a lack of dignity or respect. Rumours, possibly apocryphal, further report that Prince Philip responded, 'He is Italian, my dear, how else would he sell his ice-creams?' All this had become too much, and the Italian businessman turned politician was no longer able to laugh matters off. On 23 October 2011 Berlusconi was summoned to a meeting with Angela Merkel and Nicolas Sarkozy.

For over a year Merkel and the conservative French President had formed a bit of a double act, and now Silvio had been summoned to the principal's office like a naughty schoolboy, and faced with a barrage of searching questions. Sarkozy did most of the talking. Merkel just looked at the Italian. At the end of the meeting, she told him that the EU would put Italy under administration unless he implemented the reform plans immediately. In effect, 'we are taking over your country'. Berlusconi was humiliated. He wanted to defend himself but Merkel and Sarkozy did not want to listen. Berlusconi was waved out with a gesture.

He was not allowed to attend the press conference afterwards. 'What did you say to Signor Berlusconi?' asked a journalist. Merkel and Sarkozy looked at each other for a moment and then laughed. Berlusconi's public humiliation was complete. He was fighting for his political life, and losing. None of his former friends came to his rescue. No one dared. His insult to the paymistress of Europe and his failure to implement meaningful reforms sealed his fate. On 9 November 2011 Berlusconi tendered his resignation to President Giorgio Napolitano. A direct connection between Berlusconi's rapid fall and the woman who was the butt of his obscene comment cannot be ruled out. The Italian President, who seemed as pleased as the rest of Europe, immediately appointed the technocrat Mario Monti as the new Prime Minister.

A GREEK TRAGEDY: ACT 2

Italy was not the only country in trouble. The previous year Ireland had received money in return for reforms in November 2010 and only a few months before, Portugal had been bailed out. But the naughty child in the class, the perennial underperformer, remained Greece. For over a year the birthplace of European civilisation had provided the gloomy mood music in the background of the other crises.

Now, in late October 2011, Greece was again causing trouble. The countries of the Eurozone needed to find a more long-term solution to the crisis. A year before, in November 2010, Nicolas Sarkozy and Angela Merkel had met in the French seaside town of Deauville. Here they agreed that private investors had to share a part of the burden for bailing out the ostensibly spendthrift Greeks. Originally Sarkozy had been against this plan, and his opposition to the scheme was shared by European Central Bank President Trichet, who – very unusually – went public with his fear that requiring private investors to take losses in a sovereign rescue would undermine market confidence. Merkel stood her ground, however, and the two Frenchmen did not try to persuade her; they accepted her plan. The political scientist Robert A. Dahl once noted that 'A has power over B to the extent that he can get B to do something that B would not otherwise do'. It may seem trivial, but it is hard to deny that Merkel exerted power over Trichet and Sarkozy.

In the spring of 2011, as Merkel was dealing with Libya and the decision to phase out nuclear power, she had left most of the issues pertaining to the euro-crisis to Wolfgang Schäuble. Merkel's Finance Minister had duly told her and the German Parliament that the situation was very far from being under control.

On 21 July, with the other issues out of the way, the German government agreed to yet another bailout for the Greeks, this time to the tune of €130 billion. It was this bailout the German federal Parliament was debating in October when Roland Pofalla was so exasperated that he could take no more of 'this shit'.

The debate showed Merkel's problem in a nutshell. She, as well as Pofalla and Schäuble, had to defend the bailout, but they were finding it increasingly hard to justify their actions to Parliament and indeed to the taxpayers. Moreover, Parliament and the voters were not the only ones who were sceptical. Germany, like the USA, is a country where judicial politics plays a large role. But unlike America, where judges are largely selected on account of their perceived political positions, the constitutional judges serving in the German Constitutional Court in Karlsruhe are less politicised and regard their task as one of strictly interpreting the letter of the law. One of the other problems for Merkel was that 'the red robed judges in Karlsruhe [had] become assertive protectors of German sovereignty'.[18] Although the Constitutional Court accepted, with some hesitation, that Germany could play a role in the rescue of Greece, the room for political manoeuvre was increasingly circumscribed by the courts.

The backbenchers and other members of parliament were no different. The FDP group in Parliament only agreed to support the measures after they had conducted a poll among their party members. Many CDU backbenchers relished the thought of giving Merkel a bloody nose and several had strong political reservations about Greece.

The CDU had come a long way since Helmut Kohl had made support for the euro and the European Union the centrepiece of all his policies. The increasingly frail Helmut Kohl was all but ignored by his erstwhile party comrades when he said, 'I am more convinced than ever that European unity is needed.'[19] He added, 'She is destroying my Europe,' to which Merkel could only respond, 'Your Europe, dear Helmut, no longer exists.'[20]

Her task was not one of philosophical principle but one of practical action lest the whole structure built up by Kohl and his colleagues should come crashing down. Merkel did not want to be the Chancellor who went down in history as the one who sank the euro. To avoid that outcome, action was needed.

The problem was that Greece, even though it had received a second bailout, was still in trouble. At the beginning of October the government in Athens had received a total of €240 billion, almost the equivalent of its entire annual gross domestic product. This was alongside its access to a €440 billion rescue fund.

After the meeting with Berlusconi, Merkel and Sarkozy summoned George Papandreou, the Greek Prime Minister, to talks. The American-educated Greek politician – whose father was an economics professor at Berkeley before becoming a politician – was pleasant, engaging and charm itself during the talks. He understood the situation, and expressed gratitude for the help he was receiving. This agreement, which would have shaved billions off the Greek debt in return for structural reforms, would buy the Greek government valuable time, according to the Greek Prime Minister.

Papandreou had reason to be grateful. During the negotiations with the Greek Prime Minister, Merkel rang Charles Dallara, the managing director of the International Institute of Finance, the organisation representing the world's leading financial institutions. Merkel told the financier that investment banks had to 'accept losses of 50 per cent on Greek government debt held in private hands'.[21] Dallara was not pleased when he turned up at the hotel, but Merkel was in no mood to compromise. She dismissed his objections with the message that unless he accepted, Greece would go bankrupt and the banks would receive nothing at all. Dallara accepted the terms.

Everything was apparently resolved. Merkel, looking as if a heavy weight had been lifted off her shoulders, addressed the world press in the early hours of the morning of 27 October. She departed from her restrained and reserved attitude on such occasions and appeared almost jubilant: 'I am very aware that the world's attention was on these talks. We Europeans showed tonight that we reached the right conclusions.' The markets reacted positively and all the relevant indices rose as the stock markets opened after what was described as 'a breakthrough'.[22]

Before departing for the meetings in Cannes, Merkel had told the federal Parliament 'if the euro collapses, then Europe collapses'. She had gambled, but it had worked; she got a deal, the euro had been saved. Or so she thought. Merkel was about to go home on 31 October. The time was just past 7.20 in the evening in Berlin. It had been a productive couple of days and everything was much calmer after the deal with Papandreou had been reached. Just as she was about take the lift down she received a phone call. It was shocking news. Papandreou had announced that the agreement reached on the 27th would be submitted to a referendum. Merkel immediately rang Nicolas Sarkozy. Papandreou's move was unexpected and had not been coordinated with anybody.

Merkel and Sarkozy were incensed. They agreed that any payment would be halted until further notice and then agreed to summon Papandreou to explain himself. But they waited until the following morning before they contacted the Greek government. On 1 November at 7.20 am Wolfgang Schäuble called his Greek counterpart, Evangelos Venizelos, who was in an Athens hospital. Schäuble told the Greek politician that Merkel wanted to see him and his boss in Cannes two days later. Schäuble tried to convince the corpulent economist to convince Papandreou that the proposal would backfire. Venizelos was opposed to the referendum and he too understood that Papandreou's gamble could make matters worse, but he was unable to convince Papandreou.

The response from the markets was unequivocal, the German DAX (the blue chip stock market index consisting of the thirty major German companies trading on the Frankfurt Stock Exchange) lost 5 per cent. Speculation was rife that Greece would leave the euro, and in the process inflict serious damage on the euro, if not cause its collapse.

Under normal circumstances, there is a red carpet and a guard of honour when a foreign leader visits France. Merkel was treated to the full spectacle when she arrived for the talks with Papandreou. But when the Greek Prime Minister turned up the red carpet had been rolled up and the Garde Républicaine (the part of the French Gendarmerie responsible for providing guards of honour) had been dismissed.

Mr Papandreou was left in no doubt that he had overstepped the mark. He maintained that he needed a mandate: 'The referendum will be a clear mandate and a strong message within and outside Greece on the European course and our participation in the euro,' he had told his ministers before he left.[23] Merkel and the other participants were in no mood to listen to these justifications. At the meeting he was not only met by Merkel and Sarkozy, there was yet another player in the room, Christine

Lagarde, the newly elected President of the International Monetary Fund (IMF). A former member of the French national synchronised swimming team, the IMF chief had carefully choreographed her policies with Merkel, and together the two powerful women told the Greek Prime Minister he would receive no money whatsoever until after a possible referendum had been held. Papandreou was met with silence when he tried to argue. He returned to Greece and tendered his resignation. The referendum was cancelled and Papandreou tried to put on a brave face as he stepped down.

The humiliated politician likened himself to Homer's Odysseus, the warrior king who came home to Ithaca after ten years at sea and many travails to win back his kingdom. The problem was that Papandreou, unlike the Homeric hero, was facing shipwreck and was very far from being safe. A more appropriate reference to ancient Greek mythology would have been to Icarus, the son of the master-craftsman Daedalus, who was punished for his hubris by the gods. When he flew too close to the sun his wings melted and he plummeted to the ground.

The markets were still jittery, and something had to be done. The solution – or at least part of it – came in December 2011 when the European Council (the heads of state and government) agreed to the European Fiscal Compact, which tightened the rules for national budget deficits, introduced automatic sanctions and empowered the Commission to set targets for individual countries. Once again Germany was in the driving seat and dictating the rules. Britain opted not to be part of the process, but this mattered little. The plan stopped the relentless run on the euro. The problem had not been resolved, but the danger of a meltdown had been reduced.

But the price for this stability had been high. Nikolaus Mayer-Landrut, a career diplomat who had recently taken over as Merkel's Head of European Affairs, had drawn up the plan for consolidation. The other countries and the European commission had wanted a system of euro-bonds guaranteed by the European Central Bank, but the Germans had rejected this. They wanted a system of tight financial control and shied away from anything that could lead to inflation. In America and Britain the German position would be described as a policy of austerity: spending cuts, reduction of budget deficits and an aversion to Keynesian welfare economics. Such policies come at a cost. Many in southern Europe and elsewhere were increasingly irate that their pensions and benefits were being cut at the behest of civil servants in Berlin. Even some of the German commentators were critical of 'Merkelomics'. The sociologist Ulrich Beck, who died in 2015, dubbed her 'Merkiavelli' and concluded: 'We are faced with a hardnosed neo-liberalism that is now to be built into the European constitution, bypassing the (feeble) European public sphere in the process.'[24] Other Germans were jubilant, perhaps ill-advisedly. When Merkel returned from her Cannes meeting, Volker Kauder, the leader of the CDU caucus declared: 'Once again German is spoken in Europe.'[25] He meant politically: the other countries had succumbed to the German version of capitalism.

Was it Merkel and her advisors who stopped the rot and rescued the euro? Not they alone. Mario Draghi's comment at a conference in London in the summer of 2012 that 'the ECB is ready to do whatever it takes to preserve the euro. And believe me, it will be enough' finally put an end to the speculation and shored up support for the euro. But Merkel's persistence had played a major role, even if the solution she came up with was not popular. Although Greece still failed to comply with the agreements made in October 2011, and was more and more adrift, the other troubled economies – Ireland, Spain, Italy, and to a lesser degree Portugal – implemented reforms and consolidated their respective positions. It was becoming clear that the euro was saved, though it was still an open question whether Greece would remain a member of the Eurozone.

GOODBYE HERR WULFF

Traditionally German political analysts have been divided between those who think that foreign policy is the driving force, like the nineteenth-century historian Leopold von Ranke, and those who believe in the primacy of domestic affairs, like Eckart Kehr in the 1920s. Developments in 2011 seemed to have vindicated the view of the former: Libya, Fukushima and the Eurozone crisis were foreign issues that required a response. To be sure, Merkel's responses were in large measure restricted, even dictated, by domestic constraints ranging from public opinion to the increasingly vigilant eyes of the Karlsruhe judges, but foreign policy issues were setting the agenda.

At the beginning of 2012 something happened that once again moved the focus to domestic politics. It was an event Merkel had not foreseen, and it was not an international crisis. It concerned the President of the Republic.

When Horst Köhler resigned prematurely as President in June 2010, Christian Wulff had quickly been chosen as his successor. As we have seen, the former Governor suited the profile Merkel had drawn up for the job and was politically attractive. Maybe this was the reason that the Chancellor did not carry out the background checks that, under the euphemism 'due diligence', are normally part of the process of vetting candidates for high office. Or maybe Merkel had just turned a blind eye.

In any case, the elegant Herr Wulff was not quite as attractive as first impressions suggested. In December 2011, *Bild* suggested that the President had misled, perhaps even deceived, the local parliament in Lower Saxony during his tenure as Governor. It was a serious allegation, especially for someone whose main function was to serve as the country's conscience and provide a moral example to his compatriots. The allegation was that Wulff had received a very favourable loan totalling in the region of half a million euros from the wife of the businessman Egon Geerkens. This in itself was a bit suspicious and smacked of possible corruption. What made matters worse was Wulff's reaction to the allegations. It was not the first time Wulff had been accused of behaviour that fell some way short of 'presidential'. A year before, *Der Spiegel* had reported that the President had secured cheap tickets for a family holiday in America. On that occasion he had repaid the money in full, but it didn't look good, and now he was at it again.

Most scandals escalate because the culprits invent lies to cover their tracks. As they weave an ever more complex web of falsehoods, the reaction to the cover-up often ends up being stronger than to the original sin. The case of Wulff was no exception. Predictably, the President denied it all. In a statement issued on 15 December 2011, Wulff reiterated that he did not have any improper business relations with Egon Geerkens. The problem for Wulff was that *Der Spiegel* already had gained access to the original loan documents, which showed that Geerkens had indeed been involved.

A week after Wulff's categorical statement that he had not had any improper dealings with Geerkens, his lawyers issued a short statement in which they acknowledged that 'Geerkens was involved in the negotiation of payment'. This, of course, did not constitute an 'improper' business relationship, but legal accuracy does not equate with political credibility, let alone with trustworthiness. And the fact that Wulff sacked his press spokesperson only made matters worse.

So far the matter had been one of personal finances, and though there was a hint of allegations of corruption, none of the documents indicated that Wulff's poor judgment had violated any law. This changed when, on 31 December, *Der Spiegel* published evidence which strongly suggested that Wulff's loans were associated with Volkswagen's takeover of the car manufacturer Porsche. Wulff's position was weakening day by day, and he did not make life easier for himself. If his judgment seemed poor, his behaviour only served to strengthen this perception. On the day the Volkswagen story broke, Wulff called Kai Diekmann, editor in chief of *Bild*.

Diekmann did not answer, so the President left an angry voice message on the tabloid chief's answerphone to the effect that he was now at war with the popular newspaper. This was not clever, given that *Bild* is the largest-selling newspaper in the Western world. *Bild* came down on him like a ton of bricks. And Wulff steadfastly refused to resign, though he did admit in a television interview that he had made some mistakes. After a month during which the media treated Germans to a daily dose of embarrassing revelations, the District Attorney finally asked Parliament to lift Wulff's immunity from prosecution so that they could formally charge him with favouritism. Wulff resigned the following day.

Throughout the media storm Angela Merkel had kept silent, apart from urging Wulff to be more transparent. Wulff's resignation was not a positive news story for Merkel. The resignations of first Horst Köhler and then defence minister Guttenberg had been unwelcome distractions. The resignation of Wulff created another headache for her: who was to replace him?

Merkel had won one of her greatest triumphs when she and Westerwelle had succeeded in getting Horst Köhler elected in 2004. Now the opposition played the same trick, once again nominating the Protestant theologian and human rights activist Joachim Gauck. To Merkel's surprise the East German was supported by the FDP and wholeheartedly endorsed by its new leader. In a snub to the Chancellor, Philip Rösler had not informed his coalition partner about his party's intention to support the opposition candidate.

Faced with a *fait accompli*, Merkel dropped her opposition to Gauck, knowing full well that it is pointless to engage in battles you are unlikely to win. On 18 March Gauck was elected President on the first ballot, 991 out of 1,228 delegates in the Electoral College voting for the 72-year-old former pastor. Merkel did not comment. It was a defeat, but she was determined to make the most of an embarrassing situation.

She was able to weather the storm, or so was the perception in the media. Two years later *Der Spiegel* commented: 'Rarely has a duo from the Chancellery and Schloss Bellevue [the President's official residence] been so close.'[26]

CHAPTER 14

UKRAINE, GREECE, REFUGEES AND BREXIT

S HE DROVE DOWN ELIZABETH STREET IN CENTRAL BRISBANE IN A BLACK
BMW. At 8.01 pm she parked. At 8.02 she stepped into the Hilton
and headed straight for his room. They had spoken 38 times over the
telephone and in July they had met briefly and stolen a few moments
alone at a football game. But tonight, 15 November 2014, was different.
What happened in the six hours in between is anyone's guess, but she left
the room at two o'clock in the morning. This was not a tryst of two romantic souls in their twilight years in a tropical city. Vladimir Putin and
Angela Merkel never really got on. How could they? He had famously
declared that the demise of the Soviet Union was 'the greatest geopolitical tragedy of the [twentieth] century'[1] and she was an anti-Communist
who had grown up in a Stalinist dictatorship.

On this evening they were alone. Putin's security advisor Yuri
Ushakov and Merkel's chief foreign policy advisor Christoph Heusgen
were not present. Nor were the ubiquitous translators or note-takers.
Just Putin and Merkel alone in an Australian hotel room. But there was
no breakthrough. The situation was as it had been since late February
2014 when Putin had reacted to the Ukrainian revolution. In November
2013 crowds gathered in the Ukrainian capital Kiev in protest against
President Viktor Yanukovych, who refused to sign an association agreement with the European Union. Instead he signed an agreement with
Russia. In February 2014 Yanukovych fled to Russia. And then it kicked
off. The Russians sent undercover soldiers to the Crimean peninsula
(a part of Ukraine since the 1950s) and after that, allegedly, to eastern Ukraine. In Germany the undercover soldiers became known as

'little green men'. These were not aliens cast in the classic science fiction mould, they were Russian armed forces that suddenly appeared in Simferopol (the main city in the Crimea) on 27 February. Meeting little resistance, they seized the Crimean Parliament and declared that a referendum would be held on the peninsula's independence. President Putin, as expected, denied knowledge of any involvement in the putsch on the peninsula. 'Local self-defence forces' was how he described the insurgents at a press conference. Few believed him, and the sceptics were right. A month later Putin admitted that the 'little green men' were Russian soldiers in disguise, that 'Crimean self-defence forces were of course backed by Russian servicemen'.

This tactic is well known by those who study Russian military strategy. The Russian word for it is *maskirovka*, or masquerade, and the German strategists and advisors who briefed Merkel on the morning of 28 February were well aware of it. The Battle of Stalingrad in 1942-1943, perhaps the turning point in the Second World War, had been won by this means: Russian soldiers without insignia appearing out of nowhere behind enemy lines. The Russians had merely done it again. The strategy could have been taken straight out of the *Soviet Military Encyclopedia*: 'Strategic *maskirovka* is carried out at national and theatre levels to mislead the enemy as to political and military capabilities, intentions and timing of actions. In these spheres, as war is but an extension of politics, it includes political, economic and diplomatic measures as well as military ones.'

Christoph Heusgen, the Chancellor's foreign policy and security advisor, seems to have been professionally impressed by the slickness of the operation. Much as the career diplomat disliked Vladimir Putin personally, he recognised the strategic brilliance of the Kremlin strongman's move. It is a part of the diplomat's ethos to recognise the craftsmanship of his opponents.

Merkel characteristically kept a low profile, at least at first. As in the euro-crisis, the Chancellor favoured her famed propensity to procrastinate. Moreover – and this was another reason for Heusgen's apparent professional appreciation of the Russian move – the German government was not terribly impressed by the Obama administration's conduct over Ukraine. Small things can reveal important underlying tensions. The

Americans were not overwhelmed by the Europeans' ostensible inactivity and it did not – to put it very mildly – help matters that the senior American diplomat Victoria Nuland was reported as saying 'fuck the EU' in a leaked document.

An expletive-laden outburst is not in itself exceptional. Merkel herself was known to use colourful language from time to time; as *Bild*'s political editor put it, 'she says "shit" way more often than any of her predecessors'. But she swore about football games and not with reference to her closest allies, and in any case she didn't use the f-word. That Merkel decided to refer, through her spokesperson, to these comments as 'completely unacceptable' was significant in the coded language of high diplomacy. There were other reasons for the relations between the USA and Germany reaching a low point. Revelations in November 2013 showed that the American National Security Agency (NSA) had bugged Mrs Merkel's phone.

Putin had thus made his move at a strategically favourable point in time, at a moment when there was a rift between the Americans and their most important European ally. However, it was soon clear that he had overestimated the discord between Washington and Berlin.

Spying goes on all the time and everyone knows it. Angela Merkel, more than any of her colleagues and predecessors with the possible exception of Helmut Schmidt, was a pragmatist with a hands-on approach to politics and to what served Germany's interests. To be sure, having your phone bugged is unacceptable, especially if you have grown up in a Communist dystopia in which the Stasi did their level best to turn Orwell's *1984* into a reality. But nothing would ever get done – and Merkel would not have succeeded in politics – if such personal issues were allowed to cloud everyday decision-making. She had no interest in prolonging the spat with Obama. Much as she regarded the American President as a bit of a lightweight, she had to do business with him. In any case, the threat posed by the Russians was far too serious to be affected by a bit of personal annoyance.

She had a problem. Germany was more dependent upon Russia than any of the other major powers in Western Europe, and this was especially true after Merkel's decision to phase out nuclear power in 2011. 'Is Germany's gas supply secure?' was the question. The short answer was No. The figures spoke for themselves. Germany alone used 90 billion of the 130 billion cubic metres of natural gas that reached the EU from Russia. If the Russians were to play hardball Germany would suffer, and with her the whole Eurozone.

High politics, the strategic chess-game that Germany had refrained from since 1945, had, it seemed, trumped the carefully orchestrated consensus on economic policy that Merkel had spent the previous years constructing. The old *Realpolitik* of Bismarck, that ultimately military might is more important than economic power, seemed vindicated.

As someone who had grown up in a state in effect run by the Soviets, Mrs Merkel was aware of the dangers of giving Putin a free rein in Ukraine. While she did not articulate it in such terms, the risk of a domino effect with Russia seizing more and more disputed territories in what the Kremlin called the 'near abroad' was a real risk to Germany, to Europe and to the world. But much as Merkel did not want to get personal, she had to recognise that Putin was a different sort of player, and that she shared more with him than she cared to admit. Politics, she knew, was also about empathy, about 'the ability to step into someone else's shoes – and then step out again', as Anna Freud is said to have defined the term. As someone who had worked with the Russians, Merkel appreciated that many of them had a deep-seated fear of encroachment by the West. This was the view ordinary Russians had expressed to her when Lothar de Maizière had dispatched her to gauge their views on German reunification almost 25 years before. She remembered the fears they expressed. Whether it was warranted or not, the fear that history might repeat itself, that Napoleon and Hitler could be followed by another army from the West, was chiselled deeply into the Russian psyche. Unlike the other leaders in the West Merkel appreciated Putin's position – though, needless to say, she did not share his analysis.

Vladimir Vladimirovich Putin, born in Leningrad in 1952, had earned his stripes in the service of the KGB in what was then East Germany. Standing at only 5 foot 7 inches, he was far from being the classic square-jawed brute of the cold war spy novels. To be sure, the Russian President held an 8th Dan in Kyokushin Karate, as the English tabloid the *Daily Mail* reported with some awe. But behind the facade of the carefully choreographed image of the KGB man was a different individual.

Putin was never an action man who abseiled down buildings, chased fast cars or suchlike: 'I have never broken the law of another country', he admitted.[2] He graduated with a first-class degree in law from the State University of Leningrad and was immediately recruited by the KGB.

At this stage, in the late 1970s, Yuri Andropov was the Head of the Soviet secret service. Andropov, later became Leonid Ilyich Brezhnev's successor as General Secretary of the Soviet Communist Party. He was in the process of reforming and restructuring the KGB into a more professional and sophisticated organisation, one that relied on modern and scientific methods and less on brute force, torture and intimidation. Asked by a friend what he did during his more than fifteen years in the intelligence service, Putin answered, 'I am a specialist in communicating with people.' It was this skill – in addition to flawless German – that Putin practised when he was posted to East Germany before and during the fall of the Berlin Wall.

Angela Merkel had experienced this ability to 'communicate' at their first meeting in 2006, and it did not endear him to her. Putin and his advisors were well prepared. She was led into his office and greeted him in Russian. He looked at her with a condescending and overbearing expression. And then, with a sly smile, he presented her with a cuddly dog. A year later, when Merkel met Putin at his Dacha by the Black Sea, the door to the room in which they were meeting had been left slightly ajar. It soon became clear why: out of the corner of her right eye, Merkel could see an oversized black dog walk into the room. The former KGB officer had done his homework. He was quietly giggling and did little to hide it. He knew the German chancellor was terrified of dogs after one had bitten her during the 1994 German federal elections. Now, at their second meeting – the year was 2007 – he decided to 'let the dog out'.

'The dog doesn't bother you, does she?' said Putin with an ill-disguised sneer, gesturing toward Koni, the black Labrador he was given when he became head of the security services in 1998. Merkel pursed her lips and looked anything but comfortable. Having grown up in East Germany, she knew his type: the cunning, bullying, Soviet security officer who knew all the dirty tricks – and used them. She also knew that Putin had, in his meetings with other leaders, used all the skills he had acquired at the 401st KGB School in Okhta near Leningrad. Politics is a mind-game, a struggle between leaders for psychological supremacy. And in this game all available means are at one's disposal. In this Putin was – and is – a master. 'I am an expert in human relations,' was his short and laconic answer to his friend Sergei Roldugin, who (back in 1975) had wondered what Putin did for a living.

He was applying his talents in his meeting with the German *Kanzlerin*. Putin's mouth smiled, but his steely blue eyes were emotionless and even cold when he continued, like a cat playing with a defenseless mouse: 'She's a friendly dog, and I'm sure she will behave herself'. Like a chess player who has made a decisive move the Russian President leaned back, kicked his legs out and looked triumphantly at the gathered press photographers and assorted journalists who had been allowed to attend the opening of the meeting. But then something happened which Putin had not expected. Merkel looked back at her Russian colleague, regained her composure and said – in a rather posh Russian accent – 'At least she doesn't eat journalists.' The response came like the crack of a whip, and apparently shook the Kremlin strongman out of his smug, self-congratulatory, conceit. (There are two sides to every story: Putin denied that he let the dog out to scare Merkel: 'I did not know that she was scared of dogs. I just wanted to make her happy by showing her my dog. I have subsequently explained this to her and apologised' he told Zvezda, the nationwide television network run by the Russian Ministry of Defence. Convincing or not, the fact that he had to comment on the story showed that his tactic had backfired.[3])

All this was, if not forgotten, then at least largely overlooked eight years later. In fact, after the first encounter their relations improved. Putin realised that machismo was getting him nowhere – if anything, the opposite.

Merkel was looking after Germany's interests, even if these clashed with those of Berlin's traditional allies. In 2008, the USA was pressing hard for Ukraine and Georgia to join NATO. President George W. Bush was quietly confident that Merkel would consent to the move. He felt he had a good relationship with her, which was true, but that was irrelevant to the decision as far as the German Chancellor was concerned. At the NATO summit in Bucharest in April, Merkel effectively vetoed the American-sponsored Membership Action Plan. Georgia's President was a loose cannon and someone whom she didn't trust, and Ukraine was too volatile to be covered by NATO's Article 5: 'that an armed attack against one or more of them in Europe or North America shall be considered an attack against them all'. She was also aware, as were her advisors, that the Russians were acutely concerned about encroachment from the West. For NATO to admit the two former Soviet states to their ranks would play into fears of the threat from the West which had been the recurrent theme in all Russian foreign policy since the Napoleonic Wars, if not before. To acknowledge this was not to kowtow to Putin but simply to recognise as legitimate a concern expressed by even Mikhail Gorbachev. When NATO was expanded to include the Baltic states, the former President said: 'Western politicians would have liked to see Russia play second fiddle in world politics . . . [Such] an arrogant attitude towards Russia and her interests is deeply insulting to the Russian people, and fraught with grave consequences.'[4] Putin's foreign policy has remained almost identical to that articulated in the late 1990s by Gorbachev: to maintain strength within the traditional heartland.

Putin had been one of the constants in foreign policy equations during Merkel's reign. When he temporarily stood down and served as Prime Minister from 2008 to 2012, Dmitri Medvedev, derisively known as 'the Teddy Bear', was selected as pro forma President. There was no doubt who was in charge: Putin was. While Merkel was not enthusiastic about Putin's return after a dubious election in 2012, and expressed concern about reported irregularities and allegations of electoral fraud, she refrained from criticising him. Merkel was not, it seemed, overly alarmed at the prospect of having to deal with the former KGB man; he was a known quantity – not someone she liked or agreed with, but at least the devil she knew. Before the 2013 election in Germany, a commentator described the two leaders as like 'an old married couple who have long got used to each other's ploys'.[5]

NEGOTIATING WITH PUTIN

Considering this background, it is hardly surprising that the German Chancellor played a major role in the negotiations with Russia after the surprise annexation of Crimea. Throughout Merkel acted to de-escalate the conflict. Many of their 38 telephone conversations had taken place in the first weeks after the annexation when Merkel, speaking in Russian, was 'counseling him [Putin] to pull back from Ukraine while the West could still help him save face'.[6]

Putin had not listened. He did not expect that Merkel, let alone the German Chancellor's respected and experienced new foreign minister Frank-Walter Steinmeier, would (or could) do more than talk, criticise and plead. Steinmeier had returned to the Foreign Office after the 2013 election ended in a stalemate and a new Grand Coalition was formed. But Steinmeier had also been Chief of Staff to Gerhard Schröder and Putin assumed that the new Foreign Secretary would never cross his political mentor and Merkel's predecessor as Chancellor. Yet while Gerhard Schröder imprudently celebrated his 70th birthday with Putin, his former sidekick and confidante, Steinmeier, was 'condemning Russia's Crimea snatch as resolutely as Merkel'.[7]

Putin had made the first miscalculation, but he was still in a strong position. Equally, Merkel was determined not to let Putin's bully-boy tactics remain unanswered. She knew she had to tread carefully, and was realistic enough to know that the Crimea was unlikely to be returned to Ukraine. The goal was containment, for any escalation of the situation could be catastrophic. She needed allies and she needed to show Putin that soft power – economics and diplomacy – was a stronger weapon than military might after all.

Her strongest card was her softly spoken diplomacy and, perhaps above all, her good relations with other smaller countries. On 17 March 2014 the EU's Council of Ministers imposed sanctions on Russia and travel restrictions on some prominent allies of Putin. Upon her return from Brussels, Merkel told the German Parliament that she was ready to tighten the sanctions. But this was not the main, let alone the most important message in her speech.

Perhaps more than any of her colleagues, Merkel knew Putin's soft spots: his vanity, his almost desperate quest to be recognised as a great statesman by an equally great power. Russia had become a member of the G8 in 1998 after Bill Clinton and Tony Blair had asked Boris Yeltsin to join. It was an informal and prestigious group of the world's eight leading industrial nations and being a member was symbolically significant. The next G8 meeting was going to be in Sochi in Russia in June 2014, and Putin was in the process of pulling out all possible stops to show off the Olympic city. This was his weak spot. Merkel wanted to deny Putin a chance to shine and she wanted to hit him where it would hurt him the most. She slowly walked up on the rostrum. She was still limping after a skiing accident on her Christmas break but she looked more determined than ever, or as determined as one can look on crutches with a broken pelvis. 'Russia is isolated in all international organisations,' she told the German Parliament. And then she dropped the bombshell: until Russia complied with international law 'there will not be a G8 summit, and there will be no G8 as such'.[8]

Merkel had humiliated Putin. Economic sanctions and other predictable reactions had formed part of his considerations. But he had not reckoned with the possibility that she would effectively exclude him from the club of the most powerful industrial nations on earth. Strictly speaking such a decision was not for Merkel to make, and not all Germans were best pleased with it. An estimated 6,000 German businesses representing 300,000 employees were dependent upon trade with Russia. Putin had calculated that Merkel, as a pragmatist, would criticise him but not impose sanctions. Once again he was wrong. She had made a move that he had not foreseen; she had been able to impose sanctions that hurt Germany far less than he had imagined.

The sanctions imposed on Russia did massively affect German business. Yes, the likes of Bayer and other pharmaceutical companies would lose an estimated €2.1 billion and the car manufacturers would lose a similar amount. But business leaders were happy, as one CEO told *Manager Magazin*, 'to make sacrifices'. In fact German companies were suffering the least. France had taken a greater hit (Paris had negotiated a lucrative contract for two helicopter carriers with Russia), and Britain was concerned that the commercial interests of the City of London would be hurt by sanctions. Neither of these two countries was able to do much about it. Once again, Merkel got her way. In large measure, she did so through alliances with smaller EU countries. Her background as an *Ossi*, and her experience as someone who had lived under Russian tyranny gave her credibility in the former Communist countries. And her willingness to stand up for north European countries such as Denmark, the Netherlands, Sweden and Finland on earlier occasions meant that she could count on support all across the European Union. Britain and France lost out, largely because they had not cultivated the same contacts.

While America, France and Ukraine were all involved in the negotiations, it was soon evident that the crisis over Ukraine was a drama whose main protagonists were Vladimir Putin and Angela Merkel. Putin was by no means in checkmate position. Militarily he still had the upper hand, but Merkel had been able to buy herself and her allies valuable time. The sanctions had been unexpected and Putin was still reeling from expulsion from the G8. It was against this backdrop that representatives from the USA, EU, Ukraine and Russia met in Geneva in mid-April. The meeting did not produce a breakthrough, but it stalled Russia's progress into the eastern part of Ukraine; the Russians refrained from attacking Novorossiya (as many Russians called the Donetsk and Luhansk regions, which they had effectively occupied).

Having hindered the attack, Ukraine was able to conduct a relatively orderly presidential election in May, won by Petro Poroshenko. This conferred a certain level of legitimacy upon the Ukrainian government, an administration the Russians had hitherto referred to as counterrevolutionary insurgents and even terrorists. Even militarily Putin seemed to be losing his grip. His *maskirovka* tactics had worked well in the Crimea and earlier in South Ossetia (part of Georgia) and Transnistra (part of Moldova with a large Russian-speaking population). But holding onto small enclaves was one thing; effectively occupying a country the size of Belgium by proxy was a rather more complex task. By the end of July the re-established Ukrainian army had pushed the insurgents back.

This was unacceptable to Putin. It was one thing for Merkel to humiliate him publicly, but to allow his proxies to be defeated by an army supported by his Western foes was a bridge too far. In the first few days of August 2014, 7,000 Russian troops overran fifteen Ukrainian brigades, or so it was reported by leading defence analysts. The facts surrounding this 'invasion' are contested – Russia maintaining that she has no troops in the country. Kiev could do nothing but sue for peace – or, more accurately, agree to a ceasefire.

Once again, however, Putin was faced with a strategic problem associated with his preferred type of warfare. In traditional military operations there is a clear command structure with equally well-defined tasks. However, when you are fighting a war by proxy you run the risk that your hired guns may get bad ideas. This is ostensibly what happened when, so it seems, Russia's allies shot down Malaysia Airlines flight MH17 en route from Amsterdam on 17 July.

Initially the Russians claimed that the civilian aircraft had suffered mechanical failure, but this explanation was firmly rejected by a group of Dutch experts. Needless to say, Putin himself was not responsible for shooting down the airliner, but it was impossible to claim that his proxies were innocent. Putin had suffered another propaganda defeat. He ordered the troops stationed near the border to return to their bases and tried another tactic. He now threatened to turn off the taps. The problem for Putin was that oil prices were falling. This was a concern, for 30 per cent of the Russian economy was accounted for by oil and gas. Not selling the commodity which in large part kept the oligarchs on side and financed Putin's foreign policy schemes would be short-sighted, especially as oil prices had fallen by more than 40 per cent since June. The markets saved Ukraine, as did the EU and the International Monetary Fund, who offered them money to pay for the gas. Putin had to try another strategy. He returned to a variant of *maskirovka* tactics. Orchestrated by Moscow, the self-styled Donetsk People's Republic and the Luhansk People's Republic held 'presidential' elections and elected pro-Russian candidates, and Kiev rescinded earlier promises to grant the two areas a large measure of autonomy. On 12 November NATO's supreme allied commander, General Philip Breedlove, told the press that 4,000 Russian troops had entered Ukraine. This was, predictably, denied by Russia.

It was immediately after this that Merkel met Putin in Brisbane. She was not best pleased, and he was not willing to give an inch. Shortly after the nocturnal rendezvous Putin left for the airport. He did not attend the official group photo of the G20 leaders, claiming that he needed to sleep before he started work the following Monday. In reality, Putin was reeling once again. The other leaders had ignored him at the meeting. Before he boarded the plane he fired a parting shot, which above all was aimed at the German Chancellor. The sanctions were beginning to work and Putin sounded desperate but also threatening:

> Do they [the EU] want to bankrupt our banks? In that case they
> will bankrupt Ukraine. Have they thought about what they are
> doing at all or not? Or has politics blinded them? As we know eyes
> constitute a peripheral part of the brain. Was something switched
> off in their brains?[9]

Whose brains had been 'switched off' was debatable. But in reality the Kremlin strongman must have known that he had failed to anticipate the moves of his opponents. The problem for the West, in particular Merkel, was that Putin was becoming unpredictable and that humiliation by other countries could tempt him into making ill-considered moves.

Matters did not get much better over the following months. Russian proxies continued to operate within the Ukraine, and Putin refused to accept what appeared to be well-established and incontrovertible facts. At the same time the Russian economy was under strain. The ruble had collapsed on the international markets, partly as a result of sanctions, though it was also attributed to the fall in oil prices. Either way, the Kremlin was in a weaker position. American lawmakers, including Republican Senator John McCain, urged that the Ukrainians be armed. These calls were resolutely rejected, Merkel maintaining her position that 'more military is not the solution'.[10] Whether there was a 'solution' was unclear, as indeed it had been from the beginning of the crisis.

After consultations with President Obama, Angela Merkel began working on a stop-gap solution. At the end of January the EU had agreed to extend the economic sanctions against Russia. Shortly thereafter Merkel met with Martin Schulz, the German President of the European Parliament. Two days later, on 6 February, Merkel travelled to Moscow with the French President François Hollande. The three agreed to meet a week later in Minsk in Belorussia. The Minsk Protocol, the ceasefire agreed in September, had not significantly reduced the fighting and all sides were getting weary. Ukraine continued to make impossible demands; the rebels likewise; Russia was able to sustain the military presence by proxy but was suffering economically. And the EU – and Angela Merkel in particular – was keen to find a temporary solution.

The Europeans had a proposal for the Russian President: talks with all parties including representatives of the breakaway republics in Eastern Ukraine. Putin was surprised, but accepted. He too was tired of his allies and he wanted to find a temporary solution. After sixteen hours of talks – most of them direct talks between Merkel and Putin – the parties agreed to an unconditional ceasefire from 15 February, withdrawal of heavy weapons from the front line, release of prisoners of war, and constitutional reform in Ukraine.

It was clear that the matter had not been permanently resolved. In politics, said former British Prime Minister Benjamin Disraeli, there is no 'finally and for ever', only policies 'which would satisfy this and perhaps the succeeding generation'. Merkel and her allies in the West had not been able to force Putin back, let alone solve the problem in the Ukraine. But she had stopped Putin in his tracks and she had showed that economic policies, sanctions and concerted diplomatic efforts could inflict considerable damage upon Russia and that such policies, when used correctly, could be every bit as effective as military might. *Foreign Affairs,* a magazine that normally espouses 'robust solutions' to international crises, recognised that Merkel and those around her had managed to get the best out of a very difficult situation: 'the well-coordinated Western sanctions, the Ukrainian armed forces' resolute defence of their homeland and Merkel's patient diplomacy have so far produced the least worst outcome – one that no optimist could have dreamed of when Putin annexed Crimea.'[11]

In Merkel's third term, foreign affairs almost entirely took over. All her rivals in the Union had been defeated and none of the other party leaders seemed to want to challenge her. The challenges she had previously met from certain local CDU Governors who wanted a more robust line against foreigners and to limit the powers of the EU had been driven into the background. Merkel had effectively outmanoeuvred politicians who held illiberal and Eurosceptic views. This left the far right open to a new political party, Alternative für Deutschland (AfD).

AfD was different from other short-lived far right parties, at least to begin with. Established by Bernd Lucke, an academic and former economist in the World Bank, it had an air of respectability. The party made its opposition to the euro its main political policy and this worked, up to a point. Although the party narrowly failed to win seats in Parliament (they fell short of the five per cent threshold by a mere 0.3 per cent in 2009), it managed to win seven out of the 96 German seats in the European Parliament in 2014. Its combination of economic liberalism, scepticism towards foreigners and a dose of patriotic language made Lucke's party an attractive proposition for conservative voters who were – to put it mildly – sceptical of Merkel's social liberalism. AfD also found an audience and a demand for their policies in the less prosperous East German towns, winning almost 10 per cent of the vote in the state elections in Saxony in 2014. But the party's stronghold was also its Achilles' heel. Its support in the East tempted it to embrace xenophobic views and it did so at its peril.

Merkel, as was her wont, did not give the AfD the oxygen of publicity; she had other things to do. Moreover, the party was not yet a threat. However, in late 2014 something changed. Demonstrations broke out in East German cities, above all in Dresden. This was not a friendly civic protest, as in 1989. The demonstrations were organised by Pegida – an acronym for Patriotische Europäer gegen die Islamisierung des Abendlandes (Patriotic Europeans against the Islamification of the West). Thousands of protesters gathered in the streets demanding tougher legislation. AfD's leader Bernd Lucke was prudent enough not to get too closely involved, but his deputy Frauke Petry disagreed. Sensing that AfD could gain votes by addressing the concerns of the many who were marching in the streets, she started a power-struggle in the party. Meanwhile the protests went on. The demonstrations were organised by Lutz Bachmann, a former soccer player with a string of criminal convictions, who maintained that his organisation was purely patriotic and had nothing to do with Nazism.

It was two months before Merkel commented on the demonstrations. Then, suddenly, in her annual New Year address, she confronted the organisation head-on. Speaking only about Pegida, but clearly indicating that AfD was cut from the same cloth, she said: 'I say to everyone who goes on these demonstrations: Don't follow the clarion call of the organisers.'[12] Then, in an audacious move, she helped organise anti-demonstrations and got some of the country's most beloved soccer stars to go on demonstrations against Pegida. And then, seemingly out of the blue, a picture surfaced on the internet: a selfie of Lutz Bachmann with a Hitler-moustache and a haircut to match. His credibility was destroyed – in this case, it seems, by some internet-savvy researchers in the Chancellor's office. The demonstrations died out.

At the same time the power struggle in AfD continued. Lucke, who still wanted to run a libertarian free-market party, was losing the battle. The press was increasingly treating the AfD as a sectarian anti-immigration party. In 2015, while Merkel was negotiating with the Greeks over yet another crisis, Lucke lost the leadership of the party. Frau Petry had won the battle for the soul of AfD and had lost it all its respectability in the process. She was now presiding over a politically irrelevant 'Pegida party', *Süddeutsche Zeitung* opined. Even after the refugee crisis later in the year, support for Pegida remained low. In November 2015, despite much public debate about immigration and Islam, 83 per cent of Germans felt no sympathy for the movement. Electorally, Merkel did not need to lose any more sleep over the far right. Germany is the only country in Western Europe (with the exception of Luxembourg) not to have a populist party. Quite a feat when you think of the country's history. However – and this was a concern – 78 per cent of those polled feared the growing influence of Islam.

Maybe she shouldn't have been so calm, even complacent. A few months later on 1 January 2016 the party hit 10 per cent approval in the opinion polls.

A GREEK TRAGEDY: ACT 3

> 'What? You can't pay? No money, no Schnapps.'
> Bertolt Brecht, *Mother Courage and her Children*

Game theory is the scientific study of decision-making between interacting individuals. The premise of the discipline is that politics, life, economics, biology, and just about everything else resembles board games where individuals make choices in anticipation of their opponents' likely moves. The discipline was established by émigré mathematicians, above all by the Hungarian-born János Neumann (later John von Neumann) and German-born Oskar Morgenstern in the 1940s. Game theory was further finessed by John Nash, whose troubled life was the subject of the film *A Beautiful Mind*.

One of the most important games is called 'Hawk-Dove' or 'Chicken' and is described thus in an authoritative book on the subject:

> Jack and Jill come across a $100 note on the pavement and each has a basic choice between demanding the lion's share (playing hawkishly or 'h') or acquiescing in the other person taking the lion's share (playing dove or 'd'). Suppose in this instance the lion's share is $90 and when they both play dove they share the $100 equally, while if they both act hawkishly a fight ensues and the $100 gets destroyed.[13]

Yanis Varoufakis, who became Minister of Finance in Greece in January 2015, wrote these lines. A brilliant academic cited extensively in the scholarly literature and a man with an impressive array of publications to his name, Varoufakis was a recognised economist. But he was a political novice.

It seemed that the game theorist was deliberately engaged in a showdown similar to the ones described in his own textbook. The Greek government and the rest of Europe were playing a 'Hawk-Dove game' and a rhetorical fight had ensued which threatened to destroy the Eurozone much in the same way as the $100 note was destroyed in the text-book example drawn up by Varoufakis and his academic colleagues. Now the 53-year-old scholar was sitting in his new office in central Athens just off Syntagma Square, contemplating what to do and how to save his country. How did he get there? The background goes back to the political realignment in Greece in 2012.

The euro-crisis had been pushed into the background while the West was engaged in its diplomatic dispute with Russia, but it hadn't gone away. This had political implications. In May 2012 no party achieved an overall majority in the legislative elections to the Greek Parliament. When none of the largest parties was able to form a government, President Karolos Papoulias, a former pole vault champion, called new elections to break the deadlock only five weeks later. The June elections did not make much of a difference, though the conservative politician

Antonis Samaras, leader of the centre-right New Democracy was able to form a minority government. His position was precarious.

Seemingly out of the blue, Synaspismós Rizospastikís Aristerás (the Coalition of the Radical Left, better known as Syriza) had emerged as the second strongest party. A coalition of 13 different parties, it had done well in May's election and even better in the June poll. Now they were almost level pegging with New Democracy and vowed not to accept more austerity policies. Throughout the rest of the year, Samaras sought to find a way through, but at every stage his efforts were hampered. Syriza's leader Alexis Tsipras, a charismatic young civil engineer, consistently and tenaciously tore into the 'old parties' whom he blamed for all Greece's ills.

When Parliament was unable to agree on a new President, it was dissolved as required by the constitution. The new elections – the third in one year – took place in January 2015. Syriza got 36.3 per cent of the votes, winning 149 of the 300 seats in the legislature. After a few days of negotiations Alexis Tsipras reached an agreement with the right-wing populist party Anexartitoi Ellines (the Independent Greeks, or Anel) and together they formed a majority coalition government.

That is how the political career of Professor Varoufakis began. He was appointed Finance Minister of the new government and he immediately went to work. With a shaved head, leather jacket and riding a Yamaha XRJ 1300, Varoufakis looked more like a thug than an academic, let alone a finance minister in an EU country. And the way he addressed his fellow countrymen, his colleagues and the journalists who interviewed him was uncompromising, tough and often populist: 'Europe in its infinite wisdom decided to deal with this bankruptcy by loading the largest loan in human history on the weakest of shoulders . . . What we've been having ever since is a kind of fiscal waterboarding that has turned this nation into a 'debt colony'.[14] The international media immediately sensed that the Greeks were playing a different game. Whereas the outgoing conservative administration had been inclined to play 'dove' in game-theoretic parlance, Varoufakis and Tsipras were showing every indication that they were playing 'hawks'.

It was clear from the very moment Varoufakis and Tsipras took up their respective posts that the opponent was one particular country, Germany. 'Go ahead, Angela, make my day' screamed the headline on the cover of the *Economist*, which also featured an image of the Greek goddess Aphrodite armed with a gun. The Syriza government talked about 'Europe' but in reality they meant Germany, and the main target of their venom, their demands and their rage was one individual, Angela Merkel.

But Angela Merkel herself was playing a different game, or rather she was engaged in what chess players call 'simultaneous exhibition': a grandmaster concurrently playing several different opponents on different boards. To the outside observer – and certainly to the Greek government – it appeared that her principal 'game' was with them. In reality the most difficult opponent was her own backbenchers. All policy is global, but all politics is still local. As anyone who has studied Merkel's career even remotely will know, her prime focus was Germany and the German electors. As one of her sharpest critics wrote, 'Her chief aim is to win votes in Germany. To achieve that, she must . . . defend German money and German competitiveness in world markets. If Europe can be rescued at the same time she will certainly not be opposed to that.'[15] Her main negotiating strategy was to find a way of appeasing the voters in Germany and more immediately the parliamentary members of her own party, who had let it be known that no more money was forthcoming. But at the same time she was aware that a Greek exit from the euro (known as Grexit) could be her legacy. And she did not want to go down in history as the woman who presided over the collapse of the euro.

The German Chancellor was conciliatory, at least outwardly. On 12 February she met with Tsipras in Brussels. The meeting was cordial. Merkel seemed to be charming the younger man, who for his part seemed somewhat starstruck. Merkel calmed him down and – to the surprise of many – struck a positive note: 'Europe is always excellent at finding compromises,' she said. But if Tsipras expected to get it all for free he was mistaken: 'However, we also have to make clear that Europe's credibility depends on us sticking to rules.'[16]

Tsipras, however, continued to play hardball. And he did so with some success, it seemed. Sometimes playing 'Hawk' has its advantages. In February 2015 the Eurozone finance ministers agreed to an extension of Greece's repayments, though only in return for a cast-iron guarantee that the country would pay the amount due by the end of June. But the reforms were not forthcoming. Instead Mr Tsipras returned to Athens with a spring in his step and announced that he – and the new government – had essentially won the negotiations:

> We will be entering a new, more substantive stage in our negotiations until we reach a final agreement to transition from the catastrophic policies of the Memoranda, to policies that will focus on development, employment and social cohesion.[17]

No reforms took place in Greece, but Merkel, perhaps surprisingly, maintained her optimism. The Greeks turned up the political heat. Instead of beginning the implementation of the reforms, Alexis Tsipras threw a political curve ball. On 7 April he demanded that Germany pay €279 billion in war reparations. This was in principle not as outlandish as some in the German establishment believed. Deputy Prime Minister Sigmar Gabriel commented: 'I honestly consider this to be a bit stupid.'[18] He was not completely right, however: Germany had not entirely settled its debts after the Second World War, and Greece had some moral claim to a modicum of compensation. But legally speaking – and this was the line Merkel took – the issue was settled.

Greece seemed to have overplayed its hand. Raising the Second World War and playing on anti-Nazi sentiments had little effect in other countries in the Eurozone who were more concerned about their own finances than about settling scores from a war that had ended 70 years before. Tsipras was getting nowhere in his negotiations and he was consistently met with a disarming smile and accompanying hot air and sweet talk from Angela Merkel. The German Chancellor, who left the more detailed discussions to Schäuble, calmly and consistently repeated her mantra that Greece needed to implement reforms and had agreed to pay the money back.

Once again Tsipras changed tack. On 8 April he went to Moscow. In international relations some scholars talk about 'linkage politics', the strategy of linking policy demands in one area to demands in another. In the 1970s Henry Kissinger and Richard Nixon successfully linked international trade policies to defence policies and gained concessions from the Russians in nuclear talks. Tsipras opted for the same strategy.

On the face of it this was a bold move. Greece, as a member of the EU, could work for the scrapping of sanctions against the Russians. It was not an empty threat. Immediately after coming to power the Syriza government had delayed an agreement on the renewal of the sanctions against the Russians, though they had quickly given in. Now they were playing the game of linking these sanctions to their own economic woes. Russia had quite a lot to gain. In addition to a potential lifting of the sanctions, Greece had ports and was exactly the kind of ally Putin wanted in the Mediterranean.

Putin seemed happy to play along, if for no other reason than to tease Merkel and Hollande. But the Russian President was also pragmatic and realistic. Greece could offer no guarantees that they could help lift the sanctions. Putin might be able to find the money Greece needed to meet its payments, yet even that would be difficult with a collapsing currency and record low oil prices. Moreover, and this was the crucial factor, Tsipras had very little to offer. Putin would not have immediate access to Greek ports no matter how much he paid Tsipras. As a member of NATO, the Greek Prime Minister was locked into treaty obligations that he could ill afford to break. In the end Putin offered Tsipras nothing and curtly noted that the euro-crisis was a European problem. He could not and would not help Tsipras. It was not in his interest.

Tsipras requested yet another meeting with Angela Merkel. She granted him one hour before the EU summit on refugees on 23 April. Merkel, as was her wont, was sweetness itself when they met. She organised the obligatory handshake for the photographers and Tsipras could do nothing but play along. Then, as in their other meetings, she once again reiterated that more money for Greece was conditional upon structural reforms: a higher pension age, public sector cuts and the end of privileges for certain industries.

The situation was getting desperate for Tsipras. The Greeks were due to make a payment to the International Monetary Fund at the beginning of June but were granted an extension to the end of the month. Once again it seemed that game theory tactics had worked; that the other countries, above all the Germans, were apprehensive as to the consequences of Greece defaulting on its loans.

GREFERENDUM

It was 9.45 am on 26 June when Alexis Tsipras entered the conference chamber in Rue de la Loi in the centre of Brussels. It was a Thursday and the following Tuesday Greece was due to make a payment of €1.5 billion to the International Monetary Fund. They didn't have the money, yet the Greek Prime Minister seemed upbeat. That, at any rate, is how he came across on the television screens.

His discussion partners were already there. Both Angela Merkel and the French President François Hollande were ready to talk. They had a clear proposal. Greece could get an extension on its bailout provided that retirement age was increased, that the Greeks increased VAT and raised certain taxes. Merkel reportedly did most of the talking. Tsipras was still smiling after he left 45 minutes later. Meanwhile in Athens Greek citizens were rushing to withdraw money from Greek banks.

But there was a sense of optimism in Brussels. At 12.30 pm, the creditors agreed to extend the bailout for another five months so that Greece would, after all, be able to pay its creditors on Tuesday the 30th when the repayment was due. Everybody seemed relieved. Jean-Claude Juncker, the President of the European Commission, and Donald Tusk, the President of the European Council, called a press conference at 2.45 pm. Both were smiling. There was, said Donald Tusk, 'a real chance' of a deal. Juncker went even further: 'I am quite optimistic . . . There is a real chance of concluding an agreement.' Maybe it was this upbeat statement that tempted fate. In any case, at 3.30 pm the Greek government, through a spokesman, announced that Greece rejected the proposal presented by Merkel and Hollande at the morning meeting.

Tsipras did not comment; he was already on a plane on his way back to an emergency Cabinet meeting in Athens. All was quiet on the Greek front until 4.30 pm when Yanis Varoufakis made a short statement. To everybody's surprise, he was upbeat and smiling. 'I see no reason why we cannot have a deal,' he said. 'Unfortunately, every time we make a concession and we get three quarters of the way, the institutions [of the EU] do the exact opposite, they toughen their stance.' What concessions the Greeks had made was not clear; when asked, he moved on and pretended that he hadn't heard the question. After six months as Finance Minister he had already learned how to react and how to avoid unwelcome questions.

Merkel and the other European leaders were left hanging. They could do very little but agree to meet again on Saturday 28th to come up with a Plan B. Merkel went back home to Berlin. She was aware that there had been protests in Athens and that there had been arrests in Syntagma Square, but that was hardly new. What was new was the statement Tsipras issued at 11 pm that same evening: 'After an emergency meeting of the cabinet the government has decided to put the package of austerity measures put forward by the creditors to a referendum next Sunday,' the Greek Prime Minister informed the world. He continued: 'After five months of hard negotiations, our partners, unfortunately, ended up making a proposal that was an ultimatum towards Greek democracy and the Greek people.'

The finance ministers in Brussels were perplexed, to put it mildly. Greece had walked out and had – by both actions and words – rejected a plan that would enable them to pay the IMF. Yet the Syriza government continued to make demands. After all, it had worked before. They asked for an extension of the bailout until after 5 July, the day of the proposed referendum. There was anger around the table and many of the smaller Eurozone countries – economies with a per capita GDP lower than Greece – were expressing frustration that they were expected to pay for the bailout. At 1 pm on Saturday 28th the euro group finance ministers rejected an extension. The situation was getting out of hand.

Once again, Merkel and Hollande tried to reason with the Greek Prime Minister. The situation was almost identical to the one Merkel and Hollande's predecessor Nicolas Sarkozy had experienced in 2011 when George Papandreou threatened to hold a referendum on a deal before Merkel and her French colleague persuaded him to rethink. Behind the scenes, Merkel was less concerned. Many in her party and in the Grand Coalition were happy to see Greece leave the euro and she knew that getting a third bailout through Parliament would be very difficult. In reality Tsipras had fallen into her trap. But still, for all that, she was also concerned that she would be blamed for the debacle; that she as the uncrowned queen of Europe would be seen as the politician who presided over the collapse of the euro.

Merkel's officials organised a conference call at 6.45 pm on that Saturday evening, but Tsipras was not Papandreou. The exchange was tense and curt. Tsipras refused to call off the referendum and he rejected the suggestion that the Greek voters be asked whether they wanted to remain in the euro or not.

The Greek banks were closed on the Monday after the momentous weekend. On Tuesday Greece became the first developed country ever to default on its loans to the IMF. It was evident that the Syriza government was still playing a variant of the Hawk-Dove game: mutually assured destruction if both parts play hardball. Indeed, even financial analysts used game theory to express their concern.

The world does not operate according to economics textbooks. Following the game theories of Varoufakis, Germany and other members in the Eurozone would – after a bit of sabre-rattling – change strategy and become more doveish. They would realise that the amount of money, all things considered, was minimal and that it would be better to grant the Greeks what they wanted and bear this rather minimal cost in return for avoiding the disaster of a meltdown of the euro. After all, Merkel herself had unequivocally stated that if the 'euro fails we all fail'. All other things being equal, as economists are fond of saying, this analysis was correct. But the problem was that all things were not equal and that the world had moved on. The European Financial Stability Facility and more recent stability mechanisms meant that the other Eurozone economies were relatively sheltered from the Greek contagion. A Grexit, the markets reckoned, was not necessarily a disaster. Indeed, there was a sense in the financial markets that the Eurozone would probably be better off if Tsipras and his band of radical leftists went back to the old Greek currency, the drachma. The euro rose one per cent in New York the day after Alexis Tsipras announced that a referendum would be held.

This was the flaw in Varoufakis' analysis. The Greeks played hardball, they acted like Hawks, but, unlike in the simplified world of game theory, there was *not* mutually assured destruction; German taxpayers would not suffer from a Grexit. Rather they would save money in lower tax bills and might even have more holiday money if they chose to go on vacation in the Aegean or in Athens.

On 4 July, 61 per cent of the Greek voters voted No to the austerity package in the referendum. The following day Yanis Varoufakis lost his job, sacked by Tsipras. The outgoing finance minister complained via

Twitter that he had been given his marching orders because the other European countries could not accept him. The markets reacted positively to the news.

In 2010 the prospect of a Greek exit from the Eurozone would have sent seismic shockwaves through the financial markets and sent the euro into a tailspin. In 2015 things were different. The financial stability regulations espoused and forced through by Angela Merkel had worked. The day after the Greek referendum the euro rose against the US dollar. Not by much, a mere 0.05 per cent. The *Financial Times* reported that 'Yields on the 10-year German Bund edged down just three basic points.' In plain English, the cost of borrowing money was down; the risk of lending money was lower. The policy had worked. Markets had gained trust in the Eurozone. The German politicians were adamant that there would be no more money for the Greeks. Wolfang Bosbach, the conservative and influential CDU backbencher, was clear: 'You don't solve this with more money. What matters is structural reforms.'[19] Merkel did not contradict him. Up to a point her tactics had worked, though there was still a momentous crisis. The first part of it had been weathered but a solution was still necessary. That was her next task.

It had become clear over the weekend that Merkel and Schäuble were not singing from the same hymn-sheet; far from it, in fact. Merkel wanted Greece to stay in the Eurozone. Her finance minister, by contrast, was ready to show them the door. The next four days became dramatic.

FOUR DAYS TO SAVE EUROPE: ANOTHER BATTLE BETWEEN MERKEL AND SCHÄUBLE

Varoufakis' successor, Euclid Tsakalotos, an Oxford-educated economist with aristocratic origins, did not seem able to square the political circle of getting a deal. His country was heading for the dreaded Grexit and he called on France for help. President Hollande seconded some of his economic advisors to Greece to write up a plan, but the mood was not positive. The Greeks as well as their French bureaucratic mercenaries knew that any deal had to be sealed in Berlin before anything was decided in Brussels. All seemed quiet on the eastern front, however; Merkel said little.

On the Thursday morning following Sunday's referendum Merkel met Wolfgang Schäuble, Sigmar Gabriel and Frank-Walter Steinmeier. Schäuble began the conversation. He presented what he called 'the plan' in concise, legalistic terms. He urged a Grexit. Not a fully blown one – that would be legally difficult, he admitted – but a time-limited exit which would allow Greece to re-enter the euro when – or if – the Tsipras government implemented the necessary reforms. Merkel, Steinmeier and Gabriel did not oppose the plan, but characteristically none of them said anything publicly.

The following day, the German Ministry of Finance published a paper, written in English. Schäuble's head of department, Thomas Steffen, authored the document, 'Comments on the Latest Greek Proposal'. The paper concluded that Greece could be excluded from the Eurozone for a minimum of five years if the country did not comply with the decision made by a majority of the Eurozone finance ministers. Yet, when Schäuble landed in Brussels on Saturday morning, he realised that the clause regarding the time-limited Grexit was *not* included in the document which was sent to the European finance ministers by the German Foreign Office. Schäuble was incandescent with rage. He knew Merkel was behind it. The Chancellor had overruled him and left out the key element of the plan.

Schäuble did not give up. Before the meeting with the finance ministers he was due to attend a meeting with colleagues from the European Peoples' Party – the loose confederation of Conservative and Christian Democrat parties in the European Parliament. Most of his colleagues wanted to make the conditions so tough that Greece had no choice but to leave the euro. His talks to conservative colleagues from other EU countries had the desired effect. He mentioned the plan and won approval for it.

The battle-lines were once again drawn: Schäuble versus Merkel. The former put the plan back on the agenda. Meanwhile Merkel talked to other colleagues among the heads of state and governments. They were not pleased with the prospect of a Grexit, and they were concerned that Schäuble and the other finance ministers were in the process of forcing Athens out. The Italian Prime Minister was particularly concerned: 'I say this to the Germans. Enough is enough.'

Merkel did not speak to the public. She allowed her Finance Minister to conduct his own diplomacy. After all she would have the last word. As so often before, she held back and played a waiting game. Twenty-four hours passed without her saying anything. Then finally, at 4.15 pm on Sunday, Merkel met President Hollande, Tsipras and Tusk in the latter's Salon du Président on the eighth floor of the Robert Schuman Building in Brussels. Tsipras asked if he could bring Euclid Tsakalotos with him. Merkel said yes, but only on the condition that she could bring Schäuble. But then she paused. She spoke to Tusk and Hollande, and then let Tsipras know she had changed her mind. Tsakalotos could come along, after all. Schäuble had to wait outside.

The parties talked until 4.45 am on Monday morning. Schäuble's plan was no longer in play and the discussion was now about another proposal, namely that the EU would control the money earned from the privatisation of Greek assets. Tsipras regarded this as 'absolutely unacceptable', but there was the outline of an agreement.[20] As in the negotiations over the European budget at Merkel's first summit in 2006, it was now a matter of finding the right number everybody could accept. Merkel proposed that Greece could control 10 per cent of the assets. Tsipras demanded 50 per cent. Donald Tusk, in a move choreographed with Merkel, proposed 12.5 per cent. Tsipras accepted. The Greek Prime Minister also accepted that he had to implement the reforms to the pension system. It was a humiliating deal for Tsipras as well as for Schäuble, who had wanted Greece to be forced out of the euro. It was vintage Merkel; she waited to the last minute before she agreed.

'Hegel noted somewhere that all historical events and individuals appear twice but he forgot to mention the first time as tragedy and the second time as farce,' wrote Karl Marx. His latter-day disciples in Syriza were painfully aware of the fact that the tragedies of the first and second bailout were repeated by the farce of the third crisis: the Greek government agreed to a proposal that was tougher than the one the voters – on their recommendation – had rejected only days before. The Queen of Europe had forced her will through – again.

Tsipras, the man who less than a week before was railing against the evils of capitalism, had to give in; Angela Merkel dictated the terms, seconded by smaller countries like Finland and Estonia. The other small countries could not justify a third bailout to their voters. Nor could Merkel, not unless she got significant concessions. She got them.

At the end of a classical Greek tragedy a *deus ex machina* often descends to the stage to resolve a seemingly insoluble problem. The great Greek dramatist Euripides could not have written it better.[21]

EXODUS

'The stranger that dwelleth with you shall be unto you as one born among you.'

Leviticus 19:34

The ink was barely dry on the Greek loan document when Europe woke up to a predicament as momentous as the euro-crisis: a wave of mass migration not seen for decades, perhaps even centuries. In 2010, Angela Merkel said that multiculturalism had 'totally failed'.[22] But refugees and migration were not issues she often spoke about. In fact, in the summer of 2015 she was criticised for trying to comfort a young Palestinian girl named Reem on a television programme. The girl, a refugee, had eloquently and in perfect German told the Chancellor that she would like to stay in Germany and go to university. Merkel responded that it might not be possible. 'Politics can be tough,' she said, adding, 'You are an extremely nice person but you also know that there are thousands and thousands of people in Palestinian refugee camps in Lebanon.'[23] When the girl started to cry Merkel evidently took pity on her and tried to comfort her, but she did not alter her statement. She felt the plight of the young woman, but she could not change policy just because of a single case. Bureaucratic and inflexible perhaps, but ultimately a rational approach in keeping with the rule of law. Many criticised her for being heartless, not least the international media. Reem, however, backed Merkel: 'Personally it would have hurt me more if she had not been honest. I like honest people like Frau Merkel.'[24]

It was a completely different Angela Merkel who emerged a month or so later. The reason was the exodus of refugees from Syria. Largely as a result of the conflict in Syria, the number of refugees from the war-torn country grew exponentially from 142,000 in 2012, to 2.3 million in 2014, to an unprecedented 4 million on 1 August 2015, and still more were arriving. The presence of the mostly Muslim refugees caused concern, consternation and even violent clashes in parts of southeast Germany. Far-right groups attacked a refugee centre in the small town of Heidenau southeast of Dresden, in the state of Saxony, and 31 policemen were injured.

Sinister attacks happened in other countries too, but politicians in neighbouring nations seemed reluctant to criticise the mob. In Denmark, a country famous for having saved its Jewish population during the Second World War, the newly elected Liberal Prime Minister Lars Løkke Rasmussen had promised a tough zero-tolerance policy on hooligans, but when neo-Nazis painted swastikas on the wall of an asylum centre he did not respond.

Merkel took a different approach. She travelled to Heidenau and was met with angry cries from skinheads who denounced her as a traitor. In fact, that is putting it mildly. 'Cunt! Get back into your ugly car!' shouted a protester. Her spokesperson Steffen Seibert said he feared for his life but Merkel remained calm. She denounced the protesters and then struck a more conciliatory note. Germany had a moral duty to help the immigrants.[26] She also proposed that Germany, in this hour of need, would lead the way and welcome a large number of refugees into the country.[25]

The international media, even those who had traditionally been sceptical of the Chancellor, hailed what they saw as her brave intervention. In an editorial *The Economist* described her speech as 'brave, decisive and right', and the paper continued:

> Angela Merkel may be the most powerful politician in Europe, but she has rarely shown much inclination for bold leadership. Both in domestic politics, and especially during the euro-crisis, the German chancellor's style has been one of cautious incrementalism . . . against this background; Mrs Merkel's approach to Europe's immigration crisis is remarkable. As throngs of African and Arabs turn Greek and Italian islands and eastern European railway stations into refugee camps (and are found dead in Austrian lorries),

> the chancellor has taken a brave stand. She has denounced xeno-
> phobes, signalled Germany's readiness to take more Syrian ref-
> ugees and set out a European solution to a politically explosive
> problem . . . In a crisis where Europe has little to be proud of,
> Merkel's leadership is a shining exception.[27]

Of course, it could be argued that Merkel had little to fear politically. Whereas politicians in Scandinavia, the Low Countries, and to an extent Britain were under electoral threat from the far right, Merkel was operating in a different context. It was politically easier for her to criticise xenophobic protesters. Germany might have had the likes of AfD, but that party was in disarray and there was no credible party to the right of Merkel's CDU – and no alternative to her as Chancellor. Even two months after the refugee crisis had started Merkel's CDU/CSU were on 37 per cent in the polls (down three percentage points from August). The Social Democrats were stuck on a paltry 23 per cent.

Merkel had previously stated that Germany could not house all the poor people fleeing poverty in Africa. She maintained this position, but the refugees from Syria were something else: they were people fleeing death, destruction and the barbarous Islamic State. Not all countries saw it like that. Hungary, Serbia and many other eastern European countries refused to take more than a token number of refugees. The same was true for Britain who would take in a mere 6,000 a year. Throughout August and well into September, the immigration crisis showed no signs of abating. And, much as the German government tried to push, cajole and pressure other countries into taking what Berlin regarded as their fair share, the other EU countries refused. Some German politicians openly defied the Chancellor. Thus Horst Seehofer, the leader of the CSU and Governor of Bavaria, met with the Hungarian Prime Minister Viktor Orban in a 'show of solidarity' – and to signal his opposition to Mrs Merkel.

Merkel ignored the provocation and dealt with the crisis as she had dealt with others. She dispatched one of her trusted allies and avoided making remarks that could stir up controversy. When the EU interior ministers met in Brussels on 22 October 2015 the positions were entrenched. The countries in central and eastern Europe, above all the Czech Republic and Poland – but also Denmark in the north and

Ireland in the west – refused to take more than a token number of refugees. Germany (backed up by France and the Netherlands) suggested it would be necessary to decide the issue through a majority vote. That decisions regarding immigration, border control and asylum could be decided through majority voting was one of the changes adopted in the Lisbon Treaty.

However, in the EU majority voting is not a mere fifty plus one. Ever since the establishment of the European Community (the precursor of the EU) in 1957, votes in the Council of Ministers (which represents the governments of each of the states) had been allocated votes according to their size. After the Lisbon Treaty, Germany had 9.55 per cent of the votes. To force through a decision following these so-called Qualified Majority Voting rules (QMV) required that two conditions were met: the proposal had to be supported by 55 per cent of member states, and the majority of votes had to represent at least 65 per cent of the population of the EU.

For the uninitiated, the EU's rules for qualified majority voting are byzantine, and in any case rarely used. Indeed, even where QMV is required, the Council prefers to reach a consensus. There are good reasons why the Council would seek to reach decisions through consensus rather than through the tyranny of the (qualified) majority. Any decision that smacks of a diktat from Brussels is bound to be met with hostility in countries with populist anti-EU parties.

Further, forcing through a decision in one area may poison the atmosphere when the EU is discussing other vital issues. Angela Merkel, a politician who made her career out of reaching decisions through agreement, consensus and accommodation both domestically and in the EU, had little appetite for a fight. That was not the way she operated. She was acutely aware that using the QMV rules on an issue as sensitive as immigration could have unforeseen consequences for the EU. But these were desperate times, and something had to be done. For the time being, hinting that a decision could be reached through a majority vote was a sensible bargaining position.

Commentators seemed sure that the meeting between interior ministers – they were to discuss the allocation of some 80,000 migrants – would be a tame affair; a demarcation of the countries' respective positions before a more substantial meeting of the heads of government on 23 September. To everyone's surprise, however, Germany played it tough. In a move that is certain to have been carefully choreographed with Mrs Merkel, interior minister Thomas de Maizière took an unusually hard line: 'Europe cannot afford an inconclusive meeting today.'[28] Germany insisted on a vote. All the countries, with the exception of Romania, the Czech Republic, Slovakia and Hungary, voted for the German plan. Finland abstained. The German Interior Minister had signalled that enough was enough for Berlin; Germany needed burden-sharing. Some of this was pure common sense. Germany, her superior economic position notwithstanding, could not go it alone. The EU was, after all, a community, an organisation based on some level of solidarity. Further, at home some voices of discontent were becoming evident. The Chancellor, who had enjoyed stratospheric poll ratings, was becoming less popular. On the day of the EU summit, her approval rating slipped below 50 per cent for the first time that year. More disconcerting still, commentators began warning that the failure to reach a consensus, let alone a solution to the whole migrant crisis, could spell the end of the European Union.

Merkel – while she did not show it – was acutely aware of the crisis and its depth. But she had staked her reputation on approaching the refugee crisis in a humane way. Moreover she had the backing of many major German companies. Germany, one of the world's largest exporters of goods, was facing a shortage of skilled workers. Dieter Zetsche, CEO of Daimler-Benz, spoke for many when he declared that the refugees would be a help rather than a hindrance for economic growth; that the many refugees could lay the foundations for a new economic miracle.

> I can imagine that we could go into the refugee reception centres and provide information on the possibilities and requirements involved in getting work in Germany, or specifically at Daimler . . . Most of the refugees are young, well trained and highly motivated. That's exactly the kind of people we're looking for.[29]

It was also the case that Germany, faced with an aging population, needed more young people to pay for the older ones. The short-term problem of finding housing for the 800,000 refugees was offset by the long-term prospect of pension contributions to the more than 80 million Germans. While the influx of migrants – according to the German Ministry of Finance – would cost €20 billion (or 0.6 per cent of GDP), their arrival would increase demand, German shops and companies giving more customers. The net result of the migration would, so the Ministry argued, lead to almost one per cent more growth in the German economy by 2020, and the EU estimates agreed.

Sometimes long-term thinking is prudent, and in this case also humane. When Merkel came back from the summit in Brussels she once again reiterated her mantra, 'We'll sort it out.'

Horst Seehofer did not take this lying down. The Bavarian Minister President demanded that the migrants be placed in detention camps and the German borders closed. Merkel said relatively little. She established a special unit in her office headed by Peter Altmaier, Chief of Staff of the Federal Chancellery and former chief whip in Parliament, who coordinated the immigration policy. Seehofer kept up the pressure. His demand for camps was vehemently opposed by Sigmar Gabriel and all but ignored by Merkel. The Bavarian politician was reminiscent of a boxer who had started a fight with a flurry of punches but was losing his pace and his stamina. On 4 November Merkel called a meeting between the three party leaders: herself, Seehofer and Gabriel. She was polite and accommodating. Seehofer found it difficult to keep up the pressure and was seemingly taken aback by Merkel's accommodating approach. 'She is a total professional', and 'Yes, we are in agreement, in total agreement,' the Bavarian told *Süddeutsche Zeitung*. Only days after he had criticised Merkel in the strongest possible terms, he and she were suddenly the best of friends. Merkel had conceded little. She had agreed that the refugees from countries other than Syria could be held in immigration centres and would be sent back if they did not have a right to asylum, which was the case for most migrants from Afghanistan and Africa. Merkel was back to her position earlier in the autumn, that Germany could not take in 'the whole world' but was willing and indeed morally required to take in refugees from Syria. This policy was accepted by all the parties. Merkel had seemingly won again by keeping calm. Gabriel reluctantly had to concede this: as he told his party caucus before the meeting, 'We have to learn to keep cool – just like Mrs Merkel.'

The Chancellor herself reiterated her mantra, albeit in a slightly different form. 'I would wish,' she said, 'that people in a couple of years' time will say, they did it well and we could do it.'[30] At the beginning of November, after the aforementioned compromise, Merkel's popularity had fallen, but not by much. Before the crisis 54 per cent had approved of her. After two months of constant crisis and chaos her approval rating stood at 49 per cent.

Many had expected the refugee crisis to ease in the winter. It did not. The unusually warm weather meant that refugees could still travel across the waters. Moreover, the agreement to share the refugees among the countries of the EU was not being implemented. The Italian government refused to play along with it. Merkel was no longer able to impose her will with the same ease as earlier. Things did not go to plan – let alone as expected. For a start, Merkel had underestimated the opposition towards the refugees in some quarters in Germany. She also underestimated the problems associated with the influx of people from a different culture; individuals who had different norms and who occasionally behaved in a way that was utterly unacceptable to the Germans. On New Year's Eve migrants in Cologne sexually assaulted several young women. The authorities tried to cover up the fact that some of the perpetrators were refugees. Merkel was not directly implicated, but couldn't avoid a faint whiff of a cover-up. She sought to regain control by sounding tough. She condemned the acts and expressed her 'outrage at these disgusting assaults and sexual attacks'.[31] But she did not go further. The New Year's Eve attacks could have provided Angela Merkel with an escape route. She did not take it and perhaps that was a mistake; certainly others saw it as such. Some speculated that Julia Klöckner, an outspoken member of the Bundestag and candidate for the post as premier of Rheinland Pfalz, could take over from Merkel. Wolfgang Schäuble was also mentioned as a possible successor if Merkel was forced to resign.

The Chancellor seemed to face these rumours with equanimity. For a start, any challenger from within her party would have to be acceptable to the Social Democrats, whose leaders supported Merkel's immigration policy.

In her New Year message Angela Merkel had repeated her mantra that Germany was 'a strong country', and she added, as if to emphasise that she was in no mood to compromise, 'What matters is that we, also in the future, want to be a country in which we will be free, compassionate and open to the world.' Challenged or not, she had made her position clear. The events on New Year's Eve had not fundamentally changed her attitude towards the refugees. This was not an issue like the decision to phase out nuclear power stations in 2011.

Perhaps her determination to see it through, even risk her career, was a sign that she had finally found her passion; that she had discovered an issue that was more important than her own career; that she had returned to the beliefs and values that had shaped her upbringing in the Waldhof in Templin.

It was early January 2016 and Angela Merkel and her husband Joachim were attending a charity event for refugees. She was chatty and polite, talking to the organisers in the way expected of a guest of honour. Suddenly she spotted an old friend, excused herself and went over to him. It was Pastor Reiner Eppelmann. The retired clergyman had been a friend of Angela's father Horst and was one of the founders of the DA, the short-lived political party in which Merkel began her career. The pastor was pleased to see Merkel, and he congratulated her on pursuing a policy of openness towards the refugees. He half warned, half counselled his former protégée not to change course and then he cited the former Czech President, the playwright and dissident Vaclav Havel: 'Hope is not the conviction that something will turn out well, but the certainty that something makes sense, regardless of how it turns out.' The words seemed to resonate with the Chancellor.

Angela Merkel, a woman who had previously been reluctant to appeal to the Christian values of her childhood home and the spiritual beliefs upon which her own political party supposedly was founded, had rediscovered her true self. She now confidently justified her policies by reference to her faith, her upbringing under Communism and with a recognition that she was doing the right thing, regardless of how it turned out.

'She is standing firmly on the solid foundations of the values of her childhood home,' Pastor Eppelmann told the magazine *Der Spiegel*, 'Every day, Jesus and God were discussed in the Kasner household. The daily message was: "Love thy neighbour as yourself." Not just German people. God loves everybody . . . She understood what it must be like for people fleeing the Islamic State.'

Merkel had rediscovered why politics was important; why it was necessary to show commitment to causes that are greater than ourselves. Whether she herself would survive or not was immaterial; her actions 'made sense'. That was also the message when she addressed her party during the middle of the refugee crisis in December 2015. She was clear and direct, she spoke of her party as one that 'finds its basis in Christianity; in the God-given dignity of every individual. This means that it is not masses that arrive but individuals. For every human being has the dignity which is given to him by God.' She received a nine-minute standing ovation. Only one of the delegates, Wolfgang Schäuble, seemed unimpressed. Whether he was plotting his revenge could not be determined. But Merkel had at long last presented her credo, revealing to the world her deepest beliefs.

BREXIT AND 2016

In the famous, if apocryphal, anecdote, a journalist asked Harold Macmillan: 'What makes being a Prime Minister so difficult?' 'Events, dear boy. Events,' came the reply.

Governing Germany in the autumn of 2016 was as demanding as governing Britain in the late 1950s – and undoubtedly more so. 'Events' kept happening. Donald Trump's election as the 45th President was unexpected – and an unwelcome 'event', from a personal standpoint. The New York businessman-turned-politician had tweeted angrily about Mrs Merkel; the day following his surprise election, Angela Merkel took to Instagram to (sort of) congratulate the President-elect. Instead of sending a direct message to @realdonaldtrump, Merkel posted her conditional congratulations publicly to her followers, first in German and then in English. And no, her message didn't contain the usual platitudes about undying friendship, at least not in the traditional sense. Rather, it was a conditional invitation, a message that stopped short of congratulating him: 'Democracy, freedom, respecting the rule of law and people's dignity regardless of their origin, the colour of their skin, religion, gender, sexual orientation or political views. Based on these values, Chancellor Merkel offers to work closely with the future President of the United

States.' Seemingly listing all the issues that divided them, Frau Merkel tentatively extended the hand of friendship by daring Mr Trump to renounce many of the ideologies he flirted with during his presidential campaign. None of the other leaders publically challenged him in this way. No wonder the BBC news reported that 'Mrs Merkel is now the world's sole champion of liberal values'. Trump did not respond. But he and his staff knew that he could not afford to upset her. Six million jobs in the American 'Rust Belt' rely on exports to the EU. Trump has to work with Merkel – and she sets the agenda.

But Trump's election remains a smaller issue – for now. One problem persisted throughout 2016: the refugees continued to arrive, though their number dropped slightly after the EU struck a deal with the Turkish government in March 2016. Once again, sweeteners – in the form of an easing of visa restrictions for Turkish citizens travelling to Europe – were the price Merkel and her colleagues were forced to pay. A small price, it would seem, and yet, once again, one with unforeseen implications. In this case, the unwelcome news came not from the Aegean, nor from Greece, let alone from Bavarian opponents of Merkel's *Willkommenskultur*. The new headache came from the United Kingdom.

In a move to placate the Eurosceptics, Prime Minister David Cameron had called a referendum on continued British membership of the EU. The deal with Turkey was not welcome news for the Conservative Prime Minister. Far from it. Having earlier in his premiership secured relatively easy victories in previous referendums – one on Welsh devolution, one on a new electoral system and one on Scottish independence – Merkel's political ally in London was facing an uphill struggle; and he was losing it. The economic arguments were going nowhere. Worse still, the 'Leave' campaign sought to use the prospect of what they claimed would be millions of Turkish citizens entering the EU to their advantage. This was an effective, and ill-disguised xenophobic, argument for ending 43 years of British membership.

Merkel was in a bind. Britain had been a good, if sometimes awkward, ally for Berlin. Personal antipathies aside, Germany and Britain had formed an efficient partnership in the drive towards less regulation ever since the British had joined the European Community in 1973.

True, Margaret Thatcher and Helmut Kohl had not seen eye to eye, but they had nevertheless collaborated on market liberalisation and deregulation. Similarly, relations between Tony Blair and Gerhard Schröder had been mostly positive, as had the relationship between Merkel and her various counter-parts in Downing Street. But many Germans, both citizens generally and those working in industry, were relaxed about Brexit. With Britain outside the EU, they believed that Frankfurt was likely to become the financial centre of Europe. Merkel had made her views clear well in advance of David Cameron's decision to hold a referendum. In 2014, while addressing the House of Parliament in English, Mrs Merkel stated bluntly: 'Some expect my speech to pave the way for a fundamental reform of the European architecture which will satisfy all kinds of alleged or actual British wishes. I am afraid they are in for a disappointment.'[32]

Notwithstanding her warning, David Cameron had begun to renegotiate Britain's relationship with Europe shortly after he was re-elected. He achieved very little. The deal to block eastern Europeans from sending child benefit payments on to their offspring back home was the most eye-catching of his meagre achievements. Merkel was not in a position to give further concessions, nor did she consider it necessary. In spite of the polls, neither Merkel, nor the Prime Minister expected the result that thundered in, in the early hours of the 24th of June 2016. Britain had voted to leave the EU, and the European continent had yet another crisis to deal with.

Once again, Merkel handled with the problem with grace and diplomacy. The new Prime Minister, Theresa May, was greeted with full military honours when she travelled to Berlin within days of taking office. The British press seemed relieved, elated even, by the friendly welcome. '*Vielen Danken*', said Mrs May, making a slight grammatical error but at least trying to speak the language of her host. 'We are two women, who, if I may say so, just want to get on with the job', she continued. Merkel replied with a disarming girlish smile and a rather noncommittal '*Genau*' – 'certainly'. The German television station ZDF, too, seemed bowled over and quoted Merkel as saying that 'we two daughters of vicars [will reach] an understanding'. And why shouldn't they? Merkel stated that she 'was happy to grant Britain a bit of time' and even stressed that she 'understood' May. But the conciliatory words could not be misunderstood as softness or a lack of determination. As in the case of Tony Blair's negotiation over the EU budget in 2006, honeyed words were no indication of a willingness to accommodate. Not all papers reported that Merkel added the words: 'Of course, we have to follow the rules when Article 50 is invoked'.[33]

It gradually became clear that the Germans, like the other countries in the European Union, would not allow Britain the luxury of staying in the single market without accepting the free movement of people. While May made it her mantra that 'Brexit means Brexit', Merkel was no less adamant in her reiteration that she would not allow any 'Rosinenpickerei' – a slightly stronger equivalent of 'cherry-picking'; and whatever concessions she was willing to give would have to be in Germany's economic interest.[34] While Wolfgang Schäuble complained that the EU would be thrown into economic chaos when Britain left, and, by implication, that Germany would have to pick up the bill, Merkel seemed content with the situation, at least for the time being. Brexit was not her immediate concern.

It was hard to blame her for her lack of concern about Britain's decision to leave the EU. Merkel's position at home, while not directly challenged, was still precarious. The main reason for this was the continued infighting between the CSU and CDU, which in turn was exacerbated by the revival of Alternative für Deutschland. Horst Seehofer was anything but loyal to the Chancellor, and it was understandable why he seemed so mutinous. The 67-year-old Bavarian Premier – and former errand boy in the local administration – had a popular touch, but this counted for little among the younger politicians who wanted to succeed him; politicians who wanted to fireproof themselves against the electoral threat from Alternative. Like Merkel, who was under constant pressure from Seehofer, the latter was constantly being criticised by his own finance minister, Markus Söder, who ceaselessly demanded a tougher line against refugees and migrants.

The problem for the CSU was that it would be difficult to find an alternative to Merkel. In the local elections in March 2016, Julia Klöckner – a photogenic 43-year-old who had once been crowned *Deutsche Weinkönigin* (German Wine Queen) in a beauty pageant – had stood for election as Premier of Rheinland Pfalz. Her veiled criticism of Merkel suggested to some that it would be possible to replace the Chancellor, but the challenger was beaten by the Social Democrat Malu Dreyer, a politician who had supported the Chancellor's refugee policy. The CSU – and the right wing of the CDU – had lost their chance.

Whether Merkel's position was ever really under threat is debatable. Much as the CDU/CSU's right wing was opposed to her, no one contemplated an alliance with AfD. It would be difficult to govern without the Social Democrats, and finding a leader who was acceptable to the SPD – especially when they might be able to form a federal government with Die Linke and the Green Party – meant that the CDU could not simply ditch the Chancellor.

The weakness of the established parties had one cause: the AfD and especially their leader, Frauke Petry, who had unseated the bookish Bernd Lucke and used the refugee crisis to good effect. By September 2016, the far-right party not only scored over 15 per cent in the national polls, but also managed to beat the CDU into second place in the regional elections in Mecklenburg Vorpommern – the state where Merkel's own constituency is located. Frauke was different from previous opponents, but at the same time shared some of Merkel's background. Born into a Protestant family in Dresden in 1975, Frauke too grew up in East Germany. Like the Chancellor, she also earned a doctorate in Chemistry, and also got divorced before she entered politics. But that was where the similarities ended.

Der Spiegel, the news magazine that normally wrote positively about the Chancellor, concluded that Merkel was 'the victim of a negative mood caused by her own mistakes'.[35] Petry benefited from this. A year after Merkel opened the borders to Syrian refugees, 77 per cent of Germans were 'afraid of radical Islamists', and a full 71 per cent were not happy with the integration of refugees. Not all was negative, however. Some papers may have been preparing Merkel's political obituary, but an increasing number of Germans considered the prospect for the economy to be 'very good' – an increase from 49 to 54 per cent in a single year.[36] Further polls suggested that 75 per cent found Merkel 'competent' and 62 per cent thought her 'trustworthy'. By contrast, the figures for Mrs Petry were, respectively, 14 and 9 per cent.[37]

Complacency is the source of many a political downfall. The ability, let alone the willingness, to change course is not part of most politicians' DNA. There is a reason for this: U-turns smack of opportunism, and, even worse, a lack of conviction. True, Merkel had flip-flopped over nuclear power in 2011 – and had got away with it. In late September 2016, almost exactly a year after the refugee crisis, Merkel seemingly changed tack again: 'I wish I could turn the clock back by several years', she said, and admitted, self-critically, that 'the sentence "*wir schaffen das*" ["we can do it"], has almost become an empty formula'.[38] She also stressed that the numbers of actual refugees had remained below the expected one million. Even critics such as the Bavarian finance minister Markus Söder said that she was 'on the right track'[39] (perhaps the ambitious CSU politician wanted to mend fences with the Chancellor in case he became Premier while she was still in office).

Was this yet another U-turn; an admission of guilt, lest the voters punish her? Electoral opportunism is a motive for all politicians. While not willing to abandon her policy entirely, Merkel showed that she was not, after all, willing to sacrifice her career for principle.

CHAPTER 15

THE LAST LIBERAL...

THERE ARE TWO CONSTANTS IN GERMANY, THE EDITOR OF *BILD ZITUNG* quipped, 'Bayern München wins the *Bundesliga* and Angela Merkel is Chancellor'. And, certainly, the Bavarian soccer team was remarkably successful, especially during the 2000s. *Die Bayern*, as the Munich based football-giants are called, won the national championship uninterruptedly from 2013 to 2019. (This is in sporting terms the equivalent of the *Yankees* winning the *World Series* for over half a decade.) During these years, Merkel was unchallenged. Every national election was won by her party and her popular approval rating was never below 40 per cent.

But in the autumn of 2019 something happened. The Bavarian football team began to lose. International star players, the likes of Robert Lewandowski, Manuel Neuer and Jérôme Boateng, were not up to their usual standard and the head coach Niko Kovač left, officially by 'mutual consent' (read was sacked!) and was replaced by his rather anodyne deputy Hans-Dieter Flick, who had never played for the national team.

It was tempting to make the comparison with the Chancellor. Many – not least abroad – were quick to draw the conclusion that her days were numbered and that Germany's most successful politician was going the way of the country's greatest football team; down. Not catastrophically so but sinking into mediocrity. Depending on political persuasion this was either a cause for concern or, on the other side of politics, Merkel's predicament provided an opportunity to gloat; to revel in a good dose of *Schadenfreude*.

Certainly, things were not going as well as they used to. 2019 was a difficult year. The *CDU* sank to unprecedented lows in the opinion polls – they dipped below 30 per cent and stayed there. Moreover, at one stage the Party was even outpolled by a resurgent *Die Grüne*. In the *Land* elections in Thüringen, the CDU finished third behind the far-left *Die Linke* and the even further right *Alternative für Deutschland*. The party system in Germany, once so stable, was changing rapidly as voters' loyalties gave way to fickle consumerism and political shopping around.[1]

A British columnist summed up the general perception. Reflecting on the beginning of her fourth term in office, he wrote that 'Merkel was almost toppled' and a 'charismatic French President, Emmanuel Macron, elected in 2017, swiftly moved into lead position in the EU'.[2] Perhaps superficially so, but even this assessment proved somewhat premature. The Frenchman's emphatic victory was secured on a low turnout (only 42 percent turned out to vote in the 2017 legislative election in which Macron's *La République En Marche!* won 53 per cent). And his ambitions to lead Europe were hampered by the the the *Yellow Vest Movement* a grassroots uprising that began in November 2018, in protest against Macron's proposed reform of the French welfare state, rising fuel costs, and a tax reform that (so it was said) disproportionately hit the working classes.

This was a difficult time in politics with the Brexit debacle still unfolding in Britain and the continued rise of far-right and lesser democratic governments in Hungary and Poland. So, were things really that bad in Germany? After more than fourteen years in office, Merkel was on her fourth French Président de la République, and her fifth British Prime Minister. Despite the declining fortunes of her party, she remained the most popular politician in Germany. But there was still a sense of doom on the horizon. But her focus on her third US President. Donald Trump.

Merkel was not enthusiastic about the former reality TV-star. How could she be? During the 2016 election, Trump has blamed Merkel personally for all Europe's ills. And now he was President. Before he took office, Merkel met with Barack Obama. She had become the American's most trusted ally, and he needed to talk to her before he left office. The two met on the 16th of November in Berlin, only eight days after Trump had defeated Hilary Clinton. Obama knew that Merkel intended not to contest the 2017 federal elections. That meeting made her change that decision. The two met at *Hotel Adlon* in Berlin. They were alone. None of the advisers were in the room. We do not know the details of their discussion. But Obama's speech writer saw Merkel as she left the room. 'There was a tear in her eye', reported the former White House staffer. Obama had persuaded Merkel that it was her duty as the queen of the west, as the last champion of the liberal and democratic west, to protect the liberal order from the onslaught of Donald Trump's populists. On leaving Merkel, Obama was heard saying, 'now she is all alone'.[3]

THE 2017 ELECTIONS

On 4th of March 2018 scattered storm clouds were gathering over the German capital and a strong wind was blowing from the south. The thermometer showed 4 degrees Celsius but it felt colder, almost frosty. The mood inside the Bundestag was not much different.

For a moment there was quiet. The 709 members of the Federal German Legislature held their collective breath for a second that seemed like an eternity. For some reason the ever so reliable technology was playing up. And then, finally, the result came up on the screen: 364 had voted for the new *GroKo* (or Grand Coalition) government, the fourth CSU/SPD government in the history of the Federal Republic of Germany – and the fourth government headed by Angela Merkel. Not everybody was happy. Thirty-five of the SPD and CDU/CSU backbenchers voted against 'their' government. But, then again, the same had also been true in 2005.

It had been an eventful year for *Die Kanzlerin* – too eventful for some, even though compared to previous years nothing of substance had happened; no refugee crises, no Eurozone collapse and no Russian invasion of neighbouring countries. Merkel's trademark was calm and stable. The Chancellor was ready for another turn, though some suggested (mostly behind her back) that she had seen better days politically. She kept a brave face. After all, she had been underestimated before.

On this cold Spring day, Merkel exchanged pleasantries with the new Social Democrat leader Andrea Nahles, the combative former federal minister of employment, who weeks before had replaced Martin Schulz as leader of the SPD. For the first time in history, the two largest parties were headed by women. The weekly political magazine *Der*

Spiegel ran the headline *Die Frauenrepublik* ('the republic of women').[4] And there was certainly something to be said for this slightly exaggerated headline. In addition to the SPD and CDU/CSU, Alice Elisabeth Weidel, the parliamentary leader of the far-right *Alternative für Deutschland* was also a woman. On the other side of politics, Sahra Wagenknecht was co-leader and the most prominent politician from the far-left *Die Linke* party. At 38 per cent, the proportion of females in the Bundestag was miles ahead of America where only 18 per cent of the members of the House of Representatives were female, and Britain where the equivalent figure was 23 per cent before the 2019 election. And yet, this had not significantly improved the economic position of female workers. Women in Germany were still paid 20 per cent less than men, and the figure had only fallen by 1 per cent since 2011.

Merkel's career had been reeling for weeks, yes, even for months. The election in September 2017 had not exactly gone to plan. Winning a mere 32.9 per cent, the lowest in German history, CDU/CSU fell well short of the 41.5 per cent won in 2013. But more concerning still 13 per cent of the voters had opted for *Alternative für Deutschland*, the xeno-phobic far-right party, which included prominent members who, some believed, found it difficult to contain a certain nostalgia for the bygone days of the 'Reich'.

'We will hunt her down', said a buoyant Alexander Gauland, the far-right AfD politician about Merkel. Germany was in for a rocky ride. Not since the 1950s had a far-right nationalist party been elected to the Bundestag. Back then the remnants of *Deutsche Partei* had been swal-lowed up by the CDU. But Merkel's move to the centre had created space for a nationalist party. This was a concern for some. Others saw it as an opportunity. Friedrich Merz, the man Merkel had forced out before she became Chancellor, had re-emerged after over a decade of self-imposed exile as a corporate lawyer for the asset management firm *BlackRock*, which made him a multimillionaire. Now he was beginning to make in-terventions from the side lines. What he was up to was not clear.

Yet, in other ways, the new coalition was a sigh of relief for Merkel and her party. The migrant crisis had not led to a massive exodus of votes to the right. The Social Democrats had an even more catastrophic result winning only 20.5 per cent, or almost half of what the party polled in the days of Gerhard Schröder. Cutting her main rival down to size – or even below that – was no mean feat. And Merkel and her inner circle had, once again, utilized her cunning – and her opponent's self-inflicted wounds.

It all seemed very different a year before. In February 2017, foreign minister and SPD leader Sigmar Gabriel fell on his sword. The rotund former high school teacher realised that his party was stuck on 23 per cent in the polls. The prospect of winning the election even against a weakened Merkel seemed fanciful.

Self-sacrifice is not uncommon among the Social Democrats. Like Oskar Lafontaine gave way to Gerhard Schröder in 1998, so, Gabriel gave way to Martin Schulz, the president of the European Parliament. The latter was unusual among Germany's highly educated political elite. A former footballer, who hadn't even finished high school, he was a popular figure. The 61-year-old could speak in *Klartext*, the German word for calling a spade a spade. At a special party convention the bearded, balding and bespectacled Schulz was elected party leader and *Kanzlerkandidat* by an astounding 100 per cent of the delegates. This rattled the CDU. Merkel, though, seemed calm.

The once hapless Social Democrats, who weeks before seemed destined to disappear into oblivion (or at least be relegated to the status of a minor party), experienced a surge in the polls never previously seen in the Federal Republic. Having languished in the low twenties, the SPD rose in the polls. Within a month of Schulz taking over, the party was supported by more than 30 per cent. And, more sensationally still, in early March the party overtook the CDU/CSU as the most popular party in Germany.

This popularity created a whiff of *Hochmut* – a combination of hubris, superiority and arrogance, and one which is fatal for a political career. Schulz declared that he would never serve under Merkel, though he hinted that he was happy to lead a government with CDU/CSU as a junior party. This would not be his only miscalculation.

In the Spring of 2017, there were three *Land* elections in key states where the Social Democrats had traditionally been polling well. It seemed likely that SPD could wrestle power from CDU's Annegret Kramp-Karrenbauer, the somewhat self-effacing Premier in Saarland.

And, the Social Democratic Party was all but certain of winning re-election in North Rhine Westphalia and in Schleswig-Holstein. These expected victories would then – this was the theory – propel Schulz into the summer with a commanding lead. In practice, it was different.

Premiers in Germany are mighty politicians. And Hannelore Kraft, who had ruled North Rhine Westphalia since 2010 was no exception. With 18 million citizens, her state had a population that surpassed countries like Sweden, Belgium and Austria. She was not happy to play second fiddle to Martin Schulz. She told the new leader to stay away.

Astonishingly he abided by her request. This became his downfall. After his astounding rise in the polls, Schulz all but disappeared. Merkel, by contrast, flew in to support her underdog CDU comrades. Social Democrat complacency and the party's failure to find credible responses to a series of attacks by migrants gave Merkel's party a surprising chance. To the astonishment of everyone CDU's Armin Laschet defeated Kraft and in Schleswig-Holstein the CDU's Daniel Günther (a soft-spoken junior politician who had only become leader of the local party a year before) was able to wrestle power from SPD's Torsten Albig. Even more surprisingly, the youthful former psychology student formed a coalition with the Green Party and the Liberal FDP.

Few knew it at the time but the result in the Saarland was the most important. There, Annegret Kramp-Karrenbauer (known as AKK) won re-election. Merkel seemed especially pleased with the latter result although the state only has a population of one million and is the smallest of the German *Länder*.

Schulz was on the ropes even before he had entered the ring. He tried to regain strength and sought to fight back. The 'Schulz effect has a defect', opined one blogger. The man whom news magazine *Stern* had described as the 'conqueror' was falling faster than he had risen.

But it wasn't all over. As a member of the European Parliament, he was not part of the Grand Coalition and thus not bound by collective responsibility. Hence, he was free to take views that departed from the Union-SPD government. He knew that his party's policies – especially on social issues – were closer to those of the majority of voters. It was the Social Democrat Labour Minister Andrea Nahles who had shepherded a new minimum wage through parliament and had done so against the initial wishes of Angela Merkel. But that battle was won and there was little to gain from revisiting the issue.

Schulz chose another one: gay marriage. This was a clever move. Merkel herself was known to be sceptical and the CDU/CSU leadership was out of step with the population at large. A poll by the *German Federal Anti-Discrimination Agency* from January 2017 found that 83 per cent of voters supported same-sex marriage. For the CDU/ CSU, a traditional family values-oriented party, which had members who came close to expressing homophobic sentiments, the issue was a problem. For the SPD, it was well-suited for showing that the Christian Democrats belonged to yesteryear, whereas Schulz, by contrast, stood for a modern, inclusive and tolerant Germany.

The issue came to a head when the Green Party declared that they would not enter into a government unless the coalition agreement included a commitment to introduce marriage equality. A few days later, on June 24th, FDP leader Christian Lindner pledged his party to the same position, should they enter the Bundestag.

Merkel was in a bind. She was known to favour a 'Jamaica' coalition. But this option was now slipping away. For a politician who is known for caution and timidity, her next move was unexpected. On the 27th of June, she proposed a free vote on the issue in the Bundestag.

With one single stroke, she had shot Schultz's remaining fox. By promising a free vote she had effectively neutralized his last remaining popular policy. The vote recognised popular opinion and showed that she was willing to listen to the people, and at the same time it was an opportunity for her to show her party colleagues that she was one of them as she personally would vote against the Bill. On the 30th of June, the Bundestag voted 393–226 for the right of gays and lesbians to get married. Merkel voted against, but stressed the vote, 'not only promotes respect between different opinions but also brings more social cohesion and peace'. Schulz could find no response. His party was back at an average of 23 per cent and worse showed a downward trend. Once again, the election campaign was uneventful; there was no viable alternative to Angela Merkel.

'Oh my God! What does this mean?' CNN anchor Hala Gorani looked perplexed. The exit polls did not match her briefing notes and she turned to the author of this book, who was invited to analyse the result for the viewers. No answer was forthcoming.

The CDU/CSU had suffered historic losses, as had the SPD. FDP had re-entered the Federal Parliament but with fewer members than expected. But the cause of confusion was the exceptionally strong showing for the AfD. It was unexpected. Many had thought the party would do poorly.

The fear among liberals – that the election of Donald Trump would herald a rise of the populist right across the world – began to die down in the Spring of 2017. Centrist Emmanuel Macron beat Marine Le Pen in the French presidential election in May and just prior, far-right Dutch politician Geert Wilders lost the parliamentary election in March And yet, by September those fears would be confirmed as the German federal elections demonstrated the far-right was still a formidable force.

In politics, it is prudent to pause for thought. Martin Schulz did not. The SPD leader declared that his party would go into opposition to regain its strength. The dejected Schulz left the parliamentary leadership to Andrea Nahles.

This was not a surprising move. The 47-year-old daughter of a bricklayer from Rheinland-Pfalz had proved to be an efficient administrator as well as a good speaker. In many ways, she seemed like a female version of the likes of Roland Koch and Jürgen Rüttgers. Like the two former CDU politicians, Nahles had the same uncompromising style and followed the maxim that the 'goal justifies the means', as it was expressed by Ignatius of Loyola, the founder of the Jesuit Order. Perhaps it was not a coincidence that she shared the motto of the founder of *The Society of Jesus*. Nahles was a practising Catholic (a rarity among SPD politicians). She claimed to be in politics 'because of Jesus Christ', and she had expressed scepticism regarding abortion and fiercely defended Pope Benedict.

But what was happening among the Social Democrats seemed rather academic. In a sense Merkel was where she wanted to be – a politician with a preference for social market economics, a liberal stance on foreign affairs and a commitment to environmental issues; she was keen to pursue the 'Jamaica' option.

Admittedly, the Bavarian CSU and the Greens did not see eye to eye on many issues. Moreover, the new liberal leader Christian Lindner was something of a loose cannon. But then again, so too was the late Guido Westerwelle and Merkel had effectively neutralized him. The parties were not miles apart on economic policies and then there was the prospect that Cem Özdemir, one of the two Green leaders, could become foreign minister. To have a secular Muslim of Turkish descent as foreign minister would send a strong signal to the world. It looked as if things were going according to Merkel's plan.

The negotiations between the Greens and 'Union' went well, at least initially. But Lindner proved to be a somewhat difficult customer. Suddenly, and without any warning, the young liberal leader called a press conference on the 16th of November. He declared that it is 'better not to govern than to govern wrongly'.[7] Why wasn't entirely clear. He had been given what he wanted, but perhaps understandably he feared that his party would become invisible just as they had been from 2009 to 2013.

Germany was suddenly in deep crisis. Schulz had ruled out another Grand Coalition, and Merkel ruled out a minority government. But as in 2005 when Schröder refused to govern with Merkel, Schulz was not in control of the party and Nahles effectively forced him to change his mind.

Shortly before Christmas, the SPD agreed to negotiate with Merkel, but – at Nahles' instigation – it was stipulated that the result had to be approved by the SPD members. The *volte face* once again damaged Schulz's credibility – but further strengthened Nahles' grip on power. At least at the time. Like Merkel in 1999–2000 when she abandoned her mentor Helmut Kohn, a new SPD leader was in a similar way undermining the man who made her parliamentary leader. This was not to last, but no one knew this at the time.

Unlike the Jamaica-negotiations, the two sides quickly made headway. In late January, SPD and Union agreed on stronger European cooperation and integration, and lower health contributions for employees (both red-line issues for the Social Democrats). In return, the Christian Democrats were promised that the number of refugees coming into Germany would be far fewer.

This agreement was supported by a special conference of the Social Democrats. But the members still had to be convinced. Merkel's party had won significantly more votes than the Social Democrats, and yet Nahles was in a strong position. She pointed to the opposition against the coalition among the rank-and-file. Merkel had to give further concessions, and so she did.

The Chancellor accepted that the Social Democrats got *both* the ministries of finance and of foreign affairs, with the former going to Olaf Scholz, Hamburg's Erster Bürgermeister (the premier of the city-state). A few days later, Sigmar Gabriel was effectively fired. At the urging of Andrea Nahles, former Justice Minister Heiko Maas took over at the Foreign Office. Nahles was consolidating her position as leader of the SPD. At this stage Schulz had already handed over the position as party leader to her. Nahles was now both parliamentary spokesperson and party leader, the same roles Merkel had held after the 2002 federal election.

The situation seemed different in the CDU. The concessions to the SPD were not met with approval within the CDU. Jens Spahn, one of Merkel's fiercest critics in the parliamentary party, was especially vocal. He criticised both her economic policies and her stance on immigration. But others voiced the same opinion, though (tellingly) only on condition of anonymity.

The situation was also slightly different in the Bavarian sister party. After months of manoeuvring, Horst Seehofer (the Premier) effectively lost the internal battle to his conservative rival Markus Söder. (The latter became premier in 2018, and leader of the CSU the following year.)

There was less criticism from the CSU, perhaps because Söder and Seehofer had been given concessions over immigration that Merkel had previously ruled out. The Chancellor effectively accepted an upper limit on immigration and made Seehofer Minister of the Interior with direct responsibility over refugees. The battle over immigration had been won by the right. A few weeks later, Seehofer even declared that 'Islam does not belong in Germany'. That such views can be expressed by a senior cabinet minister in a western democracy with religious freedom is, perhaps, telling – and alarming – and shows how far the debate had moved since Merkel opened the doors to nearly a million mostly Muslim refugees.

Merkel was in a weak position, not because of external pressures, still less because of policy developments. Like British Prime Minister

Margaret Thatcher, she was weak because she had seemingly lost control over her party. Some began to talk about a *Putsch* against Merkel in the event that the coalition agreement was rejected. The coup never came because Merkel moved before her foes. On the 19th of February 2018, Merkel called a press conference and presented Annegret Kramp-Karrenbauer, the woman who surprisingly had won the Saarland election a year before, as the new secretary general of the CDU. And she let it subtly be known – though not in so many words – that the *Saarlanderin* was her anointed successor. AKK was invited to the weekly planning sessions in the *Kanzler Amt*, where only the inner circle of Merkel's closest advisers were invited. These continued to be Eva Christensen, Beate Baumann, Steffen Seibert, and the new kid on the block Dr Helge Braun, her new head of the Chancellery, a former medical doctor. He was later to play an important role.

Her opponents were surprised and before the right of the party had a chance to regroup, Merkel appointed Jens Spahn to the post of Secretary of State for Health. This was, objectively, an inspired choice – the thirty-seven-year-old had previously been the CDU's spokesperson on the issue – but it was also a wise political move. A critic of too much state intervention was now in charge of a large bureaucracy at the heart of the welfare state. That would keep him busy and would force him to make unpopular decisions. Merkel, it seemed, had rediscovered her stride.

A week later, a majority of 68 per cent of the members of the Social Democrats voted for another Grand Coalition. The turnout was 78 per cent. But that endorsement from the rank-and-file did not end the woes of the once powerful party and its standing in the polls continued to fall.

Like the Social Democrats, Merkel was not rewarded for securing yet another term. Now trouble was brewing within the parliamentary caucus.

For thirteen years, Volker Kauder had served as her right-hand man and problem solver. As the leader of the parliamentary party (a position similar to that of Chief Whip in British and American political systems) he was a bruiser. As noted in Chapter Eight, Kauder was literally a Rottweiler. He had served Merkel with skill and tact. But you do not get loved by enforcing discipline. Many in the party were upset and disappointed. Only six months after the Grand Coalition had been sworn in, the members of the CDU Caucus took it out on the *Fraktionsvorsitzende*. Kauder was normally elected unopposed. But in the autumn of 2018 Ralph Brinkhaus challenged him. Despite – or perhaps because of – warnings from Merkel and CSU leader Horst Seehofer, Brinkhaus received 125 to Kauder's 112 votes. The new leader of the Caucus outwardly swore fealty to Merkel. No one was fooled by this, least of all the political opponents.

'The beginning of the end of the Grand Coalition. The Chancellor's authority within her own party has been officially destroyed', tweeted Alexander Lambsdorff, one of the deputy leaders of the Free Democrats. He would say that of course. That is what political opponents are expected to say. Except in this case he had a point and Merkel herself knew it.

She had always vowed to stay on. She had also promised that she would never step down as party leader while she was Chancellor. Gerhard Schröder had done so with devastating consequences. Merkel was determined not to do the same. But she was running out of options. She was forced to change her mind.

THE RETURN OF FRIEDRICH MERZ

The 29th October is an important date in history. It is the shared birthday of Microsoft founder Bill Gates and the renaissance philosopher Erasmus of Rotterdam. On 29th October 1420, Beijing was officially designated as the capital of the Ming Dynasty. On this date in 1922, Benito Mussolini led his infamous 'March on Rome'. And on 29th October 1962, Soviet leader Nikita Khrushchev ordered the removal of Soviet missiles from Cuba. And again, on the 29th October 2018 Angela Merkel announced that she was stepping down as leader of the Christian Democratic Party. Her statement was historic, but delivered with a matter-of-fact assuredness and – it seemed – without hint of regret, resignation or any other r-word that could come to mind: 'Firstly, at the next CDU party conference in December in Hamburg, I will not put myself forward again as candidate for the CDU chair,' she told reporters at her party headquarters in the capital, Berlin. Then she continued, 'Secondly, this fourth term is my last as German Chancellor. At the federal election in 2021, I will not stand again as Chancellor candidate, nor as a candidate for the Bundestag and I won't seek any further political offices'.

There were no prizes for guessing who would step up to replace her; Annegret Kramp-Karrenbauer. AKK had clearly coordinated this with Angela Merkel. What surprised everyone was that the Party General Secretary was joined by a blast from the past; a politician whom no one had expected to play a role in national politics.

'My name is Friedrich Merz. That is with an "e"', said the slim, tall and balding man as he stood up at a press conference. The former judge, and latterly successful businessman, was aware that not everyone was familiar with him, and was keen that the gathered journalists – and those in the Twittersphere – should not misspell his name *März* – the German name for the month of March. Maybe there was a point to this. The German phrase *merz aus*, means to clear up, to cull or even to obliterate. And that was what he – albeit subtly – promised to do in the CDU.

Merz had previously been an exponent of the so-called *Leitkultur*, and had (as we saw in Chapter Eight) been flying the flag for German values. Though in his early sixties (and only a year younger than Merkel), the new contender for the CDU Party Chairmanship, portrayed himself as a new man; but also, as a patriot who was willing to listen to – and act on – the demands of the right-wing of the party. He pledged to combine national pride with free-market liberalism, plus a dose of traditional values. Merz, who holds a pilots' licence, in short presented himself as an action man who could get things done. His problem was that he was not the only one to represent the right-wing of the party. Jens Spahn, the Secretary of Health, also threw his proverbial hat in the ring. This notwithstanding, Merz was suddenly becoming the favourite to take over from Merkel.

Even prominent politicians were endorsing the prosperous prodigal son. Wolfgang Schäuble had been elected as Speaker of the Bundestag, but still seemed bitter. It was as if endorsing Merz was a way of getting his own back. The former finance and interior minister was clear that Merz was 'a true European, a reliable fighter for the Atlantic partnership'. He is 'someone who supports the social market economy,' Schäuble told the free-market liberal newspaper *Frankfurter Allgemeine Zeitung*.[9]

Some even hinted of the prospect of Chancellor Merz; suggesting that Merkel's old nemesis would move into the Chancellery immediately after being elected as party leader. This was mostly idle talk. For starters, Merz was not an elected member of the Bundestag, let alone any of the state assemblies. To be sure, Article 63 of the Basic Law allows individuals to be elected to the highest office without being a member of the Bundestag, but only one of the previous holders had not been a member of the Federal Legislature. The odd one out was Kurt Georg Kiesinger in the 1960s, but he had been a premier of Baden-Württemberg. Merz was not elected to anything. But, more importantly, it seemed far-fetched that the Social Democrats should accept to be a junior member of a coalition headed by a politician from the right of the CDU.

Nevertheless, Merz had momentum. AKK was almost written off. Instead of a high-profile campaign, she followed Merkel's formula of touring the country. As secretary of the party, and as someone who had recently served in regional politics, she was closer to the grassroots than Merz.

It was clear that this was a two-horse race. Spahn was under pressure to withdraw and leave the field open to follow right-winger Merz. But he refused to do so. Representing the socially liberal wing of the party, he would not leave the contest to two Catholic traditionalists. The thirty-eight-year-old Spahn stayed on.

That this was a battle between Merz and AKK proved to be correct. But the contest was still closer than expected when the 999 delegates voted on the 7th of December 2018. Surprisingly, Kramp-Karrenbauer won a plurality of the votes in the first round (45 per cent). Merz secured second place (39 per cent), while Spahn, as expected, was eliminated with a mere 15 per cent.

Conservatives in the party were feeling optimistic. Surely, Spahn's supporters would go to Merz. This confidence was premature. In the second round, AKK won 517 votes to Merz's 482 – a mere 51 per cent majority.[10] Kramp-Karrenbauer, had won by the narrowest of margins. But a win is a win.

The new party leader was not surefooted. Nor was she politically prudent. Friedrich Merz had not gone away. Behind the scenes he contacted AKK and urged her to form an alliance with the aim of removing Angela Merkel before the next Federal elections.

This was unknown to the public at large at the time. What was evident for all was that the Union was in trouble. CDU was challenged in regional elections, and in the national polls they momentarily sank below the Greens. The joint leaders of the environmental party Annalena Baerbock and Robert Habeck both appealed to young people and to the voters who were alarmed about the rising global temperatures and the climate emergency.

While many in the media, especially abroad focused on the reported rise of *Alternative für Deutschland*, this party was largely stagnant. The same could not be said for the Social Democrats. The once so powerful party fell back behind the Greens and were tied with AfD for the third spot.

After a string of defeats in regional elections, SPD leader Andrea Nahles resigned in June 2019. The party decided to have a joint leadership of a male and a female. But emulating the Greens' power-sharing model did not improve their fortunes. After a bitter contest, the Social Democrats elected the largely nondescript Norbert Walter-Borjans and Saskia Esken in late November of the same year. Walter-Borjans, a former finance minister of North Rhine Westphalia, had executive experience but was an academic economist in his late sixties. His co-chairwoman had no executive experience at all. During their campaign, Esken had suggested that SPD should leave the Grand Coalition. Once elected, and with the opinion polls suggesting that the party was more unpopular than ever, the Social Democrats decided to stay put. But it was clear that the old established political system was drifting down a political cul-de-sac.

Meanwhile the internal battles continued unabated in the CDU. Merz outwardly pledged his support for Merkel, but in the following year he didn't do anything except describe the CDU-led government as 'abysmal'.

As a new party leader Kramp-Karrenbauer, began with bravura. Or so she thought. The polls began to go up. And, behind the scenes, she accepted Merz invitation to chat. Only two weeks after her election the two met. He pledged that the right of the party would support her

– if she moved against Merkel. Merz and AKK were not aware that they were being watched. The Chancellor had sensed that a distance was building up between her and the new party leader. But she waited.

Merkel stayed in the background. At least officially. The press reported that the two were good friends. 'There is not a cigarette paper between them' reported the otherwise well-informed Süddeutsche Zeitung. In reality, she was planning her move.

On the 10th of January AKK met with Merz. Afterwards, she was invited out for a meal with Angela Merkel. The two met at Jolly, a moderately priced restaurant serving traditional Asian food in Berlin Mitte.

Merkel got straight to the point, 'So, you want to unseat me, do you?' Kramp-Karrenbauer blushed, went quiet, and tried to deny the story. Merkel ignored her and continued, 'Well, by all means, you can try that.'

Merkel could see through her successor's deceit. AKKs ambition to follow Merkel as chancellor effectively ended over Dim sum and Peking Duck only 34 days after she had taken over as party leader.

But the public did not know about this. And Merkel did not ask her successor to resign. Quite the contrary. She allowed her to stay on. Or, to change the metaphor, she gave AKK enough rope to hang herself. The next few months showed that Kramp-Karrenbauer had an extraordinary talent for self-destruction.

AKK had always been politician with a popular touch. Not someone who listened to Wagner or read modernist novels but a woman who was at ease with 'common people' over a Pilsner in a Bierkneipe, as the German pubs are called.

It was not surprising, therefore, that she did a stand-up routine in Baden-Württemberg in March 2019. Dressed as a cleaning lady, she poked fun at 'latte macchiato' leftists in Berlin who want gender-neutral toilets, 'You know they make toilets for the third-sex. Yes, you know the men who don't know if they are allowed to stand up when they take a piss, or if they must sit down'. The words were folksy. To put it mildly. The audience erupted in cheers. Finally a politician who was happy to speak her mind. But when a 43 second clip went viral, it caused a furore, or what the press called *Ein Shitstorm*.

When AKK challenged her enemies to 'back her or sack her' at the CDU party conference in November 2019, Merkel did not come to her aid but seemed preoccupied looking at her phone. Kramp-Karrenbauer was able to face down Merz, and she even won an eight-minute standing ovation from the party delegates. But the game was up. A few weeks later, she declared that she would succeed Merkel as Chancellor. The CDU had to find a new leader, and a new candidate to succeed Merkel. But this was soon to be overshadowed by something no one had foreseen: COVID19.

CHAPTER 16

THE PLAGUE

'Honesty is the only way to fight the plague'
Albert Camus, La Peste *(1947)*

D R HELGE BRAUN CAME IN EARLY ON 3 JANUARY 2020. KNOWN AS the 'Buddha of the *Bundesamt*' on account of his large frame, not inconsiderable gut and Zen approach to crises, the Minister for the Chancellery was relaxed as he took the lift to the seventh floor. The big man sat down in front of his computer. The Chancellor was on holiday, and there were few stories that required his attention. Australia was ablaze with seventeen killed in out-of-control bushfires, and Donald Trump had sent a tirade of tweets about a militant leader who had been killed by an American missile strike. Newsworthy stories, perhaps, if you were the editor of a broadsheet, but not issues that mattered to the daily lives of voters in Wuppertal, Wiesbaden, or Wolfsburg.

A former anaesthesiologist, Braun was proud of his profession, and used to say, 'People think I am an expert in making people go to sleep. But my main responsibility is to make them wake up again.' On this day he would read something that he regarded as a wake-up call.

Some of his colleagues found it mildly annoying that he had never quite been able to stop following developments in his field. He knew this. But today there were no urgent tasks to undertake. And so, he found himself browsing the *Newsletter of the Global Health Security Initiative,* or *GHSI*, as it is called by those in the know. He knew that his boss would approve. After all, Angela Merkel had specifically chosen him because he – like the *Kanzlerin* herself – was a scientist. She had wanted someone who could give robust – that is, evidence-based – feedback.

Dr Braun flicked through the PDF file, and a small note caught his attention. It reported on an acute and severe respiratory condition that had been identified in Central China. He was intrigued, and casually contacted the Ministry of Health. But no one had heard about it.

Perhaps it was his passion for his old métier, or perhaps a touch of boredom? In any case, Dr Braun wrote a memo on the novel disease, which would await Angela Merkel when she returned to her office on 6 January. In the meantime, the disease had been named COVID-19.

Helge Braun quickly became borderline obsessed with the novel disease. He had a feeling that this new infection could become catastrophic. He contacted Professor Lothar Wieler, the head of the Robert Koch Institute. Named after the Nobel Prize winner for Physiology (1905) and founder of modern bacteriology, this institution was then largely unknown to the public. It was soon to take centre stage in German politics. Originally founded as the Royal Prussian Institute for Infectious Diseases in 1891, the RKI (as it is usually called) is tasked with detecting and preventing infectious diseases. Professor Wieler immediately agreed with Braun about the threat the outbreak in China could pose. They set up a crisis group. At a time when most governments were hardly aware of the condition, German scientists were already analysing samples. Thus, it was scientists at Berlin's Charité hospital who first identified the genome and developed the first test for the virus. This happened at the end of January 2020.

The Chancellor immediately understood the severity of the situation. The woman who had been forbidden to study medicine in East Germany in her youth shared Helge Braun's interest in infectious diseases. This was an issue that could be analysed scientifically, and one where there were clear-cut answers to concrete problems.

Merkel – alongside the Foreign Minister Heiko Maas (a Social Democrat) – organised for an eight-tonne shipment of PPE equipment and protective gear to be sent to China in early February.[1] Partly as a result of the fortunate circumstance that Merkel had a medical doctor as her right-hand man, Germany was ahead of the curve, and unusually prepared when the COVID-19 pandemic broke out.

The politicians reacted in different ways. Merkel, Braun and the Federal Health Minister Jens Spahn were largely in agreement with the Social Democrats in the Grand Coalition. But others saw it differently. The most serious disagreement was between the premiers of Germany's two largest states, Bavaria (population: thirteen million) and North Rhine Westphalia (population: seventeen million). Between them, these two *Länder* account for nearly 40 per cent of the total population of the German Federal Republic. And the two leaders of the two largest states were ambitious men who – while they both denied it – were keen to succeed Angela Merkel.

The Bavarian Premier, Markus Söder of the CSU, was one of Merkel's strongest critics during the refugee crisis in 2015. He had forced out Horst Seehofer for being too weak. The 6'4"(193cm)-tall Bavarian was a character. Merkel's concern was that the fifty-two-year-old would play the populist card, though, in many ways, Söder was not the typical run-of-the-mill right-wing politician. A Protestant in a strongly Catholic state, he had occasionally dressed in drag as Marilyn Monroe. His wife, Karin Baumüller-Söder, was one of the owners of Baumüller, among Germany's most innovative manufacturers of electric automation and drive systems. Söder therefore, though a nationalist, also had a claim to being an environmentalist and often spoke with gravity about green issues. Despite being politically conservative and an admirer of Franz Josef Strauss, the controversial leader of the CSU in the 1970s and 1980s, Söder was ideologically close to Green politicians.

Merkel was less apprehensive about Söder's opposite number in North Rhine Westphalia. The leader of that state was Armin Laschet, a fifty-nine-year-old father of three who was married to his childhood sweetheart. The diminutive (only 5'6") Rheinländer was one of the few CDU politicians who stood by Merkel during the refugee crisis. Known locally as 'Turkish Laschet' for his exceptionally good relations with the immigrant community, he was previously editor of the small religious newspaper *Kirchen Zeitung Aachen*. The Premier from Düsseldorf (the state capital) was ideologically close to Merkel.

At the party conference in 2019, the two men were overheard talking about who should succeed Merkel. Standing on a balcony in Dresden, the two premiers were teasing each other, along the lines of,

'So when are you going to declare your candidacy?' It was bonhomie. Superficially, both pretended to be happy where they were. And both knew the other was *not* being truthful. It was part of the well-worn ritual whereby those in pursuit of high office strenuously deny their ambitions.

Merkel was aware that the aspirations of the two men could cause problems. But there was little she could – or rather would – do. Her attempt to anoint a successor had failed when AKK had turned out to be – at best – incompetent and disloyal. The Chancellor had work to do and would instead focus on policy. That, after all, was her strength. Or rather, it was how she like to be perceived.

COVID-19 consumed her days. But, for the time being, she kept in the background, making few public appearances. The daily work was – on the surface – delegated to Jens Spahn. Merkel herself was nowhere to be seen. But behind the scenes, she was reading up on the subject as if she were studying for an exam.

Letargo is the Italian word for hibernation. In typical academic fashion, it was this word that the philosopher Peter Sloterdijk used to describe Angela Merkel's style of government. Germany, remarked the author of *Critique of Cynical Reason*,[2] is a 'Lethargokratie' – government by hibernation.[3]

But just as there is a reason for seasonal heterothermy among bears, bats and box turtles, there was a reason Merkel was locked away. She was plotting her strategy. It was the classic pattern for her. As during the Euro Crisis and indeed practically all the challenges she has faced, she pursued her tried and trusted strategy of 'merkeln'. Only during the influx of refugees had she acted on instinct, and that was a thing she wanted to avoid repeating at all costs. So, she focused and, literally, did her homework.

After almost two months during which she largely avoided any mention of COVID-19, Merkel started publicly to address the issue on 10 March, dedicating an entire press conference to the subject on the following day. As usual, she stressed that a European response was imperative: 'We will do the necessary, as a country and in the European Union.'[4] In reality, her government was not quite as committed to a common European solution as she claimed. Her stress on a coordinated response was a reaction to the severe criticism she had faced two days earlier when – for the first time – the heads of the twenty-seven EU countries met via Zoom. In the historic meeting, Merkel was taken to task for having introduced a ban on the export of PPE equipment. In reality, the ban wasn't her doing. But the buck stops at the top. On 26 February a working group had drawn up a document that stated that, in case of a shortage of face masks and other protective equipment, no one should be able to export these to other countries. The aim was to prevent entrepreneurial spirits from capitalising on the crisis. But the decision was short-sighted and not thought through.

When the pandemic hit Italy, and the television screens showed desperate scenes from Bergamo, southeast of Milan, German companies were still barred from exporting to Italy. In the increasing febrile atmosphere, the French President Emmanuel Macron then introduced a similar export ban. Only a month after the United Kingdom had left the European Union, the solidarity among the remaining members of the EU was reduced to a scramble for face masks. This looked bad, and it was bad. Hence Merkel's emphasis on a 'European' solution.

The woman who was the frequent subject of criticism for inaction and hibernation swung into action, and into overdrive, announcing that there would be extraordinary financial support for businesses during the crisis, and ordering ministers to relax the export ban to other European countries. Her finance minister – the Vice-Chancellor and Social Democrat Finance Minister Olaf Scholz – led the initiatives, but Merkel was able to take credit. At least at this stage. Her deputy was an ambitious man. But he had surprisingly lost a bid to become co-chair of the party with Klara Geywitz. (The post went to the rather nondescript duo of Norbert Walter-Borjans and Saskia Esken in 2019.) Scholz was seen as a political has-been, though this was later to change.

For the moment, Merkel took charge. She moved quickly in parliament. Exceptional times call for exceptional measures, so she won approval for a constitutional change that allowed the central government to run a deficit. With a stroke of a pen, a cornerstone of German economic policy since the 1920s was changed in an afternoon.

The European part of the pandemic was business as usual for Merkel, at least at the diplomatic level. A week later, the first round of frantic phone call and the by now ubiquitous Zoom meetings bore fruit when the European Union countries began work on a collective tender for medical equipment.[5]

But more was needed. The markets were beginning to react to the crisis, and the prospect of the greatest economic depression since the 1929 Wall Street Crash called for a radical approach. And this had to be an international effort.

Thanks to her protégée Ursula von der Leyen as President of the European Union and a good relationship with Emmanuel Macron, Merkel was able to be instrumental in pushing through the European Recovery Fund. As so often before, the programme was a result of long and detailed negotiations. After Italy and Spain had requested help, Christine Lagarde, the President of the European Central Bank, had adopted the Pandemic Emergency Purchase Programme (PEPP) as a temporary measure – a kind of overdraft facility – to prevent governments from running out of money. Despite protests from the so-called Frugal Four (Austria, Sweden, the Netherlands and Denmark), Merkel and Macron were able to cajole, convince and coax the smaller countries into adopting a plan that allowed the EU to borrow money, and to establish the conditions under which countries were eligible to receive funds.

It was a classic Merkel stroke. It solved an immediate problem in a way that tied the European Union together – and thus helped heal the rift that had emerged early on in the pandemic. In addition, the recovery fund also managed – albeit in a limited way – to bind in countries like Hungary and Poland, who were challenging the liberal consensus of the European project. When presenting the plan, Merkel could almost triumphantly say, 'The nation state alone has no future.'[6]

But the pandemic was not a challenge that could be met solely at the European, let alone at the international level. That was Merkel's habitat, where she was the undisputed master. But unlike all her predecessors, Merkel, as we have seen, was not steeped in politics at state level; she had never governed a state (like Helmut Kohl and Gerhard Schröder) or even been a state minister like Helmut Schmidt. And this was her problem.

Germany is also a country with a federal constitution. Health is one of the issues over which the federal and the state governments share competencies. The *Länder* governments are governed by fourteen different coalitions, consisting of seven different constellations. In most of these cases, the ministers of health are not from the same party as the Premier. And what is more, the cabinet position of Minister of Health is one of the lowest ranking in the pecking order. For this reason, the sixteen health ministers are, as Robin Alexander, the editor of *Die Welt*, bluntly put it, 'not only lightweights but also politicians who were not in a trusted relationship with their heads of government'.[7] Germany's greatest health crisis since the plague in the Middle Ages was now to be coordinated by second-ranking politicians with little influence, and often with precious little knowledge and scientific expertise. A coordinated response was hard to find. Indeed, it was non-existent. At least at first.

Merkel had expected to go into battle with the usual foes. That was how it had played out in Berlin, where Horst Seehofer – now Minister of the Interior – was using every opportunity to disagree with the *Kanzlerin*. But at state level, another pattern emerged. Merkel's natural ally, Armin Laschet, was opposed to the restrictions the Chancellor found necessary.

Concurrently with the crisis, Annegret Kramp-Karrenbauer announced that she would not stand for the chancellorship and would step down as leader of the party (see chapter 15). Despite telling Markus Söder – and everyone else – that he would not be a candidate for the post as Merkel's successor, Laschet now threw his hat in the ring on 10 February 2020. COVID-19 was still not yet dominating the headlines, and, once again, the battle for the crown of the CDU was leading the news in a way that made the CDU/CSU look disorganised and weak. As in 2018, Friedrich Merz declared his candidacy. In addition, Norbert Röttgen – the foreign affairs spokesperson of the CDU in the Bundestag and a former cabinet minister of the environment – joined the fray. It was immediately clear that the latter – often known as the George Clooney of German politics thanks to his supposed resemblance to the heartthrob American actor – would have little chance. It was going to be a battle between Merz and Laschet. Since Merz had played down fears over coronavirus, Laschet felt it opportune to do the same. But it was not merely opportunism that drove the *Ministerpräsident* of North Rhine Westphalia. He was a committed European and his wife was a Francophone of Belgian descent. To close the borders to neighbouring countries was against both Laschet's instincts and his convictions – and would be politically dangerous. For these reasons, he decided against any closure of the borders with Belgium and the Netherlands.

But there was another – more sinister – reason for Laschet's hesitation. It was Markus Söder. The former television journalist and Bavarian *Landesfürst* governed the state with the highest number of COVID-19 cases. In neighbouring Austria, Chancellor Sebastian Kurz had already shut down the schools and introduced drastic measures. Having failed to win a clear majority in the most recent state elections, Söder was under pressure to follow suit. Yet to introduce measures in his state alone would draw attention to the higher number of cases, something for which Söder could be held responsible. The Bavarian tried to get the other premiers to agree to a lockdown in all the states, but to no avail. In the end, he had little choice but to go it alone. On 16 March, Söder declared an emergency in Bavaria. All non-essential shops were ordered to close.

For the rest of Germany, the Bavarian became the supposed standard-bearer for harsh lockdown measures. This outcome suited Laschet well. Söder would be blamed for the harsh measures, and Laschet would be seen as the liberator once things had quietened down. That was the Rheinländer's plan, anyway.

But the unfolding crisis did not follow this script. For starters, developments in other neighbouring countries created problems for Laschet – and for Germany. The Dutch government believed that herd immunity was the best way forward. While there were restrictions in trade even in North Rhine Westphalia, citizens could freely cross the border into the Netherlands. As a result, the number of cases exploded in Laschet's state. Under pressure from Merkel and the other premiers, Laschet was forced to agree to the closing of the borders.

Thus, within two weeks the professional relationships between, respectively, Merkel and Laschet, and Merkel and Söder changed completely. Söder became Merkel's ally, but this altered dynamic was in large part also due to a completely unforeseen circumstance.

On 22 March, Merkel stalked back into her office after yet another online press conference. She had sided with Söder, and she was enervated. Not because of the newfound alliance with the Bavarian, but because her statement had been unclear, muddled, and – according to her trusted Chief of Staff, Beate Baumann – downright misleading. Merkel prided herself on getting the facts right, and this time, well, she had not distinguished clearly enough between 'social distancing' and social gatherings.

Even Helge Braun seemed concerned when she saw him in her office. The big man was not normally someone who would criticise the Chancellor. 'There is something urgent I need to tell you,' he began.

Merkel appeared irritated. As if to say that she knew she had messed up. But Braun stopped her. 'I have spoken to your doctor,' he reportedly said. 'You need to self-isolate. You have tested positive.'

Merkel immediately went home (though finding a car that allowed for social distancing was difficult, and in the end she had to be driven in a VW minibus). The following day, she tested negative. But for two weeks she governed her country from the living room – and in close contact with the current President of the Premiers, namely Markus Söder.

The two got on well, but it was a significant change, and a surprising one for two politicians who, less than a year before, had been sworn enemies. But it was not just the crisis that brought them together. The once-boisterous Bavarian had changed. Or so he liked to say.

The real reason was perhaps more prosaic, and it cannot be ruled out that Söder was being strategic. The CSU had lost votes en masse – especially to women and younger voters – in the most recent *Land* election. At the time, in 2018, Söder sought to court voters who would otherwise have voted for the AfD. But, in the process, he had lost support from those who stressed the word 'Sozial' in Christian Social Union. Having won only 37 per cent of the votes in the state elections – a loss of 10 per cent and the worst result for his party since 1950 – Söder decided to change tack. Once a nationalist who claimed that Islam had no place in Germany, he now confessed – almost apologetically – that he had changed. He spoke of a 'near-death experience' which occurred when citizens had demonstrated against the 'politics of fear' in Bavaria. The experience, Söder declared, made him change his mind.[8] Opportunistic? Too good to be true? Convenient? Perhaps, but for the time being, he seemed sincere. Besides, his new image suited his new friend Angela Merkel.

However, the softer, kinder and gentler Söder was still sharp, and focused on his political goal. During a joint press conference hosted by the Bavarian premier, a young journalist asked a question about Merkel's successor as party leader. 'So, will you go to the press conference with Friedrich Merz and Norbert Röttgen too?' asked the reporter, who wanted to quiz Merkel about her joint appearance with the CSU leader. The journalist made an involuntary pause, perhaps out of nervousness. Söder immediately seized the moment: 'I think you have forgotten someone,' said the Bavarian. 'Armin Laschet.'

By the end of spring, Germany was in better shape than many other countries. But internally there were differences. In Bavaria, Söder was more popular than ever. In North Rhine Westphalia, Laschet's wait-and-see strategy was largely viewed as a failure. He had said that he would contest the leadership of the CDU with Jens Spahn as his deputy. Many in the party were worried. And behind the scenes, Volker Bouffier – the influential Premier of Hesse – suggested that Laschet should step aside. He refused.

At the time it seemed like a mistake not to nominate the up-and-coming health minister. Jens Spahn was more popular than ever. As so many politicians learned during the pandemic, this popularity was not to last. Having been a safe pair of hands, the youngish conservative and openly gay minister did exceptionally well at first. Merkel even warmed to him, and began to see him as a potential successor. The two began to use the informal 'du' rather than the formal 'Sie', and they were even seen together at the *Wagner Festspiele*, though Spahn joked that he had 'been dragged there by my husband'.[9]

Later in the pandemic, the Spahn star started to wane. It was more than alleged that the politician had profited from the sale of PPE equipment.[10] Moreover, *Der Spiegel* revealed that he had taken part in a fundraiser at a time when he had publicly told citizens not to meet at social gatherings. At the dinner he attended, against official government advice, he had raised close to €10,000, which he failed to declare to the authorities.[11] That he also tested positive a few days later could be interpreted as instant karma. These missteps made him toxic, though Merkel kept him in the cabinet. It is always good to have a lightning rod, someone who can be blamed when things go wrong.

All this was far in the future. When Spahn got in trouble, the CDU was choosing another leader. This contest was a bit of a sideshow, but important all the same. When the election was finally held – in an all-postal ballot – Laschet won 521 votes. Only 55 more than Merz's 466 votes. The millionaire businessman conceded defeat, but declared that he would run as a candidate in the 2021 federal elections.

COVID MARK II

However, the main issue in 2020–21 was not the internal politics of the CDU. Germany did relatively well during the first phase of the lock-down, but it was not all due to Merkel, let alone to any of the premiers. Often, the true key to success lies not in individuals but in institutional memory. And public health agencies are not created but grow. Over 129 years, disease monitoring had built up a knowledge base that simply could not be replicated elsewhere. Moreover, during the 2009 swine flu epidemic Germany was harder hit than her neighbouring countries, and the Robert Koch Institute had had to rethink their approach. As a re-sult, Germany was in a better position than other countries to deal with COVID-19. For instance, PPE equipment was readily available from the moment the pandemic started.

In addition, the German health system is arguably in better shape than the UK's much-eulogised NHS. Thanks to investment over many years, Germany has one of the highest numbers of hospital beds per 100,000 people – 8.3; in Britain, the number is only a third of this. There was also proportionally twice as many doctors and nurses, and about 200 labs could carry out COVID-19 testing at the beginning of the pandemic. The Germans were spending 11.3 per cent of GDP on health. In Britain, the figure is just above 9 per cent. It is not surprising, there-fore, that Britain proportionally had nearly four times as many deaths as Germany.[12]

The relatively astute handling of the crisis – at least at this stage – benefited Merkel and her party immensely. The CDU gained 17 percent-age points in the opinion polls within only one month. From languishing on a miserable 24 per cent in early March 2020, by early April Union ap-proval ratings were up to 41 per cent. In Bavaria, Söder's gamble seemed to have paid off: nearly 50 per cent of the state's voters would support Die Christlich Soziale Union. Over the summer of 2020, Germany was able to relax the rules. The Chancellor spoke of a conditional success. Travel to other countries – including Britain – was opened up. It seemed as if the pandemic was beginning to get under control. This impression was premature. Though the first vaccine against COVID-19 was developed by Dr Uğur Şahin and Dr Özlem Türeci – a husband-and-wife team of second-generation German scientists of Turkish descent – in what should surely have been a clear-cut German success story, scientific prowess was not matched by administrative capacity: Germany was slow to begin its immunisation programme. Around Christmas-time another lockdown was necessary. And, once again, many of the states were unhappy about the decisions taken by the central government.

Bodo Ramelow played Candy Crush. With some success – he was up to level ten. This leisurely activity was not, perhaps, the most common pursuit for a far-left politician. But, then again, not all Marxists indulge in reading *Das Kapital*. True, Marx had suggested that people should go hunting in the morning and read poetry at night.[13] But then again, that was before online gaming had been invented. So, perhaps the Premier of Saxony-Anhalt and member of Die Linke could be excused for his indulgence in this decadent capitalist pursuit. In fairness, the politician was bored. Who wouldn't be after a six-hour Zoom call? So, while on mute, he was swapping coloured pieces of candy on his smartphone. Managing the Covid pandemic in the Federal Republic of Germany was a challenge, and indeed its 'federal' nature was at the root of the issue. In other countries with a similar decentralised constitutional system, Australia for example, health was a matter for the central government. In Germany, it was almost the other way around. The devolved nature of German health policy had not shifted massively despite a change in the law that allowed the central government to take time-limited control over decisions made at state level.

'The sovereign is who decides on the exception' reads a famous line from a controversial legal philosopher.[14] And this, in a way, summed up Merkel's predicament. For in Germany, it was not entirely clear who was 'the sovereign' as sovereignty was divided between the states and the central government. So, on the particular issue of health, no one could 'decide on the exception'.

Merkel sought to act as if she was in control, but the *Ministerpräsidents* were not willing to be bowled over once again. By early 2021, many of them had had enough. Merkel could not have it her way.

And the federal government could do very little. All legislation initiated by the federal government must go through the upper house, that is, the *Bundesrat*. That was nothing new, it was simply the nature of German federalism.[15] After all, even Helge Braun had said that decisions of this nature belonged to the state governments. The Minister for the *Kanzleramt* was – everyone agreed – a brilliant doctor, and it was good to have a medical man in a health crisis, but he was not a lawyer and it showed. At the height of the pandemic, in the spring of 2020, he had written a memo which was later agreed with the states. Dr Braun's note read:

> In regions and federal states that are showing signs of dynamic outbreak, postponing the start of the semester at universities and temporarily closing kindergartens and schools, for example by bringing the Easter holidays forward, is another option. The decision on this is incumbent on the respective federal states.[16]

That was it. In black and white. The decision belonged to the states. Merkel had no authority to boss the premiers around. And so, Ramelow could continue to play Candy Crush uninhibited.

The lockdown introduced before Christmas had not been entirely lifted. And now, in March 2021, a growing number were protesting against the restrictions, while Merkel wanted to extend them. The pop singer Nena (of 1980s hit *99 Red Balloons* fame) led the charge. Politically, Merkel had worn out the Premiers. In the spring of 2020, the heads of the *Länder* had conceded that the Federal government could be given more powers on a temporary basis. But the population at large was not happy. Another lockdown was scheduled for Easter, but the outcry made Merkel change her mind.

With her back to the proverbial wall, Merkel made an unexpected move. She said sorry to the people. 'I apologise to all citizens. To put it bluntly, the idea of an Easter shutdown was designed with the best of intentions . . . But it was a flawed idea. This mistake is solely my fault, because in the end I have the ultimate responsibility as Chancellor.'[17]

Of course, it was not her idea alone. But by taking responsibility, she, paradoxically, looked stronger, and she projected the image of a resilient leader even at a time when she was weak and powerless.

THE GREENS TAKE FLIGHT – AND THE CDU CHOOSE A SUCCESSOR

Throughout the pandemic there was only one effective opposition party: the Greens. Although the environmentalist party was the smallest in the Bundestag, neither the AfD, Die Linke, or even the Free Democrats amounted to much. It was different for Die Grünen.

After the FDP had pulled out of negotiations to form a Jamaica Coalition in 2017, the Greens had struggled in the polls in early 2018. The coalition with the CDU and FDP was seen as a done deal. It was not. Robert Habeck – one of the two new leaders of the Greens – was particularly dispirited. A cerebral politician from the north with four children, he had served as an environment minister in Schleswig-Holstein, and latterly as Deputy Premier. The forty-eight-year-old politician with a doctorate in Philosophy had studied at the University of Roskilde in Denmark, and represented the values of liberal Nordic social democracy rather than those of radical environmentalism. He spoke fluent Danish, and dressed as if he were an extra in *The Killing* or one of the other Scandi-noir television series.

Immediately after the 2017 elections, the Greens had begun to regroup. And this proved popular: the party surged to 24 per cent in the polls – more than double what they polled a year before. Meanwhile, the Social Democrats slumped to 10 per cent.

It was Habeck who stole the show. His co-chair was Annalena Baerbock. A former competitive trampolinist (she had won bronze in the German championships in 1999), she had never served as a minister. Born in 1980, the year her party was founded, she was young, but she looked very much like the typical career politician. After studies in law at the London School of Economics, she had been an intern in the European Parliament before she became a member of the Bundestag in 2013 at the tender age of thirty-two.

When Habeck became the new co-leader, it was widely assumed that Baerbock would play second fiddle to the charismatic northerner. That was not how it turned out. Habeck was keen to change the image of the Greens from being a fringe party, and for this reason he suggested that the two joint leaders shared an office and staff and took joint positions. In this way, the perceived split between pragmatic (so-called *Realos*) and doctrinaire (*Fundis*) would be relegated to the history books and the party would be seen as a credible and unified alternative to the internally divided CDU and the – at the time – struggling SPD.

However, as a result, Baerbock became more visible. The photogenic female leader soon moved into the spotlight. As a mother of two, she was able to appeal to many of the voters who previously had voted for the CSU in the south. During the Covid pandemic, it was suddenly Baerbock, and not the less charismatic Habeck, who was requested for interviews.

At the national and regional level, the Greens were pragmatic. The only serving Green premier, Winfried Kretschmann – a former Maoist turned pragmatic politician – was cooperating closely with Marcus Söder in a way that suggested that the two were allies. In Berlin, Merkel herself briefed the Green politicians, above all Baerbock.

Polls suggested that Baerbock was one of the most popular politicians in Germany. And, for the first time in history, Die Grünen overtook the CDU/CSU's position as the largest party. At a time when the two sister parties were tearing themselves apart over who should succeed Merkel, the Greens needed to move fast. In contrast to the combative struggle between Laschet and Söder, Die Grünen decided to choose one candidate. With apparent grace, Habeck stepped aside. Baerbock was declared candidate for the highest office on 19 April 2021. The choice of the psychologically significant first deadline date was no coincidence. It was chosen to further gain momentum – and to unnerve the CDU/CSU.

The CDU had taken a hit in the polls, and the Greens were on the up. And the former had still not settled the K question: who was going to be their candidate for the soon-to-be-vacant spot as Merkel's successor? In the same week when the Greens showed unprecedented unity, Union did anything but.

Armin Laschet had declared his candidacy after he won the party leadership, and his victory over Fredrich Merz had put him in a strong position, but he continued to make gaffes. What about Söder? The Bavarian had finally declared on 11 April 2021.

But as a CSU leader, he needed the support of the CDU. History was not on his side. The failed attempts by, respectively, Franz Josef Strauss (1980) and Edmund Stoiber (2002) had made it the conventional wisdom that a CSU candidate could not win a federal election. Yet Söder was different. His poll ratings were second only to Merkel's and miles ahead of Laschet's. The two men met to find a compromise. But Laschet was in no mood to concede. Why should he? He knew that he had the support of the hierarchy, if not the rank and file of the CDU. Söder was popular, but the German system was not a presidential one, and in a parliamentary system it is not the people but the parliamentarians who elect the head of government. As the first deadline to find a compromise candidate passed on 19 April, Laschet was still not willing to concede an inch to his Bavarian rival. It was getting critical. Volker Bouffier, the Hessian premier, was asked to mediate. Whether he did so of his own volition, or was asked to do so by Angela Merkel, remains unclear. As we have seen, it was not the first time Bouffier had been dispatched to change Laschet's mind. And, as on the previous attempt, it failed. Laschet could, with some justification, claim that polls go up and down. Previously he had been asked to step aside for Jens Spahn. But now the health minister was embroiled in trouble. No, he had been right *not* to concede the first time. And he was not going to budge. Laschet might not possess the popular touch, but he had cultivated his contacts in the party hierarchy, and he knew when to trade in old favours. He called a meeting of the board of the CDU to be held on 20 April. The result was a fait accompli: twenty-four of the thirty-one board members opted for Laschet, and Söder conceded defeat.[18] But the victory for Laschet was overshadowed by the hype over Baerbock. That the Social Democrats – as early as August 2020 – had decided that Olaf Scholz would be their *Kanzlerkandidat* was seen as largely irrelevant. Sure, the former state leader of Hamburg had been instrumental in negotiating a plan for global taxation of internet companies, but nevertheless the SPD was viewed as pathetic. No one gave him any chance.

So, the Green *Kanzlerkandidatin* could do nothing wrong. Or so it seemed. The CDU were slipping in the polls and began to play dirty. It was alleged that Baerbock had plagiarised passages in a book she had published. Although she was able to show that the sources were public ones and that she had duly referenced other authors, the media (many of which were close to the CDU) wasted no opportunity to criticise the new female leader. It seemed clear to many that the criticism was sexist and that Baerbock was being targeted because she was a woman. Although Merkel had served over sixteen years as Kanzlerin, and arguably a successful one at that, Germany was still a sexist society. In February 2021, *Der Spiegel* found that 69 per cent of female members of parliament in Germany had experienced 'misogynistic hatred as members of the Bundestag'. And that no less than 36 per cent had experienced physical 'attacks on themselves, their offices or their home'.[19]

But Baerbock's troubles did not help Laschet. During 2021, large parts of Germany were flooded. Laschet had already made a number of gaffes, and he continued to make them: at a memorial service for the 196 people who died in the flooding, he was seen laughing and joking. Everything he did went wrong.

To everyone's surprise, Olaf Scholz began to gain in the polls. The socialist appeared balanced, serious, and had perfected Merkel's ability to say very little. At the beginning of September 2021, he overtook both the CDU and the Greens in the polls.

TAKING STOCK

In 2021, the bestselling novel in Germany was *Miss Merkel*. With a subtitle that translated as 'murder in the Uckermark', David Safier's novel was a spoofy and unserious flight of fancy about Angela Merkel's retirement job as a private detective. At best light-hearted, it portrayed the (in the book) former Chancellor as a kind of Agatha Christie character in the Miss Marple mould.[20] Leaving aside whatever literary qualities the novel might have, the key thing to note is the almost universal affection for the fictional portrayal of the *Kanzlerin*. Rarely has there been such universal love for a democratically elected leader. To imagine that anyone would write a loving book about any other serving or former German leader seems fanciful.

Was Merkel all that she was cracked up to be? Was she the Queen of Europe? Or even the leader of the free world?

It is natural to take stock and assess what Merkel had accomplished in office. Some remarked that hers was a quiet power, that she changed the style of politics in the German Federal Republic. She did. Before she became Chancellor in 2005, no woman had held high political office. Her own Christian Democrat Party was dominated by socially conservative, southern, Catholic lawyers. The party's view was – as earlier chapters of this book have chronicled – that women should concentrate on *Kinder, Küche, Kirche* – children, kitchen, church. This all changed with Merkel: a divorcee, the daughter of a Lutheran pastor and the holder of a doctorate in Quantum Chemistry, she did not conform to the standard of female Christian Democrat politicians.

'I must follow them, the people, for I am their leader,' said the French politician Alexandre Ledru-Rollin, a socialist candidate who is now only remembered as the losing candidate in the 1848 French Presidential election. (He lost to Napoleon III, who later staged a coup.) It is likely that the Frenchman, had he lived in the twenty-first century, would have commissioned polls, focus groups and online surveys to gauge the 'will of the people'. But many in the German political establishment were taken aback when it was revealed that Angela Merkel, a cerebral politician with a knack for policy detail, was equally fickle. Every week, so it was reported, she (and her staff) would commission opinion polls to find out what the people wanted. The phasing out of nuclear energy was a result of this research.[21] Perhaps more surprisingly, the decision to take in a large number of refugees in 2015 was reached after a survey showed that this was a popular policy. That this controversial decision, in the end, was a success, and that the immigrants were generally fully integrated less than five years later, is another story. Officially, she would lambast Donald Trump's 'America First' policy – albeit in her trademark understated style. In reality, Merkel *always* put 'Germany First'. She was just better at making friends, had a better image, and was a better politician.

History will probably remember her for her role in resolving the euro debt, for opening the borders to no less than 1.4 million refugees between

2015 and 2017, and for creating Europe's strongest economy. But her principal legacy lies in social policies. Her first legislative achievement as a minister in the 1990s was to introduce a more liberal abortion law. It is often overlooked that West Germany effectively banned women's right to choose before the unification of Germany in 1990. While Merkel is not a flag-flying feminist, her policies tell a different story.

On her watch, Germany became a more social democracy – with a small 's' – which included better provisions for childcare and a higher minimum wage as issues she more or less stole from the centre left Social Democrats. And while Merkel was herself sceptical, she oversaw the legalisation of same-sex marriage in 2017.

All these changes impacted not only social but also political life. More women rose to prominent positions, as did politicians with same-sex partners. The late Guido Westerwelle became Germany's first openly gay cabinet minister when he served as Merkel's Foreign Secretary in 2009–13. Merkel's methods sometimes went against the prevailing political culture: she was able to deflect criticism because she was clever enough to admit mistakes at critical junctions, for instance. Admitting in one official speech that her policies had 'generated quite a shitstorm'[22] (she used the English word!) made her look stronger, and more grown-up and responsible.

Was Merkel still Europe's most influential politician when she left office? That she was able to install Ursula von der Leyen as the first female President of the European Commission in 2019 – and the first German in that post since Walter Hallstein in the 1960s – suggests that she still played *the* dominant role in Europe. Power never lasts for ever. After some years, lethargy always sets in. That was also the case with Merkel, though more for institutional reasons than for reasons that had anything to do with her political character or ability.

Do all political careers end in failure? Not in the case of Angela Merkel. She remained Europe's most influential leader until the end.

EPILOGUE

Merkel was nowhere to be seen on the night of the election on 26 September, 2021. And perhaps her decision was wise. The CDU lost. They lost big, capturing less than 25 per cent of the votes. It was understandable that Merkel stayed away from the limelight. But then again, her absence wasn't entirely unexpected. She had hardly been seen on the campaign trail at all, making only three appearances.

The Social Democrats finished ahead of the CDU for the first time since 1998. The Green Party achieved their best result ever. The parties on the right lost uniformly. And in Bavaria, the CSU dropped to an unprecedented 32 per cent of the votes. Neither Armin Laschet nor his nemesis Markus Söder could spin themselves out of the brute electoral facts. The opinion polls suggested that voters wanted more social justice, a higher minimum wage and more equality, as espoused by the SPD.

Laschet's insistence that his party could still form a government sounded desperate, bordering on pitiful, and was immediately undercut by Söder, who acknowledged that it was time to go into opposition. With friends like that, who needs enemies?

Had the voters turned their backs on Merkel and her values? Certainly, they believed it was time for a change. Even in Merkel's Stralsund constituency, Anna Kassautzki – a twenty-seven-year-old self-declared 'young socialist' – prevailed. A bitter defeat? Perhaps so! But in a democracy, nothing is static, and yet there is stability. And thus, a woman of Polish origin was succeeded by another with the same ethnic roots. Always a bookish person, perhaps on this night Merkel might have reflected on Johann Wolfgang von Goethe's words:

That which ends and was in the beginning[1]

GLOSSARY

AfD: *Alternative für Deutschland*. Right-wing political party opposed to mass immigration. The party was founded by former World Bank Economist Bernd Lucke in 2013. The party narrowly failed to win representation to the Federal Parliament in 2013. However became the third largest party – and the main opposition party – in 2017 with 12.5 percent and 94 members of the Bundestag. The party has been kept under surveillance for pursuing policies that are unconstitutional (verfassungswidrig). The party is currently chaired by Jörg Meuthen and Tino Chrupalla.

Bundespräsident: President of the Federal Republic of Germany. The role is mostly ceremonial, but the Head of State has the power to veto legislation as Horst Köhler did during Merkel's first coalition government.

Bundesrat: The Upper House in the German federal Parliament. The members are leaders of the states and not directly elected representatives. Larger states like Bavaria have six votes, smaller states like Saxony have four votes, and the smallest city states, Bremen and Hamburg, have three votes. The Bundesrat can veto legislation in areas of shared responsibility, including refugee policy, but has no say over foreign affairs, the budget or defence.

Bundestag: The Lower House of the German federal Parliament, equivalent to the British House of Commons. 299 of the 630 members are directly elected in single member constituencies, the rest are elected by proportional representation. The Bundestag meets in the Reichstag building in Berlin. The Bundestag formally elects the Chancellor.

Bundesverfassungsgericht: The German federal constitutional court, situated in Karlsruhe in Baden-Württemberg, in southwest Germany. The court famously struck down the abortion legislation in the 1970s and is considered an activist court. Members of the Bundestag as well as all citizens can ask for the court to review legislation. This is known as a *Verfassungsbeschwerde*. The court receives about five thousand complaints every year.

Bundesversammlung: Federal council that elects the federal President. Membership consists of the entire Bundestag, and an equal number of representatives from each of the states. It is customary for the states to select non-politicians. In 2012 the football coach Otto Rehhagel and the comedian Ingo Appelt were among the members of the Bundesversammlung.

CDU: Christlich Demokratische Union Deutschlands, Christian Democratic Union of Germany. Centre-right political party founded by Konrad Adenauer. Angela Merkel became a member of this party in 1990, two months before becoming a cabinet minister. The first female leader succeeded Wolf gang Schäuble as leader of the party in 2000.

CSU: Christlich-Soziale Union, Christian-Social Union. The CDU's Bavarian sister party. Conservative party with strong ties to the Catholic Church. Under Franz-Josef Strauß the party briefly severed the ties with CDU in 1976 at a meeting in Wildbad Kreuth. The decision was reversed a month later. The leader of the party is Marcus Söder, the Premier of Bavaria.

DDR: Deutsche Demokratische Republik. Communist German state also known as East Germany. Established in 1949 and formally disbanded after the German reunification in 1990.

FDJ: Freie Deutsche Jugend. Socialist youth movement for young people aged between 14 and 25. Membership was not compulsory but in practice necessary for obtaining a place at university. FDJ had a membership of 2.3 million. Angela Merkel was a member of the FDJ.

FDP: Freie Demokratische Partei. Free market political party with liberal views on civil rights, abortion and religion. In a coalition with CDU and CSU 2009-2013. It failed to win the required 5 per cent of the votes and lost its representation in the Bundestag in 2013. The party re-entered the federal parliament in 2017

Grosse Koalition, Die: Grand Coalition. A government formed by the two largest parties who typically compete for power. The first Grand Coalition was formed in 1966 and lasted until 1969. Angela Merkel was Chancellor in a Grand Coalition 2005-2009 and again from 2013.

Grundgesetz: literally 'Basic Law'. The constitution of the Federal Republic of Germany, enacted in 1949. The constitution contains an eternity clause ('Ewigkeitsklausel') stating that the system of democracy cannot be changed, not even by constitutional amendment.

Grünen, Die: officially Bündnis 90/Die Grünen, the Green Party. Ecological and centre-left party formed as a merger between the Greens in the West and the East German Alliance 90. The party's leaders are Annalena Baerbock and Robert Haveman. Winfried Kretschmann from the state Baden-Württemberg became the first Green Ministerpräsident in 2011.

Kanzler/Kanzlerin: Chancellor. The head of the cabinet of the federal government. Four of the eight holders of the office since 1949 have been from the CDU. Ludwig Erhard (1963-1966) was not formally a member of the CDU but was elected by this party.

Länder: States. There are 16 states in the Federal Republic of Germany. Three of these, Berlin, Bremen and Hamburg, are so-called city-states or *Stadtstaaten*.

Linkspartei or **Die Linke:** The Left Party. Founded in 2007 as the merger of the former Communist Party PDS and the former SPD leader Oskar Lafontaine's WASG (Arbeit und soziale Gerechtigkeit – Die Wahlalternative, 'the Electoral Alternative for Labour and Social Justice'). The party represents the far left in German politics. Its current leader Gregor Gysi was the last leader of the SED, the East German Communist Party. The party is strongest in the former East Germany. Die Linke's Bodo Ramelow is currently Ministerpräsident in the state of Thüringen in southeast Germany. Its joint leaders are Janine Wissler and Susanne Hennig-Wellsow.

SED: Sozialistische Einheitspartei Deutschlands. The ruling Communist party of East Germany 1946-1989. In 1990 the party changed its name to PDS.

SPD: Sozialdemokratische Partei Deutschlands, Social Democratic Party of Germany. Centre-left political party founded in 1869. Traditionally the main opponent of the CDU, the party was in government with the FDP 1969-1982 and with the Greens 1998-2005. SPD formed a Grand Coalition with CDU and CSU 2005-2009 and again from 2013.

Stasi: Formally, Ministerium für Staatssicherheit, or MfS, the secret police and security service of East Germany. The Stasi had a permanent staff of 91,015 officers in addition to 173,081 unofficial informants. There were an estimated 1,553 informants in West Germany.

Vergangenheitsbewältigung: An often used term for how modern Germany and Germans are coming to terms with the Nazi past.

Union: Shorthand for the CDU and the CSU, who usually form a block in the Bundestag.

Notes

Preface

1 'Egal wie es ausgeht ...', *Der Spiegel*, 26 January 2016.

Chapter 1

1 R.G. Reuth and G.L. Lachmann, *Das erste Leben der Angela M*, Munich: Piper Verlag 2013, p. 19.
2 Reuth and Lachmann, *Das erste Leben der Angela M*, p. 21.
3 Gerd Langguth, *Angela Merkel*, Munich: DTB Verlag 2007, p. 41.
4 Angela Merkel, *Bericht der Vorsitzenden der CDU Deutschlands*, Bundespartietag, 6 December 2004.
5 Langguth, *Angela Merkel*, p. 408.
6 Merkel quoted in H. Koelbl, *Spuren der Macht: Die Verwandlung des Menschen durch das Amt*, Munich: Knesebeck 1999, p. 99.
7 Merkel quoted in Koelbl, *Spuren der Macht*, p. 52.
8 'Es gibt kein Recht auf Glück', *Bild am Sonntag*, 10 June 2001.
9 Langguth, *Angela Merkel*, p. 40.
10 Archive, Bezirkstag/Rat des Bezirkes Schwerin, 4163b.
11 Landeshauptarchiv Schwerin; 7.21-1, Bezirkstag/Rat des Bezirkes Schwerin 4163a, 3 July 1957.
12 Landeshauptarchiv Schwerin; 7.21-1: Analyse über die kirchlichen Amsträger and Gemeindekirchenräte, 25 October 1961.
13 Langguth, *Angela Merkel*, pp. 40-1.
14 Rainer Eppelmann, *Fremd im einigem Haus. Mein Leben im anderen Deutschland*, Cologne: Kiepenheuer und Witsch 1993, p. 105.
15 Angela Merkel quoted in Koelbl, *Spuren der Macht*, p. 49.
16 Angela Merkel quoted in Koelbl, *Spuren der Macht*, p. 48.
17 Evelyn Roll, *Das Mädchen und die Macht: Angela Merkels demokratischer Aufbruch*, Berlin: Rowohlt Verlag 2001, p. 35.
18 Langguth, *Angela Merkel*, p. 51.

19 'Sie war mit Abstand die Beste', *Deutsches Allgemeines Sonntagsblatt*, 7 April 2000.

20 G. Bärtels, 'Russisch Olympiade – 1.Platz', *Cicero*, no. 12, 2004, p. 68.

21 Moritz von Uslar, *Hundert Fragen an ... Angela Merkel*, Cologne: Kippenhauer and Wietsch 2004, p. 109.

22 Langguth, *Angela Merkel*, p. 52.

23 Angela Merkel, *Mein Weg*, Hamburg: Hoffmann und Campe 2004, p. 43.

24 Merkel, *Mein Weg*, p. 44.

Chapter 2

1 Langguth, *Angela Merkel*, p. 55.

2 Langguth, *Angela Merkel*, p. 61.

3 Merkel, *Mein Weg*, p. 51.

4 N. Blome, *Angela Merkel – Die Zauder-Künstlerin*, Berlin: Pantheon Verlag, 2013, p. 1.

5 Langguth, *Angela Merkel*, p. 67.

6 Institut für Geschichte der Arbeiterbewegung, Zentrales Parteiarchiv der SED (IV A2/14/2), quoted in Besier, *Der SED-Staat und die Kirche*, p. 607.

7 Roll, *Das Mädchen und die Macht*, p. 25.

8 Professor Schröder quoted in Langguth, *Angela Merkel*, p. 64.

9 Langguth, *Angela Merkel*. p. 62.

10 Spiegel, 'Interview mit Angela Merkel: "Ich muss harter werden"', 3 January 1994.

11 Horst Kasner, 'Im Vergeßen liegt Vernunft', quoted in Langguth, *Angela Merkel*, p. 70.

12 Roll, *Das Mädchen und die Macht*, p. 54.

13 Landesarchiv des Landkreises Uckermark Prenzlau, Z 24/90-1663. Rat des Kreises Templin: Gespräch mit Pharrern zur Lage in der ČSSR, 23 August 1968.

14 Roll, *Das Mädchen und die Macht*, p. 54.

15 'Das Leben ist erbarmungslos – es deformiert', *Stern*, 20 July 2000, p. 46.

16 Langguth, *Angela Merkel*, p. 50.

17 Langguth, *Angela Merkel*, p. 60.

18 'Das Mädchen Angela und ihre Freundinnen', *Berliner Zeitung*, 20 February 2000.

19 'Das eiserne Mädchen', *Der Spiegel*, 1 March 2000.

20 Langguth, *Angela Merkel*, p. 46.

21 Merkel, *Mein Weg*, p. 51.

22 Langguth, *Angela Merkel*, p. 55.

23 Reuth and Lachmann, *Das erste Leben der Angela M*, p. 57.

24 *Bild an Sonntag*, 10 June 2010, quoted in Reuth and Lachmann, *Das erste*

Leben der Angela M, p. 57.

25 Reuth and Lachmann, *Das erste Leben der Angela M*, p. 69.

26 Reuth and Lachmann, *Das erste Leben der Angela M*, p. 70.

27 Reuth and Lachmann, *Das erste Leben der Angela M*, pp. 69-70.

28 Das eiserne Mädchen', *Der Spiegel*, 1 March 2000.

29 Reuth and Lachmann, *Das erste Leben der Angela M*, p. 70.

Chapter 3

1 Merkel, *Mein Weg*, p. 55.

2 M. von Uslar *100 Fragen an ...*, Cologne: Kiepenheuer und Witsch 2004, p. 107.

3 'Interview', *Frankfurter Allgemeine Zeitung*, 15 September 1991.

4 G. Hofmann, *Essay: Willy Brandt – Porträt eines Aufklärers aus Deutschland*, Hamburg: Rowohlt 1988, p. 49.

5 Daniela Münkel, 'Der Feind meines Feindes ...', in Christian Staas (ed.), *Willy Brandt: Visionär, Weltbürger, Kanzler der Einheit, Zeit Geschichte*, 2013, p. 46.

6 Probably a reference to Brandt's chief of staff (Staatssekretär) Egon Bahr.

7 Egon Krenz quoted in Ulrich Mählert, *Rote Fahnen: Die Geschichte der Freien Deutschen Jugend*, Berlin: Opladen 1996, p. 207.

8 Angela Merkel, *Daran glaube ich: Christliche Standpunkte*, Leipzig: Benno 2013, p. 10.

9 'Interview mit Ulrich Merkel', *Focus*, 5 July 2004.

10 Jacqueline Boysen, *Angela Merkel: Eine deutsch-deutsche Biographie*, Munich: Ullstein Verlag 2001, p. 329.

11 Merkel, *Mein Weg*, p. 56.

12 'Interview mit Ulrich Merkel', *Focus*, 5 July 2004.

13 R. Der, R. Haberlandt and A. Merkel, 'On the Influence of Spatial Correlations on the Rate of Chemical Reactions in Dense Systems. II. Numerical Results', *Chemical Physics* 53(3), 1980, pp. 437-42.

14 Angela Merkel quoted in Reuth and Lachmann, *Das erste Leben der Angela M*, p. 109.

15 Quoted in Ulrich Mählert, *Rote Fahnen: Die Geschichte der Freien Deutschen Jugend*, Berlin: Opladen 1996, p. 207.

16 Merkel, *Mein Weg*, p. 71.

17 Markus Wolf, speech at the University of Copenhagen, April 1999. The author interviewed Herr Wolf.

18 Angela Merkel quoted in W. Stock, *Angela Merkel: Eine politische Biographie*, Munich: Olzog 2000, p. 49.

19 Boysen, *Angela Merkel*, p. 44.

20 'Interview mit Ulrich Merkel', *Focus*, 5 July 2004.

21 'Merkel: "Wir schaffen das"', *Frankfurter Allgemeine Zeitung*, 31 August 2015.

22 Koelbl, *Spuren der Macht*, p. 49.

23 Koelbl, *Spuren der Macht*, p. 49.

24 Evelyn Roll, *Die Kanzlerin: Angela Merkels Weg zur Macht*, Berlin: Ullstein 2009, p. 63.

25 Ernst Jünger, *Siebzig Verweht III*, Stuttgart: J.G. Cotta'scher Buchhandlung Nachfolger GmbH 1993, p. 179.

Chapter 4

1 Horst Kasner quoted in an interview with Angela Merkel: 'Das Leben is erbarmungslos – es deformiert', *Stern*, no. 30, 2000, p. 46.

2 Reuth and Lachmann, *Das erste Leben der Angela M*, p. 136.

3 Koelbl, *Spuren der Macht*, p. 49.

4 Mündlicher bericht des IM 'Bachmann' von 22.9, Bachmann Bd. 1, 7768/91 BStU (file in the Stasi Archive).

5 'Michael Schindhelm: Zweimal täglich Mokka mit Angela', *Berliner Morgenpost*, 8 March 2000.

6 'Michael Schindhelm: Zweimal täglich Mokka mit Angela', *Berliner Morgenpost*, 8 March 2000.

7 http://www.lmz-bw.de/fileadmin/user_upload/Medienbildung_MCO /fileadmin/bibliothek/weizsaecker_speech_may85/weizsaecker_speech may85.pdf (Accessed 13 May 2015).

8 'A Size-Up of President Nixon: Interview with Mike Mansfield, Senate Democratic Leader', *U.S. News & World Report*, 6 December 1971, p. 61.

9 Gorbachev quoted in Milan Svec, 'The Prague Spring: 20 Years Later', *Foreign Affairs*, 1988, p. 982.

10 S. Kornelius, *Angela Merkel: The Chancellor and her World. The Authorized Biography*, Croydon: Alma Books 2013, p. 126.

11 Schindhelm, *Roberts Reise*, p. 373.

12 Angela Merkel, in Uslar, *100 Fragen an ...*, p. 107.

13 Merkel quoted in Langguth, *Angela Merkel*, p. 100.

14 Merkel, *Mein Weg*, p. 69.

15 Ulrich cited in Langguth, *Angela Merkel*, p. 117.

16 Merkel quoted in Stock, *Angela Merkel*, p. 56.

17 Merkel quoted in Stock, *Angela Merkel*, p. 56.

18 Merkel quoted in Stock, *Angela Merkel*, p. 56.

19 'Interview mit Kurt Hager', *Stern*, 9 April 1987.

20 Erich Honecker quoted in *Neues Deutschland*, 11 September 1987.

21 K.R. Korte, *Die Chance genutzt: Die Politik zur Einheit Deutschlands*, Frankfurt am Main: Campus Verlag 1994, p. 40.

22 Krenz in ZDF Nachrichten, 1 November 1989.

23 R. Eppelmann, *Fremd in eigenen Haus: Mein Leben im anderen Deutschlands,* Cologne: Verlag Kiepenheuer & Witsch 1993, p. 341.

24 Merkel, *Mein Weg*, p. 72.

25 Merkel, *Mein Weg*, p. 72.

26 'Interview mit Angela Merkel', *Berliner Morgenpost*, 12 January 2003.

27 'Interview mit Angela Merkel', *Berliner Morgenpost*, 12 January 2003.

28 Merkel, *Mein Weg*, p. 73.

Chapter 5

1 Horst Kasner cited in Reuth and Lachmann, *Das erste Leben der Angela M*, p. 160.

2 Angela Merkel quoted in Boysen, *Angela Merkel*, p. 88.

3 Christofer Frey quoted in Reuth and Lachmann, *Das erste Leben der Angela M*, p. 163.

4 Reuth and Lachmann, *Das erste Leben der Angela M*, p. 164.

5 Angela Merkel quoted in *Stern*, 20 July 2000.

6 The letter is on file with the West German theologian Christofer Frey and was published in Reuth and Lachmann, *Das erste Leben der Angela M*, p. 203.

7 Merkel, *Mein Weg*, p. 77.

8 Langguth, *Angela Merkel*, p. 127.

9 Walter Kohl, *Leben oder gelebt werden: Schriffe auf Weg zur Versöhnung,* Munich: Heyne 2011, p. 135.

10 Helmut Kohl quoted in Reuth and Lachmann, *Das erste Leben der Angela M*, p. 221.

11 Merkel, *Mein Weg*, p. 79.

12 Quoted in Reuth and Lachmann, *Das erste Leben der Angela M*, p. 228.

13 Merkel, *Mein Weg*, p. 80.

14 Thomas Schwarz quoted in Stock, *Angela Merkel*, p. 26.

15 Merkel, *Mein Weg*, p. 88.

16 Maaß quoted in Stock, *Angela Merkel*, p. 29.

17 Maaß quoted in Stock, *Angela Merkel*, p. 29.

18 'Meine Wende: Matthias Gehler war Regierungssprecher', *Thürigische Allgemeine*, 2 October 2010.

19 Langguth, *Angela Merkel*, p. 143

20 Margaret Thatcher was 'horrified' by the prospect of a reunited Germany: *Daily Telegraph*, 2 November 2009.

21 Quoted in Philip Short, *Mitterrand: A Study in Ambiguity*, London: Bodley Head 2013, p. 476

22 Mitterrand quoted in Philip Short, *Mitterrand*, p. 473.

23 Mitterrand quoted in Short, *Mitterrand*, pp. 474-5.

24 Cabinet minutes quoted in Attali, *Verbatim*, p. 322.

25 De Maizière quoted in Langguth, *Angela Merkel*, p. 143.
26 Zemke quoted in Reuth and Lachmann, *Das erste Leben der Angela M*, p. 271.
27 Kinder, Küche, Kabinett', *Focus*, 27 June 2005.

Chapter 6

1 Angela Merkel, *Mein Weg*, p. 97.
2 'Ich muß härter werden', *Der Spiegel*, 3 January 1994.
3 Geisler cited in Langguth, *Angela Merkel*, p. 158.
4 Angela Merkel, *Mein Weg*, p. 85.
5 Angela Merkel, *Mein Weg*, p. 85.
6 Angela Merkel quoted in 'Wer grüßt mich dann spatter noch?', *Märkische Oderzeitung*, 2 December 1992.
7 Ahlers quoted in Langguth, *Angela Merkel*, p. 160.
8 Merkel, *Mein Weg*, p. 86.
9 Merkel, *Mein Weg*, p. 91.
10 Helmut Kohl quoted in Hans-Peter Schwarz, *Helmut Kohl: Eine Politische Biographie*, Munich: Pantheon 2014, p. 635.
11 Helmut Kohl CDU Bundesvorstand, *Archiv für christlich-demokratische Politik der Konrad-Adenauer-Stiftung (KAS), Sankt Augustin*, 12 November 1990.
12 Gespräch des Bundeskanzlers mit dem britischen Premierminister Major (im Rahmen der deutsch-britischen Konsultationen)', Montag 11.3.1991, im Bundeskanzleramt, Bundeskanzleramt 21-Ge 28, Bd. 83.
13 Merkel, *Mein Weg*, p. 86.
14 Langguth, *Angela Merkel*, p. 167.
15 Cited in Langguth, *Angela Merkel*, p. 167.
16 Lothar de Maizière quoted in 'Angela Rennt', *Der Spiegel*, 4 November 2002.
17 Angela Merkel in *Süddeutsche Zeitung*, 21 February 1992, quoted in Langguth, *Angela Merkel*, p. 174.
18 'Interview', *Frankfurter Rundschau*, 19 November 1992.
19 DPA-Meldung, 16 May, 1993.
20 Angela Merkel interviewed in Koelbl, *Spuren der Macht*, p. 51.
21 'Rühes Kritik war heilsam', *Hamburger Abendblatt*, 14 December 1991.
22 Kornelius, *Angela Merkel*, p. 42.
23 Schwarz, *Helmut Kohl*, p. 658.
24 M. Jung and D. Roth, 'Kohls knappster Sieg. Eine Analyse der Bundestagswahl 1994', *Aus Politik und Zeitgeschichte* 23, 1994, pp. 51-2.
25 Kornelius, *Die Kanzlerin und ihre Welt*, p. 57.
26 Merkel quoted in Kornelius, *Die Kanzlerin und ihre Welt*, p. 58.
27 Merkel, *Mein Weg*, p. 99.
28 Schröder quoted in Kornelius, *Die Kanzlerin und ihre Welt*, p. 59.

Chapter 7

1 Schwarz, *Helmut Kohl*, p. 484.
2 Schröder quoted in Baring and Schöllgen, *Kanzler, Krisen, Koalitionen*, p. 285.
3 *Der Spiegel*, 14 December 1987.
4 DPA-Meldung, 26 November 1999.
5 Margrit Gerste, 'Die junge Frau von Helmut Kohl', *Die Zeit,* 12 September 1991.
6 Heriman Schwan and Tilman Jens, *Vermächtnis: Die Kohl-Protokolle*, Munich: Heyne 2014, p. 20.
7 Angela Merkel, 'Kohl hat der Partei Schaden zugefügt', *Frankfurter Allgemeine Zeitung*, 22 December 1999.
8 Angela Merkel quoted in Koelbl, *Spuren der Macht*, p. 54.
9 W. Schäuble, *Mitten im Leben*, Munich: C. Bertelsmann Verlag, 2002, p. 212.
10 Helmut Kohl, *Mein Tagebuch 1998-2000,* Munich: Droemer, 2000, p. 141.
11 Kohl quoted in Schwan and Jens, *Vermächtnis*, p. 22.
12 Kohl quoted in Schwan and Jens, *Vermächtnis*, p. 22.
13 Kohl quoted in Schwan and Jens, *Vermächtnis*, p. 30.
14 Interview with Wolfgang Schäuble, *Phoenix*, 7 April 2000.
15 *Bild*, 9 September 1993.
16 Angela Merkel quoted in Langguth, *Angela Merkel*, p. 212.
17 *Bunte*, 24 January 2002.
18 http://www.reuters.com/article/2012/05/16/us-germany-sauer -idUSBRE84F07420120516 (Accessed 19 February 2015).
19 Interview with Angela Merkel, *Bunte*, 24 January 2002.
20 Langguth, *Angela Merkel,* p. 214.
21 Langguth, *Angela Merkel,* p. 403.
22 *Bunte*, 24 January 2002.
23 DPA-Meldung, Rücktrittserklärung Wolfgang Schäubles, 16 February 2000.
24 Verena Köttker and Henning Krumrey, 'Königin der Macht', *Focus,* 5 July 2004.
25 Jutta Falke and Hartmut Kühne, 'Die Unterschätzte', in *Rheinisher Merkur*, 6 April 2001.
26 *Stern*, August 2000.
27 *Der Spiegel*, 26 June 2000.
28 Michael Schindhelm, 'Halbschwester von Parsifal', *Die Welt*, 16 June 2004.

Chapter 8

1 Martina Acht quoted in 'Geißler will Merkel mit neuem Outfit sehen', *Frankfurter Neue Presse*, 11 July 2003.
2 Udo Walz quoted in 'Geißler will Merkel mit neuem Outfit sehen', *Frankfurter Neue Presse*, 11 July 2003.

3 'Mehr Eleganz wagen', *Welt am Sonntag*, 6 March 2005.

4 Mary Fulbrook, *A History of Germany 1918-2014: A Divided Nation*, London: John Wiley & Sons 2015, p. 285.

5 Polenz quoted in Langguth, *Angela Merkel*, p. 224.

6 'Der Mann mit dem Missgriff', *Süddeutsche Zeitung*, 20 November 2000.

7 'Westfälische Zuverlässigkeit und rheinischer Frohsinn', *Frankfurther Allgemeine Zeitung*, 20 November 2000.

8 'Angriffen egal wie', *Süddeutsche Zeitung*, 21 November 2000.

9 Quoted in M. Morjé Howard, 'The Causes and Consequences of Germany's New Citizenship Law', *German Politics*, 17(1), 2008, p. 42.

10 Bodo Strauss, 'Anschwellender Bocksgesang', in *Der Speigel*, 8 February 1993.

11 *Die Zukunft der menschlichen Natur*, Frankfurt am Main: Suhrkampf 2001.

12 '"Leitkultur": Merz gegen Kopftücher im Unterricht', *Der Spiegel*, 2 December 2000.

13 Manfred G. Schmidt, *Das politische System Deutschlands*, Munich: Verlag C.H. Beck 2011, p. 162.

14 'Merz gegen Kopftücher im Unterricht', *Der Spiegel*, 2 December 2000.

15 Manfred Schmidt, *Das politische System Deutschlands,* Munich: C.H. Beck 2007, p. 169.

16 Susane Höll, 'Die Frau mit Maske', *Süddeutsche Zeitung*, 7 May 2001.

17 Interview Stoibers mit dem Nachrichtensender N 24, DPA-Meldung, 18 November 2000.

18 http://www.n-tv.de/politik/dossier/Euphorie-und-Depression-article816704 .html (Accessed 19 June 2015).

19 Presse- und Informationsamt der Bundesregierung, quoted in Langguth, *Angela Merkel*, p. 234.

20 Goppel quoted in Langguth, *Angela Merkel*, p. 235.

21 Merkel braucht Stehvermögen', *Die Tageszeitung*, 12 November 2002.

Chapter 9

1 'Ein gutter Tag für die Küchin', *Süddeutsche Zeitung*, 18 August 2005.

2 Langguth, *Angela* Merkel, p. 308.

3 'Die Situation des Wahlkampfs: Merkels Kompetenzteam: Frischer Wind für CDU/CSU', *Handelsblatt*, 16 September 2005.

4 Langguth, *Angela Merkel*, p. 311.

5 'Ihr wisst gar nicht, wie viele sozialistischen Elemente ihr habt', *Frankfurter Allgemeine Zeitung*, 28 May 2005.

6 'Neoliberale Konzepte bringen keinen Wahlsieg', *Tagespost*, 30 September 2004.

7 'Stoiber lehnt Kirchhof-Model als unrealistisch ab', *Süddeutsche Zeitung*, 30 August 2005.

8 Schröder quoted in 'Kirchhofs Rentenpläne stossen auf Widerstand', *Süddeutsche Zeitung*, 1 September 2005.

9 '25 Perzent Steuer für Alle. Das ist die Obergrenze', *Frankfurter Allgemeine Zeitung*, 31 August 2005.

10 'Ich bin ein emotionaler Typ', *Der Kölner Stadt-Anzeiger*, interview with Merkel, 1 September 2005.

11 'Höhere Mehrwertsteuer trifft vor allem Familien', Deutschlandfunk, 8 July 2005.

12 'Was ist von diesem Mann zu halten?', *Die Tageszeitung*, 20 September 2005.

13 'Merkel gewinnt ihre Vertrauensfrage – und kann vorest verhandeln', DPA, 20 September 2005, italics added.

14 H. Herzog, 'Minor Parties: The Relevancy Perspective', *Comparative Politics*, 1987, pp. 317-29.

15 Fischer quoted in *Frankfurter Allgemeine Sonntagszeitung*, 25 September 2005.

16 'Merkel gewinnt ihre Vertrauensfrage – und kann vorest verhandeln', DPA, 20 September 2005.

Chapter 10

1 Gerhard Schröder, Regierungserklärung von Bundeskanzler Gerhard Schröder am 10. Dezember 1998 zum Thema Vorschau auf den Europäischen Rat in Wien, 10 December 1998.

2 Heisenberg, 'Merkel's EU Policy', p. 113.

3 http://www.theguardian.com/commentisfree/2015/mar/13/beware-the-superman-syndrome-politicians (Accessed 28 March 2015).

4 Kornelius, *Angela Merkel*, pp. 94-5.

5 Kornelius, *Angela Merkel*, p. 204.

6 'Merkel Tries to Act as Dealmaker in Change of German Style', *The Guardian*, 18 December 2005.

7 Campbell, *Winners and How they Succeed*, p. 47.

8 The relevant articles of the Basic Law are: Art. 70 (Länder), Art. 73 (Centre) and Art. 74 (Shared jurisdiction).

9 Bruce Ackerman, 'The Storrs Lectures: Discovering the Constitution', *Yale Law Journal*, vol. 93, 1984, p. 1022.

10 Föderalismus: Große Mehrheit für Reform', *Die Zeit* (2006), 1 April

11 Kornelius, *Angela Merkel*, p. 42.

12 http://www.n-tv.de/politik/dossier/Kurskorrekturen-der-CDU-article200885.html (Accessed 2 April 2015).

13 U. Merkel, 'The 1974 and 2006 World Cups in Germany: Commonalities, Continuities and Changes', *Soccer and Society* 7(1), 2006, pp. 14-28.

14 This account of Merkel's helicopter flight is based on information from Margaret Heckel, *So regiert die Kanzlerin: Eine Reportage*. Munich: Piper Verlag 2011, p.1

15 Rede von Bundeskanzlerin Merkel anlässlich des Kongresses 'Finanzmark-tregulierung nach der Krise – eine Zwischenbilanz' der CDU/CSU -Bundestagsfraktion.

16 Angela Merkel quoted in A. Crawford and T. Czuczka, *Angela Merkel: A Chancellorship Forged in Crisis*, Winchester: Wiley 2013, p. 49.

17 'CSU Faziniert mich immer wieder', *Münchner Merkur*, 22 September 2008.

18 Angela Merkel to the author, December 2008.

19 Walter Eucken, 'Vorwort', *Ordo: Jahrbuch für die Ordnung von Wirtschaft und Gesellschaft*, vol. 1, no. 1, 1948, p. 1.

Chapter 11

1 *Der Spiegel*, 11 March 2009.

2 http://www.welt.de/politik/article3338318/Ministerin-Schavan-nennt -Merkel-einen-Gluecksfall.html (Accessed 2 April 2009).

3 'Christlich geprägte Beliebigkeit', *Süddeutsche Zeitung*, http://www .sueddeutsche.de/politik/neues-buch-ueber-angela-merkel-christlich -gepraegte-beliebigkeit-1.390161 (Accessed 2 March 2012).

4 The clip in which Bishop Williamson made these remarks can still be found on Youtube, https://www.youtube.com/watch?v=k6C9BuXe2RM (Accessed 9 March 2015).

5 Kornelius, *Angela Merkel*, p. 184.

6 Speech to the Knesset, 18 March 2008, cited in Kornelius, *Angela Merkel*, p. 180.

7 http://www.merkur-online.de/politik/georg-ratzinger-verteidigt-seinen -bruder-benedikt-69088.html (Accessed 18 February 2010).

8 http://www.zeit.de/online/2009/07/merkel-papst-vatikan-lob (Accessed 18 February 2010).

9 'Ministerin Schavan nennt Merkel einen Glücksfall', *Die Welt*, 8 March 2009.

10 V.O. Key, *The Responsible Electorate: Rationality in Presidential Elections*, New York: Vintage Books 1968, p. 30.

11 'Westerwelle will geschichte schreiben', *Der Tagesspiegel*, 20 September 2009.

12 http://www.spiegel.de/spiegel/print/d-17322733.html (Accessed 15 March 2013).

13 http://www.spiegel.de/international/germany/spiegel-interview-with-fdp -leader-westerwelle-i-consider-a-coalition-with-the-spd-and-greens-out -of-the-question-a-643586.html (Accessed 19 March 2014).

14 Kornelius, *Angela Merkel*, p. 61.

Chapter 12

1 'Merkels Routinestart und eine Mahnung', *Deutsche Presseagentur*, 28 October 2009.

2 http://www.c-span.org/video/?289781-1/german-chancellor-address-joint -meeting-congress (Accessed 20 March 2015).

3 Z. Havlas et al., 'Ab initio Quantum Chemical Study of the S_N2 Reaction, CH_3 F+ H– → CH_4 + F–, in the Gas Phase', *Chemical Physics* 127(1), 1988, pp. 53-63.

4 A. Crawford and T. Czuczka, *Angela Merkel: A Chancellorship Forged in Crisis*, Winchester: Wiley 2013, p. 65.

5 Crawford and Czuczka, *Angela Merkel*, p. 71.

6 Crawford and Czuczka, *Angela Merkel*, p. 71.

7 http://www.euractiv.com/priorities/greek-crisis-brings-village-poli-news -494452 (Accessed 20 March 2013).

8 Crawford and Czuczka, *Angela Merkel*, p. 61.

9 Merkel quoted in Crawford and Czuczka, *Angela Merkel*, p. 61.

10 http://www.spiegel.de/politik/deutschland/kinder-statt-inder-ruettgers-verteidigt-verbalen-ausrutscher-a-68369.html (Accessed 20 March 2015).

11 'Köhler tritt mit Tränen in den Augen zurück', DPA, 31 May 2010.

12 http://www.deutschlandradiokultur.de/koehler-mehr-respekt-fuer -deutsche-soldaten-in-afghanistan.1008.de.html?dram:article_id =163260.

13 'Nach heftiger Kritik: Bundespräsident Köhler tritt zurück', *Frankfurter Allgemeine Zeitung*, 1 June 2010.

14 Volker Resing, *Angela Merkel: Die Protestantin*, Leipzig: Benno Verlag 2009, p. 21.

15 http://www.bild.de/ratgeber/gesundheit/christian-wulff-mutter-multiple-skle-rose-hg-11128936.bild.html.

16 http://www.nachrichten.at/nachrichten/society/Deutschlands-neue -First-Lady-Bettina-Wulff-ist-jung-gross-blond-und-taetowiert;art411, 422809 (Accessed 21 May 2013).

Chapter 13

1 '"Wir wollen nicht auf die Kanzlerin schießen": Konservativer "Berliner Kreis" will andere CDU', *Rheinische Post*, 2 November 2012.

2 'Pofalla wegen Beleidigungen in der Kritik', *Die Zeit*, 2 October 2011.

3 '"Ich wollte es nicht glauben"', *Die Zeit*, 24 February 2011.

4 'Merkel sichert Guttenberg "volles Vertrauen" zu', *Die Welt*, 18 February 2011.

5 chavan quoted in 'Schavan: Plagiatsaffäre ist keine Lappalie', *Süddeutsche Zeitung*, 27 February 2011.

6 http://www.spiegel.de/politik/deutschland/guttenbergs-erklaerung-ich-habe-die-grenzen-meiner-kraefte-erreicht-a-748372.html (Accessed 23 June 2015).

7 http://edition.cnn.com/2014/02/19/world/asia/japan-fukushima-daiichi -water-leak/ (Accessed 23 June 2015).

8 Roland Pofalla quoted in Ralph Bollmann, *Die Deutsche: Angela Merkel und Wir*, Klett-Cotta 2013, p. 69.

9 Merkel quoted in Bollmann, *Die Deutsche*, p. 64.

10 Merkel quoted in Bollmann, *Die Deutsche*, p. 79.

11 Quoted in the *New York Times*, http://www.nytimes.com/2011/05/31 /world/ europe/31germany.html?_r=0 (Accessed 25 June 2015).

12 Merkel quoted in Bollmann, *Die Deutsche*, p. 79.

13 'Cicero to Lentulus Spinther', in D.R. Shackleton Bailey (ed.), *Cicero's Letters to his Friends*, Penguin 1978, p. 67.

14 Wikileaks quoted by Reuters: http://www.reuters.com/article/2010/11 /29/ us-germany-wikileaks-idUSTRE6AR3EC20101129 (Accessed 25 July 2015).

15 Kornelius, *Die Kanzlerin und ihre Welt*, p. 113.

16 Ludger Helms, 'Political Leadership', in Stephan Padgett, William E. Paterson and Reimut Zohlnhöter (eds), *Developments in German Politics Four*, Basingstoke: Palgrave 2015, p. 113.

17 As reported in 'Einmal Asiat, immer Asiat', *Die Tageszeitung*, 27 September 2009.

18 'Europe's Reluctant Hegemon: Special Report on Germany', *The Economist*, 15 June 2013.

19 Bollmann, *Die Deutsche*, p. 27.

20 Cited from Nikolas Blome, *Angela Merkel: Die Zauder Künstlerin*, Munich: Pantheon 2013, p. 150.

21 Crawford and Czuczka, *Angela Merkel*, p. 9.

22 'Gipfel-Durchbruch: Asiatische Börsen feiern den Euro', *Der Spiegel*, 27 October 2011.

23 George Papandreou quoted in 'Papandreou wins backing for referendum', *Financial Times,* 2 November 2011.

24 Ulrich Beck, *German Europe*, Cambridge: Polity 2013, p. 52.

25 Volker Kauder quoted in 'Kauders Euro-Schelte: "Jetzt wird in Europa Deutsch gesprochen"', *Der Spiegel*, 5 November 2011.

26 'Der Mann an ihren Seite', *Der Spiegel*, 21 July 2014.

Chapter 14

1 Vladimir Putin's address to the Nation, April 2005, quoted in Fiona Hill and Clifford G. Gaddy, *Mr Putin,* Washington DC: Brookings Institution Press 2013, p. 55.

2 Putin quoted in Fiona Hill and Clifford G. Gaddy, *Mr Putin: Operative in the Kremlin*, Washington DC: Brookings Institution Press 2013, p. 191.

3 http://tvzvezda.ru/news/vstrane_i_mire/content/201601110935-kh6x.htm (Accessed 10 November 2016; I am grateful to Bjørn Qvortrup for help with the Russian translation)

4 Mikhail Gorbachev, 'Russia Will Not Play Second Fiddle', *Moscow News*, no. 37, 22-28 September 1995.

5 Kornelius, *Die Kanzlerin und ihre Welt*, p. 198.

6 Elizabeth Pond, 'Germany's Real Role in the Ukraine Crisis', *Foreign Affairs*, vol. 94, no. 2, 2015, p. 173.

7 Pond, 'Germany's Real Role in the Ukraine Crisis', p. 174.

8 'Krim-Krise: Merkel kündigt neue Sanktionen gegen Russland an', *Der Spiegel*, 20 March 2014.

9 Vladimir Putin quoted in 'Vladimir Putin Leaves G20 After Leaders Line Up to Browbeat Him over Ukraine', *The Guardian*, 16 November 2014.

10 'Mehr Militär ist keine Lösung', *Der Tagesspiel*, 7 February 2015.

11 Pond, 'Germany's Real Role in the Ukraine Crisis', p. 176.

12 Angela Merkel quoted in 'Dokumentation: Neujahrsansprache von Angela Merkel im Wortlaut', *Der Spiegel*, 31 December 2014.

13 Shaun Hargreaves-Heap and Yanis Varoufakis, *Game Theory: A Critical Introduction,* London: Routledge 2004, p. 36.

14 Varoufakis quoted on the BBC News: http://www.bbc.co.uk/news/business-31111905 (Accessed 5 July 2015).

15 Ulrich Beck, *German Europe*, Cambridge: Polity 2013, p. 48.

16 'Merkel hofft auf Kompromiss mit Tsipras', *Die Zeit*, 12 February 2015.

17 'Greece and Eurozone Agree Bailout Extension', *Financial Times*, 20 February 2015.

18 'Gabriel rügt Athen für "dumme" Debatte um Reparationen', *Wirtschafts Woche*, 7 April 2015.

19 Bayern 5-Aktuel, 5 July 2015, 8.20.

20 This account is based on the events as chronicled in *Der Spiegel* ('Das Diktat', 18 July 2015) and *Die Zeit* ('Held des Konjunktivs'), 23 July 2015.

21 See Francis M. Dunn, *Tragedy's End: Closure and Innovation in Euripidean Drama*, New York: Oxford University Press 1996.

22 'Kanzlerin Merkel erklärt Multikulti für gescheitert', *Die Welt*, 16 October 2010.

23 http://www.bbc.co.uk/news/world-europe-33555619 (Accessed 18 August 2015).

24 'Worte der Woche', *Die Zeit*, 23 July 2015.

25 '"Wir sind das Pack" – Merkel wird ausgebuht', *Die Welt*, 26 August 2015.

26 'Merkel: "Wir schaffen das"', *Frankfurter Allgemeine Zeitung*, 31 August 2015.

27 'Merkel the Bold', *The Economist*, 5 September 2015.

28 http://www.dw.com/en/refugee-controversy-heats-up-ahead-of-eu-emergency-summit/a-18731170 (Accessed 23 September 2015).

29 'Flüchtlinge könnten Wirtschaftswunder bringen', *Frankfurter Allgemeine Zeitung*, 15 September 2015.

30 'Der Polit-Transformer', *Süddeutsche Zeitung*, 5 November 2015.

31 'Merkel verlangt harte Antwort des Rechtsstaats', *Frankfurter Allgemeine Zeitung*, 5 January 2016.

32 https://www.parliament.uk/documents/addresses-to-parliament/Angela-Merkel-address-20130227.pdf (Accessed 12 October 2016).

33 'Keine Eile beim Brexit', *Der Tagesspiegel*, 20 July 2016.

34 'Merkel will keine "Rosinenpickerei" bei Brexit-Verhandlungen zulassen', *Süddeutsche Zeitung*, 28 June 2016.

35 'Die Entrückten: Wie späte Kanzler ihr Volk verlieren', *Der Spiegel*, 9 September 2016.

36 Renate Köchner, 'Eine Erosion des Vertrauens', in *Denk ich an Deutschland: Eine Konferenz der Alfred Herrhausen Gesellschaft und der Frankfurter Allgemeine Zeitung*, 2016, p.8.

37 'Angriff von Rechts', *Stern*, 15 September 2016.

38 'Merkel räumt Teilschuld für schlechte Wahlergebnisse ein', *Die Zeit*, 19 September 2016.

39 'Ein Kurswechsel kündigt sich an', *Die Zeit*, 20 September 2016.

Chapter 15

1 Russell Dalton (2014) 'Interpreting partisan dealignment in Germany', *German Politics*, Vol. 23, pp. 134-144

2 Simon Jenkins (2018) *A Short History of Europe: From Pericles to Putin.* London: Penguin, p. 299

3 Die Welt, '"Sie ist nun ganz allein", sagte Obama nach seinem letzten Treffen mit Merkel', 31st May, 2018

4 *Der Spiegel*, 'Die Frauenrepublik', 10th March, 2017

5 Robin Alexander (2021) *Machtverfall*. Munich: Siedler, p. 94

6 *Frankfurter Allgemeine Zeitung*, 'Lesben und Schwule in der Union fordern Entschuldigung' 3rd March 2019.

Chapter 16

1 *Die Zeit*, 'Bundesregierung schickt weitere Hilfslieferung nach China', 18 February 2020.

2 Peter Sloterdijk, 1983, *Kritik der zynischen Vernunft*. Frankfurt, Suhrkamp.

3 Peter Sloterdijk cited in Robin Alexander, *Machtverfall*, p. 208.

4 *Die Welt* 'Merkels politisch gefährlicher Satz zu Corona', 11 March 2020.

5 *Die Welt,* 'Einreiseverbot in EU-Staaten – jede verfügbare Hilfe für die Wirtschaft', 17 March 2020.

6 *Der Spiegel*, 'Merkel und Macron haben doch noch genug Kraft für Europa' 22 May 2020.

7 Alexander, *Machtverfall*, p. 199.

8 *Merkur*, 'Politische Nahtoderfahrung: Söder-Biografie gibt Einblick in dunkle CSU-Stunden – und wirft brisante K-Fragen auf', 23 March 2021.

9 Alexander, *Machtverfall*, p. 193

10 *Merkur*, 'Interessenkonflikt? Nach Masken-Eklat – Linke fordert Spahns Rücktritt', 21 September 2020.

11 *Der Spiegel*, 'Wie Minister Spahn auf die eigenen Mahnungen pfiff', 26 February 2021.

12 https://coronavirus.jhu.edu/data/mortality (Accessed 17 August, 2020).

13 Karl Marx and Friedrich Engels, 2010. *Die deutsche Ideologie* Berlín: Akademie Verlag, p. 54.

14 Carl Schmitt, C. 1922. *Politische theologie: vier kapitel zur lehre von der souveränität* (Vol. 1). Berlin: Duncker & Humblot, p. 11.

15 Werner J. Patzelt, 1999, 'The Very Federal House: The German Bundesrat', in Samuel C. Patterson and Anthony Mughan (Editors) *Senates: Bicameralism in the Contemporary World. Columbus: Ohio State University*, p. 61.

16 Helge Braun's note quoted in Alexander *Machtverfall*, p. 223.

17 Süddeutsche Zeitung 'Die Entschuldigung Merkels im Wortlaut', 24 March 2021.

18 *Handelsblatt*, 'CDU-Bundesvorstand stimmt für Armin Laschet als Kanzlerkandidaten der Union', 20 April, 2021.

19 *Der Spiegel*, Feindbild Frau 12 February 2021.

20 David Safier, 2021, *Miss Merkel: Mord in the Uckermark*. Hamburg: Kindler.

21 Constanze Stelzenmüller, 2021, 'The Singular Chancellor: The Merkel Model and Its Limits', *Foreign Affairs*, Vol. 100, No, 3, 161–172, at 65.

22 https://www.srf.ch/news/international/coronavirus-in-deutschland-merkel-erntet-shitstorm-wegen-diskussionsorgien (Accessed 18 August, 2021).

Epilogue

1 Johann Wolfgang von Goethe (1818) 'Daß du nicht enden kannst, das macht dich groß', *West-östlicher Divan*

INDEX

Abortion, 141-143
Academy of Sciences, 77, 84, 97, 118, 122, 163, 255
Acht, Martina, 171, 172
Ackermann, Bruce, 219
Adenauer, Konrad, 21, 29, 31, 39, 67, 208, 214, 225, 233, 254
Adorno, Theodor W., 175
Ahlers, Detlev, 123, 134
Ahlreich, Reinhart, 99
Ahtisaari, Martti, 156
Albert Camus, 351
Albrecht, Ernest, 207
Alexandre Ledru-Rollin, 368
Alternative für Deutschland (AFD), 304-306
Althusius, Johannes, 218
Altmaier, Peter (Ministerpräsident Rheinland-Pfalz), 86
Altmaier, Peter, Head of Kanzleramt, 86
Andropov, Yuri, 92-102, 297
Annalena Baerbock, 347, 364
Arab Spring, 18, 51, 272
Arendt, Hannah, 46, 116
Armin Laschet, 338, 353, 357, 360, 365, 371
Article 50, 330
Ash, Timothy Garton, 109
Asmussen, Jörg, 263-264, 332
August Ferdinand, Prince of Prussia, 252

Bachelet, Michelle, 225
Backmann, Lutz, 341
Bahr, Daniel, 282
Bahro, Rudolf, 73-74, 114
Baker, James III, 135
Ballack, Michael, 210
Balzac, Honoré de, 335
Barschel, Uwe, 145

Barthle, Norbert, 210
Barzel, Rainer, 76, 86
Basisdemokratie, 114
Baumann, Beate, 147, 165, 218-222, 227, 330
Bay City Rollers, 56
Beck, Kurt, 278
Beck, Ulrich, 289, 339
Beckenbauer, Franz, 210
Beckstein, Günter, 206
Benedict XVI, Pope (Joseph Ratzinger), 233, 234, 235, 237, 253
Berlin Wall, 38-40, 50, 67, 113, 106-107, 111, 114, 169
Berliner Kreis, 271-272
Berlusconi, Silvio, 282, 283, 284, 286
Biermann, Wolf, 74, 75, 104
Bismarch, Otto von, 152, 273, 296
Blair, Tony, 153, 156, 191, 212, 214, 215, 216, 217, 226, 300, 333
Bliss, Peter, 59
Bloch, Ernst, 74
Blockpartien, 22, 116, 117
Blüm, Norbert, 134
Bodo Ramelow, 362
Böll, Heinrich, 175, 335
Bonaparte, Napoleon, 296, 336
Borrusia Dortmund, 178
Bosbach, Wolfgang, 181, 182, 271, 272, 315
Brandt, Willy, 38, 40, 65-71, 75-76, 116, 155, 173, 178, 195, 208, 233, 247, 252, 333, 334
Bravo, 56
Brecht, Bertolt, 23, 208, 306, 339
Brexit, 293, 329, 330
Brezhnev, Leonid, 50, 83, 92, 297
Bründerle, Rainer, 264, 282
Bundesrat, See Senate
Bundesversamlung, See Electoral College

Burckhardt, Jacob, 108
Burgfriedenspolitik, 154, 155
Bush, George Herbert Walker, 41st President of the United States, 115, 119, 123, 135
Bush, George W., 43rd President of the United States, 171, 173, 184, 215, 218, 225, 226, 297

Caesar, Julius, 208
Callas, Maria, 172
Cameron, David, 328, 329, 336
Campbell, Naomi, 172
Common Agricultural Policy, 211, 212, 216
Carter, Jimmy, 83
Cassidy, David, 56
Catherine the Great (Yekaterina Alexeyevna), 328
Catholic, 25, 29, 30, 70, 87, 141, 142, 162, 177, 198, 207, 233, 234, 239, 267, 281, 331, 340
Cato the Elder, Roman Senator, 19
Ceaußescu, Nikolai, 109
Cézanne, Paul, 56
Channel 5, 49
Channel 7 (West), 49
Charité Hospital, 352
Charles Windsor, Prince of Wales, 153
Chernenko, Konstantin, 92, 93, 94
Chicken Game, 307
Chirac, Jacques, 214, 216, 217, 254, 333
Chopin, Fréderic, 92
Christ, Jesus, 25, 325
Clausewitz, Carl von, 243
Clinton, Bill, 42nd President of the United States, 232, 300
Clinton, Hillary Rodham, 334
Constitutional Court of Germany, 141, 142, 145, 193, 266, 272, 285, 339
COVID-19, 349, 352, 354, 357-358, 361-362, 365
Crimea, 293, 294, 299, 301, 304, 328, 334
Cuban Missile Crisis, 49

Dahl, Robert A., 282
Dallare, Charles
DAX, (*Deutscher Aktienindex*), 217
De Gaulle, Charles, 69, 254
de Maiziére, Lothar, 117-121, 123, 127, 139, 342

de Maiziére, Thomas, 121, 122, 207, 214, 296, 322
Delors, Jacques, 95, 96
Demokratischer Aufbau (DA), 113-123
Dempsey, Judy, 205
di Lampedusa, Guiseppe Tomasi, 191
Dibelius, Otto, 45, 46, 47
Diekmann, Kai, 291
Dietrich, Marlene, 172
Disraeli, Benjamin, 304
Donath, Wolfgang, 37
Donnersmarck, Florian, 54
Dorbrindt, Alexander, 19, 20
Double Track Decision, 83, 85
Douglas, Michael, 261
Dow Jones Index, 227
Draghi, Mario, 283, 289
Dreyer, Malu, 331
DSF (German-Soviet Friendship Organisation), 64, 72
Dual Citizenship Law, 175
Dubček, Alexander, 50, 52, 108
Dylan, Bob, 74

East German Parliament (*Volkskammer der DDR*), 116, 120, 127
Ebeling, Hans-Wilhelm, 118
Ebert, Friedrich, 154
Ehrman, Ricardo, 105
Eichel, Hans, 155, 196
Einstein, Albert, 256
Eisenhower, Dwight D.
34th President of the United States, 222
Electoral College (*Bundesversamlung*), 49, 145, 188, 269, 292
Engels, Friedrich, 64
Engholm, Björn, 145
Eppelmann, Rainer, 33, 48, 119, 120, 325, 326
Erhard, Ludwig, 29, 30, 49, 178, 234, 341
Euchen, Walter, 229, 332
Euripedes, 318
European Financial Stability Mechanism, 271, 288, 314
European Recovery Fund, The, 356
Eurozone, 13, 18, 42, 251, 253, 258, 259, 282, 289, 309, 313, 315, 316
Evangelische Kirche in Deutschland, 27, 45, 46, 47

Faust (Goethe's), 171
FDJ (East German Communist Youth Organization), 36., 53, 56, 57, 58, 64, 71, 75,90, 100, 327
Federal Election Commission, 157
Federalism Reform, 218-222
Feldmeyer, Karl, 158
Fink, Ulf, 140
Fischer-Lescano, Andreas, 273
Fischer, Joschka, 151-152, 156, 203, 247
Flat Tax, 197, 247
Flemming, Klaus, 60, 61
Flick Corporation, 88
Flick, Friedrich Karl, 157
Forbes, 225
Ford, Gerald, 38th President of the United States, 82
Foreign Policy Committee (of the German Bundestag), 174
Four-Plus-Two Agreement, 126-127
Four-Plus-Two negotiations, 125-126
FRELINO, 59-60
Freud, Anna, 296
Freud, Sigmund, 34
Frey, Christofer, 112
Friedrich II (See Frederick the Great), 138, 252

G20, 283, 302
G7, 228
G8, 300, 301
Gabriel, Helga, 41
Gabriel, Sigmar, 18, 20, 264, 269, 310, 323
Gaddis, John L., 83, 93
Game Theory, 306
Gandhi, Mahatma, 153
Gauch, Joachim, 103, 269, 292
Gehler, Matthias, 123
Geisler, Georg, 'Heiner', 140, 157
Genscher, Hans Dietrich, 125, 247
Gesinnungsethiker, 343
Gierek, Edward, 84
Giscard d' Estaing, Valéry, 213
Glasnost, 92, 97
Glos, Michael, 131, 180, 201
Gloser, Günter, 244
Goebels, Joseph, 50, 68, 126
Goethe, Wolfgang von, 62, 171
Gollwitzer, Helmut, 51

Goppel, Thomas, 180
Gorbachev, Mikhail, 91, 92, 93-100, 101-104, 123, 124, 126, 135, 298
Göring, Herbert, 31
Gramsci, Antonio, 176
Grand Coalition, 17, 67, 201ff, 222, 328, 340
Grass, Günter, 70, 195
Gresz, Maria, 231,
Grexit, 309, 314-316
Große Koalition, 17, 67, 201ff, 222, 328, 340
Grundgesetz (Basic Law), 115, 193, 218, 219, 220, 265, 341
Guilaume, Günter, 76
Guthrie, Woody, 74
Guttenberg, Karl-Theodor zu, 254, 273, 274, 282, 291, 342
Gysi, Gregor, 30, 73, 241, 269
Gysi, Klaus, 30

Habermas, Jürgen, 175, 230, 234
Hager, Kurt, 100
Hallstein Doktrin, 65
Hallstein, Werner, 65
Harms, Monika, 236
Hartz IV, 191, 193, 222, 241, 332
Hartz, Peter, 191
Hasselfeldt, Gerda, 135
Havel, Václav, 108, 325
Havemann, Katja, 111
Havemann, Robert, 74, 81
Havemann, Utz, 81
Hayek, Friedrich August von, 195
Hegel, G.W.F., 234, 318, 336
Heiko Maas, 342, 352
Heinemann, Gustav, 49
Heisenberg, Werner, 64
Heitmann, Stefan, 144
Helge Braun, 343, 351-352, 359, 363
Helms, Ludger, 281
Helsinki Declaration, 82
Herrmann, Klaus, 128
Hertz, Gustav, 64
Hertz, Heinrich, 64
Heusgen, Christoph, 293, 294
Hildebrandt, Tina, 167
Hitler Jugend, 36, 235
Hitler, Adolf, 28, 235

Hoentsch, Erika, 72, 112
Hollande, François, 303, 311, 312, 313, 315, 317
Homer, 288
Honecker, Erich, 71, 81,82, 100-105, 108, 127
Höppner, Reinhard, 203
Horenschönhausen Prison, 22
Horn, Charly, 59-61
Huber, Wolfgang, 237
Humboldt, Willhelm von, 335
Husák, Gustáv, 109
Hussein, Saddam, 126, 156
Hypo Real Estate Holding AG, 228ff, 257

Ihrke, Bodo, 35, 56
International Monetary Fund, 257, 259, 260, 288, 311, 313, 314
Iraq, First Golf War, 126, 135, 156
Iraq, Second Gulf War, 184, 191, 215
Islamic State (ISIS), 14, 320, 326, 330

Jacob, Günter, 47
Jamaica Coalition, 201, 203, 272
Jaruzelski, Wojciech, 84
Jauck, Erhard, 47
Jentzsch, Gertrud, 25
Jentzsch, Willi, 25
Jens Spahn, 342-343, 345, 353-354, 360, 366
Jeremiah, Old Testament Prophet, 253
Jintao, Hu, President of China, 263
Jochimsen, Luc, 270
John, Paul II, Pope (Karol Józef Wojtyła), 234
John, The Evangelist, 186
Johnson-Sirleaf, Ellen, 225
Johnson, Claudia 'Ladybird', 163
Johnson, Lyndon B., 36th President of the United States, 337
Juncker, Jean-Claude, 217, 312
Jung, Franz-Josef, 207, 243, 249, 254, 255, 267
Junge Gemeinde, 26
Jünger, Ernst, 86, 335

Kant, Immanuel, 197, 234, 329
Kanter, Hans-Adolf, 88
Kasner, Herlind, 21, 24, 25, 27-30, 38, 80, 251

Kasner, Pastor Horst, 24, 25, 28-36, 38, 44-48, 52-60, 72, 80, 89, 111-112, 252, 253, 325
Kasner, Irene, 28, 107
Kasner, Ludwig, 24
Kasner, Margarethe, 57
Kasner, Markus, 28, 37, 85, 111, 130
Kauder, Volker, 189, 289
Kehr, Eckard, 289
Keip, Walter, 157
Keitel, Peter, 277
KGB, 92, 96, 102, 296, 297, 298
Khruschev, Nikita, 26, 38, 49, 50, 93, 100
Kiesinger, Kurt-Georg, 49, 50, 68, 178, 208, 222, 223, 247, 252
Kirchhof, Paul (Judge), 194, 195, 196, 205, 332
Kissinger, Henry, 82, 310
Klein, (Colonel) Georg, 242, 243, 244
Klinsmann, Jürgen, 209-211, 226
Klöckner, Julia, 325, 330
Kloeppel, Peter, 231
Klose, Miroslav, 210
Klum, Heidi, 172
Koch, Roland, 167, 175, 180, 182, 187, 201, 222, 223, 237, 238, 246, 268, 271, 335
Kohl, Hannelore, 163
Kohl, Helmut, 85, 88, 94-108, 109, 115-121, 123-127, 131-149, 150-166, 173, 178, 183, 195, 208, 211, 212, 221, 233, 243, 333, 336
Köhler, Eva Luise, 265
Köhler, Horst, 186-188, 192, 238, 239, 252, 253, 265-269, 290-291, 339
Kommando Specialkräfte, 254
Koni (Putin's Dog), 291
Körner, Bettina, 268
Köster, Andrea, 129-130
Kouchner, Bernard, 244
Kraft, Hannelore, 262-263
Krause, Günter, 126-129, 135, 137, 143-144, 342
Krenz, Egon, 71, 75, 101-104, 108, 109, 120, 136, 241
Krugman, Paul, 339
Kühn, Heinz, 192
Kundera, Milan, 51
Kunduz Bombing, 242-247, 267

Labskaus, 133
Lafontaine, Oskar, 133, 146, 155, 192, 203, 241
Lagarde, Christine, 288
Lambsdorff, Otto Graff, 88
Langguth, Gerd, 341
Lehmann Brothers, 227ff, 257
Leipniz, Gottfried, 63, 76-77
Lengsfeld, Vera, 240
Lenin, Vladimir I., 22, 24, 30, 55, 101, 218
Leo XIII, Pope (Vincenzo Pecci), 196
Leopold II, 273
Lévy, Bernard-Henri, 52, 342
Liebknecht, Karl, 154
Lincoln, Abraham, 16th President of the United States, 255
Linkage Politics, 310-311
Lothar Wieler, 352
Luhansk People's Republic, 302
Luther, Martin, 26
Lutheran, 26, 27, 30, 31, 32, 33, 45, 46, 47, 48, 53, 64, 65, 80, 101, 118, 122, 207, 234, 238, 328
Luxemburg, Rosa, 101

Maaß, Hans-Christian, 122, 119, 122
Macmillan, Harold, 327
Machiavelli, Niccolò, 208, 253, 336
Major, John, 88, 136, 214
Mandela, Nelson, 153
Mann, Thomas, 25
Mansfield, US Senator Mike, 93
Markus Söder, 330, 332, 342, 353, 357-359
Marshall Plan, 22
Marshall, George, 23
Marx, Karl, 13, 112, 317
Marx, Reinhart, 237
Maskirovka, 294, 301
May, Theresa, 329
Mayer, Laurenz, 174, 188
McCain, US Senator John, 303
McCartney, Paul, 56
Médicins sans Frontiéres, 244
Medvedev, Dmitri, 298
Meinhof, Ulrike, 172
Meisner, Cardinal Joachim, 162
Merkel, Ulrich, 72, 73, 80-81, 90
Merz, Friedrich, 160, 166, 167, 177, 178, 179, 181, 182, 185, 188, 189, 192, 202, 335

Meyers, Franz, 192
Mielke, Erich, 100, 101, 116
Mill, John Stuart, 335
Milošević, Slobodan, 155
Minsk Protocol, 303
Mitscherlich, Alexander, 68
Mitscherlich, Margrethe, 68
Mitterrand, François, 95, 115, 124
Modrow, Hans, 102-105, 117
Molkentin, Wolfgang, 128-130
Möllenstadt, Oliver, 269
Monnet, Jean, 153
Morgenstern, Christian, 59
Morgenstern, Oskar, 307
Müller, Peter, 180-181, 182, 272
Multiculturalism, 175, 177, 210, 224, 318
Müntefering, Franz, 192, 202, 203-205, 221
Muslim, 79, 177, 271, 319
Myung-sook, Han, 225
Mronz, Michael, 251

Napoleon III, 368
Napolitano, Giorgio, 284
Nash, John, 307
Nath, Kamal, 148
NATO, 29, 46, 83, 85, 123, 124-126, 244-245, 297, 298, 302, 311
Nena (Gabriele Susanne Kerner), 363
Neubert, Ehrhart, 113
New Middle (Neue Mitte), 191
Nietzsche, Friedrich, 63
Nixon, Richard M. 37th President of the United States, 93, 310
Nolte, Claudia, 146
Norbert Röttgen, 272, 275, 357, 360
Norbert Walter-Borjans, 347, 355
Novalis, Friedrich von Hardenberg, 13
Novotný, Antonín Josef, 50, 52, 53
NSA (National Security Agency), 295
Nuclear Power, 88, 147, 149, 247, 274ff., 282
Nuland, Victoria, 295

Obama, Barack, 44th President of the United States, 227, 231, 295ff
Oettinger, Günter, 201, 219-222
Ohnesorg, Bruno, 69
Olaf Scholz, 342, 355, 366-367
Operation Desert Storm, 135
Operation Gomorrah, 24

Opitz, Jürgen, 18
Orbán, Viktor, 14, 320
Ordoliberalism, 335, 338
Orwell, George, 36, 90
Osmond, Donny, 56
Osten, Hans-Jörg, 81, 91

Pahnke, Rudi, 34
Papandreu, George, 253, 258, 286-289, 313, 314
Parsifal (Opera), 168-169
PEDIDA (Patriotische Europäer gegen die Islamisierung des Abendlandes), 305-306
Perestroika, 91, 96
Perez, Shimon, 204
Peter Sloterdijk, 354
Petry, Frauke, 306, 307, 331, 345
Planck, Max, 256
Plato, 234
Pofella, Roland, 271, 272, 276, 285
Polenz, Rupert, 173, 174
Politbüro (East German), 47, 71, 92, 99, 100, 110, 116
Politburo (Soviet Union), 93, 94
Poss, Joachim, 257
Powell, Enoch, 204
Powell, Jonathan, 215
PPE equipment, 352, 355, 360-361
Prague Spring, 51-53, 93, 109
Pravda, 99, 101
Pressler, Manahem, 327
Pushkin, Feodor, 37

Ranke, Leopold von, 63, 289
Rattle, Sir Simon, 327
Ratzinger, Joseph, See Pope Benedict XVI
Rau, Johannes, 144, 186, 265
Reagan, Nancy, 163
Reagan, Ronald, 40th President of the United States, 84, 87, 91-95, 96, 164, 191
Red Army (Soviet), 31
Reem (Palestinean girl), 318
Refugees, 12-14, 19, 12, 71, 79, 80, 226, 277, 319-325, 329-331, 334
Rehn, Olli, 260, 262
Reisenhuber, Heinz, 132
Rerum Novarum, 196
Rexroth, Günter, 131, 149

Rice, Condoleezza, 225
Ring des Niebelungen (Opera), 248
Ringstorff, Harald, 203
RKI, See Robert Koch Institute
Robert Habeck, 347, 364
Robert Koch Institute, The, 352, 361
Roberts, Julia, 172
Robin Alexander, 357
Rohwedder, Detlev, 137
Rolling Stones, 56, 246
Rönsch, Hannelore, 135
Roosevelt, Theodore, 26th President of the United States, 261
Rosinenpickerei, 330
Rösler, Philip, 281, 282, 292
Röttgen, Norbert, 272, 275
Rühe, Volker, 140, 144, 153, 154, 166, 201
Russian Language Olympics, 53ff
Rüttgers, Jürgen, 192, 201, 207, 221, 222, 223, 224, 261, 263, 268,271, 276

Sahwil, Reem, See: Reem
Sakharov, Andrei, 37
Sanders, US Senator Bernie, 26
Sandy Hook Primary School Shooting, 232
Sarkozy, Nicolas, 258, 262, 282-88, 313
Saskia Esken, 347, 355
Sauer, Joachim, 91, 96, 162-164, 165, 256
Schabowski, Günter, 104, 105, 106
Schalck-Golodkowski, Alexander, 108
Schäuble, Wolfgang, 18, 126, 127, 142, 153, 154, 159-161, 166, 167, 177, 180, 186-188, 208, 257-260, 263-264, 272, 284, 285, 287, 310, 315-317, 326, 340
Schavan, Annette, 207, 224, 238, 272, 274, 342
Scheel, Walter, 247
Schiffer, Claudia, 172
Schindhelm, Michael, 97, 168-169
Schlüssel, Wolfgang, 217
Schmidt, Helmut, 76, 82-83, 85-87, 178, 181, 208, 234, 247, 295
Schmitt, Carl, 50
Schnur, Wolfgang, 113, 118, 119, 120
Scholz, Rupert, 115
Schönbohm, Jörg, 269
Schönherr, Albert, 31, 32, 34, 45, 47, 100
Schröder, Foreign Minister Gerhard (CDU), 143

Schröder, Kanzler Gerhard, 11, 48, 146,
    149, 153-155, 166, 172-175, 177, 178,
    180, 181, 183, 186, 188, 191-195, 197,
    198, 201-208, 211, 212, 214, 215, 217,
    221, 222, 225, 234, 237, 241, 248,
    254, 275, 299, 331, 332, 333
Schulz, Martin, 303
Schulz, Werner, 193
Schumacher, Hajo, 168
Schürer, Paul Gerhard, 108
Schwan, Gesine, 188, 239
Sebastian Kurz, 358
Senate (Bundesrat), 67, 192, 221-222, 261,
    262, 263, 264
Shakespeare, William, 163, 171, 339
Shamir, Yitzhak, 204
Social distancing, 359
Socialist Unity Party (SED) 22, 30, 37, 45,
    47, 69, 75, 102, 103, 109, 116, 117,
    120, 341
Society of Pius X, 235
Söder, Markus, 330, 332
Solidarność, 84
Solms, Herman Otto, 131
Spengler, Oswald, 261
Stafford, Lee, 172
Stalin, Josef, 21, 22, 26, 39, 49, 126, 269
Stamtischpolitik, 175
STASI Officer 'Bachman', 90, 91
Steffen, Thomas, 316
Steinbrück, Peer, 17, 18, 19, 192, 207, 228,
    241, 257, 264, 337
Steinmeier, Frank-Walter, 18, 207, 232,
    241, 242, 244-246, 248, 255,
    299, 316
Stoiber, Edmund, 166, 179-185, 187, 188,
    194-196, 206-207, 220, 336
Stollman, Jost, 195
Stone, Oliver, 261
Stoph, Willi, 100, 103, 105
Strategic Defence Initiative (SDI), 94
Strauß, Bodo, 176ff
Strauß, Franz-Joseph, 67, 87, 108,
    157, 179
Strauß, Richard, 65
Streep, Meryl, 240
Stroetmann, Clemens, 146, 147
Süssmuth, Rita, 138, 145
SYRIZA, 308-318

Taliban, 242-247
Taraki, Nur, 83, 102
Templin Theological Seminary, 32-33
Teufel, Edwin, 180
Thatcher, Margaret, 87, 94, 115, 124, 137,
    195, 211, 255, 328, 338
The Beatles, 56
The Economist, 309, 319
Thirsty Pegasus, 75, 82
Tiananmen Square, 103
Tillich, Stanislaw, 18
Time, 225,
Timm, Udo, 129-130
Tolstoi, Leo, 37
Töpfer, Klaus, 146-148, 187
Traxler, Hans, 87
Treuhandanstalt, 137
Trichet, Jean-Claude, 283, 284
Trotha, Thilo von, 186
Truman, Harry S., 200-201
Trump, Donald J., 327, 328, 337
Tsalalotos, Euclid, 315, 317
Tsipras, Alexis, 308, 309, 310-318
Tusk, Donald, 312, 317

Ulbricht, Walter, 21,22, 23, 26, 38-40, 46,
    47, 50, 67, 68, 70
Ulrich, Klaus, 98, 114
UN Security Council, 156, 184, 272, 280,
    330, 335
Ushakov, Yuri, 293

Varoufakis, Yanis, 307, 308, 312, 314, 315
Venizelos, Evangelos, 287
Verantwortungsethiker, 343
Vergangenheitsbewältigung, 68, 342
Verhofstadt, Guy, 258
Vogel Commission, 219
Vogel, Bernhard, 219
Volker Bouffier, 360, 366
Von Beust, Ole, 276
von der Leyen, Ursula, 207, 232, 269, 272
von Neuman, John (János) 306

Wagner, Friedhelm, 129
Wagner, Richard, 63, 248, 329
Wahlkreis Stralsund-Rügen-Grimmen,
    128-130
Walz, Udo, 172

Warsaw Pact, 29

Weber, Juliane, 133

Weber, Max, 138, 343

Weidmann, Jens, 259ff, 264, 336, 338

Weil, Kurt, 206

Weizsäcker, Richard von Freiherr, 91, 92, 265

Westerwelle, Guido, 163, 183, 187, 188, 202, 242, 246, 247, 248, 251-255, 268, 272, 270-282, 335

Westpakete, 44

Whitman, Walt, 255

Williamson, Richard, 234

Willkommenskultur, 328

Winfried Kretschmann, 276-277, 365

Winnenden School Shooting, 232

Winterkorn, Martin, 19

Wissmann, Matthias, 131, 149

Wölber, Hans Otto, 27

Wolf, Christa, 74, 112

Wolf, Markus, 67, 76, 88, 102, 105

Wulff, Christian, 147, 198, 201, 207, 222, 223, 267, 276, 290

Xiaoping, Deng, 103

Yanukovych, Victor, 293

Young Pioneers, 36

Zahradnik, Rudolf, 90

Zemke, Hans Günter, 128-130, 132

Zetsche, Peter, 322

Zoom, 355, 362

Zwanzifer, Theo, 210